potatoes

corn? value
k.

will ever
t will be
can come
longs and
e two of you
work of one

-TETE:
should be plant-
day; he should
If he does, then

MARTIN: MAR
a saloon?

COUPE-TETE:
ant Jean and Mister
rhaps. Miss Catherine.
t until after Tuesday.
may 'Madame Mornet'.
there will be some hope

French dont eat corn...Coupe-Tete would be
nting potatoes... Planting potatoes ???
Not for home eat?   in May ???
takes six weeks after the publication of the banns
s before a wedding can take place. The banns
ted outside of the city hall for 42 days.

Faulkner

*A Comprehensive Guide
to the Brodsky Collection*

Volume III: The De Gaulle Story
by William Faulkner

Faulkner

*A Comprehensive Guide
to the Brodsky Collection*

Volume III: The De Gaulle Story
by William Faulkner

Edited by
Louis Daniel Brodsky
and
Robert W. Hamblin

UNIVERSITY PRESS OF MISSISSIPPI
Jackson

Center for the Study of Southern Culture Series

Library of Congress Cataloging in Publication Data

(Revised for volume 3)
Main entry under title:

Faulkner, a comprehensive guide to the Brodsky Collection.

(Center for the Study of Southern Culture Series)
Bibliography: v. 2, p.
Contents: v. 1. The biobibliography—
—v. 3. The De Gaulle story.
  1. Faulkner, William, 1897–1962—Bibliography—
Catalogs. 2. Faulkner, William, 1897–1962—Manuscripts
—Catalogs. 3. Faulkner, William, 1897–1962—Miscellanea
—Catalogs. 4. Brodsky, Louis Daniel—Library.
I. Brodsky, Louis Daniel, II. Hamblin, Robert W.
Z8288.F38 1982   [PS3511.A86]   016.813'52   82-6966

ISBN 0-87805-240-2 (set)

CONTENTS

List of Illustrations   vi

Acknowledgments   vii

Introduction by Robert W. Hamblin and Louis Daniel Brodsky   ix

"The De Gaulle Story" Materials in the Brodsky Collection   xxxv

Editorial Notes   xxxix

  I   "Journey Toward Dawn": Story Outline   3

 II   "Free France": Story Treatment   13

III   "The De Gaulle Story": Revised Story Treatment   71

IV   "The De Gaulle Story": First Complete Screenplay   91

 V   "The De Gaulle Story": Revised Screenplay   213

VI   Related Documents   335

    Textual Collation   399

LIST OF ILLUSTRATIONS

1   Warner Bros. Employee's Starting Record for Faulkner, July 27, 1942   2

2   Initial story outline of work which became "The De Gaulle Story"   4

3   Faulkner's typescript of abstract of "Free France"   14

4   Passage from "Free France" that anticipates the Nobel Prize Acceptance Speech   30

5   Page from Faulkner's intermediate draft of story treatment entitled "Free France"   39

6   Page from Faulkner's intermediate draft of "Free France"   43

7   Page from Faulkner's intermediate draft of "Free France"   46

8   First page of Faulkner's revised story treatment of "The De Gaulle Story"   72

9   Opening of first complete version of Faulkner's screenplay   92

10   Page of Faulkner's rewrite of first draft of screenplay   116

11   Page of Faulkner's rewrite of first draft of screenplay   117

12   Some of the research materials supplied to Faulkner during his work on "The De Gaulle Story"   127

13   Page from copy of "The De Gaulle Story" containing Robert Buckner's notations regarding revision and filming   217

14   Henri Diamant-Berger's critique of Faulkner's screenplay   254

15   First page of Faulkner's last known revision of "The De Gaulle Story," November 19, 1942   304

16   Memo from Faulkner to Buckner, November 19, 1942   332

17   Contract between Faulkner and Warner Bros., June 29, 1945   397

ACKNOWLEDGMENTS

The editors are extremely grateful to Warner Bros., Inc., for permission to publish the contents of this volume. We especially want to thank Stanley Belkin, Peter D. Knecht, and Marshall M. Silverman, of the Warner Bros. legal staff, for their cooperation and assistance.

We are happy to acknowledge our great indebtedness to two individuals who, more than all others, made this book possible. A. I. "Buzz" Bezzerides kindly allowed materials Faulkner had given him in the 1940s to be placed in the Brodsky Collection. These manuscripts and documents proved indispensable in enabling the editors to piece together the complicated record of Faulkner's involvement in the De Gaulle project. Warren R. Howell, regarded at the time of his death in 1984 as one of the world's foremost bookmen, not only arranged for Faulkner's Warner Bros. scripts to be added to the Brodsky Collection but also handled the preliminary negotiations regarding publication. The editors deeply regret that Mr. Howell did not live to see the fruition of his labors; we can only hope that this volume will serve as an appropriate testimony of his unselfish efforts and become a lasting tribute to his memory.

Robert Buckner, Meta Wilde, and Joseph Blotner graciously responded to the editors' inquiries and offered many helpful suggestions. Glenn Horowitz, New York bookdealer, and John C. Bierk, professor of film and literature at Southeast Missouri State University, also provided valuable help and counsel. Paul Lueders photographed the materials that serve as illustrations in this volume. To these persons, too, the editors extend our heartfelt gratitude.

We also want to thank the following individuals for their continuing support of the series of which this work is a part: William Ferris and Ann J. Abadie, of the Center for the Study of Southern Culture at the University of Mississippi; Barney McKee, JoAnne Prichard, and Hunter Cole, of the University Press of Mississippi; and Bill W. Stacy, Leslie H. Cochran, Fred B. Goodwin, and Henry Sessoms, of Southeast Missouri State University.

The editors are also appreciative of the crucial financial support and personal encouragement provided by Saul and Charlotte Brodsky; Biltwell Company, Inc., of St. Louis; and the Grants and Research Funding Committee of Southeast Missouri State University.

INTRODUCTION

I

ON JULY 27, 1942, William Faulkner went on the payroll of Warner Bros. Pictures in Burbank, California, as a scenarist at a salary of $300 per week. His initial assignment was to write a screenplay based on the career of General Charles De Gaulle, who had only recently been thrust into international prominence as the leader of the Free French/ Fighting French resistance against Germany's invasion and continuing occupation of France. The idea for the film seems to have originated with President Franklin D. Roosevelt, who convinced his good friend Jack Warner that such a movie would enhance the image of General De Gaulle, a prospective American ally, in the eyes of the American public. Warner had enlisted writer-producer Robert Buckner to oversee the project, and Buckner had written to Faulkner in mid-July 1942, asking him to do the script.[1]

As it turned out, Buckner was more perceptive about Faulkner's compatibility with the De Gaulle material than the producer probably realized. Buckner knew, of course, about Faulkner's interest in war stories and his previous involvement with two successful war films, *Today We Live* (Metro-Goldwyn-Mayer, 1933) and *The Road to Glory* (Twentieth Century-Fox, 1936); but the producer may not have known that Faulkner, for several months prior to his arrival in California, had actively sought a commission in the United States navy in the hope of acquiring his pilot's wings and being assigned to combat duty.[2] Frustrated in these efforts, and severely strapped by lack of money, Faulkner turned to Hollywood, where he would discover in the De Gaulle project not only a measure of financial security but also a means to communicate his patriotic zeal.

Writing for Warner Bros. in the early 1940s could understandably

---

[1] See *Selected Letters of William Faulkner*, ed. Joseph Blotner (New York: Random House, 1977), p. 157.

[2] In a letter written in late March 1942 to Robert Haas, Faulkner explained: "I am going before a Navy board and Medical for a commission, N.R. I will go to the Bureau of Aeronautics, Washington, for a job. I am to get full Lieut. and 3200.00 per year, and I hope a pilot's rating to wear the wings. I dont like this desk job particularly, but I think better to get the commission first and then try to get a little nearer the gunfire, which I intend to try to do." *Selected Letters of William Faulkner*, p. 149.

be viewed as active participation in the nation's war effort. As Jack Warner has noted, Warner Bros., like the other Hollywood studios, had been converted into "a sort of war industry."[3] Scriptwriters were granted draft deferments, and the studios produced hundreds of movies—training films for both military and civilian personnel, documentaries, and newsreels, as well as feature pictures—designed to contribute in one way or another to the winning of the war. One Warner Bros. film, *Rear Gunner,* was specifically calculated to entice air force recruits to volunteer for the dangerous assignment of manning the machine guns on fighter planes. Jack Warner's commitment to the national cause was greatly strengthened by his personal friendship with President Roosevelt. Predictably, much of Faulkner's work for Warner Bros. related to the war effort—not only his authorship of "The De Gaulle Story" but also his assignments in 1943 and 1944 on "The Life and Death of a Bomber," *Air Force,* "Battle Cry," *God Is My Co-Pilot,* and *To Have and Have Not.*

It is not at all surprising that Faulkner was strongly attracted to the story of Charles De Gaulle and the Free French movement. From his earliest days Faulkner had been enamored of romantic heroes who embodied courage and action. As has frequently been noted, the prototype for Faulkner's heroic ideal was his great-grandfather, William Clark Falkner. In the image of this Confederate officer, landholder, railroad builder, lawyer, politician, and author, Faulkner discovered the apotheosis of the heroic man of action and gallant deeds. Actually, this ancestor's achievements in a variety of endeavors merely provided additional justification for festooning laurels on him; for Faulkner his great-grandfather was first and foremost a soldier: "Colonel" Falkner. Even a clear recognition of the serious defects in the man's character (as evidenced in Faulkner's interview statements and the derivative characterizations of Colonel John Sartoris, Thomas Sutpen, and L. Q. C. McCaslin) could not diminish the tremendous admiration Faulkner felt for his famous forebear.

As a young man, even before he actively committed himself to following the great-grandfather's example as a writer, Faulkner sought to emulate the Old Colonel as a soldier—or, rather, the poetic, heroic counterpart, a flier in the First World War. To this end Faulkner attempted, like so many other romantically inclined youths of his generation, to enlist in the armed services with the hope of fighting on foreign soil. His initial rejection by the American forces because of his small stature, his ultimate acceptance as a flight training cadet in the

---

[3] Jack Warner (with Dean Jennings), *My First Hundred Years in Hollywood* (New York: Random House, 1965), p. 282.

RAF in Toronto, his stint of service from July to December, 1918, his return to Oxford with the signing of the Armistice, and his unassuagable disappointment at not getting into battle—these are all commonly accepted biographical facts. So, too, are the apocryphal tales that Faulkner concocted regarding his dogfights in European skies, his crack-ups, and his near-misses. Clearly, twenty-one-year-old Billy Faulkner, back home in Oxford, chose to project himself—or one of his selves—as a heroic flier returned from the Great War, wounded to the extent of sporting a "steel plate" beneath his skull. Such early works as "Landing in Luck" and "The Lilacs," as well as his first novel, *Soldiers' Pay,* reflect the degree to which the role of the military hero dominated Faulkner's psyche at this stage of his life. Even as late as the 1940s Faulkner would still be alluding to himself as a pilot who saw action over Germany; in fact, he wrote to his nephew Jimmy Faulkner, it was in that vicinity that he had lost his dog tag. "I think the Gestapo has it," Faulkner fabricated; "I am very likely on their records right now as a dead British flying officer-spy."[4]

Just as Faulkner's dream of becoming a flier in World War I is mirrored in the recurrence of airplanes, pilots, and war in his early poetry and fiction, so, too, his failure to become a front-line combatant in World War II led Faulkner to project his heroic ambitions onto various characters in his fiction of this period. Uncle Ike McCaslin's contention in "Delta Autumn" that "when the time comes" America "will cope with one Austrian paper-hanger"[5] mirrors not only a national belief but also Faulkner's own personal commitment to the cause. That commitment is expressed also through the McCallums of "The Tall Men," who consider it a disgrace to have to be drafted (but who willingly volunteer) to serve their country, and through Pete Grier and his younger brother in "Two Soldiers" and the Grier and de Spain families in "Shall Not Perish." Foremost among Faulkner's World War II heroes, however, are General Charles De Gaulle and his Free French loyalists.

II

Indicative of Faulkner's enthusiasm for the De Gaulle project is the fact that he went immediately to work on the story the day of his arrival at Warner Bros. Following a story conference with Buckner, Faulkner produced a nine-page typescript (I.A),[6] dated "7/28/42,"

---

[4] *Selected Letters of William Faulkner,* p. 170.
[5] William Faulkner, *Go Down, Moses* (New York: Modern Library, 1942), p. 339.
[6] The numbers in parenthesis throughout the text refer to the bibliography printed at the end of this introduction.

outlining the projected plot line. To this set of notes Faulkner affixed two pairs of possible titles: "Journey Toward Dawn" or "Toward Dawn" and "Journey Toward Hope" or "Toward Hope." The brief narrative is divided into two sections. The first opens with a reference to De Gaulle's early career and his developing quarrel with General Philippe Pétain and "the hide-bound military establishment" that has ignored De Gaulle's pleas for a mobile, mechanized French army. Following the invasion of France by Germany (according to the very tactics De Gaulle had predicted), De Gaulle travels to London, where he secures the friendship and support of Winston Churchill and uses the BBC airways to call upon other Frenchmen to join his opposition movement against the conquering Germans and their collaborators, the Vichy French government. As time passes, De Gaulle's Free French organization flourishes, and his agents scatter from London to all parts of the Empire to enlist sympathetic defenders of freedom and democracy.

Section II, which, Faulkner explains, "will be cut into Section I from time to time," traces the experiences of a typical young French soldier, Georges, who becomes a convert to Gaullist ideas, escapes from France after the German invasion, joins the Free French army in London, and eventually returns to France as a member of a commando unit. As Faulkner notes, "Georges represents the French individual as De Gaulle represents the abstract idea of Free France." Although Faulkner here presents the De Gaulle and Georges narratives in separate summaries, he makes it clear, as noted above, that he intends to interweave the two strands of plot, in much the same manner, one supposes, that he had counterpointed material in such novels as *The Sound and the Fury, As I Lay Dying, Light in August, Absalom, Absalom!,* and *The Wild Palms.*

After completing this story outline on July 29[7] and holding additional consultations with Buckner, Faulkner further developed his plot. In a two-page typescript (I.B) addressed to Buckner and dated "7/30/42," Faulkner suggested that Georges might be cast as a soldier who is captured by the Germans during the Battle of France but who later escapes to Syria and Africa, or possibly even America, where he hears of De Gaulle's growing popularity and enlists in the Free French movement. In another two-page typescript addendum (I.C), dated "7/31/42," Faulkner proposed to Buckner that "representative individuals"—for example, a peasant, a student, a musician, a bank clerk, a

---

[7] Although the outline is dated "7/28/42," Faulkner must have taken two days to complete this material, since the appendices dated "7/30/42" and "7/31/42" refer to the "notes of July 29th."

Basque, and a Breton, among others—be introduced to dramatize the tragic effect the German invasion has had upon the French people, as well as to reinforce the undying dream that France will one day be restored to "its ancient pride and glory." Even at this early stage of composition, therefore, Faulkner was keenly conscious of the need to relate the abstract quality of Free France to the everyday, concrete experiences of ordinary citizens.

By August 3, 1942, Faulkner had made considerable progress on an expanded treatment of the story, now entitled "Free France." In undertaking this version Faulkner relied heavily upon Philippe Barrès's book, *Charles De Gaulle,*[8] and possibly upon materials supplied by the Warner Bros. Research Department. By August 19 Faulkner had written enough material to fill forty-four pages of typescript (II.B), including a nine-page insert, dated "8/13/42," that incorporates suggestions Buckner had made in a memo to Faulkner on August 10 (VI.B).

In this forty-four-page segment Georges's name has been altered to Charles Mornet and, more significantly, he has been given an older brother named Jean. Employing the contrapuntal pairing of relatives that he had used years earlier in *Sartoris* and more recently in "The Bear," Faulkner places Charles and Jean on opposite sides of the De Gaulle question. Both men are soldiers, Jean a sergeant-pilot in the air force and Charles a private in De Gaulle's tank corps. But Jean is a traditionalist, staunchly defending the strategy of emplacement symbolized by the Maginot Line, while Charles, who has read De Gaulle's books on modern warfare, argues that the Maginot Line is useless, since the Germans will merely go around it. The first ten pages of this treatment are devoted to successive arguments on this subject between the two brothers—first at their home, a farm near a small village in Brittany; then at a village cafe, where others take sides in the dispute; and finally at the home of the mayor, whose daughter Catherine has been promised to the Mornet brother of her choice. This third argument is interrupted when a group of messengers rush into the mayor's house to announce that the German army has invaded the Low Countries and that all French soldiers are being recalled to active duty.

[8] This book, written to promote De Gaulle's Free French stand, was available in two French language editions (Paris: Plon, 1941; New York: Brentano's, 1941) and an English translation (Garden City, New York: Doubleday, Doran and Company, 1941). Faulkner drew upon Barrès's work not only for the broad historical pattern of the Nazi invasion and the emergence of De Gaulle and the Free French underground but also for such specific details as De Gaulle's trail of cigarette butts, the subversive role of Mme de Portes, the phrase "the little people," and De Gaulle's contention that "France has lost one battle; she has not lost the war."

At this point Faulkner shifts the focus to the Battle of France in May 1940. De Gaulle's heroic actions at Laon and Abbeville slow the invaders and enable the French infantry to retreat in safety. But De Gaulle's success is short-lived. Called back to Paris by Premier Paul Reynaud and appointed Under-Secretary of War, De Gaulle watches helplessly as the French cabinet collapses and one after another of the nation's leaders calls for capitulation and a quick armistice. Reynaud at first shows some inclination to side with De Gaulle in wanting to continue the fight, but the premier is overly influenced by his mistress Hélène de Portes, a fascist who counsels surrender to the Germans. When Reynaud resigns to be replaced by General Pétain, the aged World War I hero, De Gaulle realizes that France is lost. Even the intervention of Churchill has failed to reverse the course of events. Faulkner closes this section of his treatment by showing De Gaulle and Churchill aboard a plane headed for England. "Blood, sweat, and tears," Churchill remarks to his new ally. "But I have never yet heard you speak of hope." De Gaulle replies, "You never heard me talk of breathing, either."

Back in the Breton village a German garrison, including a Gestapo squad, has seized control from the local authorities. The mayor, frightened and powerless to resist, sees no alternative to collaboration. Jean, home again after the armistice, supports the policy of appeasement, not only out of pragmatic necessity but because, as an honorable soldier, he feels duty-bound to obey his superiors, the Vichy French government under Pétain. Charles, too, returns to the village, but as an escaped prisoner of war, still in uniform, en route to the coast and thence to London to join De Gaulle's army. Approaching the village, however, Charles is forced to kill a German soldier to avoid arrest. Jean, though furious with his brother for jeopardizing the safety of his family and even the entire village, conspires with a family retainer, Chopine, to bury the soldier's body and hide Charles from the Germans. Once again the brothers quarrel violently over their opposing loyalties; and Jean discovers, to his amazement, that others among his family and friends support Charles's contention that France must be defended, whatever the cost. Catherine is one of those who find Jean's compromising spirit intolerable. "Bretons have suffered before this for Brittany," she says. "And if there are still Frenchmen left who are willing to fight and die for France, at least we who can't fight can stay here and suffer too. And die too." Another who argues against collaboration is the village priest. Emotionally Jean identifies with these sentiments, but reason dictates that resistance is foolhardy.

When the German authorities discover the grave of the missing soldier, they barricade the village and threaten to execute a hostage each twenty-four hours until the citizens identify the soldier's killer. One hostage is shot, but the second is saved when his mother rushes forth to name Charles as the guilty party. Charles, having fled to some nearby woods, remains undetected; but the Gestapo arrests Jean, Mme Mornet, Chopine, and the cook. Chopine is severely beaten but refuses to cooperate with his captors. Jean offers himself in his brother's place, but the German commander declines the proposal and gives Jean until the next day to turn over his brother.

Returning home from hiding, Charles learns of the persecution of his family and vows to assassinate the German commander. The priest, however, discourages that action. He reminds Charles that his life must be dedicated to France, not to private vengeance. Moreover, to ensure that Charles will have a reason to live as well as a cause for which to die, the priest insists that Charles and Catherine be married before Charles departs. The priest performs the ceremony and then, the following morning, outfits Charles in a cleric's robe, supplies him with a travel permit, and sends him on his way toward England and De Gaulle.

Once Charles's escape has become known, the Gestapo official demands the execution of the priest. The German commander, who opposes the brutal tactics of the Gestapo and who recognizes that the villagers are moving closer to open rebellion, asks the Gestapo officer to rescind the order of execution. The latter agrees to do so, provided the priest will use his influence to persuade the people to abide by the conditions of the armistice. When confronted with this proposal, the priest spits in the Gestapo agent's face. Enraged, the agent pulls his pistol and murders the priest.

Here Faulkner again enlarges his perspective to present the growing developments in the Free French movement. In Bordeaux De Gaulle is declared a traitor and sentenced to death by the Vichy government, but in London he continues to rally Frenchmen under the banner of resistance. At first his is a ragamuffin army, wounded, discouraged, lacking in training and supplies, and sustained only by devotion to liberty and love of homeland. Gradually, though, more and more Frenchmen join the crusade. Many of them, like Charles Mornet, are former members of De Gaulle's tank unit. Charles, now in London recruiting Free French supporters among the refugees, has become the general's orderly. Actually, he is treated more like a member of the De Gaulle family.

In rapid, staccato shifts of scene Faulkner now shows the Free

French movement gathering momentum. On Bastille Day, 1940, De Gaulle makes a moving appeal by radio, imploring all Frenchmen to stand firm in their resistance and to continue to come to him in England. They do, in such numbers that on August 7, 1940, the British government declares De Gaulle to be the legitimate head of the French state. De Gaulle and Churchill sign an agreement of mutual support. On August 23 De Gaulle parades his troops before King George VI of England. During this ceremony De Gaulle announces that the French provinces of Tchad and Cameroon have pledged their support to Free France.

In the next-to-last scene in this segment De Gaulle, Mme De Gaulle, and Charles discuss the upcoming Dakar expedition against the Vichyites. As an example of Free French perseverance Charles recounts the story of his own village, telling of the priest's sacrifice, the courage of the women, and the son his wife may have conceived on their wedding night. The conversation ends with De Gaulle proposing a toast "to all the sons who will rise from these dark times to give light to tomorrow." The next, and final, scene shifts to Dakar, where the combined Free French and British forces, De Gaulle and Charles among them, move against the Vichy French fortress. Both Charles and his general are greatly saddened that the conflict has resulted in a situation in which Frenchmen are at war with fellow Frenchmen. The scene fades out with Charles watching the Vichy battleship *Bretagne,* named after his native province, being sunk by British guns.

As evidenced by the unresolved handling of De Gaulle's disastrous and questionable attack on Dakar, this forty-four-page typescript, though it appears at quick glance to be self-contained, is actually only an installment on what was undoubtedly even then perceived as a longer work. A penciled note in an unidentified hand on the title page indicates that Faulkner submitted this material to the Warner Bros. Story Department on August 19, 1942. He spent the remainder of that month expanding and revising his treatment.

III

Faulkner's advancement of the story at this stage of composition can best be traced by examining materials only recently discovered by Louis Daniel Brodsky at the home of A. I. "Buzz" Bezzerides, with whom Faulkner lived briefly in 1944 and again in 1945. Sometime during this period Faulkner gave to his friend Buzz some seven hundred pages of manuscripts and other documents relating to the De Gaulle project. Almost half of these materials relate to the expanded treatment of "Free France." Included are 132 pages of Faulkner's typescript drafts, with holograph corrections (II.A), and twenty-nine miscellaneous carbon pages from at least two previous versions, typed by a Warner Bros. secretary but revised in hand by Faulkner as he incorporated those pages into subsequent drafts (II.A.). Also found in Bezzerides' home was a carbon copy of the seventy-nine-page completed treatment (II.E), accompanied by forty-four pages of carbon typescripts (II.C) that apparently represent discards from Faulkner's progressive revisions. While most of these materials are fragmentary and possibly derive from as many as five different versions of Faulkner's treatment (or portions thereof), they provide a clear indication of Faulkner's concept of the story at this point in time, as well as a remarkably intimate view of Faulkner's actual process of composition.

In completing his treatment (II.D), Faulkner not only extended but also revised the material he had submitted on August 19. Most significantly, he altered the characterization of Jean, casting him as an opportunist and an active collaborator of the occupying German forces. This shift accounts for the insertion of a new scene in which an unidentified villager seeks to assassinate Jean as a traitor. Faulkner also made other changes. The execution of the hostage and the arrest of the Mornets and their servants were deleted, and General Georges Catroux's defection from the Vichy French was added. Moreover, Faulkner shifted certain scenes—for example, the marriage of Charles and Catherine, the murder of the priest, De Gaulle's Bastille Day speech, and Charles's conversation with General and Mme De Gaulle—to other positions in the manuscript. Textual critics familiar with Faulkner's method of composition in producing such novels as *Sartoris, Sanctuary, Light in August, Absalom, Absalom!*, and *A Fable* will hardly be surprised to learn that Faulkner similarly rearranged and rewrote his "Free France" treatment.

Sometime during his work on the story treatment Faulkner took time out to produce a brief abstract of the work (II.A), perhaps for his own use but more likely for Buckner or someone else interested in the project. Typed (with Faulkner's typical strikeovers) on the verso of a discarded ribbon typescript page from a previous version of the treatment, and beneath four canceled ribbon typescript lines from the same or another treatment, the abstract is a single paragraph of 139 words. Faulkner begins by noting, "This is the story of Free France, told in the simple terms of a Breton village: the collapse of France and the hopes and struggle for rejuvenation as seen through the eyes of villagers, told by means of village characters who are themselves the common denominator of France." Faulkner goes on to identify the action in the village as the "strophe" of the plot, with the "antistrophe" being the broader events affecting the French nation as a whole. Faulkner concludes his summary by identifying the "thesis" of the work as the belief "that lust and greed and force can never conquer the human spirit."

In resuming the narrative, Faulkner substituted a Syrian confrontation between the Free French and the Vichy French for the raid on Dakar, possibly because the latter had proved an embarrassment for De Gaulle. In the altered version Charles has been assigned to accompany General Catroux on a mission to Syria. Ironically, Jean has also been sent to Syria, as a Vichy officer in a frontier fort, following the attempt on his life in his native village. When the Free French capture the outpost, Jean is taken prisoner and delivered into Charles's custody. Charles grants his brother freedom and invites him to join the Free French cause. Jean refuses, still insisting that Charles is a traitor. Shortly thereafter, in a scene subsequently deleted (II.C), the brothers meet again in Brazzaville, Africa, and this time Charles arranges for Jean to meet with General De Gaulle. Jean is impressed with the general's sincerity and humility but still declines to align himself with the Free French.

Back in France, Jean uses his position with the Germans and the Vichy government to direct food, coal, and other supplies to his mother. But he finds himself more and more isolated and alone, increasingly distrustful of both the Germans and their Vichy puppets yet still unable to support the resistance. Jean's only friend is a young sewing-woman whose father is a musician with little opportunity for work. Jean provides them with food and occasionally visits in their apartment, located beneath his own. Of Jean's relationship to the young woman Faulkner notes: "By proxy she is Catherine, though there is no thought of love or sex between them."

Jean's duties require him to inspect enforced French laborers at a munitions factory. Coincidentally, he arrives just prior to the time set for an RAF bombing raid. Several of the workers who are members of the Free French underground know about the planned attack, but they remain at their work stations in order not to jeopardize the mission. One of these laborers knows and recognizes Jean; and, "divin[ing] what so far nobody else has: that in his heart Jean is troubled and uncertain and is on the road to changing his beliefs," this young man privately warns Jean to leave the factory immediately. A few minutes later Jean and the German plant manager watch from an office across the river as the bombs begin to fall on the factory. In the midst of the attack Jean can hear the Gaullists, including the man who saved his life, singing the Marseillaise as they die in the bombing.

Gradually, Jean is influenced more and more by the bravery and loyalty of the Free Frenchmen. Another model in this regard is Chopine, the crusty old family servant.[9] Chopine has distinguished himself in a game in which the men of the village bargain and gamble for the privilege of someday cutting the throats of the Gestapo troops who occupy the village. When Charles and Catherine's son is born, Chopine defies the German sentries to take the good news to Charles, whom Chopine finds participating in a commando attack on the coast. Chopine not only delivers the message but also assists in the raid of a hotel and the arrest of some German staff officers.

Following this battle Charles convinces his superior officer to allow him to return with Chopine to the village, ostensibly to gather intelligence information but actually to see his child. This decision, however, proves to be unwise, as Charles is captured almost immediately upon his arrival back home. The remainder of Faulkner's treatment describes Jean's successful plotting to effect Charles's escape, Jean's conversion to the Gaullist side, and the coordinated raid by the Free French underground and De Gaulle's forces in England on a German military installation in France.

In manipulating Charles's escape from the Nazis, Faulkner apparently wrote one account, then discarded it in favor of another. In the first version (II.C) Jean rescues Charles in a fashion reminiscent of the climax of Charles Dickens's *A Tale of Two Cities*. With the aid of a German soldier who is indebted to Mme Mornet, Jean arranges Charles's escape through an underground viaduct and then takes his brother's place in the cell. In the revised version (II.D) Jean and Charles fight their way to freedom, steal a plane, and head toward London. On the way Charles parachutes to earth near his home village to assist with preparations for the upcoming raid.

In England Jean is taken to De Gaulle, who invites the Vichy defector to look around and judge for himself what Free France is all about. Witnessing once more the enthusiastic manner in which people of all nationalities have rallied to the support of freedom under De Gaulle, Jean finally decides to cast his lot with the Free French. In the last scene Jean is with De Gaulle as the general radios a warning to

---

[9] In addition to his role in the French underground, Chopine (later Coupe-tête) serves as a choral commentator who offers opinions on a variety of subjects. Biographers interested in Faulkner's relationship to his wife Estelle will pay particular attention to one observation attributed to Chopine: "Chopine says the best thing to do is to arrange to get Catherine off Charles's mind and the best way Chopine knows to change the idea of a woman in a man's mind from a dream to a nightmare is for the man to marry her."

Frenchmen that an air raid is about to begin. As the general speaks, the scene dissolves to the French village, where Charles, Chopine, and other freedom fighters prepare to light fires to serve as flight markers for the approaching bombers. Mme Mornet, Catherine, and the cook stand on a nearby hill, watching the raid begin. Catherine holds her newborn child, an obvious symbol of an emerging hope for the future. The story fades out with De Gaulle, Jean, and others huddled about a radio, listening to a pilot's voice reporting the sighting of the fires. "And still more!" the pilot shouts. "Still more! All France is on fire, blazing!"

IV

On September 1, 1942, Buckner left on a two-week trip to New York to work on another assignment, but he instructed Faulkner by memo (VI.C) to complete the "full treatment of the De Gaulle story," if possible, "by Friday or Saturday," September 4 or 5. Buckner added: "I have told Geller[10] that I wish you would begin immediately next week on the actual screenplay, without waiting for any word from De Gaulle, which in any case will take several weeks." It seems that Faulkner followed Buckner's instructions to the letter. The title page of Faulkner's completed, revised treatment (II.F), mimeographed by the Warner Bros. Stenographic Department, carries the date "September 4, 1942." The content of this copy corresponds to the version described above, with one exception: Charles's name has been changed back to Georges,[11] the name used in the original story outline. Having completed his treatment, Faulkner now directed his attention, as Buckner requested, to writing the first draft of the screenplay.

By the second or third week in September Faulkner had turned in roughly one-third of the eventual screenplay, now entitled "The De Gaulle Story,"[12] for the secretarial pool to type. The first forty-two pages of this segment (IV.A) focus on the Mornet brothers and the situation in their village just prior to the German invasion of France. Included are the successive arguments about the Maginot Line and General De Gaulle, the brothers' wooing of Catherine, and the announcement at the mayor's home of the start of the war. The follow-

---

[10] James J. Geller was at this time the head of the Warner Bros. Story Department.

[11] In this mimeographed copy of the treatment the English form "George" is used instead of the French "Georges." Since the English spelling appears in no other version of the treatment or screenplay, one may presume that Faulkner intended the French form of the name to be used in this copy also.

[12] Faulkner's shift of title probably derived from the recent change of the name of De Gaulle's organization from the "Free French" to the "Fighting French."

ing sixteen pages present brief vignettes of De Gaulle—receiving command of the tank corps from Premier Reynaud and General Pétain, leading the retreat and engaging the Germans in holding actions at Laon and Abbeville, and being summoned by Reynaud to return to Paris.

At this juncture Faulkner's progress on the screenplay was retarded by the intervention of Adrien Tixier, the Fighting French representative in Washington, D.C., De Gaulle's principal agent regarding the film project. Upon his return from the east coast Buckner had conferred by telephone with Tixier about Faulkner's story treatment. In a subsequent four-page memorandum (VI.D) Buckner summarized for Faulkner some of the objections Tixier had registered. Most of the complaints related to errors of fact. For example, Tixier pointed out that no two-week furloughs were granted at this time in the French army, which was on continuous alert. A Breton peasant family would have no cook. Bretons would play cards, not dominoes, in cafes. Chopine's name should be changed to one more typical of Brittany. Moreover, Tixier insisted, Faulkner had taken too many liberties with actual history in the description of De Gaulle's early days in England. In particular, De Gaulle's first troops were not wounded, ill-trained refugees but "several thousand who were well uniformed and equipped." Beyond such questions of accuracy Tixier argued that the Syrian incident, a highly sensitive matter to De Gaulle, should be eliminated; the German soldier should be presented less sympathetically; and a larger role should be assigned to the French underground. In passing along these points from his conversation with Tixier, Buckner also noted: "Tixier is sending out a complete point-by-point criticism of the entire treatment, which should be in our hands shortly. I will have it translated at once and we will go over it together." Buckner added that Henri Diamant-Berger, another De Gaulle representative, would be available in Hollywood for consultation as the project proceeded.

With the follow-up critique from Tixier (VI.E) in hand, Faulkner temporarily laid aside his partial screenplay to produce a new twenty-eight-page story treatment. This revision (III.A), while remaining true to the broad design of the previous treatment, incorporated almost all of the suggestions contained in Buckner's and Tixier's memos. Chopine's name was changed to Coupe-tête, and De Gaulle's actions during the fall of France and later in England were altered to conform to Tixier's account. The naval encounter between the British and French fleets at Oran was substituted for the objectionable Syrian incident—a shift that necessitated Jean's assignment to the navy rather than the air force. With regard to the main story line, the most significant changes resulted from the increased attention given the French underground, representative, in Faulkner's words, of "the immortal human spirit which not even death can put in bonds." In this new version Georges returns to France as a De Gaulle agent to organize underground cells of resistance. Faulkner also casts the sewing-girl and her musician father (both still unnamed at this point) as members of the underground, thereby making these characters more central to the main action of the plot.

The other principal alterations in this revised treatment concern the handling of Georges's escape and Jean's ultimate fate. As in the first treatment, Georges is captured by the Germans and rescued by his brother; but Faulkner now revived his previously-discarded plan of having Jean take Georges's place in the jail cell. However, since Tixier had objected to the use of the German soldier as Jean's accomplice in the escape plot, Faulkner needed a different strategy of operation. The scheme he settled upon was to have Jean enter into a marriage of convenience with the seamstress, summon Coupe-tête to drive the bride and bridegroom to the village to visit Mme Mornet, and then arrange for Georges to be disguised and slipped past the authorities as the new husband. When Jean is discovered in Georges's cell, he is arrested and sent to work as an enforced laborer in the munitions factory at Dieppe. In the final episode Jean dies, like his boyhood friend earlier, singing the Marseillaise with other Free Frenchmen, during a bombing raid on the factory.

It is presumably this revised treatment that Faulkner mentions in his letter to his stepdaughter, Victoria Fielden, on September 19, 1942. "The script I did," Faulkner wrote, "now has the official O.K. of De Gaulle's agent and of the Dept. of State, so nothing to do now but write in the dialogue."[13] He would spend the next two months in completing the screenplay.

In resuming his work on the actual script, as the drafts given to Bezzerides demonstrate, Faulkner first rewrote (IV.B) the material he had previously submitted to the Story Department. He changed Chopine's name to Coupe-tête, altered the brothers' furloughs to two days, and incorporated De Gaulle's quarrel with his superiors on how best to deploy his three thousand tanks. All these details were drawn straight from Tixier's list of suggestions. In addition to such alteration of specific fact, Faulkner also made numerous, if minor, stylistic changes, revising his phrasing in both narrative and dialogue. For example, Marthe's remark to Chopine, "You'll never have the last

---

[13] *Selected Letters of William Faulkner,* pp. 163–164.

word because you won't even come to it until you expel your last breath," is reworded: "You'll never have the last word anywhere because you won't even come to it until you are expelling your last breath." The many changes of this type seem to have derived from Faulkner's long-established practice of experimenting and rewriting any time he edited previous copy. However, despite his revisions, both those of his own making and those requested by Tixier, Faulkner was able to retain the basic content and structure of his first draft. By October 5, 1942, he had completed the revision of the first fifty-eight pages of the screenplay and added another seventeen pages (IV.C) tracing the debate of the French war ministry following the Battle of France, as well as De Gaulle's early negotiations with Churchill and England.

Throughout October Faulkner made steady progress on his script. As he wrote, he continued to draw upon materials supplied by the Warner Bros. Research Department and the Free French representatives. One group of such aids was contained with the manuscripts Brodsky found in Bezzerides' home. Included are separate chronologies (VI.F, G) of De Gaulle's activities during 1940 prepared by the Research Department and by the French Research Foundation, a West Hollywood-based Fighting French support organization. Also included are transcriptions of some of De Gaulle's radio speeches (VI.H); selected pages from various issues of *Free France,* a biweekly newsletter (VI.J); and a twelve-page, first-person narrative (VI.K) by an unidentified person (apparently an American), describing conditions in France under German occupation during June and July, 1940. Except for the chronologies and speeches (the latter of which he significantly edited), Faulkner seems to have made little, if any, use of these materials. Their existence, however, suggests the extent to which Faulkner was being inundated with "facts" as he worked on the screenplay.

On October 13 the Research Department responded to Faulkner's request for a list of typical first names and surnames of Breton men and women. Since all nine of the surnames on this list (VI.L) are introduced on page 101–109 of Faulkner's finished screenplay, it would appear that by the middle of October Faulkner had completed roughly two-thirds of his script. By October 30, the date that appears on the revised page 115 of the script, Faulkner had presumably finished the work, now numbering 153 pages in typescript (IV.D).

V

After three extremely busy months of consultation, writing, and revision that had produced possibly as many as 1,000 pages of typescript,

Faulkner could hardly have been prepared for the response of De
Gaulle's Hollywood representative to the finished screenplay. In a
nineteen-page report (VI.N), poorly typed and expressed in awkward
English, Berger delivered a devastating attack upon Faulkner's script.
Many of the objections were of the type previously cited by Tixier:
Faulkner had been grossly inaccurate with regard to French custom,
politics, and history. But Berger also faulted the handling of plot and
characterization. The two brothers, Berger argued, were not convincing: "Georges seems rather uninteresting and Jean, who has become
the hero of the film, is really shown as too stupid for words." Why not,
Berger asked, cast Jean as Georges's father, an industrialist who col-
laborates with the Germans out of fear and self-interest? Moreover,
Berger insisted, Coupe-tête's ploy of unnecessarily stealing food
packages just to remove the Vichy curse from them is "childish" and
scarcely appropriate for a film "whose magnitude is the first condition." Having members of the underground gamble for the right to
kill Germans was equally offensive. "The situation of the peasants
under oppression," Berger noted, "is no joke. . . ." What obviously
bothered Berger most, however, was that Faulkner had shifted the
focus of the story away from De Gaulle. "General De Gaulle," Berger
wrote, "disappears practically from the story after the first third and
the Fighting French movement with him. This was the strongest objection made by London[14] on the first story, and it should be even
more stronger [sic] in the second, which has practically nothing to do
with De Gaulle nor with the movement." Berger continued: "De
Gaulle does not insist on having his 'part' increased, but he thinks that
he can lend his name and personality [only] to a picture which shows
the accomplishments done by his movement and being at least spiritually inspired by his activities." Berger's overall judgment was a re-
sounding rejection of the script as written: "It seems that this second
scenario, although more complete in certain aspects, [has] gone more
far away from the right track than the first one, and it seems that
radical changes have to be considered to make it acceptable."

Faulkner probably received Berger's evaluation on November 9,
along with a memo (VI.M) from Buckner that contained further suggestions from Berger. Faulkner's real feelings about Berger's remarks
would surface ten days later in a two-page memorandum (VI.O) to
Buckner, but for the time being the author held his peace and set
diligently to work once more (V.A) to placate the Free French contin-

---

[14]"London" here refers, of course, to De Gaulle's London headquarters. An intrigu-
ing question concerns whether General De Gaulle himself read Faulkner's treatment.

gent. In response to Berger's assertion that the French citizenry was not at all concerned about the cost of the Maginot Line, Faulkner deleted many of the references to that matter and substituted a new opening that concentrates on the arrangement of a wedding contract for Georges and Catherine. Faulkner also reworded his references to De Gaulle in this section, again in accordance with the corrections made by Berger. Another revision involved the debate in the Chamber of Deputies following the collapse of France. Berger had taken issue with Faulkner's depiction of the officials as "arguing, anxious, bewildered." If there were any such meeting as Faulkner described, Berger insisted, "it was not panicky nor even extremely violent." In his rewrite of this scene, Faulkner, now obviously straining to please Berger, notes: "The scene is orderly, though tense. There is no panic nor violence." In similar fashion, Faulkner lifted verbatim from Berger's notes Weygand's anti-semitic retort to Mandel, "Of course, you, as a Jew. . . ."

Faulkner acceded to Berger's wishes on still other points. He eliminated the role of Madame de Portes, showed General Catroux as coming to De Gaulle by way of the United States, and correctly identified De Gaulle's strategy of retreat. He made Jean an official of Vichy, not Germany, and incorporated Mme Mornet's opposition to her son's collaboration. Taking note of Berger's observation that "Doriot is the name of a very well known traitor," Faulkner changed the name of the musician to Moellens.[15] For the card game Coupetête and his companions play for the right to kill Germans, Faulkner substituted a more credible underground activity, the derailing of an enemy train. Moreover, by placing Georges coincidentally on the train and having him rescued by the saboteurs, Faulkner managed to return Georges to his village without having him violate the order that, according to Berger, forbade any De Gaulle secret agent from visiting his family.

By November 18 Faulkner had rewritten sixty-nine pages of the script in response to Berger's criticisms. In the copy of the screenplay reassembled on this date by the secretarial pool (V.A.), all of the revisions except the thirty-two-page opening carry the dates on which they were rewritten and/or retyped. Pages 33–35, 40–41, 45, 45a, 46–50, 50a, and 54 are dated "11/13/42"; pages 70–72, 79, 79a, and 80–84 are dated "11/16/42"; pages 85 and 92–95 are dated "11/17/42";

---

[15] However, Faulkner failed to change the name in all instances in which this character appears. Thus, in the subsequent versions of the script both "Moellens" and "Doriot" are used. A similar oversight occurred in the case of the character Guezonnec, who continues to appear in the text even after he has been killed in Faulkner's revised pages.

and pages 99–101, "102–112" [one page], 113–114, "116–117" [one page], and 119 are dated "11/18/42." A retyped, repaginated copy (V.B) of this version, omitting the above dates, was routed to Buckner for his consideration.

The next day, November 19, 1942, Faulkner made one more (apparently his last) revision of "The De Gaulle Story."[16] Accepting Berger's clarification of the status of conscripted French laborers under Nazi control, as well as the relationship between Vichy French officials and the Gestapo, Faulkner rewrote the scene depicting the encounter between Jean and Kereon at the Renault factory. In a carbon copy of the script completed the previous day (V.A) and subsequently passed on to Bezzerides, the earlier version of this scene (pages 120–124) was removed and the new pages (120–124, 124a–b), each dated "11/19/42," were inserted.[17] Thus, some sixteen weeks after his initial story conference with Buckner, and following countless revisions, many of them forced upon him by the Free French consultants, Faulkner had ended his work on "The De Gaulle Story." Undoubtedly there would have been further revisions had the project continued, but circumstances largely beyond Faulkner's control shortly led to the shelving of the script and rendered additional changes pointless.

VI

An examination of "The De Gaulle Story" ultimately leads to the question: Why was the film never produced? One possibility, of course, is simply that Faulkner's screenplay was not good enough, that, despite the weeks and months of laborious effort, Faulkner had not been able to deliver a workable script. Certainly "The De Gaulle Story" has its defects. The opening that Faulkner finally settled on seems tediously long and not altogether germane to the story. The motivation for Jean's collaborationist activity remains weak and unconvincing, and his eventual conversion to the true faith of resistance smacks of melodrama. The dialogue is frequently stodgy, almost lifeless; and certain speeches, especially Emilie's extended metaphor about ants and elephants, seem inappropriate for the respective characters. More important, the separate strands of the plot—the events in the life of the Mornet family, the clandestine operations of

---

[16] Warner Bros. files show that Faulkner was assigned to "The De Gaulle Story" from July 27 to November 22, 1942, and again from March 11 to March 19, 1943. However, there is no evidence that Faulkner did any additional writing during the latter period.

[17] This final revision is not included in any of the Warner Bros. file copies the editors have seen. Nonetheless, since the version left with Bezzerides is a carbon copy typed by someone other than Faulkner, one may presume that the ribbon copy was submitted to Buckner or the Warner Bros. Story Department.

the French underground, and the international political activities of General De Gaulle and the Free French—are never quite integrated into a unified whole. The question of the role of De Gaulle, in particular, presented a special (and perhaps insoluble) dilemma. The result is that the famous general very nearly becomes a minor character in the story that bears his name.

Furthermore, Faulkner, novelist that he was, did not always consider the practical and economic imperatives for filming particular scenes. These technical deficiencies are evidenced in the notes Buckner affixed to one copy of "The De Gaulle Story" now in the Brodsky Collection (V.B). For example, one note paper-clipped to the page recording the priest's sermon reads: "Priest lines are very good, but we should cut them down—350 feet of film in there." A similar judgment ("Good but so long!") Buckner penciled beside one of Emilie's lengthy speeches. In another attached note Buckner pointed out that, since it would be infeasible to photograph the Chamber of Deputies, the debate among the French leaders should be presented through montage, with the use of a stock shot of the exterior of the Chamber at the beginning of the scene. Faulkner, of course, was unaccustomed to thinking in such cinematic terms.

Yet, despite its weaknesses, "The De Gaulle Story" remains a poignant, moving account of one of the central events of twentieth-century history. Its very contemporaneity could presumably be counted upon to attract a wide audience, as a host of other war films of this same period had already demonstrated. Though Faulkner's script hardly qualifies as a great work of art, it does appear to have been deserving of production. In any event, the decision to kill the movie almost assuredly had little, if anything, to do with matters of quality or marketability.

Joseph Blotner traces the cause of the project's demise to the "unexpected circumstances" of wartime politics. As he explains, "De Gaulle was proving himself a troublesome ally to Winston Churchill. As their relations became more abrasive, Churchill's attitudes were communicated to Roosevelt, whose interest in the picture cooled. This was followed immediately by a similar cooling on the part of the brothers Warner. The picture was closed down."[18] While this assessment accurately reflects the mercurial nature of De Gaulle's status with his two principal allies, as well as the close personal ties of President Roosevelt and Warner Bros., such an explanation overlooks other factors that had some bearing on the situation.

As Robert Buckner recollects, one of the major difficulties encountered in the project concerned finding an actor who could be cast as a convincing De Gaulle. This matter is alluded to more than once in the

[18] Joseph Blotner, *Faulkner: A Biography* (New York: Random House, 1974), p. 1130.

notes Buckner affixed to his copy of the temporary script (V.B). To the battlefield scenes at Laon and Abbeville, Buckner attached a note reading: "Why show De Gaulle? Why not just talk about him? He has so little to do in the picture, and he would be ten times more important if we didn't show him. And what a casting problem!" Regarding a scene in which Mme De Gaulle appears, Buckner further noted: "Is it necessary to bring Mme De Gaulle in[to] the picture? Won't it be tough enough to cast the General without trying to bring his family in for a scene?"

The question of casting, though, was not the only problem. For another thing, even as Faulkner was busily putting the finishing touches on "The De Gaulle Story," Buckner and Warner Bros. were already turning their attention to another project deemed far more crucial to the American war effort. On September 1, 1942, Buckner left Hollywood for New York to meet with Joseph E. Davies, the former United States ambassador to the Soviet Union, regarding the proposed film version of Davies's book, *Mission to Moscow*.[19] On September 7–8 Buckner and scriptwriter Howard Koch held discussions with Davies at his camp in the Adirondack Mountains. In the weeks that followed, Buckner, as producer, devoted considerable time to the *Mission to Moscow* project. Actual production began on November 10, 1942; and the film was released on April 30, 1943. Ostensibly a documentary based on Davies's experiences in Russia in 1936–38, *Mission to Moscow* was designed by Davies and Warner Bros., with the encouragement and full support of President Roosevelt and the Office of War Information, to sell the American public on the idea that Joseph Stalin would be an acceptable ally in the struggle against Adolf Hitler. To accomplish this purpose, however, the makers of the film played fast and loose with important historical facts, most notably by justifying both the Soviet purge trials of the 1930s and the Soviet invasion of Finland in 1941 as appropriate and necessary responses to the threat of Naziism. Judging by Stalin's willingness to allow *Mission to Moscow* to be shown in the Soviet Union, the film apparently succeeded in presenting the Russian dictator and his country in a favorable light; but one consequence of that success was a vociferous protest from many Americans who deplored the distortions of history calculated to make a terrorist regime palatable to a democratic society. Even today *Mission to Moscow* remains one of the most controversial propaganda

[19] For a detailed history of this film project see David Culbert, "Introduction: The Feature Film as Official Propaganda," *Mission to Moscow*, ed. Culbert (Madison: University of Wisconsin Press, 1980), pp. 11–41.

films in the history of American cinema. One measure of the extreme pro-Stalin, pro-Communist bias of the film is that in 1947, during the early days of the Cold War between the United States and the Soviet Union, Jack Warner was called before the House Committee on Un-American Activities to defend the making of the film.

Just what may have been the relationship between the production of *Mission to Moscow* and the termination of the De Gaulle project remains a matter of speculation, but at least two observations may be safely advanced. First, there can be little question that in late 1942 and early 1943 the European military situation dictated that Stalin and the Soviet Union were considerably more vital to American interests than were De Gaulle and the Fighting French. While Buckner's and Warner's commitment to *Mission to Moscow* did not necessarily preclude a continuing involvement with "The De Gaulle Story," the studio's priorities obviously favored the former work.[20] Secondly, the loud public outcry raised against *Mission to Moscow* almost certainly generated second thoughts about a proposed movie concerning another contemporary leader, De Gaulle, who, though in quite a different way, was nearly as controversial as Stalin. In defining the lesson derived from the furor surrounding *Mission to Moscow,* Jack Warner has written: "There are some controversial subjects that are so explosive and so open to misinterpretation by well-meaning supporters of one side or the other, that it doesn't pay for anyone to be a hero or martyr. You're a dead pigeon either way."[21] Having learned this lesson with *Mission to Moscow,* Warner was probably reluctant to test its validity with "The De Gaulle Story."

Easier to document is the problem Faulkner encountered with the Free French consultants who advised him on the screenplay. Notice was taken previously of the manner in which Faulkner extensively revised both his treatment and the completed screenplay in response to the criticisms offered by De Gaulle's representatives, Adrien Tixier and Henri Diamant-Berger. A two-page memorandum Faulkner forwarded to Buckner on November 19, 1942 (VI.O), reveals how tense and precarious the working relationship between Faulkner and his French advisors had become. In this letter, significantly written on the day he made his last known revisions to "The De Gaulle Story," Faulkner made a startling proposal to his producer. "Let's dispense," he began, "with General De Gaulle as a living character in the story."

---

[20] In *My First Hundred Years in Hollywood* (p. 290) Jack Warner records that President Roosevelt said, "Jack, this picture *must* be made, and I am asking you to make it." Warner replied, "I'll do it. You have my word."

[21] Warner, p. 293.

Only by so doing, Faulkner asserted, could the studio "gain the free-dom" to produce an entertaining movie for an American audience, rather than a propaganda tool to serve the political purposes of the Fighting French. To proceed under Free French supervision, Faulk-ner stated, "we must either please them and nobody else, or probably please nobody at all." The problem was that these advisors would continue to require "an absolute adherence to time and fact, no mat-ter how trivial the incident nor imaginary the characters acting it." This position was one that Faulkner would encounter again from time to time, as when in 1945 Malcolm Cowley challenged the discrepan-cies in the Compson family "Appendix" and Albert Erskine in 1959 quarreled with the inconsistencies in the Snopes trilogy.[22] Unfortu-nately, the Free French critics proved less willing than these other editors to grant Faulkner a considerable degree of poetic license in his handling of fact.

This November 19 memo to Buckner also confirms what the text of the screenplay implies: that Faulkner's interest in the story had shifted radically, even while he conscientiously sought to placate his French consultants. The real focus of the script, Faulkner had come to believe, should not be De Gaulle but the ordinary citizens who fol-lowed him. "Any historical hero, angel or villain, is no more than a figurehead of his time," Faulkner wrote. "He is only the sum of his acts, only the sum of the little people whom he slew or raised, en-slaved or made free." Thus, Faulkner advised Buckner, "Let's tell what [De Gaulle] has done by means [of] its poetic implications, in terms of some little human people, with their human relationships which an audience can understand, whose lives and destinies were affected, not by him but by the same beliefs that made him De Gaulle."

In summary, then, it seems likely that no single factor but rather a combination of causes led to the cancellation of the De Gaulle movie. The disenchantment of Churchill and Roosevelt with De Gaulle un-doubtedly influenced the decision, but so, too, presumably did the problem of casting, the higher priority assigned *Mission to Moscow,* the recalcitrant objections of the Free French consultants to Faulkner's script, and even Faulkner's own reservations about the proper focus of the work. In later years Faulkner occasionally commented on the compromises imposed upon a Hollywood screenwriter. "There's no

---

[22] See Malcolm Cowley, *The Faulkner-Cowley File: Letters and Memories, 1944–1962* (New York: Viking Press, 1966), pp. 41–47; and Louis Daniel Brodsky and Robert W. Ham-blin, eds., *Faulkner: A Comprehensive Guide to the Brodsky Collection, Volume II: The Letters* (Jackson: University Press of Mississippi, 1984), pp. 250–251.

chance," Faulkner said, "for the individual to make something as he himself thinks it should be made." Movies, he continued, are "made by too many people, too many forces. . . ."[23] His experience with "The De Gaulle Story" undoubtedly provided Faulkner with a major case in point.

VII

One of the most impressive features of "The De Gaulle Story" is the manner in which it anticipates content and themes treated in later Faulkner works. One somewhat surprising example is the link between the screenplay and the Compson "Appendix" that Faulkner wrote in 1945 for Cowley's use in *The Portable Faulkner*. Drawing upon his stint in Hollywood, only recently terminated, Faulkner has Caddy Compson divorce her second husband, "a minor movingpicture magnate," disappear "in Paris with the German occupation, 1940," and then reappear in a photograph with "a handsome lean man of middleage in the ribbons and tabs of a German staffgeneral."[24] These last two quotations coincidentally place Caddy in precisely the same milieu Faulkner utilized in "The De Gaulle Story." More significantly, Faulkner's concluding commentary on the fate of Dilsey and her progeny reiterates the dominant theme of "The De Gaulle Story." "They endured," Faulkner notes of Dilsey and her kin; and one can only wonder to what extent the recent example of the French resistance to Nazi occupation, as well as the long struggle of Southern blacks, may have influenced Faulkner's justly-famous line.

"The De Gaulle Story" has even stronger ties to *A Fable*, the 1954 Pulitzer Prize novel structured on the biblical story of Christ. Faulkner's screenplay similarly employs the Christ myth as a controlling motif. From his early treatment through the finished screenplay Faulkner draws numerous parallels between General De Gaulle and Christ. Labeled by Reynaud "an obscure dreamer, servant of an illusion," De Gaulle has been, according to Georges, "crucified" by the nation he sought to warn of impending doom. Not only in his rejection and unjust death sentence but also in his power to effect miracles is De Gaulle identified with Christ. "I thought you were dead," De Gaulle says to one soldier. "What brought you back to life?" "France, General," the soldier replies. A comrade adds, "Someone whispered

[23] James B. Meriwether and Michael Millgate, eds., *Lion in the Garden: Interviews with William Faulkner, 1926–1962* (New York: Random House, 1968), p. 153.

[24] Malcolm Cowley, ed., *The Portable Faulkner* (New York: Viking Press, 1946), pp. 745–746. The "Appendix" also appears in Modern Library and Vintage editions of *The Sound and the Fury*.

De Gaulle in his ear." "Does that raise the dead in France?" De Gaulle inquires. The soldier responds, "It will do better than that now. It will raise the living." In another scene that recalls a passage in Christ's parable of the great supper (Luke 14:20), a sailor temporarily abandons De Gaulle with the excuse, "I have a wife. We have been married only a year." An indirect link between De Gaulle and Christ is also found in the priest's dying words, "God, not [the fuehrer], is my leader." By identifying the Free French cause with God, the priest is following Christ's injunction (Matthew 22:21) to distinguish between obedience to God/Christ (De Gaulle) and obedience to Caesar (Hitler).

There are still other Christian elements in "The De Gaulle Story." When Jean switches his allegiance to the Free French, he has, in Emilie's words, "saved his soul." In a passage appearing in the story treatment but deleted from the screenplay, De Gaulle welcomes Jean to the resistance movement by recalling Christ's words in Luke 15:7: "What does the Bible say? More rejoicing in heaven over one sinner that repents than over a hundred who did not sin." By taking Georges's place in the jail cell and then later giving his life for the cause of freedom, Jean has symbolically equated the Free French mission with the Christian ideal that leads one to lay down his life for another. In the contention that "there is something of the little people in the very great: as if all the little people who had been trodden and crushed had condensed into one great one who knew and remembered all their suffering," Emilie indirectly parallels De Gaulle's role with the Christian concepts of incarnation and substitutionary atonement. Georges, De Gaulle's most fervent disciple, enunciates the Free French version of the Great Commission (Matthew 28:19–20): "There are many more like me, that he has sent, to go among the villages and towns as I have come here, to bring his message. He says, 'Be secret and be strong, and wait and hope, and above all, work'." Coupe-tête, distributing the stolen caviar along with bread and wine, in commemoration of two freedom fighters, becomes a secular priest administering the political equivalent of the mass. And, finally, the anticipated triumph of the Free French is repeatedly conveyed through images of resurrection.

In *A Fable*, on which Faulkner actively worked during his tenure at Warner Bros. and not long after his writing of "The De Gaulle Story," the application of the Christ story has admittedly undergone a distinct metamorphosis. Instead of the allusive technique of the screenplay, Faulkner adopted for his novel an allegorical method. Moreover, in *A Fable* the Christ figure is an obscure corporal (one of "the little people") who opposes a war rather than a famous general who seeks to promote one. Nevertheless, the fact remains that the narrative designs of both script and novel depend heavily upon the gospel pattern. That being the case, one might argue that "The De Gaulle Story" must be included in any consideration of the evolution of *A Fable.*

Doubtless the most important connection between "The De Gaulle Story" and Faulkner's later work is to be found in the priest's remarks in the original story treatment. In lines substantially altered in the finished screenplay, the priest observes:

> . . . the land is constant. It will remain. Earthquake and flood and drought come and pass as this man [Hitler] will pass, and there is still the land. Oppression and suffering come upon mankind and even destroy him as individuals. But they cannot destroy his immortal spirit. That endures. It is more than the simple will to freedom and contentment. It is his immortality, his hope and belief that out of his suffering his children and all the children of man to follow him will be free. In his suffering and his resistance to tyranny and evil and oppression he finds himself.

When Jean questions the priest's militancy, saying, "This from you, a priest?," the cleric replies:

> Yes. Look. This man, this Hitler, is nothing: a little clod of rotten dirt before God. He will pass. We may not see it. Some of us will not—we who are old, and many of you young men who are yet to die because of him. But somewhere in the long annal of human suffering our suffering will remain, fixed: one little rock at least in the foundation of our children's security and peace.

Faulkner readers will quickly note the remarkable similarities between the priest's lines and Faulkner's remarks, eight years later, upon receiving the Nobel Prize for Literature. Not only the priest's sentiments about suffering, enduring, and prevailing but even the use of a rock metaphor (though in a different context) and an accretional prose style recur in the Stockholm speech.

This link with the Nobel Prize address may well supply the key to the ultimate significance of Faulkner's unproduced screenplay. As the priest's speech demonstrates, Faulkner was greatly moved, even inspired, by the courageous and sacrificial struggle of the Free French to resist the tyranny and cruelty of Nazi Germany. Such heroism Faulkner equated with the invincible, immortal qualities of the collective human spirit. Critics have long noted how a faith in this spirit, as well as a public voice raised on its behalf, increasingly came to characterize the work of Faulkner's late years. What can now be recognized, however, is that the first full expression of that faith and voice is not to be found in the Nobel Prize acceptance speech in 1950, or *Intruder in the Dust* in 1948, but in "The De Gaulle Story" in 1942.

Robert W. Hamblin
Louis Daniel Brodsky

"The De Gaulle Story"
Materials in the Brodsky Collection

(Items from the Warner Bros. Story Department files are designated by the initials WB; materials acquired from A. I. Bezzerides are labeled AIB. Items included in the present volume are indicated by asterisks.)

I. STORY OUTLINE

*A. "Journey Toward Dawn." Carbon typescript with ink corrections in Faulkner's hand, 9 pages, dated "7/28/42." WB

*B. "From William Faulkner to Robert Buckner: Appendix to Notes of July 29th." Carbon typescript with ink corrections in Faulkner's hand, 2 pages, dated "7/30/42." WB

*C. "From William Faulkner to Robert Buckner: Appendix #2 to Notes of July 29th." Carbon typescript, 2 pages, dated "7/31/42." WB

II. STORY TREATMENT

A. ["Free France"]. Faulkner's drafts (mixed ribbon and carbon typescripts with holograph revisions) of parts of at least three early versions, 161 pages (135 leaves), undated (c. August 1942). AIB

B. "Free France" (partial). Carbon typescript, 45 pages (title page, [1]–13, 13a–13e, 14–39), dated on title page, "August 3, 1942," and on pages 10–13e, "8/13/42." WB

C. ["Free France"] (out-takes). Carbon typescript, 44 pages, undated (c. late August 1942). AIB

D. "Free France." Ribbon typescript, 79 pages (title page, [1]–13, 13a–13e, 14–24, "25–27a" [one page], 28–31, 31a, "31b–31c" [one page], 32–38, 38a, 39–41, 41a–41d, 42–44, 44a, 45–46, 46a, 47–66), in blue wrappers with brass clasps; dated on title page, "August 3, 1942," and on pages 10–13e, "8/13/42." (These dates were brought forward from the partial treatment described in B above; much of the material in this version represents work of a later date, probably late August 1942.) WB

E. "Free France." Carbon copy of item D. (This copy was grouped with the out-takes described in C above.) AIB

*F. "Free France." Mimeographed typescript, 79 pages (same pagination as *D* and *E* above), in blue wrappers with brass clasps; dated "September 4, 1942." (Charles's name has been changed to George [*sic*] in this copy.) WB

III. REVISED STORY TREATMENT

*A. "De Gaulle Story: Treatment." Ribbon typescript, 28 pages, in blue wrappers with brass clasps; dated on cover, "10/20/42." (This date apparently represents the day that the treatment was filed in the Warner Bros. Story Department; Faulkner probably wrote this treatment in late September 1942.) WB

B. "De Gaulle Story: Treatment." Carbon copy of item *A*. AIB

IV. SCREENPLAY

A. "First Draft / Screenplay / 'De Gaulle Story'" (partial). Ribbon typescript, 58 pages ([1]–47, "48–49" [one page], 50–59), in brown wrappers with brass clasps; dated on cover in unknown hand, "9/?/42." WB

B. ["The De Gaulle Story"]. Faulkner's draft of rewrite of item *A*, 63 pages (mixed ribbon and carbon typescripts with holograph revisions), undated (c. late September 1942). (On verso of thirty of these pages are miscellaneous ribbon and carbon typescript pages from at least two earlier versions.) AIB

C. "Second Draft / Screenplay / 'De Gaulle Story'" (partial). Ribbon typescript, 73 pages ([1]–52, 52a, 53–54, "55–56" [one page], 57–73), in blue wrappers with brass clasps; dated on pages 40, 41, 46, and "55–56," "10/3/42," and on pages 51, 52a, and 54, "10/5/42." WB

*D. "The De Gaulle Story." Carbon typescript, 153 pages, in brown wrappers with brass clasps; dated on page 99, "10/28/42," and on page 115, "10/30/42." WB

V. REVISED SCREENPLAY

A. "De Gaulle Story." Ribbon typescript, 153 pages, ([1]–32, 32a–32f, 33–45, 45a, 46–50, 50a, 51–79, 79a, 80–101, "102–112" [one page], 113–115, "116–117" [one page], 118–153), in blue wrappers with brass clasps; dated on cover in unidentified hand, "11/18/42." WB

B. "De Gaulle Story." Carbon typescript, 146 pages (retyped, renumbered copy of item *A*), in blue wrappers with brass clasps; undated (c. November 18, 1942). (Paper-clipped to pertinent pages of this copy are sixty-one typed notes by Buckner, listing suggestions for revision and/or filming. Handwritten marginal notations, also by Buckner, are scattered throughout the text.) WB

*C. ["The De Gaulle Story"]. Carbon typescript, 153 pages (text

and pagination identical to item *A*, except for pages 120–124, 124a–124b), in blue wrappers with brass clasps; dated on pages 120–124b, "11/19/42." AIB

VI. RELATED DOCUMENTS

*A. Warner Bros. Employee's Starting Record for Faulkner, dated "7-27-42." WB

*B. Warner Bros. Inter-Office Communication from Buckner to Faulkner, August 10, 1942, ribbon typescript, 2 pages. AIB

*C. Warner Bros. Inter-Office Communication from Buckner to Faulkner, September 1, 1942, ribbon typescript, 1 page. AIB

*D. "Free French Story." Summary report from Buckner to Faulkner, undated (c. September 1942), ribbon typescript, 4 pages. AIB

*E. "Observations on Inexact Details." Critique of Faulkner's story treatment by Adrien Tixier, undated (c. September 1942), carbon typescript, 5 pages. AIB

*F. Warner Bros. Inter-Office Communication from Research Department to Faulkner, September 30, 1942, ribbon typescript, 3 pages. AIB

*G. Information supplied by French Research Foundation, West Hollywood, California, undated (c. October 1942), ribbon typescript, 6 pages. AIB

*H. Transcribed copies of four of General De Gaulle's BBC radio broadcasts, carbon typescript, 4 pages, ribbon typescript, 1 page. AIB

I. Transcribed copy of cable message from General De Gaulle to the American Jewish Congress, carbon typescript, 1 page. AIB

J. Selected pages from various issues of *Free France: A Fortnightly Bulletin Published by the Free French Press and Information Service,* August–October 1942, 18 pages (9 leaves). AIB

K. First-person narrative by an unidentified person (apparently an American) describing conditions in France under German occupation, June–July 1940, ribbon typescript, 12 pages. AIB

*L. Warner Bros. Inter-Office Communication from Research Department to Faulkner, October 13, 1942, ribbon typescript, 1 page. AIB

*M. Warner Bros. Inter-Office Communication from Buckner to Faulkner, November 9, 1942, ribbon typescript, 1 page. AIB

*N. Critique of Faulkner's screenplay by Henri Diamant-Berger, undated (c. early November 1942), ribbon typescript, 19 pages. AIB

*O. Warner Bros. Inter-Office Communication from Faulkner to Buckner, November 19, 1942, carbon typescript, 2 pages. AIB

*P. Signed contract between Faulkner and Warner Bros., dated June 29, 1945, assigning ownership of "The De Gaulle Story" to the studio. WB

EDITORIAL NOTES

UNLIKE MOST OF his other movie work, in which he actively collaborated with other authors, for "The De Gaulle Story" Faulkner himself did most of the plotting and all of the actual writing. Thus the successive stages in the development of this work provide a rare and intimate view of Faulkner's working technique in crafting a screenplay. For this reason the editors have elected to produce not only the final script but also the original story outline, the initial and revised story treatments, and the first complete draft, as well as various out-takes, memoranda, and other documents relating to the project. Since these combined materials provide the most detailed record yet made available of Faulkner's efforts to create an original screenplay, this volume is indispensable to anyone seeking to understand and assess Faulkner's ability and practice as a scenarist.

One happy result of the decision to publish the progressive versions of "The De Gaulle Story" is that the editors have been relieved of the necessity of judging which of the two versions of the finished screenplay—Faulkner's first complete draft or the revision incorporating the changes recommended by the Free French consultant—constitutes the "definitive" version. Each reader will undoubtedly have his own preference between these two works, and the editors are content to allow each reader that choice. For those who might be interested in knowing, however, we here record our own personal preference for the first of the two versions—in part because the first seems closer to Faulkner's actual intent but also because the first is, in our opinion, more successful in engaging the reader's attention and interest.

In preparing these materials for publication, we have been guided by the principles of clarity, consistency, and readability. Obvious typographical errors have been silently corrected; spelling, punctuation, capitalization, and indentation have been regularized; and the basic format of the scripts has been slightly altered. In those cases in which the typescripts employ variant but equally acceptable forms, the most prevalent form has been adopted. The relatively few instances that have required substantive editorial interpolations and emendations have been duly noted in the textual collation printed at the end of the volume.

Faulkner

*A Comprehensive Guide
to the Brodsky Collection*

Volume III: The De Gaulle Story
by William Faulkner

EMPLOYEE'S STARTING RECORD — WARNER BROS. PICTURES, INC

MAN NO. _____

SOCIAL SECURITY NO. _548-05-8158_

DATE _7-27-42_ NAME _FAULKNER, WILLIAM_

HOUR STARTED _____ ADDRESS _____

RATE _300._ CITY _____

_____ PHONE _____

DEPARTMENT _____ OCCUPATION _Writer_

DATE OF BIRTH _____ PLACE OF BIRTH _____

NATIONALITY _____ MARRIED _____ SINGLE _____

LEGAL RES. (STATE) _____ CITIZEN OF U.S. _____

IF NOT CITIZEN (DATE OF ENTRY) _____ QUOTA NO. _____

UNION _____ EVER EMPLOYED HERE BEFORE _____

13 weeks - 3 idle. (Make MPRF deductions)

APPROVED _R. J. OBRINGER_ EMPLOYEE'S SIGNATURE

ML-149

1. Warner Bros. Employee's Starting Record for Faulkner

I

Journey Toward Dawn
Story Outline

SECTION I

We begin with the Tank School which De Gaulle commands. It is the nucleus of what he hopes will be a powerful tank corps someday. The reason for starting here appears in Section II.

We follow De Gaulle up to the start of war, show him with his Tank School and reveal his aim to build it into a tank corps. We show his struggle to gain this end. It will be necessary to show something of the politics of France at the time, to explain his struggle and its foredoomed failure.[1] We can refrain from personalities. We will not need to make Pétain[2] a villain. We can show that De Gaulle considers him a villain, but if necessary we can show Pétain as simply an old, tired man who had no business with that much power. We can use some symbol to represent the hidebound military establishment of most democracies as being the villain.

We will show in parallel the other side of this picture. We will show the younger, stronger, livelier men who see the writing on the wall, which the old men do not. This can be done by taking up Churchill at this point. He does not know De Gaulle now, possibly has never heard of him nor of his struggle with the old French generals for a mechanized army. These two lines will be

---

1. Throughout the 1930s, as Adolf Hitler steadily increased Germany's capabilities for war, De Gaulle, then an obscure junior officer, publicly challenged the French military reliance upon fixed fortifications and huge numbers of civilian draftees. De Gaulle argued that modern warfare required a mechanized, mobile, professional army employing the tank as its principal weapon.

2. Phillipe Pétain (1856–1951), French army officer, gained recognition as the "savior of Verdun" during World War I. From July 1940 until the liberation of France from German occupation in 1944, Pétain served as chief of state for the Vichy French government and, in that capacity, opposed the Free French policies of General De Gaulle.

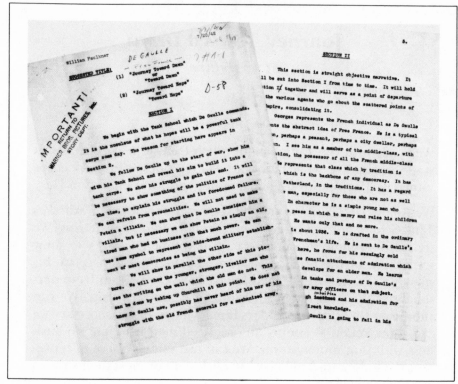

2. Initial story outline of work which became "The De Gaulle Story"

parallel and antithetical, but they will not touch yet. This will be simply turning over the medal to see the other side of it for a moment.

De Gaulle loses his argument with the generals about tanks. He has no tank corps and realizes that he probably never will. But he still struggles for it. He makes his prophecy in print as to how the Germans will conquer Europe.[3] He gets into hot water about this. The war starts. De Gaulle's prophecy comes true to the letter. De Gaulle does the best he can with what he has. France collapses. De Gaulle alone insists on further resistance.

3. As early as 1934, in his book *Vers l'Armee de Metier,* De Gaulle warned that France's greatest vulnerability to military attack was created by the broad but shallow plain linking the country to Belgium. In May 1940 the Germans invaded France from this direction.

Now he and Churchill meet. Churchill is also trying to persuade the French to keep on fighting. They fail. The final betrayal comes with the armistice. De Gaulle and Churchill leave France for England.

We will point up the tragedy of De Gaulle's position now. He has been repudiated by the army to which he has given his life. He has chosen exile rather than surrender. He has been proscribed by his own countrymen and is forced to flee his fatherland, which he loves. He and Churchill take a plane for England. Neither of them sees any hope in sight for France. After the speed with which France was conquered, there is every reason to believe that England will fall, too, but Churchill and De Gaulle do not give up although there is no hope in sight.

They sit opposite each other across the aisle in the plane. Churchill is a nervous man. He is chewing an unlighted cigar. He is worried, baffled, aghast at the future. De Gaulle is a stolid man. He sits motionless, like a stone, staring ahead. Off scene, the pilot tunes his radio and picks up a German broadcast. The voice is saying how quickly France fell and that England will fall within ten days. The voice stops. Churchill chews his cigar. De Gaulle stares ahead. Churchill leans across the aisle and asks De Gaulle for a match. De Gaulle gives him one. Churchill lights his cigar. They stare ahead again. This is to indicate how the future looks so dark that there is simply nothing for them to say to one another. Each knows that the other has not given up.

FADE OUT.

We follow the growth of the Free French movement from London. De Gaulle reaches England with no money and only a pair of pants and a few shirts in a briefcase. We will see Frenchmen escaping from France and fleeing to England. Most of them have not heard of De Gaulle yet. They simply gravitate toward anyone who still intends to resist.

His name and his purpose spread, by word of mouth, by underground. It leads to France, and we will see all sorts of French people responding. We see those who can and do escape from France and those who cannot and never will be able to escape. We see the young men who can fight and old men and women who cannot. We see five schoolboys with their book satchels who escape from France and cross the Channel in canoes. We see nuns writing letters, expressing their hope that the Germans will still be resisted. We see peasants writing letters. Veterans of 1918, who have not yet heard of De Gaulle either, hear the British broadcast; and they write these letters in the hope that they will reach someone who can still pull France together.

We will show this as first a trickle, then a stream, then a tide of hope and resistance, flowing toward England and De Gaulle. Then we will show it in reverse, the trickle, the stream, the tide setting out from De Gaulle's little house in England back into conquered France and then Africa and India and the Pacific, giving something of hope to whatever Frenchmen can and will listen.

We can use the method Mr. Buckner suggested.[4] We can show De Gaulle's agents setting out toward all the scattered parts of the Empire on their errands of consolidation. Then we will show a changed map to indicate that their purpose was accomplished. We will indicate that some of these are risky jobs, that sometimes the agent loses his life in the effort. It may be more effective not to show that he does lose his life, to indicate that these men believe that their lives are nothing in balance with the freedom of France and the restoration of its proud name.

This sounds episodic as written here, but I think it will tighten itself up in the telling. Also, Section II which follows will hold it together. I am trying now to follow a suggestion of Mr. Buckner's. This was to paint a big canvas to show the growth and scope of the Free French movement and to indicate that its limit is boundless, that one strip of film cannot possibly contain it, that it will run over the edge and will go on and on until its aim is accomplished.

4. Robert Henry Buckner (1906–   ) was born near Richmond, Virginia, and educated at the University of Virginia, Edinburgh University, and École Polytechnique in Paris. As a journalist and fictionist Buckner lived in London, Paris, Brussels, and New York before becoming a Hollywood screenwriter in 1936. Selected by Jack Warner to produce a film based on the career of General Charles De Gaulle, Buckner held a number of conferences with Faulkner regarding the story line for the script.

SECTION II

This section is straight objective narrative. It will be cut into Section I from time to time. It will hold Section I together and will serve as a point of departure for the various agents who go about the scattered points of the Empire, consolidating it.

Georges represents the French individual as De Gaulle represents the abstract idea of Free France. He is a typical Frenchman, perhaps a peasant, perhaps a city dweller, perhaps a Parisian. I see him as a member of the middle class, with some education, the possessor of all the French middle-class virtues. He represents that class which by tradition is democratic, which is the backbone of any democracy. It has pride in its Fatherland, in the traditions. It has a regard for its fellow man, especially for those who are not as well off as it is. In character he is a simple young man who looks forward to peace in which to marry and raise his children and do his work. He wants only that and no more.

The time is about 1936. He is drafted in the ordinary course of a young Frenchman's life. He is sent to De Gaulle's tank school. While here, he forms for his seemingly cold commander one of those fanatic attachments of admiration which a young man sometimes develops for an older man. He learns of De Gaulle's belief in tanks and perhaps of De Gaulle's trouble with the superior army officers on that subject. This may be partly through intuition and his admiration for De Gaulle more than any direct knowledge.

He thinks that De Gaulle is going to fail in his campaign to get a mechanized army. He begins to ape De Gaulle. Inside the small group with which he lives in contact he becomes a replica of De Gaulle himself in De Gaulle's broader scope of struggle with the army to get his tank corps. His very sincerity will make this sequence comic. He spends most of his time defending De Gaulle and preaching mechanized force, about which he really knows nothing. He wrangles so much with his fellow soldiers that finally a sergeant tells him he talks too much and orders him to shut up.

Georges serves his time and is discharged. He marries his
sweetheart, takes up his job again and is buying a little house
with a garden. He talks to his wife about the man he still ad-
mires. His child is born and they're quite happy, paying for the
house.

The war begins. Georges does not wait to be called to serve. He
volunteers. He tries to return to De Gaulle's command. He fails
in this. But he is still trying to save France, which to him means
his little house and garden, which he hasn't quite paid for yet.
We follow him through the Battle of France, to the collapse of
the French armies, while he sees his beloved commander's
prophecies come true, one by one. We can see in other soldiers
of Georges's age, peasants, clerks, young professional men, stu-
dents, the soil on which De Gaulle's Free French movement will
sprout and grow.

Georges escapes from France. His wife and child are still in
France. They and his little house represent to George what the
old fine name of France now cast into the dust represents to
De Gaulle. From now on Georges works to save France in order
to save his home and his life as he had wanted to live it. He, too,
has not surrendered and never will. He is only waiting until he
can return to France and drive the conqueror out of his house
and yard.

By means of his subsequent adventures, we can tie into the
story the scattered phases of the struggle between the Free
French and the Vichy French. He escapes into Syria. We can use
the episode in which the Free French captured the Syrian post
without firing a shot. We could see him next in Africa when De
Gaulle makes his expedition to the Cameroons and the Tchad.
We can show now the movement spreading and growing. We
can indicate that the Empire, the colonies, are at least safe and
that now all the French who want to be free are waiting only for
the time to come to invade France itself and drive the Germans
out. To Georges of course this still means to drive the Germans
out of his little house and garden, which he hasn't been able to
pay for yet.

Georges is now in England, once more with his beloved commander. His wife has escaped from France, and they are to-

gether again. Now he has only to drive the Germans from his house. We show here that the tide has turned to the extent that the bombings of England have failed and have ceased, and that the next step will be an invasion of France, though this of course is still in the future.

Georges has never failed in his belief of ultimate victory. The future to him is simply tomorrow, not days or weeks or years away but just tomorrow. He belongs to a commando unit. He goes on a raid on the French coast. At last, after many years, he is about to invade France. To him it is as though this little expedition is the one which will drive the Germans out. He tells his wife goodbye. He is going to drive the invader out of his little house, maybe not this time but the next time. He is exalted. He seems almost happy to go. He doesn't think for one moment that he may lose his life. His wife, though, considers this, but he has imbued her with something of his fanatic belief in De Gaulle and in a Free France. The expedition departs.

De Gaulle and Churchill together. The expedition has gone. Some of the men won't come back. De Gaulle sits at his desk, looking at papers or writing. He is still the calm, emotionless man of the scene in the airplane. Churchill is still the nervous man, chewing his cigar, walking up and down the floor.

CHURCHILL Blood, sweat and tears. But I never once heard you speak of hope.

DE GAULLE You never heard me talk about breathing, either.

The home of the English people with whom Georges's wife and child are living. The expedition is on the Channel now, perhaps reaching France. Georges may return and he may not. It is as though his wife and the English people were standing at a window, looking out over the Channel where Georges has disappeared. Georges's wife takes no part in the dialogue.

FIRST VOICE Yes, hope.

SECOND VOICE We can always hope.

THIRD VOICE We will always hope.

FADE OUT.

[NOTE: It seems to me more effective to let this ending be by implication. This seems to me even stronger than to base it on some historical success, which of course we do not have and may not have for some time.]

FROM WILLIAM FAULKNER TO ROBERT BUCKNER: APPENDIX TO NOTES OF JULY 29TH

The Battle of France. Georges is a member of a small group of soldiers which still try to defend the Maginot Line after the French armies have collapsed. This will point up the folly of the generals who counted on a defensive war and who repudiated De Gaulle and mechanization. It will also show the spirit of the men who later did work and die for Free France, who continued to resist the enemy after the men who betrayed them had surrendered and were safe.

He is captured. He is in a prison in Germany. We can show how the will to freedom exists even among the prisoners. We will see men making desperate efforts to escape, even when they know that failure means death—not just to escape from prison but to try later to reconquer France. They do not try to escape to France to return home because the German jailers tell them that France is no more. They want to escape to some free country where they can arm and return and drive the enemy from France. This idea is alive in their minds even before they have ever heard that there is a movement of this nature and a leader for it.

Georges escapes. He can escape to Syria and then to Africa and meet De Gaulle as in Section II of the notes of 7/29, or he can escape to America. We can show him enduring incredible hardship, trying to get back to England, where he has now heard of De Gaulle's movement, to join it and drive the enemy from his home and his garden and his Fatherland. We will see him escape from a prison within a few miles of his lost home and then have to travel halfway around the earth in order to return and prepare to drive the intruder out. He does not yet know where his wife is. He does not even worry about her. His feeling is almost mystic. He takes it for granted that she hates the conqueror as he does and that nothing can happen to either of them because all French men and women must and will live to resist until the last German is driven out of France.

He manages to reach England at last. He finds his wife and child and hardly stops long enough to say hello to them before he joins commando and leaves again to invade France. His good sense tells him this can only be a hit-and-run raid, but there is still the invincible hope and belief and his passionate admiration for De Gaulle and the cause. It is as though the simple will to drive out the invader will be enough to sweep even a handful of men on to Paris and beyond it to the frontier until the crooked cross no longer flies anywhere over French soil.

FROM WILLIAM FAULKNER TO ROBERT BUCKNER: APPENDIX #2 TO NOTES OF JULY 29TH

We symbolized all France by means of representative individuals. One is a peasant; one a Parisian Apache; one a student; one an artist of some kind, actor, musician, painter, poet, etc. One is a bank clerk; one is a southerner from the Medi; one is a Basque; one, a Breton; one a Picard, etc. We see them all together as soldiers in the same company during the Battle of France. One or two of these representative types are in the little group which still defends the Maginot Line, even after France has fallen and they know their cause is hopeless and can end only in death or capture. We can show that all of them prefer death, but they are captured instead. One of these might be the officer commanding this group. We can show how at this point they're no longer officer and men but are all simply men who will resist to the last, even to death, rather than to surrender and accept the dishonor of France.

Before this time the other two or three or four of these representative types have become scattered into other parts of the army. When they can fight no longer, they flee from France and escape to England. They hear of someone who still intends to resist. They gravitate toward him, ready to sacrifice their lives to restore France.

We can follow these separate individuals after they become De Gaulle agents and are sent by him to the remote parts of the

Empire to work to consolidate resistance there. We see some of them lose their lives to accomplish their leader's orders.

We can go into their various backgrounds and thus personalize the desire for freedom which De Gaulle champions, showing that it already existed and is waiting only for a leader. We can see their families, their parents, wives, etc., their homes and their jobs, what sort of life each had hoped to lead and just what freedom and the eviction of the Germans mean to each particular one of them. Each one wants to restore and preserve the old life, of course, but we show how this desire is tied into one same love and grief for the betrayed Fatherland and its ancient pride and glory.

II

Free France

Story Treatment

A small village in Brittany, May, 1940: Jean and Georges are brothers. They are soldiers, conscripted as they reached the proper age. Jean is the older. He is a sergeant-pilot in the air force. Georges is a private in the tank corps. Their mother is a widow. She has been running the farm in their absence with the help of a crochety old peasant hired man whose wife is the cook.

Interior of the kitchen on the morning after the night the boys arrived home on two weeks' leave. Mme Mornet and the cook are preparing breakfast while the boys are still asleep. The table as set for this first meal, even though it is breakfast, has a slightly festive air. Mme and the cook are happy to have the boys home again, but they show it only indirectly. Mme is quite calm. The cook even fusses about the extra work, dirt in the house, etc., where the two women had got along so well. They are Bretons. They look upon the rest of France as being a foreign country almost. The cook says that now that the Germans have overrun Scandinavia, perhaps people will stop this foolish and unnecessary war and go back to work and the boys can come home for good and attend to the farm. Not that the farm needs them, of course, but on the contrary. But this business of living with a lot of irresponsible soldiers, drinking wine and gambling all day and all night, too, will be the ruination of the boys, if it has not already ruined them. Mme Mornet wants to know why the cook thinks the Germans will be content to stop now with Scandinavia conquered. The cook is perfectly serene about it.

> **COOK** Where else can they go? They have gone South, East, and now North. There is only the West left. And on the West is our Maginot Line that cost us 3000 francs.
>
> **MME MORNET** You mean 3 million francs.

Jean and Charles enter. ~~They wear their everyday, civilian~~
~~clothes, farm~~ clothes though not peasant's smocks. ~~Jean is~~
~~25, Charles 23. Jean has his mother's calmness. Charles is more~~
~~volatile, free-hearted, reckless~~ even, ~~lively and merry.~~

This is the story of Free France, told in the simple terms of
a Breton village: the collapse of France and the hopes ~~of~~ and
struggle for rejuvenation as seen through the eyes of villagers,
told by means of village characters who are themselves the common
denominator of France. The village is the strophe, with its passions and bafflements and ~~dxix~~ divisions of brother against
brother and blood against blood, that it may continue to exist
as a symbol of home, security, happiness and peace which is man's
heritage;~~xXxxx~~ France is the antistrophe, with its passions and
bafflements and division of ~~brxtkxxxxgxixxt~~ Frenchman against
Frenchman in the national terms of a people struggling to survive
and to keep alive their traditions and glory as a nation. It is
a thesis that lust and greed and force can never conquer the human
spirit.

3. Faulkner's typescript of abstract of story

COOK 3 million? 3 million? For a fort? The politicians could have bribed all Europe to let us alone for 3 million francs.

MME MORNET Well, let us hope it will save France even in the way the politicians did spend it.

COOK Let the Germans invade France. France is not Brittany. Even Boches will think twice before they try to invade Brittany, even though Bretons are no longer the men they were when I was a girl—

The boys enter in time to hear the end of this argument. Jean tells the cook not to worry, that the French have their Maginot Line and the Germans have their Siegfried line and neither one can cross the other and will not waste men trying. Georges says the Germans won't have to cross the Maginot Line because they will go around it. Jean wants to know who says so.

GEORGES My colonel says so. He has been saying so for three years.

JEAN And what colonel is this?

GEORGES Colonel De Gaulle. He has written books about it to warn us.

JEAN I never heard of these books.

GEORGES Few in France have. The generals do not want them to. Only the Germans have heard of them. Let's hope they don't believe them either. Because if the Germans have believed them, all we will have left is hope.

This is becoming a hot argument, still a boyish one. It is merely the forerunner of a possible flare-up between the brothers. It will show the difference in character between them. It will show Georges's naturally hot-headed disposition, on which is superposed a young man's fanatic admiration for his commander, De Gaulle. Jean is calmer, more rational, with more self-control. Mme Mornet stops the argument before it goes any further, shows the command which she still holds over them even though they are grown men and soldiers, too. They sit down to breakfast, the argument forgotten or at least forgiven.

We follow the brothers through the day about the farm. In company with the old peasant they examine the tools and live-stock and the barns and the condition of the growing crops, etc. The old peasant will lend a comic note as the brothers squabble with him in mock seriousness about the way he farms, etc.

They return to the house for dinner. This is really the festive meal, celebrating the boys' return. Catherine is present. She is the mayor's daughter. She and the brothers have known each other all their lives. Both the brothers are interested in her, and both families intend that someday she will marry one of the brothers. But the boys will have to complete their services first and peace will have to return to Europe. The matter has not even progressed far enough for anyone to consider yet which brother it will be, since the girl herself has not yet expressed a definite choice. But we see at once that she is drawn, even without being quite aware of it, toward that hot-headed, reck-less, aliveness in Georges, in comparison with which Jean's calmness and dependability seem simple dullness to a young girl.

After dinner the brothers intend to go to the cafe to spend the evening with the other men who will gather there on Saturday night. A byplay shows that Jean had just as soon linger with Catherine. But Georges wants to go to the cafe, to meet the friends he has not seen in some time, and to find noise and movement. He is not yet interested enough (and never will be) in any girl to want to spend an evening just courting her. And Catherine does not show any particular desire to have Jean stay. So Jean follows Georges.

They walk through the village, toward the cafe. We begin to see the village now. Jean and Georges are greeted and welcomed home by the people who have known them and their parents, and by young men and girls they have grown up with. We see these people who are the backbone of the village just as the village is one integer in the backbone of France. They enter the cafe.

The cafe. A domino game is in progress between two older men, with other men watching it. There are men at other tables and at the bar, smoking and drinking and talking. All the representative types of the village are present: the apothecary, the postmaster, the constable, the mayor, the schoolteacher, etc. The younger men gather about Jean and Georges. One of them makes a remark which sets Georges off again on the subject of tanks and the Maginot Line. This is a puerile sort of argument, too, though at the word Maginot the older men begin to listen. Jean tries to cover up for Georges, wants him to shut up, but Georges is riding his hobby horse again. He says the Maginot Line is not going to stop the Germans because they probably won't even see it except from the back. All the older men take fire at this, to the extent that the mayor himself answers. He considers himself, and at this time he actually is, speaking in the name of all Frenchmen.

> **MAYOR** What? The Maginot Line no good, that cost us 30 million francs?

Georges tries to reply by quoting his beloved Colonel De Gaulle. Now he has the whole cafe down on him, all the old men who have had to pay their tithe of taxes to build the Maginot Line. This is right up Georges's alley. He sees himself embattled with all blind stupidity, fighting his beloved absent leader's cause in which he believes not because he is wiser than the others but because of his faith and admiration for his colonel.

Jean tries to slow him up; these are the elders, the respected powerful men of the village. But Georges is only too ready to take Jean on, too, even though Jean is trying to protect Georges. Jean believes Georges is wrong. When Georges refuses Jean's good-intended offices, Jean gets into the argument also. Georges now finds one or two supporters, who have read De Gaulle's books. Soon the entire cafe is in an uproar, the patronne leaning across the bar to put her voice in. The dominoes are scattered, the two old men who were playing are now shaking their fingers in one another's faces, while Georges still supports his end of the argument, trying to tell what De Gaulle thinks and has said and the treatment he got from the blind generals in payment for his warning of the danger. It is on the verge of becoming a free-for-all when the gendarme enters, sees Georges in a raging state now, realizes or learns that

Jean and Georges started the whole thing, and orders them to go home, hurries them firmly out. As they return home, Georges will not even speak to Jean. He crosses the street to walk on the other side from Jean. Georges is coldly furious and inwardly seething. Jean is angry at Georges not for what Georges believes but because of Georges's behavior. Georges strides on ahead. They go up the path to their door, Georges about ten feet in front, stomping angrily along.

Interior of house. Mme Mornet comes out of her bedroom in a dressing gown, stands as Jean and Georges enter. They do not see her. Jean attempts some placating remark; he is willing to apologize if he had a chance. Georges turns on him. They take up again where the gendarme broke them off. Jean retorts. Mme Mornet steps forward and makes them shut up, tells them to go on to bed. They obey her as always, stop, tell her good night as she has trained them to do, and mount the stairs. She stands watching them until they enter their room and close the door.

Interior of bedroom. A big old bed in which Jean and Georges have slept together ever since they were weaned. Georges undresses rapidly, in that same restrained fury, gets into bed and lies rigidly on his back. Jean undresses slower. He would still apologize for his heat if Georges would make any gesture of repentance for his own heat. But Georges makes no movement. Jean puts out the lamp and gets into bed, lies down, too, on his back, decides to make the first movement himself toward reconciliation, since he is the older and the calmer. He rises onto his elbow and turns toward Georges.

JEAN   Georges.

Georges flings out his arm, throws Jean back, slaps Jean on the rump and turns his back to him.

GEORGES   Ah, go on to sleep, you blind opinionated sap.

The hall. Mme Mornet stands looking up at the closed door. It does not open again. She turns and goes back into her room.

Next day. It is a Saint's day. The bells are ringing, the atmosphere is festive and peaceful and yet quiet, subdued because it is the Sabbath. The brothers and the mother and the cook and the peasant depart for church in their Sunday finery.

We see the village on this peaceful Sunday in which there is no hint anywhere of war. All the people wear their best, moving slowly toward the church, to gather about the entrance as the parade led by the priest enters the church. We see the ceremony inside the church, during which the priest prays for peace for France and for the world, too, soon, that the Lord's grace might descend upon Hitler and show him his error.

The mayor's house. The Mornets are there for dinner. This is a festive meal. The Mornets are more than just guests, since as soon as peace comes to Europe and France no longer has to stand to alert day and night, the marriage between Catherine and one of the boys will be arranged and the two families will then be kin. The mayor talks of this in cheerful fashion, teasing Catherine and the brothers, too, since he has forgiven the heat of last night at the cafe. He chaffs Georges about being so quick-tempered and disrespectful to his elders, but he excuses the folly of Georges's beliefs about De Gaulle and tanks because of Georges's youth. That's all Georges needs to set him off again on the old argument. Last night still rankles in the mayor, although he was willing to pass it off if Georges had seemed repentant. But when he finds Georges absolutely unshaken, the mayor takes fire. The mayor represents all individual Frenchmen who have had to pay taxes towards the cost of the Maginot Line; the idea of a whippersnapper of a boy telling him to his face that the money has been wasted is more than he will bear. Jean and his mother and Catherine all try to make Georges hush; they realize that none of them can hush the mayor, not even Catherine. But Georges will have none of it. Georges does not give a damn about the Maginot Line either. But his beloved colonel is being challenged and vituperated. At last his mother stops him temporarily by sheer force of will power and the old habit of obedience she taught both of them. She tells him that since he has so forgot his manners and the courtesy due not only to his host but to the mayor and the chief man of the village, too, that he had better apologize for his heat and excuse himself and go home. Her firmness works. Georges gets hold of himself, apologizes to the furious mayor and asks to be excused. As he turns to leave the room the door bursts open. The mayor's servant enters in a flutter, almost hurled into the room by three or four men; among them is the constable and a messenger from the nearest town with a telegraph, followed by other men whom we saw in the cafe last night, whom the hurrying messenger gathered into his train as he rushed through the village toward the mayor's house. They boil into the room in mad excitement. The message tells that the Germans have invaded the Low Countries. The message says that all French soldiers are being called up and all soldiers in the village are to report at once. All except Georges look at one another in incredulous and aghast consternation.

GEORGES   The Colonel was right! He was right!

He rushes out, Jean following.

We follow them through the village as they hurry home to don uniforms and get their kits. We see the other young men who are being called back, and the aghast and amazed older people and the women.

A group of people gathered before the cafe. A voice speaks over the radio, telling of the invasion of Holland, the bombing of Rotterdam, the retreat of the armies in Flanders.

DISSOLVE TO:

OVER DISSOLVE the voice of Reynaud[1] on the radio, telling the people to stand firm, that the army has broken at Sedan and that it is another 1914 but that Weygand[2] has been ordered in from the East and Weygand is another Foch.[3]

Battle of France—May, 1940. De Gaulle asks Pétain[4] for three

1. Paul Reynaud (1878–1966), lawyer and statesman, became premier of France on March 21, 1940. He resigned on June 16, in opposition to the armistice with Germany. He was arrested on September 6 by the Vichy regime and spent the remainder of the war in captivity. After the war he welcomed General De Gaulle's accession to power.
2. General Maxime Weygand (1867–1965) was named commander-in-chief of the French army on May 20, 1940. He declared Paris an open city on June 10 and actively sought an armistice with Germany.
3. Marshall Ferdinand Foch (1851–1929), one of France's most celebrated military heroes, served as supreme commander of the Allied forces on the western front during the final phases of World War I.
4. At this time Marshall Pétain was vice-premier in the Reynaud cabinet.

divisions [Is this divisions or battalions? Barrès[5] says battalions] of tanks and two of infantry; he will hold the German left flank, where he sees the breakthrough will come. But when the troops arrive, it is only one and a half divisions of tanks. De Gaulle is shocked, coldly enraged at the blind folly and optimism or cowardice, or whatever it is, of the staff. But he does not hesitate. He deploys what he has into battle, even though he knows it is not enough and that they could have sent him more. He holds the Germans temporarily at Laon and then at Abbeville. We will show that it was this action alone that allowed the British and French left to reach Dunkirk and be partially evacuated.

Battle of Laon. Georges is a member of one tank crew. The tanks are fighting well; they believe in De Gaulle, even though they realize there are not enough of them and that there could have been more. They are falling back, but in order, making it costly for the enemy. Georges's tank is ordered to report to Brigade H.Q. They are looking for it. They stop and ask a soldier where it is.

> **SOLDIER** Why don't you report to General De Gaulle himself?
>
> **TANK SERGEANT** There's a battle on, pig. Whoever saw a Division Commander in battle?
>
> **SOLDIER** You will now. He was fighting one of your tin baby carriages himself until he got a direct hit a while ago. He's over there now under that apple tree. Just look for a trail of cigarette butts. Follow it until you come to a man that looks like he was weaned on a shoelace. That's De Gaulle.

Georges and the others find the cigarette stubs, follow them and find De Gaulle in greasy pants and a torn leather jacket, looking like anything in the world but a general, watching the battle from beneath an apple tree in bloom. A staff officer bustles up, wants to know what the men want. De Gaulle turns,

---

5. Reference here is to Philippe Barrès's *Charles De Gaulle,* one of Faulkner's principal sources for the historical details concerning De Gaulle and the Free French movement.

looks at them. To Georges's astonishment, De Gaulle remembers his face.

> **DE GAULLE** You were at the tank school. What's your name?

Georges tells him. De Gaulle questions them rapidly about the battle and the shifting front, gives them orders what to do and dismisses them.

The battle continues as De Gaulle fights shrewdly with what he has: the only part of the whole retreat which is holding and giving the other units something to anchor on and save themselves.

Battle of Abbeville. The tanks are fighting stubbornly, still retreating but in order, holding enough for the infantry to withdraw. De Gaulle is in Georges's tank. A halt is made, other tanks come up, De Gaulle watches battle, receives messages from runners, orders the tanks out again. The crew mounts the tank again. De Gaulle gets in fast, standing up in cockpit, looking back towards the battle. If they had just given him all the tanks they had, he might have saved France. A Stuka dives at the tank, machine guns it, zooms away, another Stuka dives at it. De Gaulle still stands exposed, looking back, until Georges reaches up and catches him by the belt and tries to pull him down.

> **GEORGES** For God's sake, General!

> **DE GAULLE** You're right. Perhaps I always will be too tall for French tanks.

Night. Temporary H.Q. The battle goes on, the men weary, haggard, but still fighting. A messenger enters, brings De Gaulle a peremptory order from Reynaud to return at once to Paris. De Gaulle does not want to leave now; he cannot leave now, since only his tanks are holding at all. At first he refuses. An aide argues with him. It is an order from the head of the government, etc. De Gaulle realizes this and that he must obey.

He returns to Paris. Reynaud appoints him Under-Secretary of War. Reynaud seems confident, active, optimistic. De Gaulle is reassured. But he sees at once that the rest of the cabinet has the jitters, and that the defeatist element is steadily growing. But De Gaulle thinks first of the battle which he was forced to leave at a crucial time. He asks Reynaud to give him all the tanks the French have and let him go back to the front until the enemy can be stopped; then will be the time to discuss cabinet changes. But Reynaud says No, no, they can plan the battle better from this central point, etc. Reynaud overrules De Gaulle, partly by his position as head of France and partly by the fact that he seems confident and really appears to be doing something, as compared with the helplessness of the others. Reynaud promises De Gaulle he will back him up, support him. De Gaulle can do nothing else but acquiesce.

De Gaulle sees the whole cabinet collapsing about him. Reynaud is the only one with any ability or courage. Then he realizes that Reynaud is completely under the thumb of Mme de Portes,[6] and that she is a fascist and perhaps in German pay and is urging Reynaud to surrender. There are others, the mayor of Bordeaux, etc., who join De Gaulle in pleading with Reynaud to hold on, but De Gaulle sees that they are being beaten. He realizes at last that France is lost unless something is done.

He hurries to London in a British plane, to see Churchill. He has to borrow a coin to call Churchill on the telephone. Churchill sees the writing on the wall and De Gaulle does not even have to explain. Churchill offers De Gaulle anything in Britain. De Gaulle asks only for a microphone. The whole British Broadcasting system is turned over to him. The whole careful plan of British propaganda and communication is interrupted so De Gaulle can speak. He speaks directly to all the French people, telling them to hold on, that help is coming.

He returns to Paris. It is being evacuated, streets thronged with people walking, pushing perambulators loaded with household goods, carts, wagons, taxis, cars, etc. He learns that the government has moved to Tours. He follows in a fast car. The roads crowded with fleeing refugees. He reaches Tours and learns

6. Hélène de Portes, Reynaud's mistress, was believed to be a Fascist sympathizer. She supported the armistice with Germany.

that the government is planning to move to Bordeaux. De Gaulle realizes this will surrender all Brittany, all the Channel Coast, to the enemy. He pleads with Reynaud to stand firm. Reynaud vacillates, but at last De Gaulle seems to persuade him to resist. Reynaud takes up the telephone to rescind the order to move to Bordeaux. Mme de Portes enters, bows to De Gaulle, goes and takes telephone from Reynaud's hand and puts it back in cradle.

MME DE PORTES   Surely you will not order this move without informing the General.

REYNAUD   Of course not. *(to De Gaulle)* I must inform you that the government will definitely move to Bordeaux.

De Gaulle bows, goes out. An aide meets him as he emerges. The aide looks at De Gaulle's grim face.

AIDE   France is lost.

DE GAULLE   No. France is not lost. Never.

A single French fighter being pursued by Germans. The sky is so thick with Germans that the others do not even pay any attention to the Frenchman, save the four who are chasing him. The pilot is Jean. He turns, shoots one German down, turns and flees again, is hit, glides down to a crash landing, crawls out while the fighters still dive at him, machine gunning him, and reaches the woods.

DISSOLVE TO:

OVER DISSOLVE a radio voice, a German broadcast boasting how the British army has been trapped at Dunkirk and will be exterminated.

Georges and other French soldiers have been captured. The turmoil of the battle is still going on about them. They are questioned, their names and addresses are taken, and they are ordered back to the rear. They watch their chance, knock out the soldiers guarding them and escape, hide until nightfall.

DISSOLVE TO:

OVER DISSOLVE the radio voice telling that Paris has been declared an open city and the French government has fled to Bordeaux.

An aerodrome in the Midi. Jean and other French pilots. All have decided to take their planes and fly to Africa or England, where they can continue to fight, except Jean and two or three others. So far Frenchman has not fought Frenchman, and there is no bitterness yet. It is a matter of personal feeling, free choice yet, as nobody knows just what will happen; there is only a coldness, as if the men who once risked their lives together merely comprehended by instinct that their ways and beliefs were parting perhaps forever. But so far each man has the right to choose as his heart and mind tell him, and so there is only a withdrawal between the two groups. Jean and the other three suddenly find that they are alone, even though still surrounded by their mates. They have stolen gas to fill the tanks. Jean and the other two even help to ready the planes for the flight. Then the others take off. Jean and his two companions stand on the empty field until the planes disappear. Then they, too, separate. Suddenly they find that even they who made the same choice are somehow strangers, facing a future which they cannot yet divine.

DISSOLVE TO:

Bordeaux. Churchill, Halifax[7] and British mission have come to plead with the French government to hold on. Reynaud resigns. Pétain becomes head of the state. De Gaulle realizes this is the end. He cannot even gain access now to the men who now run things, who are betraying France. He decides to leave for England.

De Gaulle's final scene on French soil. By using what few tanks they gave him, he saved a part of the French and British armies. Yet now he cannot even gain access to the men who now run the government he saved. His only friends on his native soil are foreigners, the British, and a handful of soldiers who have

7. Edward Frederick Lindley Wood, the first Earl of Halifax (1881–1959), was viceroy of India from 1925 to 1931 and foreign secretary at the outbreak of World War II. In December 1940 he was appointed British ambassador to the United States.

escaped from the victorious enemy and have gravitated almost by instinct toward the one man whom they know who will still resist and can perhaps tell them what to do. Georges is among them; it is perhaps Georges who brought them to De Gaulle. De Gaulle welcomes them. He is going to England to organize resistance. He would take them with him, but he has no money, no influence, nothing save a pair of pants and a few shirts in a briefcase. He tells them to be of good courage, to pass the word to all Frenchmen who want to be free that there is still a France which will not surrender, and to come to him in England as they can.

De Gaulle in plane bound for England. Close shot of De Gaulle in his seat, gazing straight ahead, grim, calm, expressionless. The armrest of the seat in front of him can be seen; a plump hand holding a chewed, dead cigar lies on the armrest. The blurred shape of the co-pilot enters, bends over the seat where the hand lies.

> **PILOT** Mr. Churchill, will you sit across the aisle, if you please, to trim ship?

> **CHURCHILL'S VOICE** Yes. Quite. *(the hand with the cigar moves, a blurred shape obscures De Gaulle for a moment)*

The pilot turns, bends over the seat across the aisle.

> **PILOT** Belt all right, sir?

> **CHURCHILL'S VOICE** Quite, thanks.

Pilot exits. De Gaulle stares somberly ahead. The plane's radio cuts in: a voice says that Pétain has requested the Spanish Ambassador to ask the Germans for an armistice. Radio voice is cut off.

> **CHURCHILL'S VOICE** Blood, sweat, and tears. But I have never yet heard you speak of hope.

> **DE GAULLE** You never heard me talk of breathing, either.

FADE OUT.

FADE IN

De Gaulle's Headquarters in London. June, 1940. De Gaulle at microphone, broadcasting. In b.g. French and British officers and civilians, their faces grave and strained with worry though their spirit is still unshaken. De Gaulle speaks to all French people, telling them to be of good courage, that France will still carry on and she is not alone. He speaks levelly, without emotion. But we sense the indomitable sincerity even in the cold and inflectionless voice. His voices carries through—

DISSOLVE TO:

A small group of French people crouched about a small secret radio in a rude dark hut, listening to De Gaulle's voice.

DE GAULLE'S VOICE . . . France will survive. France will fight on. She is not alone. She is not alone. She is not alone.

The village. A swastika flag above the door to the mairie.[8]

A group of people—standing in the street before the cafe door, listening to a radio, Pétain is speaking. It is the voice of a tired old man, telling the people that France has quit fighting and asking all loyal Frenchmen and women to stand behind their chosen leaders in their effort to preserve what is left of France until the nation can rise again in its ancient pride, etc.

A German garrison has taken over the village. There is an army officer with his troops, and a Gestapo agent with a few of his men. We will show a constant conflict between the army and the Gestapo. The Gestapo is jealous of the army officer's power; the army officer with his army tradition is opposed to the Gestapo's ruthless blood lust, etc., which is stupid to the army man. The mayor has been evicted from his mairie, which is now German headquarters. German soldiers are billeted among the homes, and the cafe has been taken bodily over for an officers' mess; there is no longer any room in it for Frenchmen. There is a curfew law, and German soldiers drive the natives in off the streets.

The people are still shocked, dulled, amazed. They still cannot believe it. Yesterday they were free, secure behind their fine army and their costly Maginot Line on which they had wagered all their hopes. Today their very leaders command them to cease all resistance to and accept and collaborate with the

8. Town hall.

enemy whom they have hated and fought against for more than a hundred years.

The mayor, even though ignored and dispossessed, still holds himself to be head of the village, chief of the people. He considers his first duty toward their welfare and the preservation of their old lives and rights and property. He is convinced that the only way to do this is by obeying their leaders, no matter how shameful this seems, and staying on the best terms possible with the Germans. He has gathered about himself a clique of men who believe likewise: older men and other officials and landowners. There are others, mostly young men, who are opposed to this. But they have no voice yet. They dare not talk of resistance even to one another. The only leader they have heard of yet is in London, scarcely known, and apparently as helpless as themselves as far as they know.

Jean is the most militant one of the mayor's supporters. He is the only young man in the group. He is even more purposeful than the mayor in his intention to collaborate, which he is convinced is the only course to take. He even considers the mayor and the other older men a little wishy-washy and lacking in force. He realizes that the other young men of his age distrust him. But he does not care. He ignores them; they are helpless, don't matter in the scheme of this new France which Frenchmen must accept. He is already known to the German commander as his most dependable agent among the villagers.

Georges returns to the village. He is on his way to England to join De Gaulle. He has been hiding by day and traveling at night, begging food when he dared risk it but mostly doing without. He has stopped by home to see his mother and get clothes to replace his uniform and to get ready to make the last and most dangerous part of his journey.

While stealing into the village, he is surprised by a German soldier and is forced to kill the German. He drags the body into the bushes and goes on.

He hides in the stable and sends word by the old peasant, Chopine, to his brother. Jean is annoyed that Georges should have come straight to where the Germans are watching for him, but when he learns that Georges killed the German soldier, he is furious. Georges has not only jeopardized his own safety, he has jeopardized the security of the village and is about to ruin the good name for collaboration and some power which Jean has been building up in the village. Now Jean is not sure that even he can save his brother. Georges tells Jean not to worry. He won't need Jean's nor anybody else's saving. He is on his way to England to join De Gaulle. He and Jean can both go now. When Jean finally comprehends that Georges is going to England to keep on fighting Germans, Jean blows up completely. He calls Georges a traitor. This is the ultimate cleavage between them, as each realizes what his brother actually is. But Georges is still his brother. He must give Georges a chance to get away. He orders Georges to remain hidden until he gets back.

Jean and Chopine go and find the dead German and bury him and conceal the grave. When they return to the stable, Georges is not there. Jean knows at once what his brother's heedless and reckless temperament has led him to do. He goes to the kitchen. Georges has revealed his presence. Catherine, Mme Mornet, the cook and the priest are all present. It seems to Jean that not only do none of them realize the serious predicament which Georges has put them in, but that Catherine and Chopine think Georges has done right and are even proud of him for it. Catherine tells Jean that the whole village except the mayor's old men know Georges is here and that all the other young men are going to England with him.

JEAN And don't you know what that means? That the Germans will take vengeance on all of us that are left—old and young, men and women and children.

CATHERINE Let them. Bretons have suffered before this for Brittany. And if there are still Frenchmen left who are willing to fight and die for France, at least we who can't fight can stay here and suffer, too.

CHOPINE That is true. If Frenchmen can die for a cause, we certainly can. The Frenchman thinks first about his stove, then about his bed, then about his house, and then about la belle France. But if he can finally think about

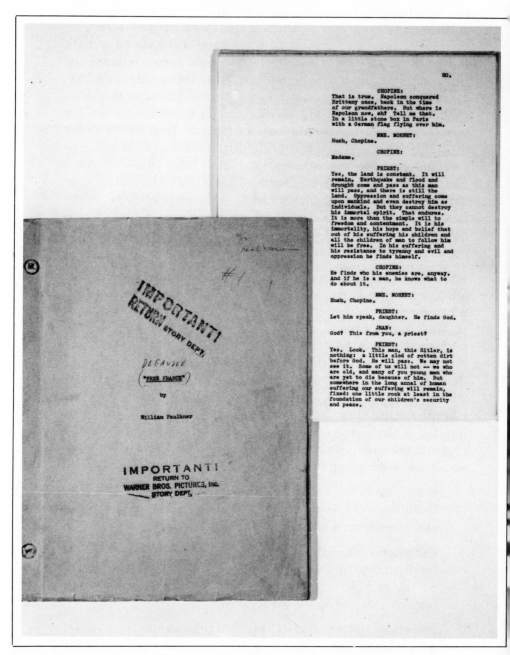

4. Passage from "Free France" that anticipates Faulkner's Nobel Prize Acceptance Speech

France and think well enough of it to be willing to die for it, then a Breton can certainly do as much.

MME MORNET   Hush, Chopine.

CHOPINE   Madame.

Jean looks at his mother. He cannot believe it.

JEAN   I am young. There is little enough in the future for men of my age, in any case. Young men have already died in this war and more of them will die. But you are old, a woman. At least we can give you peace. When by trying to resist we can accomplish nothing.

CATHERINE   But we can! We can!

MME MORNET   So much the better then. If by being an old woman and suffering to what little extent the old can suffer, I can leave a young man free to endure what a young man can endure by fighting to free our land, so much the better.

JEAN   But the land. They have overrun most of it already. If we resist, it will all be gone.

MME MORNET   Not the land. Land is constant. It will survive. It always has. It will remain no matter how many invaders pass over it and vanish, as this one will.

CHOPINE   That is true. Napoleon conquered Brittany once, back in the time of our grandfathers. But where is Napoleon now, eh? Tell me that. In a little stone box in Paris with a German flag flying over him.

MME MORNET   Hush, Chopine.

CHOPINE   Madame.

PRIEST   Yes, the land is constant. It will remain. Earthquake and flood and drought come and pass as this man will pass, and there is still the land. Oppression and suffering come upon mankind and even destroy him as individuals. But they cannot destroy his immortal spirit. That endures. It is more than the simple will to freedom and contentment. It is his immortality, his hope and belief that out of his suffering his children and all the children of man to follow him will be free. In his suffering and his resistance to tyranny and evil and oppression he finds himself.

CHOPINE   He finds who his enemies are, anyway. And if he is a man, he knows what to do about it.

MME MORNET   Hush, Chopine.

PRIEST   Let him speak, daughter. He finds God.

JEAN   God? This from you, a priest?

PRIEST   Yes. Look. This man, this Hitler, is nothing: a little clod of rotten dirt before God. He will pass. We may not see it. Some of us will not—we who are old, and many of you young men who are yet to die because of him. But somewhere in the long annal of human suffering our suffering will remain, fixed: one little rock at least in the foundation of our children's security and peace.

But Jean cannot accept this. They are worse than wrong: they are fools whom he is trying to save in spite of themselves. He won't even argue with them any more—three women, a doddering old fool of a peasant, and a monk. He says that Georges must leave tonight. But Georges is hurt; he cannot go tonight; he will be caught, found if he tries it. He must rest for a day. Jean says Georges had no business getting himself hurt. They are taking a risk by keeping him until dark. Georges must take his chance, too. The priest points out to Jean what will happen to him, Jean, and his carefully established reputation if the Germans catch Georges and learn that his brother knew of his presence in the village without reporting it. Jean agrees to give Georges time to rest. But he must remain hidden, and the other young men must not go with him.

The Germans find the soldier is missing. The whole village is barricaded, the people ordered to stay indoors while a search is made for the missing man. It is too late for Georges to try to escape now. He must lie hidden, waiting until the search begins to loosen.

The farm work must go on, to produce the food which the Germans will take. Soldiers are sent to the field to watch each group of farmers while patrols search the adjacent country for the missing man, whom they know now has been killed.

A patrol captures a starving dog, puts it on a leash. It finds the buried body by the smell of meat, food, starts digging. The body is discovered.

Chopine hurries home with the news. Jean insists that Georges must leave at once, injury or no injury. Georges leaves the village and hides at a charcoal burner's hut in the woods, waiting for night. The charcoal burner goes to the village, to find out what is going on. He returns and tells Georges that the German commander has arrested two young men as hostages and has given the village twenty-four hours to produce the murderer. Georges returns to the village. He will not let an innocent man die for his act.

Jean, Georges and Chopine meet in the house. Jean is coldly and grimly determined that Georges shall not give himself up and so reveal to the Germans that it was his, Jean's, brother who did the killing and thus bring Jean and all his family into bad repute, ruin the position which Jean has built up.

> **GEORGES**   How will you stop me?

Jean draws a pistol on Georges. Georges advances toward him.

> **GEORGES**   Shoot me, then. That's all the Germans can do. Chopine will tell your new friends the truth and the other man will not die.

Chopine watches. He is behind Georges. He realizes that Jean will shoot. He knocks Georges out, helps Jean to tie him up and hide him in the cellar. Chopine doesn't like this. Georges was doing the only thing a man of honor could have done. Chopine feels contempt for Jean, but at least Georges is saved and the old mother is saved that grief, etc.

The twenty-four hours are up. The commander has all the people brought up to the village square. He makes the two hostages draw lots, stands one of them against the wall before a firing squad and offers the village one more chance to name the murderer. The man's mother rushes out and names Georges as the killer.

Chopine rushes home and hides Georges in a secret place in a wine bin which Chopine has built against just such an emergency. Jean does not know about it.

Jean goes to the commander. He says he can get in touch with Georges, but he will not tell where he is. He asks the commander to give him time to see Georges and Georges will surrender himself. The Gestapo doubts this, wishes to send out a squad of men at once to search Jean's house. The commander stops him. Jean is of some value to the German plan of occupation. He will give Jean his chance to produce his brother.

Jean goes home. The whole village is watching him, to see if he really will betray his brother. Jean reaches home. He cannot find Georges. A scene between him and Catherine in which Catherine bitterly assails what she calls Jean's treachery, etc., but in vain against his inflexibility. Georges must give himself up. But he cannot find Georges. Jean believes that he has escaped. The Gestapo and his squad enter. Jean says that Georges is gone. The Gestapo expected nothing else. He slaps Jean. Jean takes the blow, restrains himself, is arrested and marched out.

He is taken back to the commander. The Gestapo is triumphant. He wants to execute Jean right away. The commander refuses again. Jean is worth nothing to them dead. Besides, they will catch Georges since they know now where he is going.

> **GESTAPO**   If he wishes to work with us, let him prove it. *(shouts at Jean)* Heil Hitler!

Jean looks at the Gestapo.

> **GESTAPO**   *(louder)* Heil Hitler, swine!

> **JEAN**   I obey the leaders of my country—France. When they command me to acclaim your leader, I will.

That night. The priest dresses Georges in his robes and Georges escapes.

Now Jean sees himself parted in spirit not only from his family and Catherine, but he is a stranger in his own village. They withdraw from the man who would have betrayed his own brother. But he carries on. He continues to try to collaborate with the Germans even though he knows he is suspect not only by his people but by the Gestapo agent, too, who is his enemy. One night a village man tries to kill him. He recognizes the man. German soldiers hear the shot, rush in. Jean says he does not know who the man was. He is taken before the commander. He still denies he knows who tried to kill him. The commander tells him his life is not safe, that he had better leave. The commander can recommend him for a job in Paris, perhaps in the police, perhaps as a hanger-on in Vichy. Jean says he is a soldier. That's all he has learned to do except farm. If he must fight, let him fight as a soldier.

FADE OUT.

FADE IN

Bordeaux. The chamber in which the so-called French government functions. Pétain in principal seat, his supporters about him. A clerk reads officially the order which declares De Gaulle a traitor, strips him of his rank, and proscribes him for having deserted his post of duty, etc.

DISSOLVE TO:

London. De Gaulle, penniless, almost alone among foreigners (the British), without rank in his own land, with nothing but his own indomitable will to carry on and his belief that there is a spirit among the French which has not succumbed and tamely accepted the conqueror, proclaims himself head of a people and a government which so far exists only in his hope and his own belief.

London. French soldiers and civilians, some wounded and hardly able to walk, have escaped from France and come to London. They are still dazed. They have no money, cannot speak English, do not know where to go. They know only that Britain out of all the world they once knew still resists the enemy who has conquered France, and to whom the French leaders have betrayed it. They want to resist, too, but they don't know how nor whom to turn to who can tell them how, lead them. As far as they know, there is no leader anywhere. Perhaps there is no leader. It seems to them that very likely anyone with power and rank enough to lead them has also succumbed to the Germans to save his own skin. All the high men they know have done this.

Small ragged groups of them sleep in parks, under the bridges along the Embankment with the English beggars. The British services feed them, do for them whatever is possible in this time of anxiety and disruption, though the refugees, even while recognizing the British courage, realize they are so far only an extra burden. They try to explain that they wish to fight, to do whatever they can, but they cannot be understood. Georges is among them. He talks about a man named De Gaulle. He will lead them, if they can only find him. One asks who is De Gaulle. Georges answers, a general.

> **A MAN**   Oh, a general. Well, you know where a general will be: in his fine chateau in France, licking the boots of the Vichy men.
>
> **GEORGES**   Not De Gaulle.

This is on the verge of becoming a fight almost when an English beggar intervenes. Save the fighting for the enemy, etc. The beggar tells them where De Gaulle lives. Georges is the only one of them who ever heard of De Gaulle before. The beggar, who is a pariah from his own race, who is a mendicant for his own selfish ends: food and drink, alone knows where the man lives who has been proscribed and repudiated by his country and is now a mendicant in a foreign land, not for his selfish ends but for arms to reconquer his country. The beggar leads them to De Gaulle. It is a single shabby room in a dingy street [Soho? I can't find where it was.] where De Gaulle lives on the charity of the British government who alone know about him yet and believe in him.

When De Gaulle and his lone aide come out, the street is choked with quiet anxious men, old and young, some wounded, in the ragged mixture of civilian clothes and uniforms in which they have escaped from France and have slept in parks and gutters since. De Gaulle does not recognize them as Frenchmen. The aide steps forward, says in English that the General cannot speak English and what do they want. A man answers that they are French, that they have come to him to fight again. De Gaulle speaks to them now, learns how they have lived since reaching England. He gets permission from the British to house them in an old warehouse.

The warehouse. Bedding, etc., has been supplied. Now the ragged and homeless men who had nothing but the desire to fight on have found what they sought: not only food and shelter, but a leader who will show them what to do and how to do it. They become soldiers again. They know pride and confidence again, standing stiffly at attention, each at his appointed place, the wounded men, too, while De Gaulle looks from face to face. He stops at Georges, recognizes him, motions him forward. Georges stands stiffly at attention.

> **DE GAULLE** I saw you last on the Somme, that night in front of Abbeville.
>
> **GEORGES** Yes, General.
>
> **DE GAULLE** Are there more of you who escaped?
>
> **GEORGES** A few, General.
>
> **DE GAULLE** Good. I hope they will come to me.
>
> **GEORGES** They will, General. All France will come to you now.
>
> **DE GAULLE** Good.

He dismisses Georges back to his place in the line. He makes a speech of welcome to the men in the name of Free France, says good night. He and the aide go toward the door.

> **DE GAULLE** *(to aide)* Who says France is lost?

The village. Jean is gone, too, now. To the villagers, he has gone completely over to the Germans. Catherine and Chopine think so. To the cook, this whole business is a nuisance. Jean and Georges should both have stayed at home and attended to their own business, which is the farm, instead of flying here and there about the country talking about freedom and duty, etc. Mme Mornet hides whatever her feelings are. Catherine and Chopine sympathize with her, try to be gentle and considerate.

Catherine is quite bitter about Jean. Chopine realizes what Catherine is too young to realize: that perhaps Mme Mornet is suffering, whether it shows or not. He cautions Catherine to be careful. Catherine is warm-hearted and repentant if she has hurt Mme Mornet's feelings, but she still insists that Jean has been a traitor to his country.

The attitude of the village is much the same. They are sorry for Mme Mornet, but she is not one to show grief and to accept pity. They would show their sympathy but they do not know just how. They show it in small ways, trifles of consideration and thoughtfulness, trying to conceal the fact that it is pity and shame that she would have had a son who would do what Jean did.

Armistice Day, 1940. The Germans permit the villagers to decorate with flowers the village cenotaph of the First World War. It is a bronze infantryman, a bronze plaque bearing the names of the village men who died between 1914–1918. One of the names is that of Georges and Jean's father.

>   **CATHERINE**   He should be glad he died before he had to see what we have seen.

She is referring to Jean, his treachery. Chopine smooths her remark over with some of his peasant crude wit or aptness, lest Mme Mornet be hurt.

England. Bastille Day. The exiled French soldiers parade before De Gaulle and British officers and civilians. It is still an unofficial parade. They are ragged men, in fragments of uniforms and worn civilian clothes. They have no flag yet. They are still only a mob of refugees, homeless, who have only one burning desire and a belief in the man who as yet has no power and status and authority himself.

One platoon is composed of men who have just recently arrived from France. Georges is in charge of it. De Gaulle has this platoon brought up before him. He goes along the front, speaking to each man individually. He stops before one whom he recognizes just as he recognized Georges.

>   **DE GAULLE**   I saw you that morning at Chalandry. You behaved well. It still goes?

```
Paragraph 1, page 31b
DISSOLVE TO


Bastille Day, 1940. London. De Gaulle makes his first Bastille Day
broadcast to all the French people everywhere in the Empire who
love freedom and the old proud name of France---in Africa, the
middle East, the Pacific---telling them, men and women too, to
stand firm and resist and to come to him in England as some of their
fathers and brothers

England. Bastille Day, 1940. Begin with: Paragraph 2, page 31g.

Continue: page 32.                        Last paragraph, page 31f
                                          Delete last sentence:
DISSOLVE to                               "De Gaulle: volte. Cmhvn

The village. Paragraph 1, page 31g.
Paragraph 1 and dialogue. page 33
Fade Out
```

5. Page from Faulkner's intermediate draft of "Free France"

SOLDIER It goes, General.

De Gaulle passes on, stops before another man. This man is wounded. He is still gaunt, weak.

DE GAULLE Chalandry, also. You were on the ground. I thought you were dead. What brought you back to life?

SOLDIER *(weakly, almost whispers)* France, General.

MAN NEXT TO HIM Someone whispered De Gaulle in his ear.

DE GAULLE Hah. Does that raise the dead in France?

SOLDIER It will do better than that now. It will raise the living. That's what we need.

DE GAULLE Good. Let us hope so. *(he passes on, men stare ahead, grave yet confident, proudly now)*

Georges and the other soldiers in barracks, after the parade.

WOUNDED MAN He remembered me.

GEORGES He remembered all of us. He says all men who love freedom have only one face to remember. Besides, he says there are not enough of us yet for him to begin forgetting us.

WOUNDED MAN But soon there will be.

SECOND SOLDIER True. If he just keeps on calling the dead back to life as he did you.

THIRD SOLDIER And he will remember them, too, just as he did Raoul.

DISSOLVE TO:

Night. Wine bin in Mme Mornet's cellar. A hidden radio, Chopine, Mme Mornet, Catherine, a dozen villagers, listening to De Gaulle's voice.

VOICE All of you whose sons and fathers and husbands and brothers have died, grieve for them but do not despair. All of you whose fathers and husbands and brothers and sons have merely disappeared from the places which once knew them—(*Catherine reacts, looks at Mme Mornet, who shows nothing*)—do not even grieve. Because they have come to me. They come to me here daily, and our battalions and regiments live again. They are with me today, and they tell you in my voice to believe and hope, for even you whom for a little while yet the enemies of France continue to hold, you also are not alone and are not forgotten.

FADE OUT.

FADE IN

De Gaulle's wife and children have escaped from France and have joined him. They live quietly in a small house near London, which the British government has supplied them. Georges is now the General's personal orderly, though the relationship is much closer than that of officer and N.C.O. Georges is almost a member of the family. He keeps in constant touch with the Underground by which men escape from France to join De Gaulle. He meets the men and brings them to see De Gaulle, who never fails to remember any man from his tank corps.

More and more men are reaching England to take oath with him. The movement is growing. Soon Free France in England will be a respectable military force.

One day General Catroux[9] reaches England from the far Pacific where he refused to accept Pétain's orders and to swear allegiance to Vichy. He enters De Gaulle's office unannounced. Catroux wears five stars where De Gaulle wears only two. He enters the room, rips three of the stars from his shoulder straps and salutes De Gaulle as a subordinate officer, or at least only an equal in rank. Catroux asks De Gaulle what the orders are.

DE GAULLE   There is just one: Free France.

CATROUX   Good. I know when. That is now. Where?

De Gaulle gives Catroux the field command of all Free France.

Evening. De Gaulle's home. De Gaulle tells Georges he is to go to Syria with General Catroux. Georges does not want to go; he wishes to stay with his beloved General. De Gaulle is firm. He has a reason for sending Georges, who knows him better than most soldiers, knows his, De Gaulle's, aim and purpose and his ways.

DE GAULLE   There will always be plenty of soldiers to fight for France. We will never lack those as long as men remember what France was. I need those to go from me who will carry my last command: Frenchman must not fire on Frenchman.

GEORGES   But we may have to. And why not? Do the men of Vichy hold their hands from us?

DE GAULLE   We are not the men of Vichy. We do not need to dread and fear other Frenchmen.

Aldershot. August 23, 1940. De Gaulle holds the first official review of Free French troops before the King of England. This will be in complete contrast to the shabby Bastille Day parade. The French and British flags fly side by side. De Gaulle wears

9. General Georges Catroux (1877–1969), the French governor-general of Indo-China, was an early convert to the Free French policy of General De Gaulle.

the nearest to full and correct uniform which he possesses, for the first time. The parade passes now in its separate units, according to the old corps and regiments, with their regimental colors and dressed in their regimental uniforms—Foreign Legion, Tirailleurs, Marines, Sailors, Artillery, Senegalese, Tank Corps, Chasseurs, etc. They have no arms yet and are in small, almost pitiful units, skeletons of the old battalions which they represent. But a color guard with the Tri-Color leads them and the band plays the old military tunes: "Temeraire," "March of the 11th," "Boudin," "Salut d'Emperor," etc. De Gaulle calls parade to attention, reads out reports of how the Tchad and the Cameroons have joined him, pledged to resist. The parade passes on. DISSOLVE over marching men to:

The same men in battle dress and kit, embarking in transports to sail for Syria.

FADE OUT.

FADE IN

Syria. Jean is an officer in the Vichy French force which holds a frontier fort. His company holds an outpost against the British and the Free French advance. A force of Free French approach and demand its surrender; they are Frenchmen, too, etc. Jean refuses. The Free French officer orders his men to sling their rifles on their backs. With their empty hands held out before them, they advance into the open and approach the outpost. Jean orders them to halt, or he will fire. They do not halt. Jean orders his men to fire. They refuse to fire on other Frenchmen, and on men who are unarmed. Jean leaps toward a machine gun, flings the crew aside, swings the gun to bear on the advancing troops. Three or four of his men spring on him before he can fire and hold him prisoner as the Free French enter and capture the outpost.

The fort. The British and Free French have occupied it. Georges is among them. The captured garrison is unarmed and paraded before the conquerors. Jean is called out and put under arrest and marched away. The Free French commander then gives the captives the choice between coming over to Vichy and departing. A few officers and soldiers step forward and declare to remain loyal to Vichy. The commander tells them

36

FADE IN. Syria

Jean is an officer in the Vichy French force which hold a frontier fort. His company holds an outpost ~~which~~ the British ~~and~~ and
the Free French ~~are approaching~~. A force of Free French approach
and demand its surrender; ~~because they are~~ they are Frenchmen too,
etc. Jean refuses. The Free French officer orders his men to
sling their rifles on their backs. With their empty hands held
out before them, they advance into the open and approach the
outpost. Jean orders them to halt, or he will fire. They do not
halt. Jean orders his men to fire. ~~They refuse. He springs~~ to
a machine gun, hurls the crew away and swings the gun to fire
but before he can shoot one of his men knocks him ~~out~~ down and hold him
prisoner as the Free French enter the post and capture it.

The fort. The British and Free French have taken over the fort.
The garrison and officers are ~~immediately~~ disarmed. The Free
French commander offers them the choice of coming over to De
Gaulle, or departing. A few of then step forward, officers and
men too, and decalre to stay with Vichy. They will be given food
and water to cross the desert and must ;eave the fort by sundown.

Jean has been arrested for having offered to fire on his own
countrymen. He sees the others depart, free. A guard comes for
him, takes him to the office. The room is empty save for Charles.
The guard goes out and leaves Jean and Charles alone. Charles
tells Jean that it was he, Charles, who asked Jean's life from
the Commander, because Free Frenchmen do not kill other Frenchmen.
Charles says they are not Free Frenchmen, they are traitors to
France, and if he had seen Charles himself among the attackers
~~that morning he would still~~

6. Page from Faulkner's intermediate draft of "Free France"

they will be given food and water to get them across the desert to the seacoast, and they must leave the fort by sundown.

Jean in his cell hears the others depart. He may be shot for having commanded his troops to fire, for all he knows. Guards come for him and carry him to a room where Georges is waiting. The guards go out and leave them alone together.

Georges tells Jean that it was he, Georges, who had Jean held until he could talk to him. He says that Jean is free, too, since Free Frenchmen do not make war on Frenchmen. He asks Jean once more to come over to De Gaulle. Jean refuses. He says Georges is a traitor; that if Georges himself had been in the advancing company that morning, he would still have ordered his men to fire. Georges departs to return to France.

FADE OUT.

FADE IN

France. Jean is an official under the Vichy government in his district. He is a valuable and trusted man to the Germans. He lives in the capital town of the district. He is not physically afraid to try to live in the village. He just knows how he is hated there and how his capabilities will be lessened by living there. He uses his official position and privileges to send food, coal and minor luxuries home to his mother, which she could never get any other way.

He has had personal contact with Pétain, Darlan,[10] etc., and the other men who now head France, and he has had personal dealings with the men who run it. His eyes begin to open now. He sees the cowardice and falseness of their position, their enforced subservience to their conquerors and the contempt in which the Germans really hold the puppets whom they are using. He sees France being gradually stripped of food, the factories taken over, people starving, being sent away to enforced labor with the acquiescence of the men who are sup-

10. Admiral Jean Louis Darlan (1881–1942) was named commander-in-chief of the French navy on August 28, 1939. He served as minister of foreign affairs in the Vichy French government, but resigned that position in 1942 to become the commander of all French military forces. He was assassinated in Algiers on December 24, 1942.

posed to protect France. He finds himself more and more alone, solitary, without companionship almost, without any sort of warmth in his life, even though he still believes his course is right: that the only hope for France must come from men of character inside of it. He even has nobody to whom he can tell this.

The only friend he has is a young woman, a sewing-woman perhaps, maybe had a fair job, enough to make a living, before France fell, now has little. Her father is a musician. Now he has work only occasionally. Jean supplies them with food, spends his evenings with them, because he is lonely. He cannot even talk his real thoughts to her, as he knows the Germans spy on the very Frenchmen who collaborate with them. He does not want to get the girl or her father in trouble for sedition, etc. She is the only young woman he knows. By proxy she is Catherine, though there is no thought of love or sex between them.

The village. Every man in the village has picked out a German whose throat he will have the pleasure of cutting when the day comes when France can rise up against the invader and be free again. They win and lose these Germans from one another at dominoes and cards. They swap and trade among themselves, swapping Germans for tobacco, etc., or one big German for two little ones. There is one fat German who is the prize. When he is wagered or bought or swapped, he brings five or six smaller ones. The garrison changes from time to time. When the new garrison arrives, the number of men is always slightly different. There is either one or two extra Germans, or one or two less. This always causes much swapping and arguing until the balance is struck again. From time to time another Frenchman is arrested and sent away to labor or is executed. The executed man's next of kin inherits his Germans from him, or he wills them to a friend. When a man must depart, his principal business in clearing up his affairs is to dispose of his Germans. He uses his Germans as life insurance, annuity, for his family, etc.

One young man is a shrewd trader and a lucky gambler. He begins to acquire all the Germans in the village, until he crosses swords with Chopine. By using Mme Mornet's name and position, Chopine acquires the Gestapo chief, the most hated man

The young man finally falls foul of the Germans. He is to be
sent awaybto work in the Renault factory in Billancourt. Chppine
agrees to hold his half of the corporation's stock until he can
get back. The young man departs.

The village is aware that Jean is sending his mother luxuries.
The village does not like it. Yet they still feel pity and sympathy for Mme Mornet. She tries to share the luxuries with the villagers. They admire her and grieve for her too much to refuse outright. When she brings them little parcels of food, coal, etc.
she wait until she is gone and then destroy them. One poor family
accepts and uses the gifts. The opprobrium of the village falls
upon them. At last it is too much for the peasant, whose family
needs the food, to stand. He goes to Mme Mornet and tells her he
cannot accept it anymore, haltijg and trembling and in terror of
her anger at his ingratitude. Mme Mornet shows nothing. The peasant departs. Chopine has been listening.

                    CHOPINE
     Of course we cant destroy it. It's food.
     To destroy food, even German food, is con-
     trary to God. Eating it doesn't worry me.
     But then, I am too old to be troubled over
     any priciple except that of a full stomach.
     That principle I support in the face of all
     Germany and all France too. "ay, even in
     the face of Brittany. Refuse it. Write him
     not to send it.

               MME MORNET (gravely)
     No. I cant do that.

                    CHOPINE
     Why not?

               MME MORNET
     Because that's all Jean has: sending us a
     little food. Dont you see what he has lost?
     His country, the trust of his people— everything.

                    CHOPINE
     He chose it. He likes

7. Page from Faulkner's intermediate draft of "Free France"

of all. Chopine plays this ace against the young man's long suit, holds him at stalemate so that the young man compromises. He and Chopine now hold a corner in Germans, a holding company, a trust, closed. The young man finally falls foul of the Germans. He is about to be sent to occupied France to work. Chopine agrees to hold his half of the corporation's stock for him until he can get back.

The village is aware that Jean is sending his mother luxuries. The village does not like it. Yet they still feel pity and sympathy for Mme Mornet. She will eat none of it herself, but the village does not know that she won't. She divides the luxuries among the villagers. They admire her and grieve for her too much to refuse outright. When she brings them little parcels of food, coal, etc., they wait until she is gone and then destroy them. One poor family accepts and uses the gifts. The opprobrium of the village falls upon them. At last it is too much for the peasant, whose family needs the food, to stand. He goes to Mme Mornet and tells her he cannot accept it any more, halting and trembling and in terror of her anger at his ingratitude. Mme Mornet shows nothing. The peasant departs. Chopine has been listening.

CHOPINE Of course we can't destroy it. It's food. To destroy food, even German food, is contrary to God. Eating it doesn't worry me. But then, I am too old to be troubled over any principle except that of a full stomach. That principle I support in the face of all Germany and all France, too. Nay, even in the face of Brittany. Refuse it. Write him not to send it.

MME MORNET *(gravely)* No. I can't do that.

CHOPINE Why not?

MME MORNET Because that's all Jean has: sending us a little food. Don't you see what he has lost? His country, the trust of his people—everything.

CHOPINE Except his soul. Let him finish losing that and he can become a vegetable and will no longer grieve for having lost France, because he will not know then that he has even lost it. Yes, you are right. We cannot refuse to accept this food.

From now on, each time a shipment is due, Chopine contrives to steal it before it reaches Mme Mornet, thus technically taking the curse off it. There is a young German soldier, a member of the village garrison. Through him we can show how Naziism is inherent with its own ultimate downfall to the extent that Nazis are at bottom human beings, too, when this quality can be reached. One day, by chance, Mme Mornet does him a simple kindness which recalls to him his own mother perhaps, or perhaps his childhood before trouble came to the world. Mme Mornet did it simply because she had hated Germans so much and so long that a natural reaction happened for a moment. He tries to express his gratitude, clumsily. Mme Mornet brushes him off. Apparently she no longer remembers him. He does not know whether she even sees that he wishes to repay her kindness. Nevertheless, he believes he owes her a debt that must be paid. Chopine sees the situation. He uses the young German in his schemes to steal the food which Jean sends. The German never knows exactly how he is being used. He only knows that he is repaying the debt he owes the Mornets.

Chopine shares the food out among the villagers. The curse is off it now; it was accepted not from the traitor Jean but stolen legally and justly from the German oppressor; to eat it now becomes a matter of patriotism. Mme Mornet has a good idea of what is going on. She refuses to eat any of the food herself, insists that her share be given to the needy villagers.

FADE OUT.

FADE IN

England. We see the progress of the Free French movement after a year. There are French pilots in the RAF, French naval units, French commandos, etc. De Gaulle sends Georges on a mission to France. I may be able to find some historical basis for Georges's return. Or he may go on his own hook, incidentally to accomplish something which in his estimation at least will further free France, though his dominant reason may be to see his sweetheart again.

He reaches the village, hides at his mother's. Everyone is aghast at his temerity and foolhardiness in returning, though glad to see him. The young German finds that the stranger is in the village. Chopine takes command. He never lets the German know that Georges is a spy. He merely tells the German that Georges is Mme Mornet's son. He fools the German into concealing Georges's presence. The German never knows that he is committing treason to his country by concealing the presence of a spy. Chopine contrives this by means of a drinking bout. The German believes he is repaying some of the debt to the Mornet family.

When the danger is over, Chopine and the priest both take Georges to task about his foolhardiness, etc. Chopine tells him bluntly that he, Georges, has now got away with it twice but that the next time they will catch him. Georges is in the wrong, realizes it, is defiant. Chopine says the best thing to do is to arrange to get Catherine off Georges's mind, and the best way Chopine knows to change the idea of a woman in a man's mind from a dream to a nightmare is for the man to marry her. Georges is angry at this way of putting his feeling for Catherine. Then he finds that the priest takes Chopine's suggestion seriously, though the priest's reasons are different. The priest tells Georges he is too reckless, too heedless, that in these times, when a few Frenchmen are trying to save France, recklessness and heedlessness are the same as treason because they may cost Georges his life and now his life belongs not to him but to France.

> **PRIEST** So far you have had incentive only to risk your life and sacrifice it if necessary. There is no question of courage. We know you have that. But if France is to live again, you and all the men like you must have incentive to live as well. To live, and to return.

> **GEORGES** I did come back. And look what I got for it. Everybody who has seen me yet has jumped down my throat. And I'm coming back again. With guns and men.

> **PRIEST** Yes. And blood and destruction and suffering and death. You must have incentive to return, not for destruction and battle, but to peace. Marry her.

GEORGES   When according to all of you, I may be dead tomorrow? According to Chopine, I will certainly be.

PRIEST   Even so. A man with an incentive to live is hard to destroy. Look at her. She is not afraid.

CATHERINE   I am not afraid.

The priest marries Georges and Catherine. Mme Mornet, the cook, Chopine are present.

Dawn next morning. The priest disguises Georges in priest's robes. Georges steals out of the village, escapes back to England.

England. De Gaulle's home. De Gaulle, Mme De Gaulle, Georges are talking after supper, quietly about the fire. They talk of France, of the growing movement. De Gaulle says that the courage of the Frenchmen who will fight is enough to save and restore France, but with the courage and spirit of the women and the oppressed people under the German hell in France, then France is unbeatable.

GEORGES   Yes. The women. I didn't expect them to be brave. I expected courage and fortitude from some of the men, but I didn't expect it from any of the women. Yet it was the women who showed it; not just a few of them but all of them. Because of the land, their homes, the security of their homes and children. I thought that the lives of women went no further, were centered in their households and possessions: keeping alive and having enough to eat for their children and husbands at whatever cost. I didn't expect women to be willing to risk suffering just for an idea.

DE GAULLE   What idea?

GEORGES   Freedom.

DE GAULLE   Freedom is not just an idea. Freedom is bread. Without freedom, you don't live. Why shouldn't women know that and prize it too? And suffer for it. It's from women that courage and fortitude are to be expected, when the alternative is no more than just physical suffering and death. Women are not afraid of physical suffering and death. They are used to it. They risk it each time they bear a child.

GEORGES   I know that now. I have a son there myself.

DE GAULLE   After being married only two months?

GEORGES   I was married only one day. But I have a son. The priest told me I had.

DE GAULLE   And you believe?

GEORGES   I know.

MME DE GAULLE   Of course he knows. Of course he has a son. It doesn't take one day even to make a Free Frenchman.

DE GAULLE   Well, anyway he can hope.

MME DE GAULLE   Hope? Nonsense. He knows.

GEORGES   Thank you, Madame. *(to the General)* We must do more than just hope. Old Chopine was right. Just to wait and hope is not enough. We must do more.

DE GAULLE   We will do more. We just wait for the time, the day. Come. *(he rises, approaches table, fills three glasses from a decanter, hands one to Mme De Gaulle, another to Georges)* To the Day.

GEORGES   To France.

MME DE GAULLE   To the son. He will be France.

DE GAULLE   To many sons, then. To all the sons who will rise from these dark times to give light to tomorrow.

FADE OUT.

FADE IN

Jean returns to the village in an official German car. He sees the sullen hatred of the people when he is recognized. He goes to his mother's house. He suspects something even in her pleasure in seeing him again, even though she tries to conceal anything of that nature. He thinks he sees it in Chopine and the cook, but he has expected it; he will not trouble them long, etc. He asks to see Catherine. At first she refuses to see him. Finally she does so. She is cold, too, but on Mme Mornet's account she tries to conceal it. Jean tells her of his loneliness, of his beliefs about how France can be restored; that it will have to be men like himself rather than Georges who will do it. He asks Catherine to marry him. She refuses. He has expected that, too. He leaves the village in all his official panoply. When Jean returns to the city, he finds that the sewing girl has been attacked by a German soldier. In trying to defend her, her father was killed.

The young German soldier learns that Jean is Mme Mornet's son. Thus Jean is liable to the German's gratitude also. Jean is on their side; the young German feels that Jean can openly receive the discharge of the debt which he has been unable to pay to Mme Mornet. He approaches Jean, diffidently, tries to explain the debt and how he wishes to pay it. Jean is worried, brushes him off. The German accepts the rebuff; he will have to wait. But someday maybe he can discharge the debt. Meantime he can still leave a few shabby field flowers at Mme Mornet's house now and then.

Jean returns to his office. His duties take him on an inspection of the enforced French laborers at the Renault factory at Billancourt. The young man who was Chopine's partner in the cornering of German throats to be cut is a laborer there. A De Gaulle agent has arrived at the factory. It is to be bombed by the RAF. The agent knows the day and hour. His purpose is to get in touch with the true French laborers and give them a chance to get out at the time of the bombing. He contacts the priest. The priest brings the young man to the agent. The young man says there is no way to learn just who is true and who are German secret agents. The De Gaulle man says the raid must be stopped. The young man says no. It must go on.

Jean reaches the factory. The young man recognizes him. He knows Jean's history. He makes no move until Jean recognizes him. In the scene the young man, perhaps with the clairvoyance of sensitive people who know they are on the verge of probable death, divines what so far nobody else has: that in his heart Jean is troubled and uncertain and is on the road to changing his beliefs. He dares not tell Jean about the bombing. He merely insists that Jean be out of the factory before a certain hour. Jean wants to know why, sees the young man's seriousness and sincerity. The young man still won't tell him. He just says Jean must go on back to his job.

JEAN You know what my job is.

YOUNG MAN Yes. It is the saving of France.

JEAN Which France do you mean?

YOUNG MAN There is only one.

The raid. A clock shows a few moments before the bombers will arrive. Jean is out of the factory. The young man draws the attention of all the workers to him, begins to sing the Marseillaise. Other Free French sympathizers join it; the work stops as guards and German agents rush in to see what is going on, to try to send the men back to work. The singing grows louder as the clock hand draws nearer Zero.

CUT TO:

Office across the river. Jean and German manager, etc. A telephone call comes through, telling of the near riot; no fighting yet; the men have merely stopped work and begun to sing. Jean begins to understand. He goes to window, opens it. The singing can be heard from across the river as the bombs begin to fall, grows louder and faster. Jean knows now what has happened.

Village. The priest from the factory has taken a list of all the villages where the enforced workers lived, is calling at them to tell them how their sons, brothers, etc., died. They hold a ceremony for the dead young man even though there was no body found to bury.

FADE OUT.

FADE IN

1942. London. The United States has declared war on Germany. To all the embattled allies this is the portent of hope, the beginning of the end.

House of Commons. Churchill's shadow as he makes his speech: "We have mounted the long hill and have crossed the crest and from now on the course is downgrade as the momentum of all peoples who love right and justice and freedom increases, etc."

De Gaulle's headquarters. Maps on the wall, showing how Syria, the Cameroons, Tchad, other parts of Africa and the Pacific Islands are now Free French. Georges fetches in four French schoolboys. They still have their satchels, etc. They tell De Gaulle how they left school one afternoon, stole a canoe, and crossed the Channel to serve him. We show here how Churchill's words are right: the Allied cause has crossed the crest, there is a power building up which will presently set toward enslaved Europe, irresistible; that something is getting ready to happen.

A commando raid is planned. It will be on a small scale; a dash to get quick information, etc., to prepare for what will be the Dieppe raid on a definite day later, perhaps a week or whatever lapse is necessary for chronology.

FADE OUT.

FADE IN

1942. United States declares war on Germany. The Germans begin to fear an invasion of France. They prepare for it: gun emplacements, concealed and camouflaged airfields. They build a dispersal field in the village, using the village to camouflage it: hangars under the streets and houses, fake trees, fake houses, etc. They depend on the village still looking like a village as a part of the concealment; people following their daily lives, etc. Thus the people know something is going on and perhaps what, but guards are doubled now and nobody is permitted to leave it at all. The Germans hold the villagers as prisoners in a concentration camp; they are even fed better now.

In the midst of this, Catherine and Georges's son is born. Chopine wants to get the news to Georges in England somehow; he is all for going to the coast and finding someone who is going across who will take the message. The priest dissuades him, now that the village is so closely guarded. But when the

priest and others realize that something is up and that word of
what the Germans seem to be doing all through the district
should be sent to England, too, the priest tells Chopine to try it,
gives Chopine the name of an agent in Brest who will get the
message through. Chopine departs.

He reaches the coast just in time to meet a commando raid. He
is not even surprised. He is just pleased. He thinks that sort of
thing goes on every night, is quite usual. He finds himself right
in the middle of it. He seems to have no thought of danger,
bullets, as he tries to stem the sudden horde of rushing, grim,
determined British soldiers, trying to find someone who can
understand him. He is swept up in the raid and carried along
with it, still trying to stop someone who can speak French. Then
he forgets his message in the excitement; he becomes a raider,
too. He joins a British corporal and two men, helps to garrote a
German sentry, helps to raid a hotel where a dance is being
held. The whole German staff of officers is captured. Chopine
is found on the ground, knocked out by a blow on the head.
The corporal refuses to leave him there. Chopine is carried to
the beach, where boats wait to take them off. They revive
Chopine. The first face Chopine sees bending over his is
Georges's.

CHOPINE It's a boy.

GEORGES What?

CHOPINE You have a son.

Then Chopine remembers the other information about the airfields, etc., which it had been his ostensible purpose to come to
deliver. He tells it. The British officer and Georges listen. This
is exactly the sort of thing they came to discover. Georges says
he will go back to the village with Chopine and find out about it.
Georges is really just like Chopine was. He wants to go home
and see his son. He and Chopine have both forgotten now how
Chopine warned him that the next time he risked coming back
home, the Germans would catch him. This does not occur to
Chopine now. The new Mornet heir is the most important
thing. If Georges can also do a military job while seeing his son,
he can take time out to do that, too. The British officer doesn't

quite like this. Chopine has given the information; they had better go back to England while they can get away and report what they have learned, as they were ordered to. But the British officer is young, too, and the very recklessness of what Georges intends to do overweighs his military regulation scruples. He finally tells Georges to take a look at the whole district while he is at home, and to cut away and be damn sure and change his clothes. Georges and Chopine depart for the village.

The village. Georges now wears a peasant's smock and rough pants over his battle dress. He finds the whole village barricaded and patrolled by Germans. Something really is going on.

Night. The wine bin. Men from the whole district have come to report to him. He learns how the whole district is honeycombed with similar hidden dispersal points for planes, camouflaged as villages and even built under villages, etc. Georges is jubilant. He tells them of the big raid which will come day after tomorrow night. They must go back home, warn all the villagers in the district to get out of their villages in time before the bombers arrive, and to put out lights to show the bombers where the hidden fields are. Chopine has been on watch outside. He enters hurriedly, tells them a patrol of Germans is approaching. The men scatter. Georges is caught and marched off under guard.

FADE OUT.

FADE IN

The village. The young German soldier is hanging around the village. His annual week's leave has fallen due, when he can return to Germany and go home to see his people. But he has not gone. He has not only lost out on his free transportation, he has been taken off the active list and now has no status in the mess and will have to buy his own food, and he knows that the first time some N.C.O. sees him and takes time to remember who he is, he will be in trouble. But he has not gone. His apparent reason for staying is the unpaid debt, and a member of the Mornet family now in serious trouble. But he has no idea what he can do about it. Nevertheless, he remains dodging about the village to keep from being caught as a deserter from that week's leave which he should have been looking forward to for the last eleven months and twenty-one days.

Georges has been sent to the capital city of the province, where Jean's office is, and put in the jail there to wait his trial and probably inevitable execution for spying or desertion, etc. At least everyone knows that the Germans will have no trouble finding some reason to shoot him. His mother and Catherine do not know where he is. When they try to find out from the local German authorities, they are brushed off. Catherine is frantic. Finally Chopine learns from the young German soldier what has become of Georges. Now Catherine is more frantic than ever. She is convinced in her grief and terror and alarm that Jean spied on his brother, is at least responsible for his capture if he did not do the actual catching. Catherine wants to go to Jean and plead for Georges's life, but she believes this will do no good. She even revolts at the idea: she would ask the favor of a German, but she revolts at the idea of revealing her grief to a traitor Frenchman, a man who has made a doormat of himself to the enemy who hates them, to save his own skin, etc. Mme Mornet and Chopine attempt to quiet her. Mme Mornet is too worried herself; it is finally Chopine who calms her in his epigrammatic ungentle way and tells her to go ask Jean, unless of course her pride is more precious than her husband's life.

Catherine agrees to go see Jean. Chopine arranges the trip. The first thing Catherine realizes in her frantic worry is, she has the young German soldier for a bodyguard to accompany her to the city. She doesn't know how he came there, nor care. She makes some effort to talk to him and ask him what it is all about, but he is too diffident and she is too worried to carry it through. She goes to the city, perhaps by train. The young German follows her, determined but respectful, at a distance.

Jean has been summoned to the office of the army colonel who commands the whole district. The Gestapo agent is present. He is Jean's enemy. The colonel is an army man. He feels his come-down in this job. He should be off fighting battles instead of being stuck here supervising the squabbles of politicians, etc. He also has the army's contempt for the police. He says briefly he is sorry to hear that the prisoner, the captured spy, is Jean's brother, etc. While the Gestapo listens triumphantly, the colonel says briefly and drily that since there has been a good deal of complaint lately from the French government about German interference in French affairs, that the French government seems to want to wash its own dirty linen, the German authorities have decided in this case to let the Frenchmen clean up their own mess, and that Georges's case will now be turned over to Jean for examination and briefing and examining of witnesses, etc., with the Gestapo to advise him. Jean knows what this means: that it will be a farce, and that the Gestapo is taking this chance to enjoy his sadist's revenge by making him acquiesce publicly to his own brother's execution. But Jean shows no emotion. He indicates he will obey orders, requests that all necessary authority will be given him to handle the matter, examine his brother and summon other witnesses, etc. The colonel says this will be done, dismisses Jean. Jean returns to his office. He reveals nothing. He busies himself with the dossier of the case.

Catherine enters. She is hopeful, despite herself, even though she shows her loathing to the man of whom she intends to ask the favor. But she discerns at once that she is getting nowhere apparently. He is cold, calm, inscrutable, though gentle. She loses control, ends in violent recriminations against Jean, accusing him of treason, fratricide. He accepts it, letting her exhaust herself. She wants to return home. Jean orders his official car to send her back to the village in. She refuses to accept the car. She says she has a German soldier with her who will see her safely back home. She says bitterly that the Germans will protect French women when French men fail, etc.

    JEAN What German soldier?

Catherine tells him, bitterly, still taunting him rather than trying to answer his question. Jean comprehends it is the young soldier who had bothered him about a debt to his family. He prepares to accompany Catherine to the street. She will not let him touch her.

The street. The official car which the Germans let Jean use is waiting. The young German stands beside it. Jean speaks to the soldier in German. The soldier answers. Jean speaks again in German, opens the door for Catherine to get in. Catherine refuses again to use the car. Jean says coldly she had better, since the soldier is not going back with her. Catherine is beaten. She gets into the car. Jean tells the driver in German where to take her. The car goes on.

JEAN *(to soldier)* So nobody sent you but Chopine.

SOLDIER Yes, meinheer. I have my week's leave. I can go where I like.

JEAN Why didn't you go home?

SOLDIER My mother died last year.

Jean tells the soldier he is now on duty with him, tells him to go to the bistro or wherever he wants to go, and come back at six o'clock. He can tell anyone who asks him he is on special detached duty by the colonel's orders, etc. The soldier turns obediently. Jean stops him, asks if he has any money.

SOLDIER Yes, meinheer. I have the money for my leave.

JEAN All right. Be back here at six.

The soldier goes on. Jean returns to his office.

The cell where Georges is. An armed soldier enters, orders Georges to follow him.

GEORGES This late? Don't tell me it took you all this time to decide to shoot me. No wonder it's taken you people three years to lick England and you still haven't done it, and you haven't even licked France yet.

The guard orders him to shut up and march ahead.

A corridor. The guard marches Georges to a door, opens it, drives Georges in, follows.

CUT TO:

Int. room. Georges and the guard enter. Jean is sitting on the corner of his desk, smoking. He speaks to the guard in German. The guard exits, shuts the door. Georges stands looking at Jean. This scene is almost a continuation of the one in the bistro on their first night back home in May, 1940, when they divined in one another the inevitable divergence of their paths. Much has happened since then. Each has stuck to his principles and each by the other's light is a traitor. At least, Georges believes that Jean considers him a traitor. Georges believes it is all up with him, that his goose is cooked. He begins to taunt Jean in his old reckless, heedless, courageous, devil-may-care way.

> **GEORGES** So this is what they make you do now? Are they trying to find out just how much dirt Frenchmen will eat?

Jean is calm, outwardly cold. When he answers, he begins to work on Georges, fanning his anger and his desperation until at last Georges, believing himself finished, even begins to boast.

> **GEORGES** The mistake you people make is you don't execute enough of us. That must make you rage: to know that even you can't execute enough of us to save yourselves.

> **JEAN** I can save you.

> **GEORGES** But you had better not. We don't want you to. We want you to execute more and more of us. If you stop, we will merely absorb you. We don't want that. We don't want to assimilate your fear and hatred among us. To execute one of us doesn't show power: it shows fear. Your fear is what we feed on. Your fear and dread is the thing that will conquer you and set us free.

> **JEAN** What about your fear of whom you call us?

> **GEORGES** Fear? Of what? Of who? Of men who are afraid even to lie down to sleep at night? Of men who in fear are forced to make promises to the people they claim to have conquered, and then out of that same fear fail to keep them?

He recounts what Jean already knows: the promises to free the French war prisoners and the failure to free them, the taking of food from the conquered peoples, the starving of women and children, the secret murderings, which still have not broken the spirit of the people and never will.

JEAN But they are the stronger now. We must—

Georges interrupts him. He speaks again, stating his conviction: that single fierce uncomplicated ideology which Jean has seen before in Free Frenchmen but which seemed wrong to him. Georges stops suddenly. He stares at Jean. Jean stares back at him.

GEORGES You said "they." You said "they," Jean!

Georges starts forward a step, staring at Jean. But Jean is unmoved.

JEAN Yes. The stronger. The guns, the men.

GEORGES And the fear and dread to use them.

JEAN And you have nothing.

GEORGES We have everything. We have the love of freedom and the good will of all people everywhere who love freedom.

JEAN But that is not guns. You don't even have recognition and honor and thanks yet except from England. You have a few guns, and the privilege of dying.

GEORGES That's true. But soon we will have. If your people will just execute enough of us, soon we will have that too, out of very shame: recognition and honor and thanks, as well as a few guns and the right to die. But we have that already, and that will be enough. Call your hired man and send me back to my cell. The air is bad in here.

Jean summons the guard. The guard enters, marches out.

Night. Jean's office. Jean at desk, writing. Orderly enters, speaks to Jean in German. Jean answers, orderly exits, opens the door again and the young soldier enters.

JEAN Once you tried to tell me something about a debt you owed my mother.

SOLDIER Yes, meinheer. I have tried to pay—

JEAN You can pay it tonight.

SOLDIER Yes, meinheer. I thank you.

JEAN You may not thank me later. You will be struck, maybe beaten, too.

SOLDIER Yes, meinheer. I am a soldier. Beatings are not new to soldiers.

JEAN Good, then.

He goes to a cabinet and takes out a helmet, rifle, a pack—full equipment for a soldier on guard duty. The German puts them on, he and Jean exit.

The corridor outside Georges's cell. A guard on duty passes Jean and the soldier into the cell.

CUT TO:

Interior of cell. Georges looks up as Jean and the soldier enter. The soldier suspects nothing. Jean is behind him, takes out a blackjack and hits the soldier underneath the edge of the helmet, catches him as he falls. Georges still looks on in amazement.

JEAN *(to Georges)* Come alive, you fool!

Georges comes alive. They lay the soldier on the bunk. Jean begins rapidly to undress him. Georges comprehends and helps.

CUT TO:

Corridor outside cell, sentry at door. Sentry opens door, Jean and Georges emerge, Georges dressed as German soldier. They exit.

Street. Jean's official car with the German driver. Jean and Georges approach the car. Jean opens the rear door. Georges starts to get in. Jean speaks loudly in German, jabs Georges viciously in the side. Georges gets into front seat beside driver. Jean gets into back, speaks to driver, car moves away.

CUT TO:

Road out of town, the driver and Georges on front seat, Jean in the rear. Jean speaks to the driver sharply in German. Driver stops the car. Jean leans forward, strikes driver underneath the edge of his helmet with the blackjack.

JEAN *(to Georges)* The knapsack! Hurry!

The car in motion, another angle. Georges is driving. On the back seat Jean sits beside the prisoner, the late driver. He is bound and gagged, stiffly upright, wears an officer's cap and overcoat. A general's pennon flies from radiator or wherever German symbol is carried.

CUT TO:

Another part of road. The car is going fast. A squad of German troops leaps from road to give it way, salutes the pennon.

CUT TO:

A barrier. A sentry halts the car. Jean speaks sharply in German, the sentry salutes, lets the car pass.

CUT TO:

The car is stopped. Only the pseudo officer sits in it, rigid and Prussian since he can do nothing else. A corporal and a soldier approach, flash a flashlight quickly on the car, see the officer and the pennon, salute and go on.

CUT TO:

Corner of an aerodrome. Jean and Georges crouch in hiding.

GEORGES I've got a job to do first. I'm going back home.

JEAN So you want to put your head back into the noose. What job?

GEORGES Never you mind what job. You've done enough. I'm out now. Just turn your back a minute—

JEAN What job?

GEORGES You can even put yourself in solid with them again. I'll go back to the car and I'll put a knife in that driver and then tie you up and leave you, and it will even look all right. Of course they may hold your foot to the fire a little for letting one lousy Free French traitor tie you up, but you Vichy people are used to that.

JEAN   What job?

Georges tells him about the raid tomorrow night.

GEORGES   You can even tell them that. They can't stop it now. The more of them that know about it, the more of them we will have to blast when we come ashore.

JEAN   Hush. Come on.

GEORGES   I'm going home, I tell you. I—

JEAN   Did I ever say you were not? What do you want to do: get us both caught squatting here?

GEORGES   Wait. *(he catches Jean's arm, turns him)* Where are you going?

JEAN   Where would I go?

GEORGES   Jean. Jean. Yes. Go to him. Talk to him. He never refused to see any man. He can tell you. I can't. All I can do is fight. But he can tell you. All he has to do is to say it, and any man can see it. Any man will believe.

JEAN   Even me? Come on. If you wanted to stay in that cell, why did I waste all this time?

They manage to steal a plane. It is an obsolete Ju 87. Jean shows Georges how to get into the parachute harness, how to pull the cord. Jean takes it off.

CUT TO:

Shot of plane taking off. It is seen by soldiers, mechanics.

CUT TO:

Control office. An officer tries to contact plane by radio. It doesn't answer. Alarm siren sounds.

CUT TO:

Int. cockpit, plane in flight. Jean hears the ground trying to talk to him, switches radio off.

CUT TO:

The parked car and the prisoner are found.

CUT TO:

Operations office. The officer telephones a warning toward the coast, describes the plane.

CUT TO:

The plane, hedge-hopping, going full out.

CUT TO:

The plane over the village. Jean tells Georges through the intercom that now is the time to jump and reminds him again about opening the chute, etc.

GEORGES'S VOICE Yes. All right. Go to him. Talk to him. He will tell you.

Georges jumps. Jean circles until he sees the parachute open. Then he heads the plane for England.

CUT TO:

French coast. The alarm for the escaping plane has gone out. A.A. goes into action, searchlights, etc. Jean dodges the A.A. Jean flies out over the Channel, low and fast.

CUT TO:

English coast. A listening device. Soldier speaks into phone.

CUT TO:

Control center. WAAF[11] at telephone. WAAF turns and speaks into microphone.

WAAF Bandit in x4. Bandit in x4.

CUT TO:

Squadron office. Another WAAF at telephone.

WAAF (*into loudspeaker*) Badger scramble. Badger scramble.

CUT TO:

Dispersal hut, pilots lounging about.

LOUDSPEAKER Scramble. Scramble.

11. Women's Auxiliary Air Force.

Pilots rush out.

Aerodrome, exterior. Three night fighters take off.

CUT TO:

Jean is attacked by three British fighters. He dodges as long as he can. He does not fire back. His ship takes fire. He leaves it and parachutes down.

CUT TO:

Jean lands. He is slightly wounded. He is arrested immediately and efficiently by three ATS[12] girls who think he is a German.

DISSOLVE TO:

France. The orderly office in the jail from which Georges escaped. Jean's driver and the young German whom they left tied up in Georges's cell have been brought before the frantic and raging Gestapo agent and an aide of the colonel. The driver is not blamed. It is the soldier whom the Gestapo blames for having let himself be tricked by Jean. The Gestapo questions the soldier, shouts at him, tries to browbeat him. The young soldier stares ahead, does not answer. The Gestapo loses all control, strikes the soldier in the face, shouts at him to answer. The other privates stare rigidly ahead. The German officer, the aide, does not like this, but the Gestapo has taken charge and it is a police matter. The young German answers. He tells the Gestapo some truths about it. He says we (the Germans) will never conquer the French. We are wrong to begin with. Each time we murder one, two more spring up. We will never conquer them because all we know to employ is savagery and fear, and these people don't even know what fear is. The Gestapo leaps on the soldier, beats him down with his pistol butt. The aide intervenes, makes the raging Gestapo stop, orders the men to carry the young German out.

DISSOLVE TO:

The village. Georges is back, his parachute hidden. Men from the other villages have gathered again, stealing in, hopeful,

12. Air Traffic Services.

triumphant, rallying to him. He passes the word out that to-morrow will be the night when lights must be set out so the British bombers can see to bomb. The atmosphere is tense, exalted, confident and waiting. The different men hurry away. Georges knows how the word will spread from village to village until the whole country will be waiting.

FADE OUT.

FADE IN

England. A hospital. Jean is in the hospital. His wound is only a slight one. He was merely sent to the hospital while he was investigated. The British have learned who and what he is now. While waiting in the hospital to be summoned wherever he will be, he hears about the expedition for tonight. For three years now he has associated with people who hid their every move in secrecy and behind a veil of savage bloodthirstiness. These people all seem to know about the raid, no matter how humble— nurses, other wounded soldiers, etc. They talk of it as if it were a party some were going to. The wounded talk of it with envy because they cannot go.

Night. At last Jean is brought to De Gaulle. De Gaulle welcomes him. He says nothing at all about Jean's past actions and convictions, does not criticize him nor even mention them, until Jean says something about them.

> **DE GAULLE** What does the Bible say? More rejoicing in heaven over one sinner that repents than over a hundred who did not sin. Or maybe you haven't quite repented yet?

Jean doesn't know yet, admits it. He came because he had to, because he had closed the door behind him in order to save his brother.

> **JEAN** Maybe I came to talk to you. My brother said you would convince me.

> **DE GAULLE** Maybe I could. But I won't. I don't think you want to be convinced by anyone. I think you must learn it from inside.

> **JEAN** But that will take time.

DE GAULLE   We have time. Only those who have no peace do not have time. Only those who are never free of doubt and fear have no peace.

JEAN   But so far you have neither recognition nor thanks nor honor; only a few arms and the right to die.

DE GAULLE   The courage to die.

JEAN   The courage to die. My brother says that is enough.

DE GAULLE   It is enough. We would like to have more, and daily we have more. But even if we did not, that would be enough when those who face us are armed with doubt and fear. But you must convince yourself. It must come from inside you, or you are no good to us. A man who can be sold by one demogogue can be unsold by the next one who meets him.

De Gaulle gives Jean authority to look about, see for himself what Free France is.

DE GAULLE   You will see them start tonight. They can speak to you better than I can. You were a soldier once. You will understand that language better than any one man can speak.

JEAN   Suppose I see what is to be seen and then escape from you and return to France?

DE GAULLE   Go then. We want men only by their own choice.

Presently De Gaulle says it is time to start, invites Jean to come with him.

CUT TO:

Scenes in which Jean sees the expedition getting under way. A barracks. Men blacking their faces, etc. Jean sees they are men of all nationalities, but with one single purpose, cheerful about it, even though some of them will die tonight. He sees the feeling they have for De Gaulle, which is so different from the iron-bound rigidity of the German toward his officers. He sees French privates come and speak to De Gaulle without formality, hears De Gaulle call them by name.

The coast. Jean sees the expedition debark in the raiding barges, etc.

An aerodrome. The pilots are French. Jean recognizes them all. They are his old squadron, the one he elected to quit that night in 1940 when the squadron chose to escape from France rather than submit to Vichy. The men accept Jean after the first moment as if nothing had happened. With the help of the squadron commander, De Gaulle puts up a job on Jean. A crew captain reports that one of his men is absent. De Gaulle says perhaps another one can be found to take his place. Suddenly Jean volunteers to go.

> **DE GAULLE** You see? That's what I meant by saying you must choose by yourself.

The missing crew member appears. The squadron takes off. An orderly brings in a microphone extension. De Gaulle speaks into it the message which will notify the people that the raid has started and for all the French to stay indoors until it is over.

DISSOLVE TO:

France. The village. The wine bin and the secret radio. Georges and other men from about the district. The message comes from De Gaulle. It is now time. Georges and the others exit and scatter.

Interior house. Mme Mornet, Catherine carrying the child, and the cook. A few bundles of their household effects and baskets waiting about on the floor. When the hidden dispersal point is bombed, the whole village will suffer, too. This is true of each village which the Germans have used to camouflage a field. All the people are vacating as Mme Mornet is doing. Georges says the time has come. They take up the bundles and exit. There is nothing of grief and regret about any of them.

Exterior. Night. Chopine sets fire to the barn for a marker for the bombers.

CUT TO:

A bomber in flight. The pilot speaking into his mike back to England. He reports the beginning of the fires.

CUT TO:

Mme Mornet, Catherine, carrying the child, the cook on a hill. A dozen burning houses and barns can be seen about the countryside, others spring up.

CUT TO:

Bomber in flight, pilot with mike.

PILOT *(excited)* I see more of them! They are marking the fields for us!

DISSOLVE THRU VOICE TO:

England. Squadron office. De Gaulle, Jean, officers about radio as pilot's voice COMES THROUGH.

VOICE And still more! Still more! All France is on fire, blazing—

FADE OUT.

THE END

III

The De Gaulle Story

Revised Story Treatment

FADE IN

Jean and Georges Mornet are brothers. Jean is thirty-five, a career man in the navy, from the naval academy.

Georges is ten years younger. He was a student. He would have been a farmer, farming the land which belonged to the family, after completing his legal army service. When the war broke out, he was called up again. He was put into the tank corps, where he developed a fanatical admiration for his colonel, who was De Gaulle. He has no political inclinations. He is merely a disciple of De Gaulle, preaching on the subject of tanks, and his warning to the French government of what will happen to it if tanks are not developed.

They have not seen each other for several years. They meet at home again at last by special permission on the day before the Germans invade Holland. In the village is Catherine, twenty. It was planned between the two families that some day Catherine will marry one of the Mornet sons. The war interrupted any such plan, which will now be consummated when peace returns. It is now generally accepted that Georges will be the husband. He and Catherine are nearer in age, though the principal reason is that Jean is a career man, will be an officer for the rest of his life, etc., and that when he takes a wife, it will probably be from a navy family, for the sake of his own advancement in his chosen profession.

When he returns to the village and sees Catherine again, he develops a certain interest in her, first of a big-brotherly nature, toward the woman who is to marry his younger brother. It begins to be a little sharper when he sees that Georges is apparently paying little attention to her. Georges seems to have in his mind only his and his colonel's conviction that France is to be

71

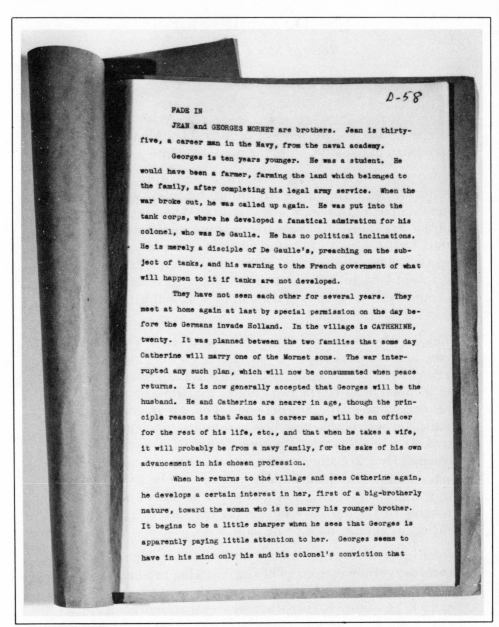

FADE IN

JEAN and GEORGES MORNET are brothers. Jean is thirty-
five, a career man in the Navy, from the naval academy.

Georges is ten years younger. He was a student. He
would have been a farmer, farming the land which belonged to
the family, after completing his legal army service. When the
war broke out, he was called up again. He was put into the
tank corps, where he developed a fanatical admiration for his
colonel, who was De Gaulle. He has no political inclinations.
He is merely a disciple of De Gaulle's, preaching on the subject of tanks, and his warning to the French government of what
will happen to it if tanks are not developed.

They have not seen each other for several years. They
meet at home again at last by special permission on the day before the Germans invade Holland. In the village is CATHERINE,
twenty. It was planned between the two families that some day
Catherine will marry one of the Mornet sons. The war interrupted any such plan, which will now be consummated when peace
returns. It is now generally accepted that Georges will be the
husband. He and Catherine are nearer in age, though the principle reason is that Jean is a career man, will be an officer
for the rest of his life, etc., and that when he takes a wife,
it will probably be from a navy family, for the sake of his own
advancement in his chosen profession.

When he returns to the village and sees Catherine again,
he develops a certain interest in her, first of a big-brotherly
nature, toward the woman who is to marry his younger brother.
It begins to be a little sharper when he sees that Georges is
apparently paying little attention to her. Georges seems to
have in his mind only his and his colonel's conviction that

8. First page of Faulkner's revised story treatment of "The De Gaulle Story"

attacked and that when it happens, the French defenses will collapse.

Holland is invaded. Jean and Georges return hurriedly to duty.

In this sequence we will show, through the people in the village, the attitude of all France at this time. They expect an attack, but they have every confidence in the Maginot Line and in the French army. They believe they need only attack the Germans and the war will be won. They have never heard of De Gaulle. To them, Georges, with his talk of De Gaulle and tanks and his prophecies that the Maginot Line will be no good, is a radical, a fanatic and a croaker of bad news who should keep his mouth shut. Jean typifies the established military contempt for all innovation and civilians, etc.

FADE OUT.

FADE IN

The Germans cross the Low Countries, into France. Sedan falls, the Germans continue to advance. The people cannot understand it. The supposedly invincible French army is being driven back, yet still the government, as typified by Premier Reynaud, seems confident.

But the government is not confident. It is becoming divided, though willing to hope still. Reynaud dominates it. He recalls Colonel De Gaulle, whom he has always defended, back from the East and gives him command of a tank group. But he fails to give De Gaulle as many tanks as he could, or as he promised even. Nevertheless, De Gaulle takes what tanks he has, stops the advance temporarily at Laon.

The Belgian king surrenders. The British and some of the French reach Dunkirk and are evacuated. The bewilderment in the French government increases; the country is more puzzled than ever, though the people still have not given up, even though Weygand and the generals seem to believe that the war is already lost. De Gaulle does not believe so. He continues to retreat and fight. He stops the Germans again at Abbeville and holds them.

In the middle of the battle, Reynaud calls him to Paris, makes him Under-Secretary of War. Now his struggle with the war cabinet begins. Reynaud and a few civilians support him. The generals are all against him, Weygand as the active commander, Pétain as the senior French marshal, and with his old reputation from Verdun in 1916. They are contemptuous of the new general, etc. But De Gaulle's presence, or at least his and Reynaud's continued confidence, bolsters up the confidence and hope of the civilian members. Reynaud and De Gaulle decide that De Gaulle will go to England and see Churchill. Reynaud is optimistic; he promises to control the situation while De Gaulle is gone.

While De Gaulle is in England, he learns that the French government has left Paris. He hurries back; Churchill promises to follow in person.

De Gaulle reaches Paris. The government has gone to Tours. But the people in Paris are still confident. They are preparing to resist; they are convinced the city will be defended and that the Germans will never reach it.

De Gaulle hurries on to Tours. Churchill joins him at the cabinet meeting. Weygand says an armistice must be asked of the Germans. The civilians, followers of Reynaud, protest. Apparently Reynaud is still against this. He allows De Gaulle to speak. De Gaulle says, retreat to Brittany, establish there, where England is only a short distance away. The generals are against this. They want to retreat to Bordeaux. Thus the whole military establishment is against De Gaulle, who has only himself and a few civilians to support his side. Reynaud weakens. He asks Churchill to release France from the agreement not to ask for an armistice. Churchill refuses. Reynaud says that the government will move to Bordeaux.

Again Weygand insists that an armistice be asked. De Gaulle and a few civilians insist on fighting on. Reynaud responds to their pressure, gives De Gaulle permission to go again to London to see Churchill.

In London Churchill offers union between France and Britain, to become one government and one people. De Gaulle returns to Bordeaux with the good news, finds that Reynaud has resigned and Pétain is Premier and that he, De Gaulle, is now proscribed as a traitor. He escapes from France just before he is arrested and returns to England.

FADE OUT.

FADE IN

We will show how De Gaulle, starting out as a stranger in London, with only a change of clothing and a microphone, became not just the chief of a small group of rebels, but became the chief and head of France itself, excepting only the group of aged traitors who sold France to the enemy and then found out when it was too late that they had merely sold themselves, since the France which they believed they had sold refused to remain sold, but gradually rose again despite almost insurmountable difficulties, getting ready for the day when they could throw the betrayers and the enemy both out.

When the armistice is signed, Jean remains true to his navy tradition, remains with the navy, not as a Vichy man but as a navy man first and last and always. He believes what he has been told by his superiors, or what he assumes they believe: that through the weakness of the French people the war was lost; that the army and navy were all right and will continue to be all right, and that only the army and navy can ever restore France, or enable France to exist at all.

Georges escapes from the Germans. He still believes in De Gaulle. The other soldiers who know him, who served in his tanks and know what he has done at Laon and Abbeville, believe in him, too. A few of them follow him to Bordeaux and would follow him to England. But he has no status now, is a proscribed traitor. He tells them to come to England to him, to tell all other Frenchmen who love France to resist always and to join him in England.

The rest of the common people in France have not yet heard of De Gaulle. They still want to resist. They only know that the army which they had been taught to believe was invincible has been defeated. Its generals have assured them that England, too, will be defeated in another week. The generals and the new French leaders have assured them that collaboration is the only out for France. There is no one to tell them anything else, no matter how they feel about it. They believe that at least their leaders are sincere, know best, have some organization behind them at this time when nobody else offers anything.

Georges will go to England, to join his beloved colonel. He will never give up. His home village is on his way. Also, he can stop there and rest and get food and get rid of his uniform, which will cause his arrest at any time, since he is now a deserter from the army.

He reaches the village, finds it occupied by a German garrison. He finds the same situation there that exists all through France. The people are bewildered. They had believed their army and Maginot Line invincible. Yet the army had been defeated, collapsed; their Maginot Line is now a German tourist resort. Their only leaders had told the people to believe in them, to obey the conquerors, that there was no help in Europe for them, since within another week England, too, would be conquered. Yet the week had passed, and England still fought on. In fact, there was a Frenchman in London bidding the French people over the radio to be of good courage, etc., that they had been betrayed. But so far they have not known what to do, how to fight on. Then Georges appears.

For the first time they actually see someone who not only has no doubt about the final outcome, but who also knows what to do about it. There are in the village two other soldiers, deserters like Georges, who got lost in the shuffle of the German occupation, and are at home simply because they don't know what else to do.

Georges tells them France is not whipped, will never be whipped; they see that England has not fallen, as they were told. The message which Georges brings, of hope, something to hope for and look forward to, spreads through the village. But there is an element in the village, the older men, property owners, etc., who still doubt that anything can be done. The first doubt of their leaders has followed the failure of their prophecy about England, but Georges's scheme seems hare-brained to them, etc., dangerous to the welfare of the village, will bring reprisals on them certainly, and perhaps he is wrong, and no single man now a fugitive in England can restore France. But there are some who believe in Georges, who accept the figure of De Gaulle as Georges's enthusiasm represents him. The two soldiers decide to escape to England with him.

On entering the village, Georges was surprised by a German soldier and was forced to kill the soldier. Georges is alarmed, but determined to go on. He does not know what situation he will find at home and in the village. He has seen his beloved leader repudiated and driven from France. He has seen things happen in France and among French people which he had not believed could happen. He does not know but what the pressure of the French authorities, combined with that of the occupying Germans, will be so strong that his own village will not dare shelter him.

But he finds that his family and others in the village are ready to help him escape, not just because he is their kinsman, but to help anyone who will still fight. Coupe-tête, an old peasant family retainer, helps him conceal the body; his whole family, his mother and Catherine and all, help him and the other young men to get away.

FADE OUT.

FADE IN

When De Gaulle reached London the first time, he was so little known that, despite the urgency of his errand, instead of going straight to Churchill, he telephoned to him first. He borrowed a coin from General Spears[1] to telephone with. When he came to London for good, from Bordeaux, a proscribed traitor, he had nothing but the clothes he stood in.

As Georges and his companions near England, he meets other Frenchmen who have escaped from all parts of France, on the same errand. He begins to see a thin stream of men drawing toward De Gaulle, the man who has offered them something beside surrender. He meets more of them in England, all

---

1. Major-General Sir Edward Spears (1886–1974) represented the British government as liaison to the French High Command following the Battle of France in May 1940.

bound toward London and De Gaulle, and finds De Gaulle at
last.

De Gaulle now has the beginning of an organization. The British government has accepted him, makes a treaty with him as
the head of the French government, to fight on, but with the
stipulation that no Frenchman is to fight against Frenchmen.
De Gaulle was first joined by the refugee troops from Narvik,
then from Dunkirk. The British have given him a headquarters
and a house to live in; his wife and family will join him as soon
as possible.

De Gaulle remembers the face of nearly every man who served
in his tanks. He remembers Georges. Georges joins his organization, is close to De Gaulle: an orderly, secretary, etc., almost a
member of the household. Georges watches the organization as
it grows. He tells De Gaulle of the spirit in his village, which
exists in all the villages and towns of France as soon as the
people know what to do, etc.

De Gaulle explains how he does not want to be a politician; he
does not even want merely to command the French forces. He
just wants to be the chief of all Frenchmen who wish to be free,
who wish that voluntarily. He proves that. Against all advice, he
permits authorities from Vichy to come with impunity to the
refugee troops of Narvik and Dunkirk and ask them to return
to France to serve Vichy. He explains again how any man who
serves him must come of his own will: that only men who love
freedom will fight to restore it to France.

One day General Catroux arrives. He has refused to accept
Vichy, given up his command in the East, walks unannounced
into De Gaulle's London office. Catroux wears five stars; De
Gaulle two. General Catroux rips off three of his stars, salutes
De Gaulle and offers to serve as a subordinate under him.

                                                    FADE OUT.

FADE IN

Jean is with his ship. His feeling is, France collapsed through a
weakness in the French people. The army, being closer to the
people than the navy, was corrupted to an extent with this

weakness, too, and when the people and the civil government collapsed, there was nothing to support the army. But the navy is something different, as its present situation proves. It is still intact. It is strong enough to be the balance of power between the conquered French and the victorious Germans. It will no longer actively support its ally, England; neither will it go against its old ally by putting its weight in with the Germans.

Oran. Jean's ship, under fire, being reduced because it is bottled up and helpless; shots of the officers and crew who believe they have been wantonly fired on by a so-called ally, without provocation, are fighting bravely back even though it is hopeless. The officers are coldly furious. Jean especially so. He had a few qualms about accepting Vichy, about quitting the fight while the fleet, anyway, was still able to fight and had done nothing yet. Nevertheless, although the fleet quit fighting, still it did not go over to the Germans, as the Germans wanted. At least it kept that faith with its old ally. Now that ally has wantonly and without warning fired on it while it was bottled up in a harbor where it could not maneuver, etc.: a blow in the back. He is wounded, falls.

DISSOLVE TO:

Hospital. Jean in bed, recovering. (Wheeled chair, maybe.) A navy officer enters to see how he is doing. Jean now has no ship. The officer mentions the fact that many officers have not, but that there is some shore duty. He is trying to find men who will take it. Jean asks idly what shore duty. The officer tells him; positions with the Gestapo, administrative, etc. Jean rouses. The officer says Jean is not well enough, etc. Jean volunteers for the job, insists. He says he is no policeman, and maybe the late allies of France might object to what he is doing, but let those who destroyed his job beneath him find him a better one, etc.

Jean becomes a member of the French Gestapo. The first thing he does is to go see his mother. When the villagers recognize him, they take it for granted that he, too, has escaped from the Germans and Vichy. They offer to hide him, help him escape, etc. When they realize that he is not only not hiding but that he has an official status with the Germans, to them he is a traitor and renegade. He realizes that he is another enemy to them, to be shunned and avoided. He learns for the first time where his brother is, because the villagers expected that he was about to do the same thing.

He goes to see his mother. The priest, Marthe, Catherine and Coupe-tête are present, or he sees them all on this visit. He learns that they not only know what Georges has done, but that they approve of it. Possibly all of them save Mme Mornet are afraid to talk about Georges to Jean after they learn that Jean is now an official in the Vichy-German collaboration. But Jean is still Mme Mornet's son. She is convinced he is to be trusted about his own blood, etc. Jean tries at first to point out how wrong their attitude is, that France can be free only by collaborating with the Germans until all Europe is finally conquered. But he soon sees that he is a stranger and even a doubtful person to his own people; Catherine is the most violent one, the most ready to state that anyone against Free France and Georges's side is a traitor and coward, etc. To his notion, they are wrong. But he sees he will never convince them of it; but they are still his people, his mother is still his mother, etc.

He attempts to show them how they are wrong: that France, the old France, is finished, the armies whipped, etc. They take him to a secret radio which they have in the cellar. Catherine and Coupe-tête are afraid to do this, but Mme Mornet says not to doubt Jean; he is her son, etc. He learns how already the people in France have kept in touch with De Gaulle, etc. He hears for the first time something of events from the other side: of the conquering by Free France of Syria, then of the African battle where French troops meet and whip Germans; he hears how Tchad, Cameroon, etc., have gone over to De Gaulle.

He is about to leave, to return to his new job. He contrives to see Catherine alone. He wants to offer her what security his position can give her. He tells her Georges is finished now irrevocably. Catherine will not even listen to him: better to wait for a brave Frenchman forever than to accept the bounty of a man who is himself the tool of traitors and a slave of his country's conquerors. Jean departs.

FADE OUT.

FADE IN—1941

We see the gradual steps by which the French people lose all faith in the Vichy government, until at last none are left who believe in it but the traitors who dare not repudiate it now for the sake of their own skins, and the politicians and opportunists who are feathering their nests.

Jean is now a member of the French Gestapo, an official: inspector, commissioner, some fairly responsible officer. He has charge of dispatching into Germany the food requisitioned, as a part of the war indemnity, by the Germans from the Vichy government.

He is aware of the unrest among the French people, of their shame and suffering under the Germans. He begins to see what sort of men compose the Vichy government. He has nothing in common with them save the job he is doing. He has a racial antipathy to the German masters of France. He knows that he is considered a traitor and a renegade by his own family and that portion of the French people which they typify. Presently, for all his power, etc., his only companionship is with an old musician out of work, and the musician's daughter, a seamstress or some such who supports herself and her father. One day the girl tells him he is very lonely and unhappy. He denies it, quicky, almost harshly, concealing it.

Through them he learns a little of an underground movement in France. He always knew of it—it would be inevitable that such would exist—just as the Germans would expect such and would be combatting it. He tells the musician and the daughter to expect nothing from such, that the weakness in the French people which caused the collapse of the French government and army will likewise prevent any organization strong enough to accomplish anything.

He will not go to see his mother again, because of the difference and conflict between them. But he keeps in touch with her to know how she fares, perhaps through Coupe-tête; perhaps he arranges for Coupe-tête to come to see him and report, during which scenes Coupe-tête will be incorrigible and saturnine as always, apparently having neither awe nor respect nor even fear of the Germans. Jean uses his position to make his mother's life easier, with the secret hope of helping Catherine, too, though perhaps only Coupe-tête suspects this.

Jean has seen the corruption among the Vichy officials, how they use their position and power to benefit themselves. He has never done this. One day he asks Coupe-tête what the family needs. Coupe-tête comments on the food, the French food, which Jean, a Frenchman, is sending out of France, for Germans to eat and grow fat and conquer Europe on; how a little of that would go pretty good at home. Jean says that all the rest of the people in France could use it. Coupe-tête says that all the rest of France is not Jean's mother: a double-entendre on what Jean knows the French people who are not Vichy call his treason, etc. He dismisses Coupe-tête without answering him.

But from now on, each time a shipment of food passes through his hands, he deflects some of it to his mother. Coupe-tête knows where it comes from, as do Mme Mornet and all the rest of the village, though they have only inference, as Coupe-tête never tells. Mme Mornet shares it among the village, will keep none of it herself, though Coupe-tête protests. Marthe will accept it, but says nothing. Catherine will not accept it at all. Presently all the village begins to refuse it, save the ones who are so poor and needy, with children, that they cannot refuse. They take it in fear and trembling, trying to conceal from the other villagers that they accept it. The village does not know that Mme Mornet takes none of it. She is a traitor also to them now. One day a load comes in. The villagers burn it. By this act, only the poor and needy suffer.

Coupe-tête takes charge of the business. He sells them the idea how, by every mouthful they eat, they are doing that much damage to the enemy. They will do the damage all right by destroying the food, but by eating it themselves they will double the injury to the enemy because then they will strengthen loyal Frenchmen with every bite which weakens the enemy. After this, to completely purify the act, Coupe-tête and others go through a ritual of stealing the food before it ever reaches Mme Mornet, so that technically it was never hers, sent to her by her renegade son.

FADE OUT.

FADE IN

The Underground movement is growing, though it is still unorganized. Frenchmen more and more are fleeing France to England, to join De Gaulle. Frenchmen are even quitting their safe positions in the Vichy government to go to England. Jean is aware of this through his association with the Vichy and German officials. One day a suggestion or maybe a demand is made upon him by the German official under whom he serves that he act as a spy on his own countrymen who are working in the Underground or are escaping to England.

Jean refuses. The German tries to threaten him with pressure, etc. Jean reminds the German that he is first of all a navy man, and that the navy is neutral—so far. Jean's character as well as his words carries enough weight for the German to desist. The German asks Jean what he will do in the case of some flagrant violation by a Frenchman of his Vichy oath to the articles of agreement with the Germans. Jean answers that he will do his duty, for the German not to worry. The German realizes this: that Jean will do his duty, keep his promise, etc., but will do no more.

Jean also keeps up with the other side of the picture through his friend, the seamstress. She trusts him. She sees through him, perhaps: that he will carry out his duty to the letter but will never betray his individual countrymen unless to do so becomes a part of his immediate duty, etc. One day she asks him why he does not betray them, knowing he will not, testing him.

As he watches symptoms of the growing Underground, as a Frenchman he can see why. He sees French children being robbed of food to feed German troops. He sees the German promise to free French war prisoners broken. He sees Frenchmen being drafted into German factories and put in concentration camps and killed in reprisals, yet still the spirit of resistance continues and even grows.

One day he meets a boyhood friend, now a laborer in the Renault factory, making German tanks. The friend recognizes Jean at once, but he knows Jean's present situation and does not show recognition until Jean does. Jean leaves. He is in the factory manager's office the next day, across the river from the factory, when the factory is bombed by the RAF. Later Jean learns that the friend and others knew the raid was coming and could have escaped. But to have done so, they would have given warning to the Germans of the raid. So the friend kept quiet, got the other Frenchmen, who also knew they were going to die, to singing the Marseillaise while the bombs came down, destroying the factory and the German guards, etc.

Jean is learning more and more about the spirit which exists in France. He is also learning something about the spirit, not alone of Frenchmen, but of the immortal human spirit which not even death can put in bonds. But he still believes he is doing right. His position, he believes, has alienated him forever from his family and the France they represent. But he still believes he is doing the only thing not only for a reasonable man to do: which is to compromise with the conquerors of his country, but he was trained to hold his navy oath, etc., above all things; and to be honorable and worthy of freedom a man must make his oath and promise good, must adhere to what he believes is right in the face of all pressure.

Then the news comes that Roosevelt has been elected President of the United States for a third time: a precedent for all time. He sees how all the French people outside of the Vichy politicians take this as a definite hope made definitely to them: that now the last great neutral has begun to lean toward the peoples who still fight for freedom even though their lands have been conquered and overrun. The Underground movement begins to coalesce. His seamstress friend indicates to him that there are De Gaulle agents in France, working toward that end, toward the time when the movement will be powerful enough to do something.

Suddenly she throws the mask aside and asks him why he doesn't come over to them. Jean asks, come over to whom? The seamstress covers up then. She has revealed no information so far and refuses now, since she realizes that Jean must stick to his beliefs. She says she knows nothing. Jean says it is too late for him to come over now, even if there was anything for him to come over to, because now nobody would believe that he had changed—granted he had changed.

His German superior summons Jean, tells him there is definite knowledge that a French agent is working in the Underground, asks Jean again to use his position as a Frenchman, etc., to find who the man is and betray him. Jean refuses.

GERMAN If you have the chance to capture him and fail to do it, then beware.

JEAN If he throws himself in my way, let him beware. But not until he does.

FADE OUT.

FADE IN

Georges is back in France, as a De Gaulle agent, organizing the Underground cells. He is not supposed to see his kin, to let them know he is in France even, so as to preserve his incognito. But he goes to the village, slips in to his mother's house, to see his mother and Catherine. That night Coupe-tête passes the word; some of the villagers come to hear what Georges has to say. He tells them how the movement is growing; it is only a question of time until it will be strong enough to rise throughout France against the traitors who sold them out and the German oppressors.

We learn here of the extent of the movement as of this date, about December 1, 1941. We see it through Georges's sanguine and confident eyes. He says that all France, all oppressed and enslaved Europe, is waiting for a sign, then it will all rise and throw off the German yoke. He does not know what the sign will be, only that it will come from the outside world—some sign from the people who are still free that they too are willing to jeopardize life and security for the sake of freeing the human spirit, etc.

He is calm, but to the villagers he seems to have been given some divine message, assurance, so that they are convinced, their hopes lifted again. The priest believes something of this, but he is wiser, calmer than Georges's fire. Mme Mornet is waiting to be shown. Catherine believes him implicitly, is exalted, too. Georges says the sign will come, after which only the poltroons and rascals will any longer hold to Vichy. That night the

priest marries Catherine and Georges—a secret ceremony in
the cellar where Georges is hidden. Georges departs to continue his work in Paris.

The United States enters the war. This is the sign which
Georges waited on. We see how only a few of the old die-hards,
with a few like Jean who have gone too far to retract, as they
believe, remain with Vichy. Georges presides at a congress of all
the secret Underground cells of France. It is held almost in the
basement of the German Gestapo h.q. in the Place de la Concorde. Delegates are chosen to go to London and offer their
organization formally to De Gaulle as the head of all France.

One day Jean sees and recognizes Georges on the street. Without divulging to the Germans who Georges is, Jean uses his
power to have Georges brought to him. Georges realizes that
Jean has him, can turn him in to the Germans. Jean tells
Georges that if Georges will give him his word to stop working
in France against the government, will leave France at once and
promise never to return, he will let him go.

Georges refuses to promise. He will work to throw the Germans
and the Vichy men out as long as he can draw breath. He says
he doesn't ask or expect Jean to let him go, but for Jean to give
him a specific time, a day say, to escape. When the time is up,
Jean can report him to the Germans and then if they catch him,
Jean will not be responsible. Jean refuses to do this. Georges
realizes that Jean really is going to turn him in. He begins to
taunt Jean, dares him to do his worst. He brags of what the
Underground now is, since America is on their side: that it is
too late to stop it now. The whole German army and the traitors
of Vichy can't stop it now. Jean has Georges arrested.

Jean goes to the village to see Catherine. He tells her Georges is
now in a German prison camp for the duration. He offers
Catherine again the protection of his name and position. When
Catherine realizes he is asking her to marry him, she blows up.
She tells him she and Georges are already married, perhaps
that the child is coming. She says she had rather be the widow
than the wife of a fratricide, had rather bear the son of a true
Frenchman who is dead than be married to a traitor who licks

the boots of his country's conquerors, etc. Jean returns to the city.

As soon as he reaches the city, he is summoned by his German superior, at the instigation of a Gestapo agent. He realizes that now he is suspected by the Germans because of the fact that he turned his brother over to them. The Gestapo wishes to know why it took him so long to decide to surrender his spy brother, etc. Jean answers as briefly as he can. He realizes that something has happened to Georges. The Gestapo tells him to be more careful in the future, etc. Jean knows that he will be watched, too, from now on.

He goes to the prison where Georges is. He finds that Georges has been third-degreed to make him talk. They will not let Jean see him. Jean restrains himself again, departs. He goes to see the seamstress, his only friend—even acquaintance—now. He asks her to marry him. Nothing of this nature has ever been suggested even between them before. The seamstress is surprised for a moment, then curious. She tells Jean that maybe he will not want to marry her when he hears her story. She tells him: she was raped by German soldiers in early days of the invasion, etc. Apparently that does not matter to Jean. There is something else in his mind. The girl realizes that as his wife she will have protection, food, peace, etc.—security with his mother in the country. But there is still some other reason in Jean's mind. Suddenly she divines what it is, though she never speaks it. But she knows what he plans to do.

    GIRL   You have come over to us!

But Jean denies it. He says that even if he had come over, if he came over at this late date, with no one left in Vichy anymore but the hated old men, nobody would believe him.

Jean notifies his mother that he is going to be married. He sends Coupe-tête a pass to come to Paris. Coupe-tête does not know what is up, but he obeys. Mme Mornet and Catherine do not know what is up either.

Jean and the girl are married, with the sanction of Jean's German superiors. His papers are altered to include his wife, etc.

Coupe-tête is present. Coupe-tête still doesn't know what is going on.

The village. Mme Mornet and Catherine are waiting for Jean to arrive with his bride and Coupe-tête. When they arrive, it is not Jean but Georges. Mme Mornet and Catherine learn then that Jean used his position with the Germans to get Georges out of the jail. Georges still suffers from the third degree, is doped also to keep him from protesting. Jean has substituted himself in Georges's cell in the jail.

The three women, Coupe-tête and the priest manage to get Georges out of the country, to return to England. This will be a tag scene or business, as strong as I can make it, to postulate the whole substance and meaning of the picture.

FADE OUT.

FADE IN—1942

MONTAGE to show how the weight of the United States has appeared and is growing in Europe: another nation of people who love freedom now in the balance against the oppressors—perhaps fleets of big bombers passing over in wave after wave, etc.

DISSOLVE TO:

Jeanneney and Herriot[2]—Close Shot.

Voice over scene, reading the joint formal letter of protest and affirmation which they wrote to Vichy:

> VOICE   . . . that liberty should ever perish from the land where it was born and spread to all the world . . .

DISSOLVE TO:

Fleets of bombers filling sky, sound of engines, bombs, gunfire.

DISSOLVE TO:

2. In August 1942 Jules Jeanneney (1864–1957), the president of the French Senate, and Édouard Herriot (1872–1957), formerly the president of the Chamber of Deputies, lodged a joint protest against General Pétain's decision to dissolve the two bureaus.

Title: DIEPPE, or some other known raid of late summer, 1942.

DISSOLVE TO:

Close Shot. Coupe-tête, crouching. He is in the middle of a commando raid. Gunfire, shouts, raiders with blackened faces running past him as he watches, shouts after them. He is excited, not at all afraid. Three men run past; Coupe-tête shouts after them, follows.

He joins a British corporal and two men, helps to attack a German sentry, is wounded. The others pick him up and carry him out as they retreat.

Beach. Landing barges, men entering, firing backward; fires in b.g., battle sound. Coupe-tête lying on the beach, mortally wounded, men bending over him. An officer revives him. When Coupe-tête opens his eyes, the first face he sees is Georges.

COUPE-TÊTE It's a boy.

He tells Georges that his son has come, dies in Georges's arms, still saturnine, courageous, whimsical. He says France will always live as long as Frenchmen continue to replace themselves like this, etc. He dies.

DISSOLVE TO:

Montage or title or voice, to indicate a time lapse, and that the weight of doom hanging over the German oppressors is growing still.

DISSOLVE TO:

An aerodrome, England. A bombing raid is departing. De Gaulle and Georges are present.

The operations office. De Gaulle, Georges, others enter, wait about loudspeaker to hear the reports from the pilots. In the dialogue De Gaulle makes a pointed speech to

DISSOLVE THRU TO:

The village. Mme Mornet, carrying small bundle, Catherine carrying the baby, watching while Jean's wife and Marthe set fire to the stable to guide the bombers. When the fire begins to burn, all four of them exit. Shouts, shots from German sentries, etc.

A hill. The four women watching as other fires begin to show about the countryside. Dialogue to indicate how the word has been passed to all the people to fire their barns, etc., to guide the bombers.

DISSOLVE TO:

Int. bomber in flight over France. The dark country spotted over with fires, others springing up, pilot speaking into his mike.

PILOT   Fires! Fires! They are springing up everywhere!

WIPE TO:

Operations office. De Gaulle and others listen as the pilot's voice comes through.

VOICE   They are lighting the way for us!

WIPE TO:

A factory in France making German munitions. The laborers are French, many German guards, etc. In f.g. is Jean, a laborer. Excitement, the approaching raid is reported, sirens. A.A. fire in b.g., the Germans shout, try to run out of building. The French laborers stop them; a German shoots one, a machine gun starts. The laborers, unarmed, overpower the guards and lock the doors. The bomber engines begin, increase, sirens, gunfire, a loud explosion as the first bomb falls. The men begin to sing the Marseillaise; the whole factory takes it up as the bombs fall. Close on Jean, singing with the others. Bombs continue to fall.

DISSOLVE TO:

Operations office. De Gaulle and Georges, others in b.g. as they listen to the pilot's voice.

VOICE   More of them! More of them! You can almost hear them, like voices singing. All France is blazing, blazing . . .

FINAL FADE OUT.

IV

The De Gaulle Story

First Complete Screenplay

FADE IN

CLOSE SHOT   TWO PHOTOGRAPHS ON A TABLE

One is a man about twenty-five, in a private's uniform, a reckless, merry, careless, open face. He is a soldier only through the force of events. The other is a man of thirty or more, in the uniform of a junior naval officer. His face is calm, grave, composed, colder. It is already stamped with the look of the professional soldier.

DISSOLVE TO:

CLOSE SHOT   TWO PAIRS OF SHOES

—sitting on floor outside a closed door. One pair sits neatly against wall. It is a pair of officer's shoes, fairly clean. The other pair seems to have been flung out the door. It is a pair of heavy, clumsy, muddy private's boots.

MED. SHOT   MARTHE

—standing close to the door beside which the shoes sit, listening. She is a peasant, about fifty. She is a servant in the house, though in an independent Breton way. Her husband has farmed the Mornet land during the sons' absence, doing the actual work which Mme Mornet cannot do. But he and his wife live in their own house, and Marthe is more a companion to Mme Mornet than a servant. She and Mme Mornet do the same work, together, etc.

Marthe is motionless, listening. After a moment, she puts her hand on the door knob and opens it.

ANGLE SHOT   PAST MARTHE   BEDROOM

—through partly open door. The end of a big, old-fashioned bed in b.g., in f.g. a chair with the navy officer's uniform hung

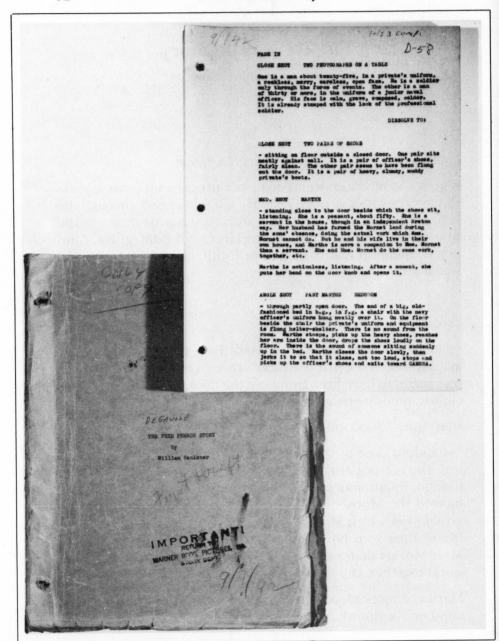

9. Opening of first complete version of Faulkner's screenplay

neatly over it. On the floor beside the chair the private's uniform and equipment is flung helter-skelter. There is no sound from the room. Marthe stoops, picks up the heavy shoes, reaches her arm inside the door, drops the shoes loudly on the floor. There is the sound of someone sitting suddenly up in the bed. Marthe closes the door slowly, then jerks it to so that it slams, not too loud, stops and picks up the officer's shoes and exits toward CAMERA.

INT. KITCHEN MORNING

It is the home of well-to-do farmers. The table is set for breakfast. It has a mildly festive air, in honor of the sons' homecoming. A vase of field flowers, small extras, fresh linen, silver, etc. Mme Mornet is busy at the stove as Marthe enters, carrying the shoes. Mme Mornet is about fifty. Her face shows strength, firmness. She has been managing the farm during the sons' absence. Marthe sets the shoes on a chair and crosses to a cupboard.

> **MME MORNET** *(without turning)* Are they up yet?

> **MARTHE** *(grimly)* They soon will be.

She takes polish and brush from the cupboard, returns and takes up one of the shoes.

> **MME MORNET** Just one pair?

> **MARTHE** Georges is a private. France is full of private soldiers. Let him clean his own shoes, if he doesn't like the way he looks in them.

CLOSE SHOT MARTHE

—cleaning a shoe, favoring Mme Mornet at stove.

> **MARTHE** Two days to track dirt through the house. Then back to the war again. Well, it will be over soon and they can come home and attend to their own affairs for a while.

> **MME MORNET** What makes you think it will be over soon?

> **MARTHE** The Boches have gone South, then East, and now North. All that is left is the West. And on the West is our Maginot Line that cost France a million francs.

MME MORNET   Five hundred billion francs.

MARTHE   Five hundred *billion?* Five hundred billion? For a fort? They could have bribed all Europe to leave us alone for five hundred billion francs.

CLOSE   MME MORNET

Her face is grave.

MME MORNET   Well, let us hope it will save France, even spent that way.

INT. BEDROOM   CLOSE   GEORGES

—favoring Jean at mirror. Georges is almost dressed, in his private's uniform. As he moves, he knocks over the chair on which Jean's officer's coat hangs. Georges picks the chair up quickly and brushes the coat off, clowning a little yet sincere, too.

CLOSE   JEAN AT MIRROR

—favoring Georges watching him. Jean wears civilian clothes, is knotting his tie.

GEORGES   Anyway, I won't have to salute and call you "sir" today.

JEAN   I thought we settled that last night.

GEORGES   Yes. But I still think it's tactful of you not to wear that uniform today.

JEAN   Well, I'm not. So break off, will you?

GEORGES   Right—sir.

Jean finishes knotting his tie, turns, finds Georges watching him, merry and quizzical, though actually glad to see him again. Jean pauses. His face doesn't change, cold and calm. He passes Georges, goes on. Georges looks after him, follows.

INT. KITCHEN   MED. SHOT

Mme Mornet at stove, Marthe turning away from the cupboard as Jean and Georges enter.

GEORGES Good morning, girls.

CLOSE   MME MORNET

—as Georges swings her half around and kisses her cheek, releases her.

CLOSE   MARTHE

—as Georges grasps her.

MARTHE Guh—

Georges kisses her before she can resist, disarranges her cap, releases her before she can slap him. She resets her cap.

> **MARTHE** Dirt! Noise! Uproar! And now violations! They call it soldiering, saving France!

> **GEORGES** We are saving France. Didn't I just save that kiss from some fat Boche with sauerkraut on his vest?

> **MARTHE** Bah! Sit down and eat, and get out of this kitchen. Go to Coupe-tête with your stupid jokes; maybe he will like them!

CLOSE   MME MORNET

—as Jean approaches.

> **JEAN** Good morning, mother.

She turns her cheek, receives kiss.

> **MME MORNET** Sit down. The omelette is ready.

CLOSE   GROUP AT TABLE

Mme Mornet, Jean and Georges seated, Marthe serving them between table and stove while Jean and Georges eat. Georges eats rapidly, talking while he eats, cheerful, glad to be home again. Jean is cold, deliberate, as always.

> **MARTHE** *(to Georges)* It won't be the likes of you that saves Brittany from the Boches. It will be that five hundred billion francs the politicians paid for the Maginot Line.

> **GEORGES** *(eating)* It might if it was still five hundred billion francs. It won't as a fort, though.

Jean is drinking. He stops, puts his cup down, looks at Georges.

CLOSE   GEORGES, JEAN, MME MORNET

JEAN   Why not?

GEORGES   They will go around it.

JEAN   Who will?

GEORGES   Any motorized army. Not us, though. We don't believe in motorized armies. We have already crucified the man who tried to warn us.

JEAN   And who was that?

GEORGES   My colonel. Colonel De Gaulle.

JEAN   I never heard of him.

GEORGES   Why should you—on a ship? Most of the army never heard of him, either. The generals saw to that.

JEAN   If you do much of this sort of talk, I'm surprised you got leave to go anywhere, even for two days. Who is this man?

GEORGES   I told you. Just a colonel. Colonel Charles De Gaulle. He's in Syria now, where he can't break the peaceful snoring of the General Staff.

CLOSE GROUP   ANOTHER ANGLE

MME MORNET   But you are not this Colonel De Gaulle nor the General Staff, either. Finish your breakfast so Marthe and I can clean up.

GEORGES   (empties his bowl) Which is too bad. Then Marthe could sweep us both out. What France needs is somebody to sweep a few generals and admirals out onto the trash heap.

CLOSE   JEAN

—standing, looking down at Georges.

JEAN   (coldly) Georges!

Georges looks up at Jean, reckless, devil-may-care.

GEORGES Sir, my admiral.

DISSOLVE TO:

EXT. A FIELD   CLOSE SHOT   GEORGES

—plowing. He shows he is out of practice, but is enjoying it.

MED. CLOSE   JEAN AND COUPE-TÊTE AT EDGE OF FIELD

—Georges plowing in b.g. Coupe-tête is an old, tough, wiry peasant, bibulous, sardonic, faithful to the farm which he has farmed for Mme Mornet while the sons were gone.

JEAN You have done well. I am grateful to you.

COUPE-TÊTE What else did you expect?

JEAN Nothing.

COUPE-TÊTE Then save your pretty speeches for a softer ear than this. *(he flips his hat brim beside his ear)* War, bah! What are all the generals and admirals, compared to giving one's dead father a successor, not to mention giving one's living mother a grandson to play with.

JEAN Not to mention giving France another soldier.

MED. SHOT   ANOTHER ANGLE

—as Jean begins to exit.

COUPE-TÊTE Produce them, then. What is valuable must be fought for. If it is valuable enough, it will be. And no enemy can beat men who will fight. *(Jean goes on; Coupe-tête raises his voice)* Try the upper lane!

Jean pauses, looks back.

JEAN For what?

COUPE-TÊTE For what you seek.

JEAN What do you think I am seeking?

COUPE-TÊTE For what you should be seeking, then.

EXT. A HILL   FULL SHOT

—as Jean mounts in f.g. In b.g. the countryside can be seen, Georges plowing in distance, the fields, the farm and its buildings, the village, church spire, etc. Jean crosses scene, exits.

MED. CLOSE

The plow halted, Georges holding it and looking at Coupe-tête.

GEORGES Now what?

COUPE-TÊTE Try the upper lane.

GEORGES All right. What for?

Georges looks at Coupe-tête a moment longer. Then he lays the plow quickly down and starts out of scene.

GEORGES The upper lane?

COUPE-TÊTE Or maybe you ground lads are not as brisk as sailors.

GEORGES (*pauses, looks back*) How do you know where Jean is?

COUPE-TÊTE You have forty-eight hours' leave. You have already spent a quarter of it arguing with me. What sort of men does France produce nowadays?

Georges hurries out. Coupe-tête goes and takes up the plow.

COUPE-TÊTE (*to the horse*) But you are no soldier or sailor, either. Advance! (*the horse moves*)

EXT. A LANE

Catherine approaches. She is about twenty—twenty-two. She is the daughter of the mayor. She wears her everyday clothes, carries a big old-fashioned satchel. She is going to spend the day at the Mornets, to welcome the two sons. She will help get the dinner, then she will change to her better clothes, which she carries in the satchel. It was arranged some time back that she will marry one of the two sons. The marriage is off now because of the war. Because Jean is a career man in the navy, Georges will probably be the bridegroom. He is nearer her in age, and Jean has been away from home more or less since Catherine was a child. She hardly knows him, and when he takes a wife, it will probably be in navy circles, for advancement, etc. But all this marriage business is off now, since all Europe is at war and everyone knows that France will be attacked soon. She looks up out of scene, recognizes someone, pauses.

CLOSE   JEAN AND CATHERINE

CATHERINE   Lieutenant . . .

JEAN   I used to be Jean.

CATHERINE   I was a child, then.

JEAN   But I should still be Jean. More than ever now. When Uncle Coudron wrote that he had got Georges leave to come home for two days, so I could meet him again, I hoped I knew why.

CATHERINE   (takes his meaning, is flustered a little) No. There's—

JEAN   Isn't Georges enough of a bargain to suit His Honor the Mayor?

CATHERINE   (recovers herself) What young man in France is a bargain now at any price?

JEAN   You, too? Of course. Georges writes you letters.

CATHERINE   Georges? Letters? Georges sends postcards.

JEAN   And postcards are not enough.

CATHERINE   (hurriedly—moves) I must go. Your mother and Marthe are waiting on me.

She goes on. Jean looks after her.

CLOSE SHOT

—the horse standing, the plow lying on its side, in the field. Georges is gone.

CLOSE   CATHERINE   ANOTHER PART OF LANE

—pauses as Georges approaches rapidly.

GEORGES   *(in burlesque falsetto)* No, Georges! No, Georges!

He takes her in his arms, while she begins to resist, holds him off. He draws her to him, smiling, devil-may-care, while she resists.

GEORGES   Now I've said it for you, so it's all right.

They kiss.

DISSOLVE TO:

EXT. FIELD   CLOSE SHOT

—Georges, plowing again. He is singing, loud, off-key, tuneless, a ribald song, to the effect that girls come and go but a good plow horse and a field that needs plowing seem to last forever.

DISSOLVE TO:

INT. KITCHEN   EVENING

The table is set for the meal to celebrate the sons' homecoming: flowers, best silver, china, etc. Mme Mornet, Catherine, Jean and Georges are seated about it, finishing the meal. Mme Mornet wears her Sunday dress, black silk with lace collar. Catherine has changed to her Sunday dress. Georges now wears his uniform coat. Jean wears a city suit and collar. He looks like a stranger, almost, among the others. Marthe moves back and forth, serving the table. She wears a fresh apron and cap. Coupe-tête sits in the b.g. in a clean, collarless shirt and an old, faded, once-elegant frock coat.

COUPE-TÊTE   You have eaten the food. You have drunk the wine. And still nothing. Can't His Honor the Mayor make up his mind which one of them he wants, or is it Catherine—

MME MORNET   Coupe-tête!

MARTHE   *(to Coupe-tête) Miss* Catherine.

COUPE-TÊTE   I'm still hoping to say Madame Mornet, someday. Miss Catherine! Yesterday she wore diapers. Someone changed them, too.

GEORGES   Not you, though.

MARTHE Hush! Have you no delicacy? *(to Georges)* Is this what the army has taught you? For shame!

MED. CLOSE GEORGES, MME MORNET, CATHERINE, MARTHE
COUPE-TÊTE IN B.G.

Georges puts his napkin on the table and rises. He turns to Mme Mornet.

GEORGES We're going to the cafe for a while. We won't be late.

MME MORNET Aren't you going to see Catherine home?

Georges hesitates.

CATHERINE *(quickly)* I don't need anybody.

MME MORNET You can take that much time.

MARTHE Coupe-tête will walk with her, since this hero cannot.

COUPE-TÊTE Certainly. I am no bear, without manners. Nor yet a wolf, that Catherine—

MARTHE *Miss* Catherine! Get the lantern . . .

COUPE-TÊTE *(rises)* That also. I'm going to the cafe, too. I want to hear something about this war myself from another point of view besides the female.

GEORGES You won't hear it from me. I'm not going to argue about the war with anybody. I'm home this time on pleasure.

EXT. FRONT DOOR NIGHT

Jean standing beside door as Coupe-tête comes around the house from the back with a lighted lantern. Jean tries to take the lantern from him. Coupe-tête resists.

COUPE-TÊTE Now what?

JEAN I'll walk home with Miss Catherine.

COUPE-TÊTE *(struggles for lantern)* Let go! Squabble with your brother. I'm not your rival.

Catherine comes out, carrying satchel. Jean and Coupe-tête pause.

> **CATHERINE** *(quickly)* No. Please. Coupe-tête always walks home with me.

She passes Jean hurriedly. He looks after her.

CLOSE   CATHERINE AND COUPE-TÊTE

—favoring Jean in doorway. Catherine goes on. Coupe-tête stops, looking back at Jean.

> **COUPE-TÊTE**   No rivals, hah? I was wrong.

> > > DISSOLVE TO:

INT. CAFE   BAR IN B.G.

—proprietor and his wife behind the bar, a few men at the bar, tables about, men sitting at tables, drinking and smoking. In f.g. and in principal place is a table with a card game in progress. At this table sits the mayor, a pompous man of fifty-odd. His opponent is another oldish man, prosperous looking also. A few men watch the game, respectfully; these are the village big-wigs, playing, two or three other important ones sitting in chairs to watch, while the hoi-polloi stand up to look respectfully on. All the village types are represented, laborers respectfully in b.g. All these men are oldish. There is not a single young man in sight yet save Jean and Georges, and one man also in uniform at bar.

CLOSE GROUP SHOT

Jean is standing at the table where the card game is in progress. The mayor is looking up at Jean, a card poised in his hand.

> **MAYOR**   Home again, I see. Is this any time for a military man to be away from his station?

> **JEAN**   I met my brother here on what I had hoped was a family matter of some importance. We will go back to duty day after tomorrow.

> **MAYOR**   Which, for all you or he either know, may be just exactly one day too late. *(he prepares to play the card, stops again)* Stand aside a little, will you? You are in the light.

CLOSE AT BAR

—Georges, the soldier, three civilians. The patron faces them, waiting for their orders.

GEORGES Isn't this one on the house?

CLOSE   ANOTHER ANGLE

The patronne leans toward the group.

PATRONNE   *(to patron)* Let them pay.

GEORGES   When we save France daily? You should be glad to give drinks to soldiers. They at least won't talk about the war in here.

PATRONNE   People who talk about the war don't stay in here long enough to drink. *(to patron)* Let them pay.

The patron shrugs, sets bottle and glasses on the bar. Georges produces a coin from his pocket, lays it on the bar. The patron looks at it, takes up coin and gives it to patronne. Patron exits.

CLOSE SHOT   GEORGES

—favoring the other drinkers. The patron fills the glasses.

GEORGES   At least we won't have to talk about the war. I was afraid I would have to give a résumé of Gamelin's whole strategy.

SOLDIER   That could be done in a nutshell.

GEORGES   Not a nutshell. You have to crack a nutshell.

The patron fills the glasses.

FIRST CIVILIAN   What do you mean by that?

SECOND CIVILIAN   That the Boche hasn't anything to crack our line with, just as we have nothing that will crack his.

SOLDIER   I thought we were not going to talk about he war.

CLOSE SHOT   FAVORING GEORGES

GEORGES   Who is? If we are talking about the Maginot

Line, who ever called that war? *(he watches the patron)* Full measure. We are paying for it.

SECOND CIVILIAN Do you really believe the Germans can break the Maginot Line?

GEORGES I don't know. I don't imagine they know either. Or care.

CLOSE   A TABLE   FAVORING BAR

Three men at the table have paused and are listening.

GEORGES They won't have to crack it. They will go around it.

GROUP AT BAR

FIRST CIVILIAN And just who is this Colonel De Gaulle?

GEORGES A better man than me or you either.

CLOSE SHOT   GEORGES

—his back to the bar, his elbows on it, easy and still reckless, devil-may-care.

GEORGES Yes, gentlemen. As far as keeping any enemy out of France, the Maginot Line might just as well be soap.

Loud crash off scene.

FULL SHOT

—the mayor standing, beside card table, his chair overturned, facing Georges, who still leans against the bar.

MAYOR Soap? The Maginot Line that has held the Germans out of France for a year now? That took five hundred billion francs out of the pockets of every man, woman and child in France? Soap?

GEORGES Better if it was soap. Because then the Germans—

A derisive whistle from the crowd.

MAYOR Who did that? *(no answer—to the constable)* Find that man!

CLOSE GROUP SHOT

—mayor facing the soldier, who has been thrust forward by the constable and one or two civilians.

MAYOR   *(to soldier)* Did you make that sound?

SOLDIER   Suppose I did?

MAYOR   *(to constable)* Arrest him!

The constable moves timidly toward the soldier.

SOLDIER   *(to constable)* Don't put your hand on me.

CLOSE   ANOTHER ANGLE   FAVORING JEAN

JEAN   *(to mayor)* He's in uniform. You can't—

MAYOR   You think your commission will protect you? You are not wearing its insignia now. *(to constable)* Arrest both these soldiers!

JEAN   On what charge?

MAYOR   Treason!

JEAN   Treason to what?

MAYOR   To the five hundred billion francs which the government spent on a concrete ditch for the army to hide behind when they should be attacking! *(to constable)* Arrest them!

The constable hesitates. The other men watch, their faces lowering at this insult to that much of French taxes. They remember 1914–1918; they have lived under the strain of this present German threat for years now, augmented by the uncertain future of which they know only that Western Europe will be next and that an attack is bound to come. The constable moves toward Georges and the soldier. As he reaches the soldier, Georges steps between them.

CLOSE SHOT

—the constable falling as Georges and the soldier between them tripped him.

CONSTABLE   *(from floor)* Help! Treason! Help!

MAYOR'S VOICE   Arrest them!

GROUP SHOT

Five or six men move upon Georges and the soldier, sounds of uproar, voices, etc.

EXT. STREET BEFORE THE CAFE DOOR   NIGHT

The shouts and uproar muffled by the walls. A gendarme enters on his bicycle, stops, listens, dismounts without haste and leans the bicycle against the wall, pauses to see if it is going to fall or not, then enters the cafe without haste, the uproar loud as he opens the door.

INT. CAFE

The noise has stopped short off; the men remain in the attitudes in which the gendarme's entrance stopped them.

GROUP SHOT   GENDARME, GEORGES, SOLDIER, JEAN, THE MAYOR
OTHERS IN B.G.

The patronne faces the gendarme angrily.

PATRONNE   I try to run a decent quiet place! And what do I get? War, war, war, until I am sick of it!

GENDARME   Peace, then, yourself. *(he turns to Jean, Georges and the soldier)* So this is how you celebrate your leave: badgering civilians.

He approaches, leans and sniffs at Georges's and the soldier's breaths, pauses, sniffs at a civilian next to them.

GENDARME   So it's you I smell. Were you in it, too?

CIVILIAN   No.

GENDARME   You don't look it. *(turns to Georges and the soldier)* Now, then. Have you done?

GEORGES   I haven't even started. I just—

GENDARME   Then start now. Both of you. Go on. Out with you.

Georges moves toward the door. The soldier follows, then Jean.

GENDARME *(recognizes Jean)* Lieutenant Mornet. Will you see that he goes on home?

JEAN Yes.

He follows, exits after Georges and the soldier.

PATRONNE They drank. Who will pay?

GENDARME Charge it to the Republic.

He follows.

EXT. STREET MED. SHOT GEORGES AND JEAN NIGHT

Georges's face is furious, seething. He glances back, sees Jean beside him, crosses the street to the opposite side. Jean hesitates, follows him. Georges looks back, sees Jean, crosses street to opposite side again. Jean watches him, shrugs slightly, goes on. They walk up the street on opposite sides, Georges striding angrily ahead.

WIPE TO:

EXT. FRONT DOOR OF MORNET HOUSE NIGHT

Georges enters, striding angrily toward door. Jean follows. Georges opens the door.

INT. HALL

Mme Mornet has just come out of a door, in her dressing gown, stands as Georges and Jean enter. They do not see her.

JEAN Georges—

Georges doesn't answer. He strides on, mounts the stairs. Jean hesitates, then follows up the stairs. Mme Mornet comes out, looks up the stairs after them.

STAIRWAY

—Mme Mornet in f.g. looking up at it. The bottom of the door to Jean and Georges's bedroom can be seen beyond the top of the stairs. Jean's and Georges's feet and legs can be seen as Georges opens the door and enters and Jean follows. The door shuts.

INT. BEDROOM

A big, old-fashioned bed, Jean lighting a lamp on the table. Georges has already begun to undress, flinging his clothes aside, exits. Jean begins to remove his coat, slowly. Georges enters, wearing nightshirt, goes to bed as Jean exits. Georges flings covers back, gets into the bed, flops down with his back to the room, draws covers up. Jean enters, in nightshirt, too, looks at bed, goes to lamp and blows it out, goes to bed and gets in.

CLOSE SHOT   JEAN AND GEORGES IN BED

Georges's back is still turned. Jean rests on one elbow, looks at Georges.

JEAN   Georges.

Georges doesn't turn for a minute. Then he flings his arm back, knocks Jean down into the bed and bangs him across the rump with a back-handed blow.

GEORGES   Ah, go to sleep, you stupid opinionated sap!

INT. LOWER HALL

Mme Mornet looking up at the closed door to the bedroom. It does not open again. She turns. Her face is peaceful again. She goes and enters her room, closes the door.

FADE OUT.

FADE IN

MONTAGE

—over sound of bombs and gunfire, on the Saturday morning when the Germans broke through the Dutch frontier, tanks in action, the bombing of Rotterdam, parachute troops landing, etc.

DISSOLVE TO:

CLOSE SHOT   CHURCH SPIRE AGAINST THE SKY   MORNING

The bells are ringing peacefully.

FULL SHOT   A PROCESSION

—the priest leading, choirboys carrying Host, monstrance, etc.

Girls in best dresses, carrying flowers. Sound of peaceful bells
OVER SCENE.

ENTRANCE TO CHURCH

The villagers, children, women of all ages, a soldier or so, a few
young men but mostly older men, all in their best clothes,
watching as the procession enters the church.

INT. CHURCH

The church is old, not large, and on the plain side as to pews,
furnishings, etc. But some of the religious furniture is rich,
though meager: the candlesticks, etc., and altar ornaments.
The villagers sit in the pews; the choir is singing.

FULL SHOT

—of priest as he comes to podium. The singing ceases. The
people in the pews kneel. The priest speaks a short brief prayer
in Latin, makes sign with his hand; the people rise and sit back
in the pews. The priest is about fifty, a peasant type by birth, but
his face is thin, ascetic, intelligent, wise, yet still strong.

> **PRIEST** In the beginning was the earth. It and all within it
> were for man's use and comfort. There was enough for all.

CLOSE SHOT   MAYOR'S PEW   MAYOR, CATHERINE AND ADJACENT
FACES IN OTHER PEWS

The mayor sits pompously erect, not listening. He doesn't need
to. He is the first man in the village, whether in the cafe or the
church either. The priest's voice continues:

> **PRIEST'S VOICE** But he was not content, even when there
> were but few of him, even when what he knew as his nation
> was just a collection of caves in a single hill, with a little fire
> to lift its puny hand between him and the darkness and the
> unknown.

CLOSE SHOT   MORNET PEW   MME MORNET, JEAN, GEORGES AND
ADJACENT FACES

Mme Mornet and Jean listen attentively. Jean is grave. Georges
has an expression of sardonic contempt on his face. The voice
continues:

PRIEST'S VOICE   Now the boundaries of what he boasts of as his nations interlock one with another across all the earth. Now he claims the air above and the seas which surround him. And still the young men of his nations face each other across these barriers, with guns in their hands which have been blessed and dedicated to patriotism and love of home, for the purpose of destroying one another in the name of ultimate peace.

MED. LONG SHOT   AISLE OF CHURCH   PRIEST IN B.G.

—facing his audience.

PRIEST   We have deposed Him. We have set up in His place rapacity and greed and power and vainglory, naming them in outrageous travesty of what He preached: love of man for man, of land and home, living space. So is it any wonder, then, with the blood of women and children, of Slav and Magyr and Jew, crying up to Him, that He has said, "So be it, then. If this is what must be, so be it, until all this blood-soaked Europe cries aloud against those who made it flow, their nights are filled with the eyes of their victims as the sky's night is with its stars, until there is no place on earth or beneath it where they can forget that choired indictment, as I Myself will not forget it!"

The priest ceases, stands motionless.

MED. LONG SHOT   ANOTHER ANGLE

Priest facing audience.

PRIEST   *(quietly now)* We must endure. Rapacity cannot be bribed. Lust and satiety are not drugs, but habits. If France were nothing, it would not have existed. To remain France, it will have to endure. If it still is France, it will endure.

He raises his hand.

CLOSE SHOT   PEW

—in which Coupe-tête and Marthe sit, adjacent faces of other peasants, etc. Coupe-tête stands up. His face is untroubled, merely frankly contemptuous, convinced.

COUPE-TÊTE Bah! Let them take France. Then let them try to capture Brittany.

Marthe pulls at his coattail. He looks around.

COUPE-TÊTE I say it again. Just let them try it.

Marthe pulls him down.

MED. LONG SHOT   AS BEFORE

Priest faces audience, his hand raised. The villagers kneel again. The priest pronounces the benediction, makes sign of cross and turns as the choir rises and begins to sing.

DISSOLVE TO:

INT. MAYOR'S HOME   DINING ROOM   AFTERNOON

Mme Mornet, Jean, Georges, Catherine and the mayor are gathered about the table, just finishing the meal.

CLOSE SHOT   MAYOR

—at head of table, his napkin tucked into his collar, as maid enters, sets bottle before him. The mayor is about to pick up bottle, stops, shows angry outrage, snatches up the bottle, turns angrily to servant.

MAYOR I said cider! Are you deaf?

MAID I thought you would want the wine.

MAYOR Do I pay you board and wages to think? Take it back!

FULL GROUP SHOT   TABLE

The maid takes up the bottle and exits.

CATHERINE Papa. Please.

MAYOR You too, eh? Perhaps you too will tell me I neither know how to conduct my household nor what is going on in France.

The maid enters, holds pitcher for the mayor to see.

MAYOR Pour.

The maid goes about the table, filling the glasses.

CLOSE SHOT   MAYOR

—standing, holding his glass up.

> **MAYOR**   For some time now, a marriage has been planned
> between our two families, depending on circumstances.
> Those circumstances were this so-called war—for which,
> incidentally, France has made an initial investment of five
> hundred billion francs, which certain high military au-
> thorities—*(he pauses, turns his head slightly and glares out of
> scene, recovers and continues)*—say has been thrown away, has
> compared, in fact, to soap. For a time we mere civilians had
> hoped that the war would stay outside our boundaries,
> even though there was only a barricade of soap to hold it
> back. But lately it seems to have entered not only France
> but this village, too, and not only the village but our homes
> and dining rooms, too—

CLOSE GROUP SHOT   FAVORING CATHERINE AND MME MORNET

> **CATHERINE**   Papa! Please!

> **MME MORNET**   Both of you hush. *(she rises, raises her glass)* It
> hasn't changed the agreement we made: that when France
> no longer needs my sons, the marriage will take place—
> provided that Catherine still wants either one of them.
> Otherwise, I'll stop it myself. I won't need a war.

CLOSE GROUP SHOT   ALL

> **MME MORNET**   So I don't know what you and Jean and
> Georges are going to drink to, and I don't care. Catherine
> and I are going to drink to the end of masculine folly, and
> to the hope that that will arrive soon.

CLOSE SHOT   MAYOR AND GEORGES

> **MAYOR**   You can drink to the end of the Maginot Line,
> perhaps.

> **GEORGES**   Have we got to start this again?

> **MAYOR**   Who did the starting of it in the first place? Five
> hundred billion francs to build a concrete pit for half the

able-bodied men in France to squat in twenty-four hours a day, playing *pelote*—

CLOSE SHOT   CATHERINE AND JEAN

CATHERINE Papa! Papa!

JEAN *(leans toward Georges)* Will you shut up?

CLOSE SHOT   GEORGES

GEORGES I'm still trying to. I'm even still hoping to. *(to mayor)* I hope you are right. Though Marthe says it only cost three thousand. That will be better still, because when the government finally decides to make a national curiosity out of it, they won't have the face to charge more than a few sous to tourists to look at it—

A sudden uproar out of scene: SOUND of feet, voices, the loud voice of the woman servant. All about the table stop, look toward the door as it bursts open. The servant enters, backward, swept into the room by the men she is trying to keep out of it, her voice still raised.

CLOSE SHOT   THE DOOR

—as maid enters backward, the constable shoving her aside, a stranger, a messenger following him, other villagers stopping still, respectful of the mayor's house, at the door.

MAID You can't come in! His Honor is eating. Eating, I tell you!

CONSTABLE Eating? Eating? This is no time for eating!

FULL SHOT   ROOM

—as the constable enters, followed by the messenger. The other villagers stop at the door, looking into the room as the constable hurries forward.

CLOSE SHOT

—mayor standing, facing constable, others in b.g. The constable is bursting with excitement.

CONSTABLE The Germans crossed the Dutch frontier this

morning! The French and British are rushing to join the Belgians—

CLOSE   FAVORING JEAN AND GEORGES   CATHERINE AND MME MORNET IN B.G.

GEORGES It has begun!

CONSTABLE *(to Georges and Jean)* And you, too. All soldiers and sailors are ordered to report.

GEORGES *(shoves constable aside)* He was right! Colonel De Gaulle was right! They are going around it!

CONSTABLE Of course they will go around it! We will hurl the whole German army into the North Sea!

EXT. STREET   AT MAYOR'S DOOR

Georges, then Jean, come out and hurry up the street. The constable and others come out. People begin to appear at other doors along the street.

GROUP SHOT

Constable, surrounded by anxious villagers, as they show reaction to the news which they have been expecting and dreading for so long.

CONSTABLE It has come. Holland has been invaded. Gamelin[1] and Gort[2] and the Belgian king are rushing—

SIDE VIEW OF WAGON

—Coupe-tête standing facing the rear end of it, writing something on the end of the wagon.

FULL SHOT   FRONT OF MORNET HOUSE

—as Jean, Georges, Mme Mornet and Catherine come out. Jean now wears a uniform, too, carries kit bag; Georges also fully equipped with pack, rifle, etc.

1. General Maurice Gamelin (1872–1958) was commander-in-chief of the French army from September 1939 to May 1940. He was replaced by General Weygand following the German invasion.
2. General John Standish, Lord Gort (1886–1946), was commander of the British Expeditionary Force in France in 1939–40.

CLOSE GROUP SHOT

Georges looks from his mother to Catherine.

GEORGES Well, which one first?

Before either can answer, Georges moves, quickly, as he did in the lane, takes Catherine in his arms, kisses her, releases her, puts his arm around Mme Mornet and draws her out of scene.

CLOSE SHOT   CATHERINE AND JEAN

JEAN *(looking out of scene, still watching Georges)* When I got Uncle Coudron's letter saying he had got Georges two days' leave to come home and for me to meet him here, I hoped it was for a reason.

CLOSE SHOT   JEAN   FAVORING CATHERINE

JEAN I hoped I was coming home to celebrate a wedding. What happened?

CATHERINE *(flustered)* This is no time for weddings. The war, France . . .

JEAN France is too loose a word. It means too much, and therefore too little. It is not enough.

CATHERINE Not enough?

JEAN For Georges—For me, yes. My course of conduct is fixed. It was already fixed long before I assumed it as my course of conduct. Any aberration from it I can make already has a name, even: treason.

CATHERINE Georges is a soldier, too.

JEAN Georges is a farmer. He is a soldier only by the force of circumstance. Fatherland will not be enough.

CATHERINE Yes. It will be. It will be. You are the one to worry—not Georges.

JEAN I?

CATHERINE Yes. I'm not afraid for the man who can commit only what people call cowardice; I am afraid for the man who believes that all he can be guilty of is what the people above him will call treason.

38 38a

                    CONSTABLE
                Eating? Eating?

Full shot Room as the Constable enters, followed by the messenger, and approaches the table. The others all stop at the door,
peering through it.

                    MAYOR
                What does this mean?

The Constable is shaking with excitement.

                    CONSTABLE
                Your Honor (struggles with himself,
                half turns toward the messenger)
                This man is from Rennes. He---
                He----

                    MAYOR
                What is this?

                    CONSTABLE
                He--- I---- God help our people.
                God help France. (pulls himself together)
                , speaks rapidly and coherently, official
                again) The enemy crossed the Dutch frontier
                this morning. Rotterdam----

Close shot Jean and Georges, Catherine and Mme Mornet in b.g.
Catherine's face is aghast, unbelieving, Mme Mornet's shocked
yet stern. Georges' face lights up, almost triumphant.

                    GEORGES
                It has begun!

Close Group shot Jean, Georges, Mayor, Constable, others in b;g.
as Georges p repares to rush out.

                    CONSTABLE (to Jean and Georges)
                And you too, You are soldiers. All
                soldiers and sailors are ordered to
                report----

                    GEORGE (shoves Constable
                aside, Jean following) He was right!
                Colonel de Gaulle was right! They are
                going around it! (He + Jean rush out)
                    Constable
He and Jean exit. Of course they will go around it! They
                will hunt the germans into the North Sea!

Ext. Street at Mayor's door. Georges, then Jean, come out and
hurry up the street. The Constable and others come out. People begin to appear at other doors along the street.

Group shot

10. Page of Faulkner's rewrite of first draft of screenplay

39

Group shot Constable surrounded by anxious villagers as they
show reaction to the news which they have been expecting and dreading for so long.

                    CONSTABLE
         ~~Rotterdam has been bombed. The~~
         ~~Queen has fled to England. God help~~
         ~~Western Europe. God help our people.~~
         ~~Hollcot~~ It his crew. Hollord hm hum invodul
         Gomilin ovl 9oRt ovl the Rlgien long one numbin, —

~~Close shot Coupe-tete sitting on seat of wagon, holding reins~~

Shot Side view of wagon, Coupe-tete standing ~~bakind~~ facing the
rear end of it, writing something on the end of the wagon.

Full shot Front of Mornet house as Jean, Georges, ᴹme Mornet
and Catherine come out. GJean now wears uniform too, carries kit
bag, Georges also fully equipped with pack, rifle, etc,

Close group shot, all. Georhes looks from his mother to Catherine.

                    GEORGES
         Well, which one first?

Before either can answer, Georges moves, quickly, as he did in
the lane, takes Catherine in arms, kisses her, re;eases her,
puts his arm around Mme Mornet and draws her out of scene.

Close shot Catherine and Jean.

                         JEAN (looks out of scene)
                    Fatherland is too loose a word. It
                    means too much, and therefore too
                    little. It's not enough for a man.

                         CATHERINE
                    So how you fight, or whether you fight
                    at all or not, depends on what you
                    leave behind you?

                         JEAN
                    On what you return to, or want to re-
                    turn to. (He looks at her as if he had
                    just understood her) No, not me. I take
                    what I wish to preserve into battle with
                    me. I am a professional maker of war. I
                    was thinking of Georges, who is ~~natxax~~
                    a soldier only because the law requires
                    it of him temporarily.

                         CATHERINE
                    So it's George you are worrying about.

                         JEAN
                    Not worrying. I'd feel better if you

11. Page of Faulkner's rewrite of first draft of screenplay

She exits hurriedly, flustered, alarmed at what she has said. Jean looks after her, gravely, shrugs at this notion of what he considers an inexperienced young girl.

MED. CLOSE SHOT

Jean embraces Mme Mornet, kisses her. Wagon in b.g. with Coupe-tête and Georges on the seat. Jean mounts the wagon. It moves.

CLOSE SHOT

—Mme Mornet and Catherine looking out of scene.

>   **MME MORNET**   Nineteen-fourteen. Again. Nineteen-fourteen.

CLOSE SHOT   WAGON IN MOTION

—as it turns, the occupants looking ahead. Back end of wagon comes into view.

CLOSE TRUCKING SHOT   REAR END OF WAGON BED

Across it in chalk, crudely printed: A BAS LA GUERRE
Two or three lines have been drawn through the words "LA GUERRE," and beneath it, in a slightly different hand: HITLER
The wagon grows smaller in—

>   FADE OUT.

FADE IN

MAP OF WESTERN EUROPE

Holland is blacked out. The black crosses the Belgian frontier, moving toward France as the front itself shifted during May. A radio voice speaks as the black moves, describing the advancing German front and the retreat of the British and Belgians and French in Flanders. The black halts, breaks through at Sedan, spreads. The voice carries over DISSOLVE to:

PLACE DE LA CONCORDE, PARIS

It is thronged with people: soldiers, civilians, police, maids, midinettes, old and young, men, women and children—a sea of faces looking anxiously upward as the voice continues. It is now Reynaud's voice.

REYNAUD'S VOICE   Do not be alarmed. It is 1914 again, but General Weygand has been ordered back from Syria to assume the command, and Weygand is another Foch. Do not be alarmed. They will not pass the Somme. They will not pass the Somme.

FULL SHOT   CHAMBER OF DEPUTIES, PARIS

—filled with men arguing, anxious, bewildered.

MED. CLOSE SHOT   REYNAUD

—standing. About him is grouped the cabinet; below him is the Chamber of Deputies. Reynaud is standing, trying to quiet the deputies. He is outwardly calm. He alone shows confidence, absence of fear and bewilderment. He is tense but forceful, commands silence at last by the sheer power of his apparent calmness.

REYNAUD   Gentlemen! Gentlemen! If you please . . .

They quiet, watch him.

CLOSE SHOT   FIRST FACE

PAN to other faces as they quiet to listen to what he will say.

CLOSE SHOT   A DEPUTY

DEPUTY   De Gaulle? De Gaulle? Who is De Gaulle?

CLOSE SHOT   REYNAUD

—-calm, forceful, standing.

REYNAUD   You may well ask that. That is a question the Marshal and General Weygand either could answer—*(his gaze moves from face to face, stops)*

CLOSE SHOT   DEPUTY

DEPUTY   Yes. I was there that day.

CLOSE SHOT   .REYNAUD

—standing.

REYNAUD   Yes. Mr. _____ was there, a member of the National Defense Council on that day in 1929, eleven years

ago, when Colonel De Gaulle advocated for the first, and
for the last time officially, as Mr. _____ will bear me out—

CLOSE SHOT   THE DEPUTY

DEPUTY   That is true.

CLOSE SHOT   REYNAUD

REYNAUD   —that the 3000 tanks which we then had be
grouped in one armored command, against such a day as
we are now facing. To be used against an enemy as the
Germans themselves are using tanks across the Somme.
And Mr. _____ will also remember what response he got
from those in whose hands the security of France lay—
(pauses)—and still lies.

A VOICE   Treason!

Reynaud pauses, looks about.

CLOSE SHOT   FIRST FACE

PAN to others, all watching Reynaud, quietly and intently now.

CLOSE SHOT   REYNAUD

REYNAUD   Will that gentleman stand? *(he looks about, waits;
no one rises)* The French people put this portfolio in my
hands. They need only ask to have it back.

ANOTHER ANGLE

—Reynaud in f.g., three-quarters, the faces watching him.

REYNAUD   Colonel De Gaulle: an obscure dreamer, servant of an illusion—little better than a poet, in fact. Why
should you know him? Why should anyone in France have
heard of the man whom the marshals and generals of
France rejected and ignored—

FULL SHOT   THE SEA OF FACES

—filling the Chamber.

VOICE   No! No!

VOICE   A nonentity! An unknown!

VOICE   Let our experienced generals—

CLOSE SHOT   REYNAUD

—facing them.

> REYNAUD Make him a general then. Give him all the tanks, all of them—

FULL SHOT   THE FACES

CLOSE SHOT   A DEPUTY AND REYNAUD

> DEPUTY No! No!

> REYNAUD I say yes!

> DEPUTY We are France!

CLOSE SHOT   REYNAUD

> REYNAUD Be it. I am the French people.

> > DISSOLVE TO:

CLOSE SHOT   MAP

SOUND of battle in b.g. The black of the German advance spreads toward Laon, pauses, begins to bulge on either side as the German advance is temporarily stopped. Sound of battle grows loud over—

> > DISSOLVE TO:

MED. TRUCKING SHOT   A MOVING TANK

The tank stops beside a French soldier, dirty and unshaven, sitting in the shelter of a fallen wall of a bombed house, eating a piece of bread. The soldier looks up for a moment, then away again, still eating. The hatch opens; Georges stands up in it, looks down at soldier.

> GEORGES Don't let us disturb you.

> SOLDIER Then take that tin can somewhere else, before a Boche comes along and decides to bomb it.

> GEORGES We intend to. Where's Brigade H.Q.?

> SOLDIER (*bites bread*) In Belgium, the last time I saw it. Will the General himself do?

The tank sergeant stands up in hatch beside Georges.

> **SERGEANT**   Now what?

> **GEORGES**   *(to soldier)* Whoever saw a brigade commander in a battle?

> **SOLDIER**   You will when you see De Gaulle. He was fighting one of your baby carriages himself until he took a direct hit on it about an hour ago.

> **GEORGES**   Who? Colonel De Gaulle? *(he begins to climb down)*

> **SOLDIER**   General De Gaulle.

The sergeant and a third man get out of tank.

> **SERGEANT**   Which way?

The soldier points over his shoulder with the bread, bites it again.

> **SOLDIER**   That way. Just look around until you find a man that looks like he was weaned on a shoelace. That's De Gaulle.

MED. SHOT   A TANK

—which has been disabled by a shell. Beside it a command car.

MED. CLOSE SHOT

The sergeant, Georges, and the third man at attention facing De Gaulle. De Gaulle wears a tank helmet, a leather coat, greasy khaki pants, no insignia. He is listening into earphones. His face is unshaven, strained. In b.g. two or three aides, radio corporal and radiomen, etc. De Gaulle listens to the progress of the battle all during scene.

> **DE GAULLE**   *(to sergeant)* I expected you last night. What happened?

CLOSE SHOT

—sergeant, Georges and third man beside him.

> **SERGEANT**   We ran into the battle yesterday afternoon and were scattered. The last order from the Commandant was

to disengage and keep radio silence and report to headquarters as we were able.

DE GAULLE   That took you until now?

SERGEANT   We ran into the battle again this morning, sir.

DE GAULLE   Ah.

PAN to Georges's face, De Gaulle's angle; then to third man. PAN
BACK to Georges's face.

DE GAULLE   *(to Georges)* You were at the tank school. What
is your name?

GEORGES   Mornet, sir.

DE GAULLE   Yes. Mornet.

PAN to sergeant.

DE GAULLE   Your tank is all right?

SERGEANT   It's all right, sir.

DE GAULLE   Grenier!

The aide enters.

DE GAULLE   Pack up. Move back to _____ village and set
up again.

FULL SHOT

The tank beside the fallen wall. The runner at attention, hiding
the piece of bread against his leg as De Gaulle, followed by
sergeant, Georges and the third man, enters.

DE GAULLE   *(to runner)* What are you doing here?

RUNNER   Taking cover, sir.

DE GAULLE   If you don't hurry, they are going to leave
you.

De Gaulle goes on to tank. The runner breaks off as Georges
passes him.

GEORGES   *(to runner)* Run! They were already serving the
dessert when we left.

De Gaulle and the three others enter the tank.

                                                    DISSOLVE TO:

THE MAP

The black moves on down the Somme toward Abbeville. SOUND
of battle, bombs, gunfire. A voice breaks in, broadcasting.

> VOICE Belgian army surrenders! The Belgian King is a
> prisoner of war . . . The British and French have reached
> Dunkirk and are being evacuated . . .

The black reaches Abbeville, stops temporarily as De Gaulle
holds the German advance again.

CLOSE SHOT   THE TANK IN MOTION   BATTLE SOUND IN B.G.

De Gaulle stands up in the hatch, looking back toward the
battle. SOUND of a bomber as it dives on the tank, zooms away.
De Gaulle pays no attention to it. SOUND of aeroplane beginning third dive at tank. Georges rises beside De Gaulle, grasps
him by belt and tries to pull him down.

> GEORGES For God's sake, General!

> DE GAULLE All right. Perhaps I will always be too tall for
> French tanks.

                                                    DISSOLVE TO:

INT. FARMHOUSE   PARLOR

—dismantled, evacuated by family. De Gaulle's field h.q., packing box for desk, camp chair, telephone, etc.

GROUP SHOT

De Gaulle, unshaven, tired, dirty, has just entered and stopped.
Grenier, the aide, stands behind the desk. Between them stands
a staff officer from Paris. The staff officer looks anxious, too,
but he is still in noticeable contrast to the battle-stained De
Gaulle and Grenier.

> STAFF OFFICER From the Commander-in-Chief, General.
> To congratulate you on the action, which at least allowed us
> to retreat in order.

DE GAULLE Thanks.

STAFF OFFICER And a message from the Premier. You are to return to Paris.

DE GAULLE Now?

STAFF OFFICER At once.

DE GAULLE It is an order?

MED. SHOT

The staff officer produces a folded paper from his pocket. De Gaulle takes it, opens it.

INSERT   LETTER

—in De Gaulle's hands. It is a note, informal:

General:
    Relinquish your command to Commandant _____ and return to Paris and receive the thanks of the Republic which has a still higher demand to make upon him who has already saved its army.
                                                Reynaud

CLOSE SHOT   DESK

—De Gaulle seated at desk, his hand on the telephone, Grenier standing beside him, holding the phone down.

GRENIER It's an order.

DE GAULLE I am fighting a battle. I have not even won it yet. Yet I am to quit it and return to Paris, to receive my reward.

GRENIER *(holds phone)* It's an order. In writing. From the Premier.

                                                DISSOLVE TO:

INT. COUNCIL ROOM   WAR MINISTRY   FULL SHOT

—Council seated around table. Reynaud standing.

REYNAUD —needs no introduction to any Frenchman. His credentials are his record; his references are the German army at Laon and again at Abbeville—

CLOSE SHOT   DE GAULLE

—seated at Reynaud's left. He now wears clean uniform, two stars of brigadier general.

REYNAUD   The Under-Secretary for War—Brigadier General De Gaulle.

CLOSE SHOT   FIRST FACE

—anxious, grave, waiting to see what the reaction will be. PAN to other faces in turn, same expression, showing how some favor Reynaud, are his yes-men, others not decided, others opposed. PAN to Pétain, who appears bored, indifferent. PAN to Weygand, who is grim, anxious, yet he is Pétain's man.

A man out of scene begins to applaud, others take it up until all join in save Pétain and Weygand. Pétain seems to shrug the whole matter off. Weygand seems grim and anxious, yet he suits his behavior to his superior.

INSERT   MAP OF FRANCE

—showing battle line as of June 8. The Somme has been crossed, the black covers all of the Low Countries, is spreading across Normandy.

GROUP SHOT AT TABLE   REYNAUD, DE GAULLE, PÉTAIN, WEYGAND

—other members of war council in b.g. The map is spread on the table. The adherents of Pétain and Weygand are reserved, inscrutable. The others are anxious, watching. The babble of voices from within the Chamber of Deputies continues. De Gaulle is grave, quiet. Weygand is grim, looking at map. Pétain is almost doddering, contemptuous, old. Reynaud watches Weygand.

WEYGAND   We will continue to retreat.

DE GAULLE   To where? The purpose of a retreat is to establish a tenable position. When it stops doing that, it ceases to be a retreat.

PÉTAIN   Does Brigadier General the Under-Secretary wish to give General Weygand a lesson in strategy, or merely in hope?

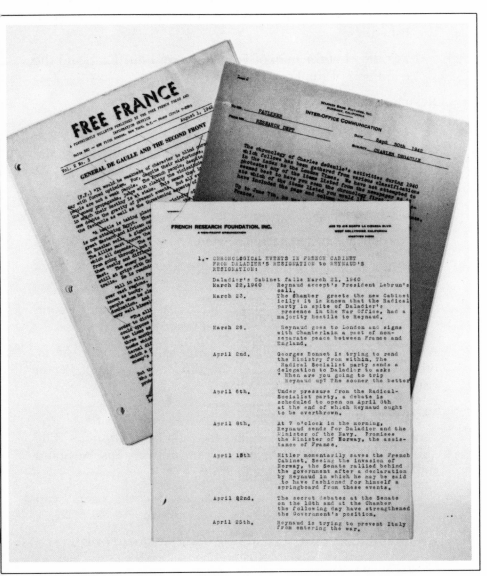

12. Some of the research materials supplied to Faulkner during his work on "The De Gaulle Story"

REYNAUD Come, come, Marshal. General De Gaulle merely wants you to answer the question we are all asking now: retreat to where? Where will our new line be established?

PÉTAIN Let the map of France answer him. That, and the condition of the French people.

Reynaud looks at Pétain a moment, rises.

CLOSE SHOT   LOUDSPEAKER ON WALL

Reynaud enters, turns switch. Out of loudspeaker comes the babble of voices from the Chamber.

VOICES Attack! Attack! We have generals; what are they doing?

FULL GROUP SHOT   WAR COUNCIL ABOUT THE TABLE

—favoring Reynaud standing at loudspeaker. Reynaud switches it off.

REYNAUD Does that sound like there is anything wrong with the condition of the French people?

A civilian begins to applaud, ceases as if aghast, another starts, others take it up, until only the army officers remain still. Pétain rises.

MED. CLOSE

Pétain standing above others, his face still contemptuous. The applause begins to die away. Pétain waits until it stops, Weygand still grimly down-looking beside him.

PÉTAIN Applaud then. Louder. So that the enemy can hear it and perhaps mistake it for gunfire.

EMPTY COUNCIL ROOM   CLOSE SHOT   REYNAUD AND DE GAULLE

Conference is over.

REYNAUD To London. See Mr. Churchill. Take all the time you need. Do not worry about us here. I myself will hold Paris single-handed until you return. The twilight of France is not to follow so short an afternoon.

INT. AEROPLANE IN FLIGHT   CLOSE SHOT   DE GAULLE AND GEN. SPEARS

SPEARS You speak no English, General?

DE GAULLE No.

SPEARS No matter. Mr. Churchill can hear and understand all men who love freedom and believe in courage.

EXT. 10 DOWNING STREET, LONDON

De Gaulle and Spears enter; sentry presents arms.

INT. CHURCHILL'S OFFICE   CLOSE SHOT

—a plump, thick hand in white cuff and black sleeve, holding a burning cigar, lying on table in f.g. De Gaulle standing facing CAMERA across the table.

CHURCHILL'S VOICE Welcome to England, General. Welcome to all that England has, as are all who stand as England stands in these dark days when all who still love liberty and freedom must league together.

WIPE TO:

MONTAGE   BULLETIN

—reading:

"French government will move from Paris to Tours"
"Paris declared an open city"

DISSOLVE TO:

EXT. STREET BEFORE FRENCH PARLIAMENT   FULL SHOT

The words: "Liberte, Egalite, Fraternite" above the door, French flag drooping above them. De Gaulle and aide mount steps and enter.

INT. CLOSE GROUP   DE GAULLE, AIDE, A SERVANT

DE GAULLE They have gone?

SERVANT Yes, General. Last night.

DISSOLVE TO:

MAP OF FRANCE

—showing the black at front of German advance on June 11. CAMERA STOPS on city of Tours.

DISSOLVE TO:

INT. COUNCIL ROOM   CLOSE SHOT

—Churchill's hand on table, the cigar has gone out, is frayed and crushed, gripped in the fingers in f.g. Beyond the hand, the length of the long table, the council sitting about it: Pétain, Weygand, Reynaud, De Gaulle, other British and French historical men. Reynaud presides, opposite Churchill. His face is self-possessed, even with all its gravity. Weygand reads aloud from a paper in his hand as others listen with varying expressions: Pétain with same almost inattentive contempt, etc., of what he knows will be the civilian reaction.

> **WEYGAND** . . . therefore, in the judgment of the General Staff, nothing remains but to ask the German High Command for an armistice.

He folds paper deliberately, lays it on the table. The other faces are quiet, intent, troubled, watching and waiting. Reynaud looks about. So far, he has been showing confidence and optimism, has said "Yes" always to anyone who spoke of resisting, fighting on. He will continue to do so. We will show in his actions the seed not so much of vacillation but of some weakness which caused him to fail where a stronger man might possibly have succeeded, or at least would never have given completely up, as De Gaulle never gave up.

> **REYNAUD** Well, gentlemen?

> **A MAN** (perhaps Mandel[3] or Compicini[4]) No!

A faint babble of other voices begins in b.g., grows.

CLOSE SHOT   CHURCHILL'S HAND WITH CIGAR

The hand crushes the cigar slowly to fragments.

---

3. Georges Mandel (1885–1944), the minister of the interior, was a relentless opponent of the armistice with Germany.
4. Faulkner probably has reference here to César Campinchi, the minister of the navy, who also opposed the armistice.

GROUP SHOT AT TABLE   FAVORING REYNAUD

REYNAUD *(looks about)* If you please . . .

The voices cease.

REYNAUD Yesterday I telephoned to President Roosevelt in America, asking for any help that can reach us quickly. I will telephone him again today—

De Gaulle rises.

REYNAUD *(to De Gaulle)* General?

CLOSE SHOT   REYNAUD   FAVORING DE GAULLE   OTHERS IN B.G.

DE GAULLE Let us help ourselves first, before we ask for help. One of our armies is still intact. The others are still serviceable forces—

PÉTAIN Bah!

DE GAULLE And there is England, as Mr. Churchill will assure you, as he has assured me. And a commander-in-chief who was a pupil of Marshal Foch—

CLOSE SHOT

Weygand, grim, cold. Pétain beside him, fretted, contemptuous, annoyed even.

PÉTAIN And what will we do with these forces?

CLOSE SHOT   TABLE   FAVORING DE GAULLE

DE GAULLE Establish our line to hold Brittany. Make all Brittany our base, with England to draw from, just across the Channel—

SHOT FAVORING REYNAUD

REYNAUD *(to Weygand)* Well, General?

WEYGAND The intact army which General De Gaulle mentioned is already isolated. The others are no longer armies. We have lost this war.

SHOT FAVORING DE GAULLE

DE GAULLE We have not lost the war. We have only lost a battle.

SHOT FAVORING PÉTAIN

> **PÉTAIN** Is the new General De Gaulle speaking as a general, or as the Under-Secretary of War?

> **REYNAUD** And if he is?

> **PÉTAIN** In the one case, he is only a civilian. In the other case, he is insubordinate.

SHOT FAVORING REYNAUD   DE GAULLE STILL STANDING

> **REYNAUD** *(to De Gaulle)* General?

De Gaulle sits down. Reynaud looks about.

> **REYNAUD** It remains only for me to request of Mr. Churchill that England release France from the obligation between the two countries that neither shall ask for a separate armistice.

CLOSE   CHURCHILL'S HAND   FAVORING REYNAUD AT HEAD OF TABLE

> **REYNAUD** Mr. Churchill?

> **CHURCHILL'S VOICE** England says "No," Mr. Reynaud.

> **TWO OR THREE VOICES** No! No!

> **CHURCHILL** More than "No." It says, "Never."

Reynaud looks about. The voices cease.

> **REYNAUD** The Government will remove to Bordeaux. Our retreat will continue. Meanwhile, I will make one more plea to the President of the United States.

WIPE TO:

REYNAUD'S OFFICE—DESK, TELEPHONE   CLOSE SHOT   REYNAUD AND DE GAULLE

De Gaulle leans over table, talking urgently, Reynaud listening.

> **REYNAUD** We can resist from Africa, where we have an intact establishment.

> **DE GAULLE** With the whole continent of Europe separat-

ing us from our only ally? No—Brittany. Brittany, with only the Channel between us. With all Brittany to fight for us, whom even the First Republic never quite conquered. Brittany! Brittany! Not Bordeaux! Countermand the move.

REYNAUD Yes . . . Yes . . . Brittany . . .

He reaches for telephone. De Gaulle sits slowly back a little as Reynaud lifts the phone, pauses, looks out of scene. De Gaulle looks out, too. Reynaud rises, De Gaulle rises.

CLOSE SHOT   DE GAULLE AND REYNAUD STANDING

—favoring door as Mme de Portes enters, approaches the desk, bows to De Gaulle, takes the telephone from Reynaud's hand and puts it back into cradle.

MME DE PORTES *(to Reynaud)* Surely you will not ratify this move without informing the General.

REYNAUD Of course not. *(to De Gaulle)* I must inform you that the Government will definitely move to Bordeaux to-night.

DISSOLVE TO:

MAP OF FRANCE

The black of the German advance spreads as of June 13–14th.

DISSOLVE TO:

CLOSE SHOT   PILOT'S FACE

—in aeroplane in flight. It is Jean, looking backward constantly from side to side, as he twists and turns.

FULL SHOT   AEROPLANE

—with French markings, in flight, chased by Germans. The whole sky seems full of Germans; they are almost in each other's way. The French plane turns and twists, shoots down one enemy as it draws further and further away. There are so many Germans that they cannot even bring their guns to bear on it for fear of shooting at one another.

DISSOLVE TO:

EXT. BATTLEFIELD

—crashed French aeroplanes, battered French tanks—all the refuse and flotsam of the retreating and routed French forces, German troops, tanks, etc., still advancing.

CLOSE GROUP SHOT

—a party of stained and bedraggled French captives under guard of two German soldiers. Again we get the sense of there being so many Germans, victors, that they are in one another's way. Georges is among the captives.

TRUCKING SHOT

—as the prisoners march on, Georges and another soldier, their faces watchful and wary.

> **GEORGES** *(from side of his mouth)* Now?

The other man glances sideways, not moving his head as they tramp on.

> **MAN** All right.

Georges and the man leap toward CAMERA.

GROUP SHOT

—as the men overpower the two guards, knock them down, run.

CLOSE SHOT

Guard on the ground fires his rifle, yells.

GROUP SHOT   A GERMAN OFFICER AND A FEW MEN

The officer shouts, the men begin to run across scene, stopping and firing, running again.

LONG SHOT

Georges and other prisoners running across a field toward woods; in f.g. two German soldiers firing at them, sound of machine gun in b.g. The prisoners reach the woods, enter it.

> DISSOLVE TO:

MAP OF FRANCE

CAMERA STOPS on BORDEAUX. Babble of voices over—

DISSOLVE TO:

INT. COUNCIL ROOM   FULL SHOT AT TABLE

—cabinet around it, Reynaud presiding, De Gaulle, Pétain, Weygand, others, etc. Babble of anxious voices from the members.

REYNAUD   Gentlemen! Gentlemen!

The noise ceases.

WEYGAND   We must ask for an armistice.

DE GAULLE   In whose name?

WEYGAND   In the name of the Army.   Of France.

DE GAULLE   Of neither. *(to Reynaud)* You are France yet. Give the order for Africa. We have time yet. We have an intact establishment already there. The fleet and transports are at Toulon—

The uproar begins again.

VOICES   No! No! An armistice!

VOICES   Yes! Yes! No armistice! We are not whipped.

The uproar grows louder in—

WIPE TO:

CLOSE SHOT   REYNAUD AND DE GAULLE

—alone. Reynaud is grave, troubled for the first time.

REYNAUD   All right. To London then. I will try to hold them until you have seen Mr. Churchill.

DISSOLVE TO:

DE GAULLE AT TELEPHONE

CHURCHILL'S VOICE IN PHONE   A Union between France and England—

DISSOLVE TO:

SHADOW OF CHURCHILL

—holding phone on wall.

> **CHURCHILL'S VOICE**   —for now and for all time. One people, with one victory to strive for and one glory to gain—

DISSOLVE TO:

CLOSE SHOT   REYNAUD'S HANDS HOLDING TELEGRAM

> MR. CHURCHILL OFFERS UNION BETWEEN FRANCE AND BRITAIN
> TO CONTINUE THE WAR
>
> DE GAULLE

Babble of voices begins in b.g.

> **VOICES**   Yes. Yes.
>
> **VOICES**   No. No. Against. Against.
>
> **LAST VOICE**   Against.

DISSOLVE TO:

INT. AEROPLANE IN FLIGHT   CLOSE SHOT   DE GAULLE AND SPEARS

—other British diplomats, listening to radio broadcast.

> **RADIO**   Mr. Reynaud has resigned as Premier of France. President Lebrun[5] has appointed Marshal Pétain to form a new cabinet, for the purpose of asking armistice terms of the German government. General De Gaulle has been declared a traitor to his country and will be arrested on sight.

DISSOLVE TO:

EXT. AN AIRFIELD   FULL SHOT   NIGHT

—the backs of a group of men, mostly soldiers, standing without order. In b.g. facing them a transport, engines idling, door open; standing before door is De Gaulle, and members of the British mission. An aide stands beside De Gaulle, holding a clumsy military-type gasoline torch which makes a murky flick-

---

5. Albert Lebrun (1871–1950) was the last president of the third French republic. A timid leader, he favored resistance to German occupation but acquiesced in the cabinet's decisions that led to capitulation.

ering light, the whole atmosphere to indicate that De Gaulle is departing almost secretly to save himself from arrest.

CLOSE SHOT   A FACE IN THE GROUP

—a soldier, unshaven, tired and strained-looking, anxious. CAMERA PANS to other faces resembling it: of soldiers who have escaped from the routed French forces. PAN to another face, then to Georges, staring anxiously at De Gaulle.

MED. CLOSE SHOT   DE GAULLE

—facing group as he recognizes Georges.

> **DE GAULLE**   I cannot take you all. I will take none of you now. There is work here in France for you to do. We have lost a battle, not the war. I am going to England, to prepare for all Frenchmen who still will fight, to come to me against the day when we can drive the enemy out again. Be of good courage, and remember: France has lost a battle, but France itself is not lost. Never!

He salutes, turns and enters plane, others follow. SOUND of engines grows loud into:

DISSOLVE TO:

INT. PLANE IN FLIGHT   CLOSE ON DE GAULLE AND SPEARS

De Gaulle and Spears are looking back and down through windows. They turn.

> **SPEARS**   Farewell to France, then.

> **DE GAULLE**   It is not farewell.

> **SPEARS**   You are right. I stand corrected, and I ask your pardon. Ah—

He takes out cigarette case, leans across aisle and offers it. De Gaulle looks down, takes cigarette.

> **DE GAULLE**   Thanks.

Spears takes out lighter, snaps it on, offers the lighter. De Gaulle leans toward it. Spears draws the lighter back slightly.

> **SPEARS**   To the day when you return.

DE GAULLE   *(raises cigarette for an instant, as if he and Spears were drinking a toast)* To the day.

                                                          DISSOLVE TO:

INT. AN AIR SQUADRON OPERATIONS OFFICE

A blackboard with scrawled operations orders, names, etc. The request for armistice has been made, the French forces have ceased fighting. This is the present base to which this navy air squadron has retreated on the day the armistice was asked.

[I will consult Mr. Berger[6] about this scene for authenticity.] It is Jean's navy air squadron, based temporarily on land to help halt the Germans. The armistice has been signed, three of the members refuse to accept the armistice, and depart. If possible, the squadron commander allows them to depart in peace, first stripping them of rank, to which one of them also adds his medal for valor, declining to wear it until France, who gave it to him, has expiated her own cowardice and treason, etc.

                                                          FADE OUT.

FADE IN

CLOSE SHOT   A GROUP OF PEOPLE ABOUT A RADIO

   RADIO   I, General De Gaulle, speaking from London, invite the French officers and soldiers, with their arms or
   without their arms, I invite the engineers and the workers
   skilled in the manufacture of armaments—

INT. CAFE   FULL SHOT

—favoring entrance from street. The patron is cleaning glasses behind the bar; a few villagers sit quietly about.

   RADIO   In the face of the confusion of French arms, in the
   face of the disintegration of a government—

The door opens quickly; a villager, a man enters. The radio

---

6. Henri Diamant-Berger, an official of the Free French organization, served as a consultant for "The De Gaulle Story." His critique of Faulkner's screenplay is printed in this volume.

voice cuts off abruptly; another voice begins, very loud as two German soldiers enter and approach the bar.

RADIO Faced with the desperate situation of the lost war and the general collapse of the French people—

The two Germans look at the men, stop at the bar. One of them points out a bottle. The patron puts glasses on the bar and fills them.

RADIO —I, therefore, Pétain, Marshal of France, took power into my own hands to obtain an honorable armistice from the enemy.

ANOTHER ANGLE

Germans drink.

RADIO There were only two alternatives in the face of the conditions imposed by the enemy: accept them and remain in Bordeaux, or refuse them and take refuge in Africa, far from our land and our people who could not depart for safety, as we, the government, could—

The Germans set the glasses down, look about again at the quiet men, turn and tramp to the door and go out. The man who entered first turns and follows them, shuts the door.

RADIO I recognize that the fate of the French people will be harsh and hard. But I, your leader, Pétain, Marshal of France—

The radio voice cuts sharply off. The second voice, De Gaulle's, begins. The patron takes the two glasses the Germans used, throws them onto the floor, where they break. The other men do not move.

RADIO I, General De Gaulle, French soldier and chief, assume the right to call upon all of you. Soldiers of France, wherever you may be, arise.

DISSOLVE TO:

CLOSE SHOT   WOODS

Georges stooping over the body of a dead German soldier. He

is unshaven, wears portions of his uniform, with other mismatched and dirty and misfit civilian garments. He is harried looking, strained. Georges drags the body out of the scene.

CLOSE SHOT

Georges hides the body in a clump of bushes, exits hurriedly and cautiously.

DISSOLVE TO:

INT. STABLE   CLOSE SHOT   GEORGES AND COUPE-TÊTE

Coupe-tête has been pitching hay. He pauses with hayfork.

COUPE-TÊTE So you killed him. If you wish to hang, why just one?

GEORGES All right, all right. Who's here?

COUPE-TÊTE One too many now.

GEORGES Don't worry about that, either. I just want to get something to eat and to get rid of this—*(indicates uniform)* Then I'll be gone, too—to England where there is still one Frenchman who will fight.

COUPE-TÊTE Good. Do that. But not until I get back. You stay right here now, until I return.

CLOSE SHOT   COUPE-TÊTE IN THE WOODS

—as he tumbles the dead German into a shallow grave and begins to cover it. He smooths the earth over the grave and removes digging traces with leaves, brush, etc.

INT. STABLE   CLOSE SHOT   COUPE-TÊTE

—as he stands looking about the stable, finds Georges is gone, turns and exits.

INT. HALL   CLOSE SHOT   CATHERINE AND GEORGES

—in one another's arms, kissing. Coupe-tête pauses in the door, looking at them with grim displeasure. Georges raises his head, sees Coupe-tête. He and Catherine break apart.

CLOSE SHOT   CATHERINE, GEORGES AND COUPE-TÊTE

COUPE-TÊTE So this is what you call concealment.

CATHERINE He must wait on the others.

COUPE-TÊTE What others?

CATHERINE Armand Micoux—

COUPE-TÊTE Paroled. To the priest. On good behavior.

CATHERINE Guillaume Hoel.

COUPE-TÊTE Paroled. To the priest. On good behavior.

CLOSE ALL   FAVORING THE OPPOSITE DOOR

—as it opens and Marthe enters and stops, still holding the door. Her face is grim, like Coupe-tête's, but it is troubled and anxious where Coupe-tête conceals his anxiety, which is greater.

> **MARTHE** *(to Georges)* His Reverence is here. And Madame would probably like a little moment with you, too, if you are done killing Germans in her back yard.

> **COUPE-TÊTE** Peace, woman.

> **MARTHE** Let him think of peace when next he comes stealing into his own home like a murderer.

> **COUPE-TÊTE** Let them think of peace who force a man to become a murderer to enter his own house.

INT. KITCHEN   MED. SHOT

—priest, others in b.g., as Georges bends one knee quickly before him, then stands again.

> **GEORGES** I would do it again. I have not surrendered.

> **COUPE-TÊTE** He in the woods received no sacrament, either. Perhaps we both need absolution.

> **PRIEST** Seek it where all Frenchmen must, and find it where all Frenchmen will: in the freeing of France.

> **MME MORNET** *(to Georges)* Come. Eat.

MED. CLOSE   AT TABLE

—Georges sitting. Mme Mornet standing beside him, Marthe setting a bowl before him, others in b.g.

> **GEORGES** It's hot. I haven't seen hot food in—

COUPE-TÊTE Eat it, then, as your mother told you. You will need it. You will need enough for you and Micoux and Hoel, all three, after that Boche sergeant calls the roll tonight and finds himself one swine short.

Georges eats ravenously.

DISSOLVE TO:

A WALL AT A CORNER   NIGHT

Four men crouching against the wall. Sound of tramping soldiers increases. A patrol passes, the tramp of feet dies away. The four men rise and steal on.

A HILL   CLOSE   COUPE-TÊTE, GEORGES, MICOUX AND HOEL
NIGHT

GEORGES *(to Coupe-tête)* You'd better go back now.

COUPE-TÊTE I just hope you don't go faster any slower.

GEORGES Don't worry about that. And we'll come back, too. The General and all of us. Don't you worry about that, either.

COUPE-TÊTE Get there first. Then talk about coming back. Go on. I'll take care of the land and of your mother, and of your wife, too, if you ever stay in a home long enough again to get one. Go on!

The three go on, vanish into the darkness. Coupe-tête turns.

INT. KITCHEN   GROUP   PRIEST, MME MORNET, CATHERINE,
MARTHE

—as Coupe-tête enters.

MME MORNET Well?

COUPE-TÊTE Three missing from the village tomorrow morning, two of whom are known, for whom His Reverence has given parole. And that Boche lying in the woods for the first stray dog to dig up.

PRIEST There is God.

COUPE-TÊTE Where?

CATHERINE If there is a Frenchman left who is willing to fight for France, we who can't fight can at least suffer to help him.

COUPE-TÊTE A Frenchman, bah! A Frenchman thinks first of his stove, then of his bed, and then of beautiful France. But if there can still be found one who still thinks of France and thinks well enough of it to fight for it, I suppose we of Brittany can still help him.

MARTHE Peace, fool! Are you deaf even to your own clacking?

FADE OUT.

FADE IN

EXT. STREET   NIGHT   CLOSE SHOT   MEN'S FACES

The street is filled with shadowy men standing in the rain. They are Frenchmen who have escaped from France and reached England. They are all staring past Camera as though waiting. They are grave, a little anxious, patient.

REVERSE ANGLE   HEADS SILHOUETTED   FAVORING AN OPEN DOOR

—lighted from inside; against the door De Gaulle and an aide stand.

AIDE The General speaks no English. He asks, what do you wish?

A VOICE We are not English! We are Frenchmen!

DE GAULLE Frenchmen?

He steps forward.

FULL SHOT   DE GAULLE AND AIDE

—on stoop, the men in the street below, looking up at him.

DE GAULLE Welcome to England then.

A VOICE Welcome to France again!

DE GAULLE Yes. Welcome again to France.

DISSOLVE TO:

INT. HUGE WAREHOUSE   FULL SHOT

—barren, filled with army cots, semi-military. Long row of cots, a Frenchman standing rigidly at attention before each cot like soldiers on parade. De Gaulle and aide in f.g. facing first man.

MAN Ledoux.

DE GAULLE *(shakes hands)* Ledoux. Welcome.

He moves on to next man; first man stares rigidly ahead.

NEXT MAN Pelletier.

DE GAULLE *(shakes hands)* Pelletier. Welcome.

He moves on to next man.

CLOSE   DE GAULLE   (FAVORING GEORGES AT ATTENTION)

DE GAULLE Mornet. I saw you last that night at Bordeaux. Did the others escape?

GEORGES A few, General.

DE GAULLE I hope they will come to me.

GEORGES They will, General. All France is coming to you.

De Gaulle moves on.

NEXT MAN Masson.

DE GAULLE *(shakes hands)* Masson. Welcome.

DISSOLVE TO:

INT. B.B.C. BROADCASTING ROOM   CLOSE SHOT   DE GAULLE AT MIKE

—operators, aides, Georges—now something between a sergeant and De Gaulle's orderly—beside him with notes, etc.

DE GAULLE Marshal Pétain, it is a French soldier who speaks to you. I heard your voice, which I know well from the old times when I was one of your subordinate officers . . . You declared that there were only two alternatives imposed by the enemy: accept his terms and remain in France, or refuse them and take refuge in the empire to continue the war. You chose to stay in France. You, who were head of our military organization after 1918, who were Generalissimo up to 1932. We didn't need you, Marshal, to obtain and accept conditions of slavery. We didn't need the conqueror of Verdun to do this . . .

You call upon France—a France surrendered, pillaged, enslaved—to go back to work; to build anew and rise from her ruins. But by what means, in the name of what, do you expect her to rise again? France will rise again. Throughout the Empire, throughout the world, French forces are forming and organizing. The day will come when our arms will join those of our allies. Then indeed we shall remake France.

He stops speaking, turns away from microphone. The operators cut switches, etc., go through routine of ending broadcast efficiently. Georges gathers up papers, etc.

CLOSE SHOT

An official holds the door open for De Gaulle to go out, Georges following.

DE GAULLE *(pauses)* Yes?

OFFICIAL Lord Halifax asks to see you, sir. He is waiting in your office.

DE GAULLE Thank you.

He exits, Georges follows.

INT. OFFICE   CLOSE SHOT   DE GAULLE AND HALIFAX

—seated at desk, aides, etc., in b.g.

HALIFAX These men came to England for refuge after Narvik and after Dunkirk—

DE GAULLE They were Frenchmen.

HALIFAX Who had no country to return to. Yet you will permit these agents of Vichy to see them and demand that they return and assume allegiance to that government which has declared you a traitor and betrayed your native land.

DE GAULLE Yes. Because those who accept Free France must do it of their own will and desire. I am not a politician and I don't want to be. I don't want to be even the commander of the French armed forces. I want to be the chief of all Frenchmen who want to be free. For how can you command a man by force to risk his life in the name of freedom? In that case, that for which he suffers has already made him a slave. You can only lead him. And only he who loves freedom so well that he is willing to die for it at need.

HALIFAX *(pauses)* I see. *(pauses again, rises)*

CLOSE   DE GAULLE

—standing, facing Halifax, standing.

HALIFAX I am not a military man, and this will be clumsily done. But perhaps you can accept the will. *(salutes De Gaulle, turns)* Shall we have it over with, then?

DISSOLVE TO:

EXT.   MED. CLOSE   DE GAULLE, AIDES, THREE VICHY AGENTS

The agents are civilians, defiant, watchful, ill-at-ease.

DE GAULLE *(to Vichy men)* Some of them are absent. They are at sea in British destroyers and trawlers, or at the airfields. But you can give your message to the ones who are here.

ANOTHER ANGLE   CLOSE ON DE GAULLE

—favoring a large courtyard outside a barracks. A small crowd of men faces him. They are Frenchmen, some in army and navy uniforms, some in misfit civvies, some in a mixture of both, some with crutches, sticks, bandages and slings, etc. They watch him quiet, curious, puzzled.

DE GAULLE These gentlemen are from Vichy. They have something to say to you. You are free men. Answer them as you desire.

MED. CLOSE   GROUP

—as De Gaulle turns and walks out. The others look after him, the three Vichy men nervously. The Vichy spokesman steps forward, speaks. Georges and others stare rigidly ahead.

SPOKESMAN I come to you from the French government, that government to which your oath of allegiance and faithful service was transferred at the instant when it came into legal being in France's hour of darkness—

DISSOLVE TO:

INT. OFFICE CLOSE SHOT

—De Gaulle seated at desk, Georges standing facing him.

DE GAULLE Well?

GEORGES One man. Will you talk to him?

DE GAULLE He's a sailor.

CLOSE SHOT FAVORING GEORGES

—as he remembers how his own brother went for Vichy.

GEORGES Yes.

DE GAULLE Tell me. Why have so few sailors left France for us?

CLOSE SHOT BOTH

GEORGES *(harshly)* They are fascists. Because their officers order them to be.

DE GAULLE Because their officers order them. Stop at that. Yes, a soldier's wife and mother is his land, his government; a sailor's is his ship, no matter what flag it flies. Let him come in.

Georges exits.

ANOTHER ANGLE DE GAULLE AT DESK

—the sailor facing him. He is about twenty-five. His face is watchful, defiant.

DE GAULLE You wish to return to France.

SAILOR I have a wife. We have been married only a year. I have a child I haven't even seen. I . . . . *(pauses, stares at De Gaulle, watchful, defiant)*

DE GAULLE   You were at Narvik. You did well there, I have been told.

SAILOR   I did what all did. What I would do again if—*(he stops abruptly, watches De Gaulle)*

DE GAULLE   *(finishes sentence for him)* If France could be so served again. *(the sailor stares at him, watchful, defiant)* Go then. You are free.

The sailor stares at him a moment, turns and exits. De Gaulle looks after him, grave and stern.

DISSOLVE TO:

INT. OFFICE   CLOSE   DE GAULLE

—seated, Georges placing pins in map on wall. PAN toward map, Europe, Asia, Africa.

DE GAULLE'S VOICE   Syria is ours.

PAN to SYRIA on map.

DISSOLVE TO:

MONTAGE

Double exposure, soldiers charging in desert.

DISSOLVE TO:

DOUBLE EXPOSURE ON MAP

—a desert fort, wall, the flag bearing cross of Lorraine flying above it.

MED. CLOSE   DE GAULLE AND AIDE

—seated, Georges at map.

DE GAULLE   And General Catroux in the Pacific. Then Africa—

A crash off scene. They pause, look out of scene.

CLOSE   FRENCH MAJOR

He has sprung to attention, his chair overturned behind him, facing door at salute. The door is open. General Catroux has entered, looks about, sees major. Catroux is travel-stained, fiercely impatient.

CATROUX Break off.

He advances.

CLOSE BOTH

CATROUX Where's De Gaulle? I've come to report.

MAJOR *(stupidly)* To report, sir?

CATROUX For duty, damn it! From damn near halfway round the world. Where is he?

MAJOR You, sir? An army-group commander, reporting for duty to a brigadier general?

CATROUX Eh? I'll fix that. Your knife.

Major fumbles at table. Catroux leans forward, takes up paper knife, rips three of his five stars from sleeve, flings the knife down.

CATROUX Well, man? Where is he?

The major comes to life, moves. He holds door open, salutes as Catroux exits.

MED. CLOSE INT. OFFICE

De Gaulle and aide risen, Georges turned from map as Catroux enters, pauses, looks quickly about.

CATROUX De Gaulle? *(sees De Gaulle)* Ah. *(he salutes)* Catroux reporting for duty.

DE GAULLE *(moves quickly forward)* Catroux is welcome.

DISSOLVE TO:

EXT. ALDERSHOT PARADE GROUND MED. FULL SHOT REVIEWING STAND

—De Gaulle, aides, British staff, King and officers; flags, French band playing (some well-known military tune for marching). Reviewers at salute.

REVERSE ANGLE   FROM STAND

—of Free France in first official parade. All the old men wear uniforms now. They march according to their old corps, regiments, and battalions. We will show Tirailleurs, Air Force, Chasseurs, etc., with their old battle flags, marching proudly now, stiffly eyes right as they pass the reviewing stand, etc. The last unit passes. PAN with it. It is a mixture of army and navy uniforms, misfit refugee civvies, and sometimes both together. The men have been wounded, on crutches, sticks, with slings and bandages. They look spent, gaunt, weak, yet happy, exalted, marching as stiff and smart as any, or trying to, helping one another. Georges is in command, gives the eyes right as they pass, then eyes front again as they pass on. Music dies away.

CLOSE   DE GAULLE

—favoring line of mismatched wounded men at attention. De Gaulle speaking to first man. Georges follows De Gaulle.

FIRST MAN   Fayol, General.

DE GAULLE   Fayol. Welcome.

TRUCK with De Gaulle to next man. Georges follows.

MAN   Dal, General.

DE GAULLE   Dal. Welcome.

TRUCK with De Gaulle to next man. Georges follows.

DE GAULLE   I saw you that morning at Chalandry. You behaved well. It goes?

MAN   It goes, General.

DE GAULLE   Good. *(he is about to pass on, looks at next man, stops; the man is on a crutch, is gaunt and weak)* Chalandry also. I thought you were dead. What brought you back?

WOUNDED MAN   *(weakly)* France, General.

FIRST MAN   Someone whispered "De Gaulle" in his ear.

GEORGES   Silence in ranks, there!

DE GAULLE *(without turning, to Georges)* That will do, Sergeant. *(to first man)* Does that raise the dead in France?

FIRST MAN It does better than that. It raises the living in France.

DE GAULLE Let's hope it will do so.

He moves on, pauses, stops dead, staring at him.

CLOSE   FAVORING THE MAN

It is the sailor who decided to go back to France with the Vichy agents. He looks haggard, desperate, grim. He is unshaven, muddy, a long unhealed recent wound across his forehead. He stares at De Gaulle, smoldering and fierce.

DE GAULLE You have come back.

SAILOR I—I—

DE GAULLE To France.

The sailor stares fiercely at De Gaulle, represses some fierce reaction.

SAILOR To France.

De Gaulle passes on.

DISSOLVE TO:

INT. DE GAULLE'S HOME   DEN OR SMALL SITTING ROOM   EVENING

De Gaulle reading, Mme De Gaulle sewing.

MED. CLOSE   FAVORING DOOR

—as it opens and Georges enters. De Gaulle looks up.

GEORGES He's here, sir.

DE GAULLE Yes. All right.

He lays book (papers probably) down and rises. Mme De Gaulle looks up.

DE GAULLE *(to Madame)* I'll go on to the studio from here. I speak at midnight.

MME DE GAULLE   Nazis don't sleep at midnight, either.

DE GAULLE   Perhaps not. But neither do the people Nazis rule.

He turns to exit, Georges holding the door.

INT. OFFICE-DEN   CLOSE   DE GAULLE AND THE SAILOR

SAILOR   Yes. I found them. I found the grave. There are three now: one for her shame and my dishonor, one for the beast that did it, and one for another beast to keep the first one company into hell. He gave me this before he died. *(touches wound on his head)* Fool, to think a bullet could stop grief and rage. So I am back.

DE GAULLE   Why?

SAILOR   Just another young woman of the people, wife to a common sailor and mother of his son—nobody. You'd think we would have been too small for them to trouble. Too small to have made them fear.

DE GAULLE   Why?

SAILOR   *(pauses)* Why? For vengeance. To kill them.

DE GAULLE   That's not enough. It's good but not enough.

CLOSE   FAVORING THE SAILOR

—as he stares at De Gaulle.

DE GAULLE   Not just for vengeance: for liberty and freedom.

He puts his hands on the sailor's shoulders. The sailor stares at De Gaulle. His face breaks. He strives against it, staring at De Gaulle. It goes completely. The sailor stares at De Gaulle, tears running down his cheeks.

DE GAULLE   For liberty and freedom. For peace.

SAILOR   For peace. Where all the little people—all the little people—

DISSOLVE TO:

INT. BARRACKS   MED. CLOSE

Five or six cots, the sailor in one, his back to the others, his eyes closed. Georges, the wounded man, two others going to bed. Window open in b.g., moon shining, air raid in distance. A man is helping the wounded man off with his clothes.

WOUNDED MAN   He remembered me.

GEORGES   He remembers all of us. He says all men who love freedom have only one face to remember.

FIRST MAN   Besides, there are not enough of us yet to start forgetting.

WOUNDED MAN   But there will be soon.

FIRST MAN   Yes. If he just keeps on calling the dead back to life like he did you.

GEORGES   And he will remember their faces, too.

INT. B.B.C. STUDIO   CLOSE SHOT   DE GAULLE AT MICROPHONE

DE GAULLE   All of you whose sons and fathers and husbands and brothers have died, grieve for them but do not despair. All of you whose sons and fathers and brothers and husbands have merely vanished from the places that once knew them—

DISSOLVE TO:

FIVE OR SIX FRENCH PEOPLE

—crouching, tense, listening, watchful. De Gaulle's voice cuts short off. Tramp of army feet increases, the shadow of a patrol, rifles slanted, legs tramping in unison, passes across, disappears, the tramp of feet dies away. The voice comes on again, the people quiet, listening.

VOICE   —do not even grieve. Because they have come to me. They come to me here daily, and our battalions and regiments live again. They are with me today, and they tell you in my voice to believe and hope, for even you who for a little while yet the enemies of France continue to hold, you also are not alone and are not forgotten.

FADE OUT.

FADE IN

Map of Europe and North Africa. PAN to ORAN on map. DOUBLE EXPOSURE on map: A French flag flying from masthead of a battleship. SOUND of gunfire, shells, burst about the flag. The flag is hit, leans over. The gunfire continues, shells continue to burst about the flag. It is hit again, falls further. Gunfire and shellbursts continue. The gunfire begins to fade in—

DISSOLVE TO:

EXT. VILLAGE SQUARE BEFORE THE CAFE

Opposite is the mayor's office and city hall, a German flag over the door. In the square is the bronze poilu commemorating the village men who died in 1914–1918.

CLOSE ON A GROUP OF VILLAGERS, MEN

—before the cafe as a German military car, Nazi pennon, etc., a German soldier driving it and Jean in back seat, rushes past. The men look after it, astonished.

> **VOICE** It's Jean Mornet.
>
> **ANOTHER** What?
>
> **THIRD** Yes. Jean Mornet. Jean Mornet.

DISSOLVE TO:

FULL SHOT   THE MORNET HOME

The car is halted in front of it.

INT. KITCHEN   JEAN, COUPE-TÊTE, MARTHE

Jean has been wounded, walks with a stick and shows other traces of recent illness.

> **COUPE-TÊTE:** Oran? You were at Oran? Then what are you doing here? In that German car?
>
> **JEAN** It's my car. Where do you expect me to be?
>
> **COUPE-TÊTE** Where your brother is. Where I would have expected any Frenchman to be, who was present at Oran.
>
> **JEAN** What do you think happened at Oran?

COUPE-TÊTE   Evidently I don't know. The official radio told us, but the official radio also said that England would fall within a month, and that was a lie, too. All we know is, someone fought at Oran for France. And if anyone fought anywhere for France, he fought Germans. So if a Mornet was at Oran, he wouldn't be coming here except to hide while he got his breath to flee again, as your brother did.

MARTHE   Hush! Here comes Madame.

CLOSE GROUP   MME MORNET, JEAN SEATED, MARTHE AND COUPE-TÊTE STANDING

JEAN   They caught us without warning, bottled in the harbor without steam up to fight and no sea-room to fight in, if we had had the steam. But no matter. Maybe they had to, or believed they had to. But we are not England, with an intact government and a home army and an island to protect us. We are France, already partly occupied, our capital lost and already under terms to the enemy because the people and the army they composed and the government they supported collapsed—

COUPE-TÊTE   Not the people. Not the army. The generals and the politicians.

MME MORNET   Coupe-tête.

JEAN   It's done now. Why doesn't matter. What does matter is that we hold together what is still strong in France, to be a bargaining factor when the day comes for a readjustment in Europe, so that we can—

COUPE-TÊTE   And to do that, you have become a German policeman.

MME MORNET   Coupe-tête!

JEAN   Let him finish. Then let him look around him and see what is happening to the people who believe and act as he sounds like he believes and seems to advocate. Let him look at Brittany today.

COUPE-TÊTE   Not all of them. Not the young, and the strong, and the brave ones.

MARTHE Silence! Hush!

COUPE-TÊTE Brittany, bah! Napoleon conquered Brittany once. And where is Napoleon? In a little stone box in Paris, with a foreign flag flying over him. As this one will be, too, in his day. This Hitler—

MARTHE Hush! Hush!

COUPE-TÊTE This nothing: a little pinch of rotten dirt before the face of God.

MARTHE Will you hush?

MME MORNET *(to Coupe-tête, rising)* Peace. *(Jean rises)* I don't understand it, nor do you. Be silent.

COUPE-TÊTE *(shrugs)* Madame.

Mme Mornet turns to Jean, anxious still. He puts his arm around her.

JEAN It's simple. We risked one battle, and lost it. We must keep what is left of France by other means. I am to be an administrator, superintendent—of what, I don't know myself, yet. I don't like it, either. *(looks at Coupe-tête)* Let them who shot my old one out from under me find me a better one.

COUPE-TÊTE They helped your brother to one.

MME MORNET Peace, Coupe-tête.

COUPE-TÊTE *(shrugs)* Madame.

DISSOLVE TO:

EXT. VILLAGE STREET

The car rushes through it; men and women turn to look after it.

CLOSE SHOT

The car stopped before the mayor's house, faces peering out from beneath lifted curtains in the adjacent windows as Jean gets out of the car, pauses, sees the faces for a second before the curtains drop and the faces are jerked away. Jean goes on toward the door, limping on his stick.

CLOSE SHOT   JEAN AT DOOR

It opens. The mayor's woman servant looks out, fearful, shrinking. She is afraid of Jean, the German car, etc. She disapproves of Jean in his present capacity. He is now an enemy. Jean enters.

INT. LIVING ROOM   CLOSE SHOT   JEAN

—standing, favoring the door as it opens and the mayor enters. He is uncertain. In his official position, he is forced by the German commander to collaborate. He must accept daily the Germans' contempt of him as a conquered Frenchman. Because of his position as official head of the village, he feels his duty is to protect his people and their property. Also, he wants to protect his own property. But he is aware of the unrest among his people, of their hatred toward the invaders, so he is not sure which side to definitely commit himself to. He is the pompous martinet he once was only on the surface. He is definitely worried, troubled.

He pauses in the door.

MAYOR   Lieutenant.

He crosses quickly, shakes Jean's hand.

MAYOR   Someone official, at last. So far they have given us nothing, nothing: no word, no contact—only the German garrison and the official radio. As if I could know what to do, what they wished. Young men escaping each night to England, the Germans taking hostages from among us in reprisal—

JEAN   I am not from Vichy. I am on duty from the navy.

MAYOR   Then you bring me no instructions at all?

JEAN   No. I stopped for a moment to speak to Catherine, with your permission.

MAYOR   Oh. Yes. I see.

The mayor turns, crosses to door, goes out, closes the door. Jean watches the door. It opens. The servant comes in just far enough to see Jean.

 SERVANT Miss Catherine is not at home.

The servant closes the door. Jean turns, walks toward Camera.

EXT. STREET CLOSE ON CAR

—as Jean approaches, gets into it. The car moves, faces appear again beneath the lifted shades.

EXT. A ROAD

A small, dirty boy at roadside, watches the car as it approaches; SOUND of car increases, the boy stoops into weeds as the car passes. The boy rises, flings something at it, ducks down again. The car goes on. PAN to the object the boy threw: a dead cat lying in the road.

FADE OUT.

FADE IN

CLOSE SHOT A DOOR

—lettered in German "Food Administrator" or whatever will indicate the bureau or office where Jean works at his job of dispatching the food requisitioned by the Germans from Vichy. It is in Paris.

DISSOLVE TO:

INT. OFFICE CLOSE SHOT

Jean seated at desk with papers, etc. A clerk enters with other papers. [Will ask M. Berger if this is a soldier or a civilian, possibly a transplanted German clerk or perhaps a woman, French or German.] The clerk lays the papers before Jean, waits. Jean examines the paper.

 JEAN You have checked them?

 CLERK Three boxes, sir.

 JEAN To Madame G. Mornet, _____, Department of _____.

CLERK To Madame G. Mornet, _____, Department of
_____.

JEAN Tonight. With priority.

CLERK Tonight. With priority.

JEAN Thank you.

The clerk exits. Jean looks out of scene until the sound of a door being closed comes. Then he takes up the paper, tears it, burns the pieces carefully over an ashtray, mashes the ash to dust, is emptying the ashes into a wastebasket, pauses, looks up.

CLOSE JEAN AT DESK

—favoring a door, open, a German orderly in the door. The orderly enters, clicks heels stiffly, though even in this he contrives to show contempt or at least disregard for Jean, the Frenchman, and as far as the German is concerned, a traitor or at least a weakling.

ORDERLY The colonel's compliments. At once.

The orderly exits without waiting for an answer. Without haste, Jean finishes emptying the ash into the wastebasket, puts the tray back on the desk, rises.

CLOSE SHOT

Jean approaches a corridor door. The door opens before he can touch it. Through the door can be seen a slightly more luxurious office, French in style and furnishings—an atmosphere rich and somehow faintly decadent. A hat-rack or -tree just inside door, a German military overcoat and sword and a helmet in grim paradox to the room. A broad desk at the far end, the German colonel seated behind it. He is Prussian, typical almost, though his face is shrewder, a little more scholarly. But he is hard. He is a soldier first, officer caste, etc. Jean enters. The orderly shuts the door behind him.

CLOSE SHOT AT DESK

Jean approaches it. The colonel is writing. He does not look up.

COLONEL Sit down.

Jean sits in a chair at end of desk. The colonel pushes a box toward him with one hand, without looking up.

COLONEL   Cigarette. Excuse me a moment.

JEAN   Thanks.

He doesn't take the cigarette. He sits quietly. The colonel signs the paper, blots it, pushes it aside, looks up, takes a cigarette from the box, looks at Jean, takes up the box and offers it again. Jean doesn't take one.

JEAN   Thanks.

The colonel puts the box down, takes up a lighter and lights his cigarette, puts the lighter down.

COLONEL   You have been sending food home to your mother. Of course you have known all the time that we have known that all the time.

JEAN   You could have stopped it.

COLONEL   I could have stopped it. I was instructed not to.

ANOTHER ANGLE

COLONEL   We expected you to send food home. I was surprised to find you content with so little.

JEAN   Then what do you want me to do about it?

COLONEL   Nothing. Continue to send it, which of course you will do. Send enough of it. If you did not have enough love of family to grieve when they suffer, and the courage to do something to rectify it, do you think you would be of any value to us? When we need rascals and poltroons capable of any act, who can be bought for almost any price, we do not need to search for them among the peoples we conquer: we breed our own.

JEAN   Just what do you want me to do?

COLONEL   There is an Underground in France. That's natural. It happens each time. We anticipate it by now. If it did not occur, we would begin to doubt human nature, and therefore ourselves. To combat it would require another army, a larger army even than was required to capture the country. So we use the people themselves, the ones among them who are intelligent enough—

CLOSE   JEAN STANDING

—the colonel still sitting.

JEAN   You use your conquered "friends."

COLONEL   Success has no friends. It has sycophants.

JEAN   I am not a spy. I am a Navy officer, under orders from my superior—

COLONEL   Until your superior orders otherwise.

Jean stares at the colonel. The colonel watches Jean. Then the colonel bends down, pulls out drawer, produces brandy bottle, sets it beside glasses on tray on the desk.

COLONEL   Drink?

JEAN   No, thanks. Was that all you wanted now?

COLONEL   Yes. Think it over.

JEAN   I have. I am a traitor perhaps, but no spy.

COLONEL   I am afraid you will discover you have gone too far to have much choice—which will be a misfortune for you, and a grief to them who love you. Someday you are going to have to obey your conscience. Then in the next moment you are going to lose your life trying to rectify the act.

DISSOLVE TO:

EXT. STREET   CLOSE SHOT

—a burst paper sack, scattered potatoes on the cobbled pavement, a girl's hands gathering them. Feet of passers as they step around the potatoes. One pair of feet stop.

CLOSE   JEAN STANDING

—Emilie kneeling, gathering up the potatoes. She is about twenty, looks poor, hungry, thin, that is. Jean stoops, begins to help gather up the potatoes. She becomes aware of him, starts as though she believed he was about to steal some of them, sees him, recognizes him.

EMILIE   Thank you, Mr. Mornet.

Jean pauses, surprised, looks at her. She watches him.

JEAN   How did you—*(begins to recognize her)*

EMILIE   Yes. On the stairs. We live on the floor beneath you. You are the lonely man.

JEAN   We?

EMILIE   My father and I.

JEAN   Oh. Then we can walk home together, if you are going that way?

EMILIE   Yes.

They finish gathering up the potatoes. The burst sack will not hold them.

JEAN   Wait.

He begins to take off his overcoat.

EMILIE   No, no. They're dirty. They'll soil it. My shawl—

JEAN   *(removes overcoat)* I doubt if any food can soil a Frenchman's clothes any more.

EMILIE   That depends on what that Frenchman has paid for it.

Jean pauses, stops, holding the coat, looking at her.

ANOTHER ANGLE

Emilie folds the potatoes rapidly into her shawl, Jean still watching her, holding his coat.

EMILIE   *(rises)* There. Come along.

JEAN   Won't you let me carry it?

EMILIE   It's not heavy.

CLOSE   BOTH

—walking along street past cafe. (Café de la Paix, or other, tables filled with German officers, etc.) French people passing, depressed, sullen. Emilie's face is calm, Jean's grave, thoughtful.

JEAN So you really do know who I am.

EMILIE Yes.

CLOSE JEAN AND EMILIE

—at a door, entrance to tenement, apartment, etc. Jean opens the door for Emilie to enter.

JEAN Then there are other French people in Paris who know it, too.

EMILIE Yes.

She enters. Jean follows.

INT. STAIRCASE CLOSE SHOT JEAN AND EMILIE

—dim and dingy. Jean and Emilie at landing, door behind them.

EMILIE Thank you.

JEAN For what little I did.

He raises his hat, turns, mounts the stairs. Emilie looks after him.

EMILIE Mr. Mornet.

Jean stops, turns, looks back.

EMILIE Come and eat them with us.

CLOSE JEAN AND EMILIE

—on landing again.

JEAN Why did you say I am lonely?

EMILIE I told you we live just under you. I can hear your feet at night. Too late at night.

JEAN Is that loneliness?

EMILIE No. It's more.

JEAN More?

EMILIE It's worse.

She turns toward the door. Jean takes hold of knob to open it. She turns, stops him for a moment.

EMILIE (*rapidly*) I won't tell Father who you are. You will excuse him—us.

Jean bows, opens door. Emilie enters. He follows.

INT. ROOM CLOSE DORIOT

—asleep in an armchair before small weak meager fire in the grate. The room is sparsely and poorly furnished, such as refugees without money would live in, rented. Doriot is old, sixty, looks weak, nervous, prematurely old, ill almost. Emilie approaches, Jean following, and stops at chair, looking down at Doriot.

EMILIE Father.

Doriot starts, wakes, looks up, sees Emilie, then Jean.

EMILIE This is Mr. Mornet, Father. He is from Brittany.

DORIOT A Breton? He has had to leave his home, too?

JEAN Yes.

DORIOT He is welcome, then.

CLOSE SUPPER TABLE

It is a makeshift table, set with mismatched china, etc. It bears the single dish of potatoes and a loaf of poor bread, which would have been the Doriots' meal, also two or three things which Jean has evidently brought from his room—obvious luxuries which he had from the Germans. There is a bottle of wine. The only wine glass is at Jean's place. Doriot has a chipped mug. Emilie is not drinking any of the wine. Doriot is pouring the last of the wine into his and Jean's glasses. He is quite shaky. He sets the bottle down and raises his mug.

DORIOT Let us drink to the guest, whose kindness supplied us with these luxuries, as well as the wine we toast him in. Though the very possession of such delicacies as these would nowadays mark any man but a Breton—or a Belgian. *(he pauses, his face darkens for a moment, recovers)* But if he were not a true man, Frenchman or not, he would not be here. *(raises mug)* To the Day. When Breton and Belgian and all the dispossessed can return. Confusion to them who robbed our nations of honor and our peoples of peace.

EMILIE   *(quickly yet firmly)* Father!

DORIOT   *(recovers)* Yes, my dear. *(raises mug again)* We will drink to our guest, then. That will be better. *(bows to Jean)* With gratitude.

Jean bows. Doriot drinks. Emilie rises, takes up a dish.

EMILIE   *(to Doriot)* Go back to your chair at the fire, while I clear the table.

DORIOT   Yes, my dear. *(raises his mug again to Jean)* Come then. The toast has been declared. We will not need to repeat it. To the Day.

Jean raises his glass. They drink. Emilie picks up another dish, exits with them.

DORIOT   —The suffering they caused, the blood they have shed, the very earth itself will take care of—the earth which drank it, the air which heard the grief, the sun which watched—all these will weigh and indict them and set the punishment and carry the sentence out.

ANOTHER ANGLE

DORIOT   But the other crimes, little crimes in the sense that neither their commission nor omission could have advanced or retarded their aims one jot: the music they banned and scattered, the books they burned and destroyed, the pictures they stole—I was a musician. I played at the Royal Opera in Brussels. I have played command performances, not only before our king but at the Hague and in London—Yes, there will be a particular providence, a small, petty, even vengeful one, which will have charge of the punishing for that, so that the greater one, the God who is God—

Emilie enters quickly, pauses, anxious.

DORIOT —will have nothing else to do but listen to the blood they shed and the suffering and the grief and the dishonor and the shame—the shame—

Emilie steps quickly up, touches his shoulder. Jean is watching her. She looks up at him, looks away.

EMILIE *(quietly and firmly)* Father.

DORIOT Yes? Yes?

EMILIE Go to your chair. It's getting cool.

DORIOT Yes, my dear. *(Emilie helps him up)*

CLOSE

Doriot seated again. Emilie spreads shawl about his shoulders. Jean in b.g.

DORIOT He is a true man, a Frenchman, or he would not be here, in this room. It is coming. All Europe will rise against them: one family, one blood, one suffering for all of us, one grief, one dishonor—

EMILIE Yes. Don't talk any more now.

DORIOT Bah! I don't need to talk to tell him. He knows it. Isn't he a Frenchman? It is all one suffering: Frenchman, Slav, Norse, all.

EMILIE Yes. Yes. No more now.

She tucks the shawl in, rises, turns. Jean is watching her, sober and thoughtful. She looks at him for a moment, grave, lowers her head a little and passes him, exits.

CLOSE   EMILIE AND JEAN

—at makeshift sink, Emilie washing dishes as Jean enters with a towel.

JEAN I can help you.

EMILIE   No. There are not many.

JEAN   You knew who I was. And you knew that—*(indicates the old man's position with a slight movement of his head)*—was going to happen. Why did you let me come?

EMILIE   Because you are not a spy. You may be a—*(catches herself, watching him)*

JEAN   Traitor? *(she doesn't answer)* There is an Underground. I know that. They do, too. But not from me.

EMILIE   Yes. It exists. Stronger than you think. It will be stronger still, as we learn better how to be Underground. We were free too long. But soon all Frenchmen will belong to it. They will have to. Or it will be too late.

JEAN   Too late?

EMILIE   Wait.

She exits, returns, hands him a paper. He unfolds it.

CLOSE SHOT

The list of proscribed Frenchmen compiled by the Underground. Among other names, PAN to:

Naval Lieutenant Mornet, Jean

CLOSE   JEAN AND EMILIE

JEAN   So you knew I was not a spy.

EMILIE   Spies are fearful and gregarious. You are just lonely and not afraid.

JEAN   Oh. How did you learn so much about men? You were married?

EMILIE   No. I was engaged. He was in Fort Emael.

JEAN   I see. He is dead?

EMILIE   I don't know. He would probably hope so.

JEAN   I see. There was something else, something your father almost said. About dishonor. *(Emilie watches him, faces him)* May I ask about that?

EMILIE No. Don't ask about that.

JEAN Yes. Goodnight. *(he turns, exits)*

DISSOLVE TO:

LANDING   CLOSE   JEAN

—sets several parcels of food on floor before the door, knocks on the door, exits.

INT. JEAN'S BEDROOM   CLOSE AT DOOR

—as it opens and Jean enters, shuts door, stands for a moment, grave, thoughtful, rouses, removes his coat, pauses as a knock sounds at door. Jean puts the coat back on, opens the door. Emilie stands there holding the parcels.

EMILIE Thank you. I accepted at supper because he needed decent food. He would forgive me for that once, but not again.

JEAN Tell him that every bite he takes is one bite less for them to get—

Emilie stands looking at him quietly until he ceases. He takes the parcels from her. She begins to turn away.

EMILIE Goodnight.

She exits. Jean closes the door.

FADE OUT.

FADE IN

EXT. VILLAGE RAILWAY STATION FREIGHT ROOM   NIGHT   CLOSE ON DARK DOORWAY

—as four shadowy men emerge, carrying a big shipping box, set the box down. One closes the door quietly, locks it, goes on along platform.

INT. DARK ROOM, RAILWAY OFFICE

A man asleep on a cot. He is a Frenchman, the agent, his uniform coat and cap on chair. A key is thrown onto the bed, wakes him. He sits up, picks up the key, looks at it, begins to get out of bed.

VOICE *(off scene, not loud)* Stay where you are, fool. Do you want all Brittany to know you have actually not been burglarized?

The agent looks out of scene, alarmed. He doesn't move. He lies back down again, draws covers up, over his head.

EXT. WOODS   CLOSE SHOT   NIGHT

The four men set the box down, hurriedly pile brush about it, hand strikes a match and lights brush.

CLOSE ON BOX

It is the box of food which Jean sent to his mother. It is addressed as he ordered the clerk in his office:

Mme G. Mornet
Saint Odile
Ile-et-Vilaine

In the corner is a sender's address, a German army symbol, etc. A hand enters with a piece of charred wood or such, scratches out the symbol, writes hurriedly beneath it:

From a Traitor

The hand withdraws. The flames begin to creep around the box.

INT. CAFE   NIGHT

Coupe-tête and another man are playing cards at a table. Every other man in the cafe is gathered around the table, watching, intent and quiet. They are so intent that a German sergeant drinking at the bar crosses to them. The ones on the edge of the group become aware of the sergeant, make way for him until he stands over the table, looking down. The others become aware of the sergeant; finally Coupe-tête and the other player notice him, look up.

SERGEANT *(with heavy accent)* What game is this?

COUPE-TÊTE A French game. You would hardly be interested in these stakes.

SERGEANT So? Why not?

COUPE-TÊTE   You would not be present when they are paid.

SERGEANT   What does that mean?

COUPE-TÊTE   You, a German, do not expect to be here when France is free enough for Frenchmen to pay their gambling debts, do you?

SERGEANT   You're right there. So, don't lose more than you can pay when the game ends. *(he turns away)*

COUPE-TÊTE   We won't. *(the sergeant exits)* Who does he belong to?

The other player is about forty-five. He has a shrewd, quick gambler's face, shrewd like Coupe-tête's but younger. He puts his hand to his pocket, pauses, turns his head and looks cautiously out of scene.

THE PLAYERS' ANGLE   THE BAR

—door beyond it, as the sergeant and two other Germans go out.

CLOSE GROUP AT CARD TABLE

The player takes out a small dingy notebook, opens it; the others all bend forward, listening and watching, intent, sober.

PLAYER   *(reading from book)* Bluch. He belonged to Thegonnec.

THEGONNEC   No, no. That was the fat corporal. That I swapped the two little lieutenants to Guerin for. That Coupe-tête beat me out of with that concealed knave last Saturday. How many have you got now, Coupe-tête?

THIRD MAN   What does it matter? He and Kereon own them all now.

THEGONNEC   It matters because a man as old and weak and crochety as Coupe-tête can't possibly cut that many throats in just one day.

COUPE-TÊTE   Bah! When the day comes, if I can't cut

them all myself, I will rent them out. That's not the question. Who owns that sergeant?

The player, Kereon, looks through the notebook. All the others wait, intently.

KEREON He's not here.

COUPE-TÊTE *(to Kereon)* And you volunteered to keep the record. How many other mistakes do you suppose you have made?

THIRD MAN Maybe he can't read that cypher he invented.

KEREON No more. And I can put him down now. *(produces pencil stub)* What's his name?

COUPE-TÊTE Put him down to who?

THIRD MAN I saw him first.

KEREON But he spoke to me.

COUPE-TÊTE But I answered him. Give me the cards.

He takes up the deck.

COUPE-TÊTE A card around, until the first spade shows. Thegonnec. *(he deals a card)* Guerin. *(he deals a card, stops, all look out of scene)*

CLOSE GROUP   FAVORING DOOR

—open. The German sergeant has just entered, excited.

SERGEANT Achtung! You! All of you! Fire!

The men begin to rise. The sergeant exits hurriedly, men following.

MED. FULL

The burning packing case. German soldiers on guard, the sergeant giving orders; the village men hurrying in with buckets of water, fling them on the fire, exit, others enter.

CLOSE GROUP   THREE MEN IN THE FIRELIGHT

—smoke blowing past them, tears running down their cheeks,

blinking and sniffing the smoke. A popping sound as something explodes in the fire. The men open their eyes, blink,
sniffing. Another pop, a tin box top sails into scene, falls; one
stoops, picks it up.

CLOSE ON BOX TOP

It says—

TRUFFLES

CLOSE GROUP   THE MEN

Sergeant enters angrily.

SERGEANT   What are you doing here?

A MAN   Smelling the smoke, Sergeant.

SERGEANT   Out of it! Grab a bucket! Jump!

The men exit slowly, the heads turned, sniffing the smoke.

INT. RAILWAY OFFICE   CLOSE   GERMAN SERGEANT

The light comes on. The sergeant's hand is on the light, two
soldiers halted behind him. The agent in the bed, cowering,
fearful.

SERGEANT   Get up!

The agent gets out of bed, stands in night clothes, undershirt
and trousers, barefoot.

AGENT   I was asleep. Someone flung the key in through
the window and waked me.

SERGEANT   Why didn't you give the alarm?

AGENT   I was afraid.

The sergeant glares at the agent.

SERGEANT   Who was it?

The agent glances fearfully right and left, wets lips.

SERGEANT   Look at me. *(agent looks at sergeant fearfully)*
Who was it?

The agent's eyes go aside again. He seems to bring them back by a physical effort, holds them, takes a deep breath. His voice is different, crisper.

AGENT I don't know.

The sergeant strikes him. He half falls backward onto the bed. The sergeant turns, shouts in German to the soldiers. They about-face in unison, tramp out, sergeant follows.

INT. CAFE   CLOSE

—favoring door, of group of men about the card table. It is the same group; they might not have moved at all: the same quiet intensity as Coupe-tête, holding deck of cards, is about to deal, when the door crashes open, the sergeant enters, a file of soldiers halted beyond the door.

SERGEANT Go home. Be off the streets in five minutes. *(the men stare at him)* Did you hear me?

The men begin to rise. The sergeant turns to the patron behind the bar.

SERGEANT Put your lights out and close up.

The patron moves slowly, to come out from behind the bar. The sergeant glares at him, steps toward the light hanging on a cord from the ceiling, draws his bayonet and bursts the light bulb.

PATRON'S VOICE You didn't need to do that.

SERGEANT'S VOICE Get out of here! All of you! One! Two! One! Two!

The men exit.

INT. MAIRIE, THE GERMAN COMMANDER'S OFFICE   CLOSE
GERMAN CAPTAIN

—seated at desk, sergeant facing him, standing. The sergeant stands stiff attention, speaks in German. The captain speaks shortly. The sergeant answers. The captain speaks again. The sergeant takes out a notebook, hands it to the captain.

CLOSE ON NOTEBOOK

A list of names, followed by the man's occupation. Some of them have been crossed out by a single line. The ones which have not been crossed out are the useful ones: miller, blacksmith, wheelwright, railway agent, etc. The next name on the list is:

Kereon, Michel. Music teacher

CLOSE

The captain hands the book back to the sergeant, speaks shortly speaking the name, "Kereon." The sergeant salutes, about-faces and exits.

CLOSE GROUP

The same men who were about the table in the cafe. They are kneeling now on a dirt floor in a crudely shored-up cave. In b.g. a box with a radio on it. The radio is tuned down. It is De Gaulle's voice, making some broadcast of this time, about August–September, 1941.

Coupe-tête has the cards, is about to deal.

    COUPE-TÊTE   Thegonnec. *(deals a card: a diamond)* Guerin. *(deals a card: a club)* Carnac. *(deals a diamond)* Trouin. *(deals a heart)* Basdavant. *(deals a club)* Plehec. *(deals a club)* Laennec. *(deals a diamond)* Kereon. *(deals a heart)* And now, Coupe-tête—

He prepares to deal. Kereon puts his hand out.

    KEREON   Give me the cards.

    COUPE-TÊTE   Eh?

    KEREON   I will deal to you.

Coupe-tête looks at Kereon, shrugs, hands him the deck. Their hands fumble for a moment; the cards almost spill but Coupe-tête catches them, pushes them into Kereon's hand.

    KEREON   Are you through fumbling with them?

    COUPE-TÊTE   Yes.

    KEREON   Then I will cut them.

    COUPE-TÊTE   I'll cut them.

KEREON Oh, you will, eh?

COUPE-TÊTE I was dealing. I surrendered without a murmur. *(he watches Kereon)* I appeal to all here.

THEGONNEC Let him cut them. The rest of us have no chance anyhow between you.

Kereon shrugs, holds out the deck. Coupe-tête cuts. Kereon deals a card to Coupe-tête. It is the jack of spades.

COUPE-TÊTE That's no news. We already knew that sergeant was a knave.

GUERIN *(glumly)* Most of us already knew you were going to get him, too.

DISSOLVE TO:

THE VILLAGE SQUARE   CLOSE   MORNING

Mme Kereon struggling with two German soldiers. She is about forty-five. She is trying to pass them. They have lowered their rifles before her, holding her back. She tries to strike at them. They restrain her. In b.g. a file of soldiers at attention, the German captain leaning on a walking stick.

MME KEREON Beasts! Animals!

A voice speaks a command in German off scene. The wooden-faced soldiers desist, merely hold Mme Kereon off with their crossed rifles. Catherine and Marthe enter, take Mme Kereon by the arms to lead her out. Marthe pauses, looks back at the two soldiers.

MARTHE *(half timorous, half daring)* Pah! Beasts!

CLOSE   VILLAGERS

—men and women, Catherine and Marthe with Mme Kereon between them, Coupe-tête, others whom we recognize, favoring Kereon, handcuffed, and the priest standing among armed guards. In b.g. other soldiers, to one side, as though having no part in what is going on but merely there because his position requires him to be. The captain leans on his stick. Kereon is disheveled a little, but is not at all chastened nor fearful. He looks calmly about, almost quizzical. The priest is grave, calm.

A German lieutenant enters b.g., marching rigidly. He is young, wears spectacles, looks like a student. He marches stiffly in, right-wheels stiffly, advances to the front, halts, claps heels, draws a paper out, opens it, reads aloud with a stilted accent.

> **LIEUTENANT** The village of Saint Odile having been found guilty of the destruction of property belonging to the German Reich, the hostage Michel Kereon, music teacher, is hereby sentenced to a term of labor for the Reich, the location and duration of which to be at the discretion of the Reich. As an example to the people of Saint-Odile.

He folds the paper, about-faces, marches, left-wheels, marches, halts beside the captain, claps heels, faces front. The German sergeant comes forward, faces the soldiers among whom Kereon and the priest stand, is about to give an order when the priest turns and speaks in German to the captain. The captain answers in German. The priest looks out of scene.

> **PRIEST** Come. It is permitted.

Mme Kereon enters, embraces Kereon. He is handcuffed, cannot lift his hands. After a moment the priest touches Mme Kereon's shoulder.

> **PRIEST** There. That will do.

Mme Kereon releases Kereon, turns blindly. Catherine enters, leads her out. The captain, still leaning on the stick, speaks short in German. The sergeant gives a command. The soldiers face-about stiffly, Kereon turning, too, his head up, as if he were a soldier, too. He keeps perfect step, his head still up, as they march out.

CLOSE   KEREON, PRIEST, SOLDIERS

—at the rear of an open German army van, favoring the villagers in the b.g., watching grim and quiet. Mme Kereon supported between Catherine and Marthe, Coupe-tête and others. Kereon faces priest, kneels, the priest blesses him. Kereon rises.

The sergeant barks an order. Kereon turns to enter the van, pauses, looks at the villagers.

KEREON   Take care of my Germans until I get back.

COUPE-TÊTE   Tenderly. And well.

CLOSE   COUPE-TÊTE AND FIVE OR SIX MEN

—facing the door to the cafe. It is closed and locked. A placard is fastened to it saying it is closed until further notice. By order. Signed by German adjutant.

CLOSE   THE MEN

Three of them we have not seen before. One of them is a gaunt, hungry-looking man, with a fanatic's face. His name is Guezonnec.

GUEZONNEC   I should have given myself up. I stole the key. I set the fire.

COUPE-TÊTE   No, I tell you. It's his own command. He told me that himself, when they came for him last night: in our tongue, not this French one, that these animals at least cannot learn. He said, "Tell Guezonnec 'No'. If he surrenders, they will merely take him, too. As it is, only one goes, and there is another one left to plague them."

GUEZONNEC   To do more than plague them: to hate them.

COUPE-TÊTE   Good. Hate them. But just be quiet about it until someone tells you when. And that will come, too.

CLOSE   CATHERINE AND MARTHE WITH MME KEREON

—in front of Mornet house.

MME KEREON   Let me go home.

CATHERINE   No. You come in with us. Marthe will give you a cup of coffee.

MARTHE   You have lost your man for a little while. Good. Let them take mine, and see how much I grieve.

They lead Mme Kereon toward the house.

INT. HOUSE   CLOSE   CATHERINE, MME KEREON AND MARTHE

—behind her, as she opens the door, is about to enter, stops.

CATHERINE   Georges!

INT. KITCHEN   CLOSE   CATHERINE AND GEORGES   MORNING

—embracing. Mme Mornet in b.g.

DISSOLVE TO:

INT. KITCHEN   EVENING

Lamp is lighted. Georges and Catherine draw apart, Georges's arm still about Catherine.

WIDER ANGLE

—to include priest, Coupe-tête and Marthe standing, Mme Mornet seated.

GEORGES   I shouldn't be here. In fact, I was forbidden to. We all are, each time: to never come back home, never let any member of our family know we are even in France—

COUPE-TÊTE   So that's why you came: because they told you not to. Catherine was not enough reason, then.

MARTHE   *Miss* Catherine!

GEORGES   But it doesn't matter now. In the United States they have elected Mr. Roosevelt president for the third time. They have been sending guns and planes and food to England all the time, but now, with Mr. Roosevelt president again, the friend to all of us in Europe who have suffered—Don't you see what that means?

COUPE-TÊTE   It means they will help us. But—

PRIEST   It means more. It means—

GEORGES   Yes! That we can help ourselves, we in France here; in all the countries they have overrun and tried to destroy. That after this, only the knaves and cowards can dare believe any longer in Vichy—only the poltroons and the knaves—

ANOTHER ANGLE

> **GEORGES** We were alone. Each little village, each man who hated them and wished to fight, was alone and could do nothing. General De Gaulle knew why. He said it was because we had been free too long. We didn't know how to organize an underground and communicate with each other. We didn't know how to combat cruelty and ruthlessness with trickery. But now we can. Now we dare. It's like all America spoke to us when they elected Mr. Roosevelt again and said to us, "We are with you. Go ahead—"

> **PRIEST** Is this true?

> **GEORGES** Yes.

> **COUPE-TÊTE** Wait. To the Day.

He turns quickly. All watch him as he darts out.

CLOSE   COUPE-TÊTE

—stooping over the woodbox, hurling wood out. He takes something from the bottom of the box, turns.

CLOSE GROUP   ALL

Coupe-tête with a bottle of wine, all looking at it. Marthe shows alarm. Bottle bears a German food administration stamp.

> **GEORGES**   *(to Coupe-tête)* Where did this come from?

> **COUPE-TÊTE** What does it matter where it came from? Can you think of a better destination for it than drinking confusion to the Boches? *(to Marthe)* The glasses, woman!

CLOSE GROUP   FACING TABLE

—wine glasses set out, Coupe-tête filling them.

> **GEORGES** Peace. No more of this—the fighting, the blood, the suffering and the grief of women and children. When a man can return in peace to the land he was born on, and work it in peace and marry—

> **PRIEST** Why do you wait?

Coupe-tête pauses, the bottle poised. All watch the priest.

GEORGES   No!

PRIEST   So far you and other young Frenchmen like you have had incentive only to risk your lives. There is no question of courage. All men who wish to be free must have courage. You need more than the incentive to die if necessary. You must need to live, as well. To live, and to return.

GEORGES   I will come back. With men and guns.

PRIEST   For still more blood and destruction and death. You must have incentive for more than that: for peace, contentment. So why do you wait?

GEORGES   Now? When I may be dead next month, next week, maybe tomorrow?

PRIEST   Look at her. Does she look afraid?

Catherine and Georges look at one another.

PRIEST   A man is almost impossible to destroy, when he has enough incentive to stay alive.

He takes their hands, joins them.

GEORGES   There is France.

PRIEST   There is no harm to France in your love.

Coupe-tête fills glasses again, splashing wine at a great rate.

COUPE-TÊTE   To love, then, France or not. If there be harm, France can bear it.

DISSOLVE TO:

MED. CLOSE   NIGHT

The ruins of an old tumbled-down medieval tower, stone, crumbled, weeds growing about it, the fallen doorway now a narrow dark crack, dark figures of men entering it.

INT. CAVE

It is the cave in which the card game took place when Coupe-tête won the German sergeant. The radio sits on the stone ledge, more crumbled stone, etc. Two or three smoky torches light it.

CLOSE   KNEELING MEN AND WOMEN

—favoring Catherine and Georges kneeling before priest. A round stone slab has been dressed with altar vestments, candles, etc. Mme Mornet, Marthe, Coupe-tête in b.g.

> **PRIEST**   —in sickness and in health, in sorrow and joy, until death. Whom God hath joined, let no man put asunder.

He makes sign of cross. Georges rises, helps Catherine up. All rise. Georges turns to face them.

> **GEORGES**   The General said we have been free too long in France; we didn't know how to be secret and be strong. But we are learning. There are many more like me, that he has sent, to go among all the villages and towns as I have come here, to bring his message. He says, "Be secret and be strong, and wait and hope, and above all, work."

> **COUPE-TÊTE**   (advances) But first, of course, is to salute the bride.

INT. HOUSE   NIGHT

Coupe-tête stooping before a closed door, cautiously hanging onto the knob a string to which is tied bottles, tin cans, an old shoe, etc., which clash and jangle together as he loops them cautiously about the knob. Marthe enters behind him, pauses. She wears her nightgown, shawl over her shoulders, her hair in papers.

> **MARTHE**   (whispers) What are you doing?

Coupe-tête starts, catches himself, merely looks back as he ties the cord.

> **COUPE-TÊTE**   I intend to remind him tomorrow he was a free man once, even if he doesn't know it yet.

He rises, pulls the string slightly, releases it. The bottles and cans clash faintly.

MARTHE   Hush! Hush! Will you wake the whole house?

COUPE-TÊTE   If some in the house need to be waked at this moment, so much the better for France, according to His Reverence. But I am not one.

He turns. Before Marthe can move, he embraces her. She struggles.

MARTHE   Let go, you old fool! You, gray as an old badger, and not two teeth in your head that meet one another!

COUPE-TÊTE   *(embracing her)* A man's teeth and hair have nothing to do with the condition of his heart nor the strength of his sap.

He draws her to him. She struggles, slapping at him. He holds her face, kisses her. She stops, clasps him a moment, turns her cheek to his, patting his back.

MARTHE   My old man.

DISSOLVE TO:

INT. CAVE   CLOSE   COUPE-TÊTE, GUEZONNEC, FOUR OTHERS

—lighted by a single torch.

COUPE-TÊTE   It is food. When we destroy it, no German will ever eat it: true. But did you ever pause to think what happens when we eat it ourselves?

GUEZONNEC   *(harshly)* No!

COUPE-TÊTE   Of course, there are our wives and children. But luckily women and children are weak creatures, and will not miss this food as we men will—

GUEZONNEC   I will not. I cannot. Not after Kereon—

COUPE-TÊTE   Kereon may not like where he is, but will he like it any the less for knowing that his wife is eating—*(he turns to another man)* What was that which came bursting out of the fire that night?

THE MAN   It said, truffles.

COUPE-TÊTE   You smelled them?

THE MAN Yes. I smelled them.

SECOND MAN Come on. Come on. *(to Coupe-tête)* What is it?

They move closer a little, intent. Guezonnec is still grim, but he is listening, too.

COUPE-TÊTE Consider then. Not only would every mouthful of it rob some Boche of strength to harm us; it would increase the strength to resist of the very ones whom he probably sees in his nightly dreams even as writhing beneath his iron heel—Ay, dreams of them at night, as a young man dreams of women—

DISSOLVE TO:

INT. RAILROAD OFFICE

The agent asleep in the cot. A shadowy man enters, stops, leans over the cot. The agent wakes, turns, raises his head.

MAN'S VOICE Go back to sleep.

The agent turns back in cot, pulls covers up over his head. The shadowy man takes a rope from under his smock and binds the agent rapidly into the cot, winding the rope about the cot and tying it. Then he goes to the chair, takes up agent's pants, puts hand into pocket, withdraws his hand, puts the pants back on the chair and exits.

INT. FREIGHT SHED   CLOSE

A packing box like the other one. Four shadowy men busy about it, hurried yet quiet. They pry a board up, remove the contents, which are various packages of food, and replace them with trash, refuse: whatever a Frenchman would admit to be refuse, rocks, pieces of wood, etc. They replace the prised-up board, load the packages of food into sacks, and steal out.

INT. OFFICE

The agent in cot, head covered. The rope is gone now; a package containing food lies on the cot with the agent. Faint sound of feet; the feet cease, die away. The agent uncovers his head, listens, looks cautiously after the feet, takes the package and draws it beneath the covers with him.

EXT. STREET   MED. CLOSE   COTTAGE

Two men, one carrying a sack, pause at the door. One takes a
package of food from the sack, sets it before the door, knocks
lightly on the door. The men go on. The door opens a crack,
someone looks out, stoops, picks up the package and withdraws. The door closes.

INT. A COTTAGE   CLOSE

—shades drawn closely. Coupe-tête sitting at the end of a table.
The table bears a candle in an empty bottle, and different kinds
of food: luxuries, jellies, pâté, a whole roast fowl, a bottle of
wine. The plates and cutlery are the poorest kind. Coupe-tête
sits motionless, a napkin tucked inside his collar, staring grimly
at CAMERA.

REVERSE ANGLE   TABLE

A woman in nightdress sitting at it; two children in nightgowns,
who have obviously just been waked up and hauled out of bed;
opposite Coupe-tête a man, dressed, too, bent over his plate,
knife in one hand, the blade of the knife loaded with food. He
is about to put it into his mouth, finds Coupe-tête staring at
him, pauses. The woman and children pause, too, look from
one to the other.

> **COUPE-TÊTE**   Do you know what that is you are shoveling
> into your maw like so much sawdust?

> **MAN**   No.

> **COUPE-TÊTE**   It's caviar.

> **MAN**   Is it?

He starts to put knife into his mouth again, finds Coupe-tête
watching him, stops again.

> **COUPE-TÊTE**   Bah!

CLOSE   ALL

Coupe-tête spreads caviar on a piece of bread, hands it to the
woman, who passes it to next child, who passes it to next, who
passes it to the man, all watching the bread as the man sits

holding it. Then all look at Coupe-tête again as he spreads another piece of bread, passes it to woman, who passes it to next child, who passes it to the next, all watching that piece, too, then all watching Coupe-tête as he spreads next piece and passes that. Coupe-tête spreads another piece, hands it to the woman. The man, the two children and the woman glance at one another secretly, start to eat.

COUPE-TÊTE   Wait. *(all stop)* Who sent you this?

FIRST CHILD   Mister Jean Mornet.

COUPE-TÊTE   Hitler sent it. By the hand of Michel Kereon.

ANOTHER ANGLE

Coupe-tête with wineglass raised; the man, the woman, the two children holding up their pieces of bread.

COUPE-TÊTE   Michel Kereon!

The man, woman, and the children cross themselves, raise the bread again.

CHILDREN   Michel Kereon.

FADE OUT.

FADE IN   CLOSE   LETTERS ON A WALL

SOCIETE ANONYME
RENAULT

Beside it, a symbol indicating German occupation: army symbol, etc.

DISSOLVE TO:

INT. OFFICE

Jean stands facing desk. A German sits behind the desk, looking at Jean. The German wears civilian clothes, is middle-aged. He looks like a factory president himself. Door in b.g.

JEAN   I am Jean Mornet. I was sent—

The German rings a bell on the desk. He says nothing.

JEAN   Am I to be told why I was sent here?

The door opens. Sound of factory comes in. A young Gestapo in uniform enters, shuts door; sound of factory ceases. The Gestapo clicks heels. The German looks down at the paper on the desk again. He does not look at the Gestapo at all.

> **GERMAN** *(to Gestapo)* Mr. Mornet is to go everywhere. He will have what time he likes. Unattended. He will leave by the front entrance.

The Gestapo opens the door. The factory sound comes in while the Gestapo holds the door open. Jean looks at the German who is reading the paper again. He turns toward the door.

INT. FACTORY   CLOSE   JEAN AND KEREON

—at Kereon's workbench. Factory sound in b.g. Kereon faces Jean. While he talks, his hand fumbles in his pocket.

> **KEREON**   It was because of the food. Your mother divided it among the women and children. But Guezonnec thought that even they shouldn't eat it. So one night he and some others burned it—

His hand comes out of the pocket and goes to the bench and fumbles on the bench as though it were writing something. He still looks at Jean.

> **KEREON**   But we are still grateful to your mother; so we want to take every opportunity to thank her because she kept none of it for herself but put every mouthful into the hand—

His hand moves across the bench.

> **KEREON**   *(accents slightly)* —the *hand* can see us; maybe can hear, too. The *hand*—

Jean is watching him, puzzled, begins to comprehend, looks down toward bench.

CLOSE   KEREON'S HAND

—holding a short piece of chalk. It has written on the bench:

OUT QUICK 1 O'CLOCK

The hand goes back, erases the words, scrawls:

GO GO MOTHER

The hand returns, erases that quickly.

CLOSE   JEAN AND KEREON

> **KEREON**   I ate some of it, too, German food or not; so I
> want to thank her *quick* before *one o'clock* we quit and *out of
> here go go—*

He turns quickly, pulls down lever of lathe motor, is at work
again as the Gestapo enters.

> **GESTAPO**   *(to Jean)* You have finished here?

Jean turns away, goes on.

MED. CLOSE   A BIG DOOR

—a German sentry at each side of it. Gestapo and Jean enter;
one soldier turns, presses lever; door slides back showing exterior, street, etc. Jean looks through it, turns and looks back
into factory, his face grave, sober, thoughtful. The Gestapo
watches him, takes a step or so toward the exit, clicks his heels
again, attracts Jean's attention. Jean turns, exits through door,
turns again. The soldier presses lever. The door slides to, shuts
Jean out. The soldier returns to his position. The Gestapo
shouts a command in German. The soldier at the door repeats
it. Two other soldiers enter, fall in behind the Gestapo. They
stride toward CAMERA.

MED. CLOSE   BIG CLOCK ON WALL

—hands at four minutes before one. The hand moves on.

CLOSE   KEREON AT HIS BENCH

—working, the Gestapo and the two soldiers behind him.

> **GESTAPO**   Mornet!

Kereon turns.

> **KEREON**   My name is Kereon.

The Gestapo speaks in German. The two soldiers grasp Kereon
by shoulders, jerk him from bench. The Gestapo goes on; the
soldiers propel Kereon behind him.

CLOSE   CLOCK FACE

—the hand at one minute past one. Voices in b.g. begin to sing Marseillaise; other voices take it up.

CLOSE   GESTAPO, TWO SOLDIERS WITH KEREON

—favoring factory room, row of unfinished tanks; the conscripted French laborers have stopped work, look toward Gestapo's group, singing. Kereon singing, too. A soldier strikes him down. Gestapo shouts in German. An alarm bell rings; more voices join the singing. In b.g. other German soldiers run in.

CLOSE   LIGHT MASTER SWITCH

A German soldier pulls it. Lights go out; singing continues. A Frenchman enters, knocks soldier away, closes switch again. Lights come on. Soldier rises to approach the German. The singing is very loud. Sound of anti-aircraft fire and sirens begin in distance, grow louder. First bomb explodes. Debris falls on the group at light switch.

CLOSE   JEAN

—crouching behind a low wall of an outdoors cafe. Chairs and tables are overturned where patrons have scattered. Air raid sirens going. A.A. fire, bombs bursting in b.g. as Jean stares out of scene. The singing can still be heard, many voices, faint.

DISSOLVE TO:

INT. GERMAN COLONEL'S OFFICE, PARIS

Jean stands facing desk. Colonel seated at desk. A Gestapo officer seated at end of desk. The Gestapo officer is youngish, about thirty-five. He is a man of power with Himmler[7] and Hitler, etc., though friction exists between him and the Army, which the colonel represents. The colonel ranks him, but the Gestapo still has the unspoken support of Himmler's police behind him, which the colonel knows.

7. Heinrich Himmler (1900–1945) was the head of the Nazi terrorist organization, the SS *(Schutzstaffel)*, from 1929 to 1945.

COLONEL *(to Jean)* Sit down.

The Gestapo speaks to the colonel in German, obviously telling the colonel to let Jean stand, since he is being requested officially to explain himself, is under a cloud, etc. The colonel answers shortly in German; he is still in command here, etc. He does not look at the Gestapo as he answers.

COLONEL *(to Jean)* Sit down.

JEAN Thanks. I'll stand.

The Gestapo speaks to the colonel in German, peremptory. The colonel pauses, seems to acquiesce, takes a cigarette from the box and lights it. The Gestapo takes charge of the investigation.

GESTAPO *(with accent)* Mr. Mornet. I cannot believe you really hoped to make anyone believe that the man Kereon was your brother.

JEAN My brother? My brother is in—

He ceases. The Gestapo watches him. The colonel studies the end of his cigarette; this must be done, but as a soldier he doesn't like what he knows is coming.

GESTAPO Your brother is in France. As a British agent, or an agent of this man De Gaulle who claims to be the leader of your people.

JEAN Then I don't know it, as you probably are aware, too. So that was why I was sent—

GESTAPO We are aware that you do not—so far. Yes. We sent you to that factory this morning to learn what you would do if you saw your brother there. You convinced an underling that the man Kereon was your brother. I do not believe that, myself, though it is beyond testing now, because the man Kereon and the underling, as well as everyone else in the building at the time, are dead. So someone there knew that bombing was on the way. If your brother really was there, it was bad for him, and it would have been bad for you. But if he was not there, it will be very bad for you indeed. We will see that you have other opportunities to reveal him. If you do not do so, beware. That is all.

EXT. STREET   CLOSE   DOORWAY

—to the apartment building where Jean lives. Emilie approaches from street, carrying market basket. As she reaches the door, Jean steps out. He is carrying a package.

JEAN   It's German food again. But I thought that perhaps one time more—

EMILIE   *(watches him a moment)* Come in.

DISSOLVE TO:

INT. DORIOTS' ROOM   CLOSE   DORIOT

—asleep in his chair before the fire, Emilie in a chair beside lamp on table, sewing. Jean in another chair.

JEAN   They all knew the bombs were coming. They even knew the hour. They could have got out just by telling the guards. But they didn't. They sang instead—*(he pauses, muses, rouses again)* At first I didn't understand why they sent me there.

EMILIE   They thought perhaps your brother was there. They intended for you to identify him.

JEAN   You knew it, too? That my brother is in France?

EMILIE   *(quietly)* Yes. We all know it. General De Gaulle sent him to us.

JEAN   We? Us?

EMILIE   If you try to force someone to do as you want them to do, and they resist you and keep on resisting until the only thing left for you to do is to kill them, they have beat you. And if you do kill them, they have beat you forever because then they have escaped from you. It's like those little ants in the jungle that nothing can stand against—not the biggest and fiercest and the most powerful—nothing. You can kill them by the millions just by stepping on them, but they keep on coming because they are so little. That's the mistake they made. They tried to force the little people. And there are too many little people. There are so many of them because they are so small. All they have to threaten us with is death. And little people are not afraid to die. The little people, and the very great. Because there is something of the little people in the very great: as if all the little people who had been trodden and crushed had condensed into one great one who knew and remembered all their suffering. And the little ones themselves are never afraid as long as they believe that the other little ants coming behind them will finally eat the elephant.

ANOTHER ANGLE

EMILIE This happened in your village; you see how well we keep in touch with one another, now that we have learned how. It was the food again, that you send your mother, after the man named Guezonnec burned the box that Kereon was taken for. It was your mother's old farmer—what's his name—

JEAN Coupe-tête.

EMILIE Coupe-tête. After that, to purify it so they could eat it, Coupe-tête and a few others would steal it, enter the station at night and pry the box open and take the food out and put rocks into the box and close it again. Then the next morning the German commander would send your mother word that the box had come, and for her to send and get it. They wouldn't deliver it, so Coupe-tête would have to come for it. It was too heavy for him to handle alone, so he would have to have help. But everybody knew the box had nothing in it now but rocks; they had eaten the food the night before. So Coupe-tête couldn't get anyone to help him. Each time he would have to pay someone with another of his and Kereon's Germans to help him load the box into the cart.

JEAN So you do know.

EMILIE We do know. Every day there are more of us who know. Because we are the little people, you see. We are

neither generals nor statesmen nor politicians. We are just
the little people and there are too many of us. Too much of
individual grief and suffering—*(she pauses an instant, looks
at Jean)*—and dishonor and shame, until, since we are little
people, the suffering and grief and dishonor and shame
belong to all of us and we can resist—

ANOTHER ANGLE

Emilie has put the sewing on the table. She sits with her hands
in her lap, looking ahead. Her face is calm.

EMILIE   We were living in a little village outside of Meche-
len. We had no warning. No more warning, that is, than all
Europe should have had. But no matter. They came suddenly. Father was in Brussels then, and my brother and I
were in the house alone, when suddenly they were there—
three of them, three young men. It didn't matter who or
which three, just as to them I was a young woman and that
didn't matter who or which one; just female and of an
inferior race created for the spoiling that could make war
and the risk of sudden death bearable. Then it was over,
and they were gone, and at least I was still alive—

JEAN   Your brother?

EMILIE   He died. Quickly. And I was still alive, and I hated
it on my father's account—an old man, just a musician, too
old and unimportant even for them to destroy. But after
we reached Paris, and they overtook us again, and it was no
use to flee again because now nothing remained that we
could be despoiled of, another musician, a Frenchman, a
young man who knew Father, would come to see us. And
one night he brought a book, an American book written by
a Mr. Hemingway.[8] He would read it to us at night and
translate it. It told about a young girl to whom that had
happened also, and about an older woman who was very
wise about people anyway, who said how, if you refused to
accept something, it could not happen to you. And I was
comforted because Jan—my brother—had died quickly be-

8. The novel alluded to in this passage is *For Whom the Bell Tolls* (1940).

forehand, and Willem, to whom I was to be married, had been in Fort Eben Emael and he would not have to hate that, too, at least. So there was only Father, and he believes, too, that some day the ants are going to eat the elephant—

CLOSE   JEAN AND EMILIE

—standing, Jean holding Emilie's hand to his lips. Emily withdraws her hand.

JEAN   So they sent me there today to find Georges. They knew I would have reported him.

EMILIE   No. They wanted to see whether you would or not. And you would have, knowing he was an agent of General De Gaulle.

JEAN   I have an oath.

EMILIE   To them, who keep none?

JEAN   To myself. I must do what I have to do, what I think is right to do, for what remains of my poor country.

EMILIE   France is not poor now. Every day all outraged Europe—

JEAN   *(quickly)* I must go. Goodnight.

He turns toward door. She watches him.

EMILIE   Mr. Mornet.

He pauses, looks back.

EMILIE   Come to us.

JEAN   *(harshly)* No. *(quieter)* It's too late now. What man or woman of what you call the true France would believe anyone now who changed to them this late? Goodnight.

He turns, advances toward Camera into—

FADE OUT.

FADE IN

MONTAGE

U.S. declares war on Germany. A secret newspaper which circulates among the French Underground. Perhaps a shot of small, clumsy hand press running off the papers. A DISSOLVE through it to—

A FEW PEOPLE IN UNDERGROUND CELL

—crouched about a secret radio, showing joyful reaction as a Free French voice tells the news and its implications of new hope and guarantee to enslaved Europe.

DISSOLVE TO:

EXT. HOTEL CRILLON

[I think M. Berger said this is Nazi Gestapo headquarters in Paris.] Nazi flag over it.

CLOSE SHOT   CRILLON

DISSOLVE TO:

INT. BASEMENT

The first general congress of the Underground cells from all of France is held. Delegates are elected formally to go to De Gaulle in London and present the alliance of the whole Underground. Georges is chairman, or at least De Gaulle's official representative.

DISSOLVE TO:

EXT. BUSY STREET   CLOSE   JEAN

Rue de la Paix, perhaps, cafe in b.g. German officers, street thronged with French civilians and German soldiers. Jean walking, somber and grave. He stops, looks out of scene, shows astonishment.

REVERSE ANGLE

Georges, walking in crowd, looks up, sees Jean and recognizes him.

INT. A BASEMENT

—known to Georges and his confederates.

CLOSE   JEAN AND GEORGES

GEORGES Don't worry. You're safe here; this is my rat-hole. The question is, am I?

JEAN Yes. For twenty-four hours. Give me your word that you will leave France and never come back.

GEORGES Or you'll report me. Go. Say it. I know you will, but I want to hear you say it.

JEAN I have an oath. I intend to keep it.

GEORGES To who? As what? As a French traitor?

JEAN To myself.

GEORGES Yes. That damned oath you took the day you entered the Naval Academy. When true France no longer has a navy.

JEAN The French navy no longer has a country, you mean. But never mind that. I'll give you twenty-four hours to get out of France.

GEORGES Not any more. Once I had to. But I have come back. And someday soon you and those who forced or persuaded you——

JEAN No man forced or persuaded me. I chose.

GEORGES All right, all right.—will have to get out of France, too, those who can. And they won't come back.

JEAN But that's not yet. Go. I'm being watched, too. They probably saw us meet; they have probably followed us here—

GEORGES In which case, you won't even have to report me. They'll find me all right with just a piece of rubber . . . *(he stops, continues)* Of course. You'll tell them first; put yourself in solid for—No, I don't mean that. God, what a time, when brother and brother—*(recovers)* No. I won't go. Tell them, or let them beat it out of you or me, either, with the rubber hose. They can't hurt us now. The United States is in this now, and all France is ready. All France is waiting. I don't need to stay any longer, actually. There's nothing anybody needs to do any more. We don't even need a martyr to help our cause. But I think I'll stay, just to see what martyrdom is like.

He rises; Jean rises, too.

GEORGES   No, that's not true, either. I'm going to stay for the fun of it. Because I don't think you and your fine Gestapo can catch me.

JEAN   So you think. So a lot of your men have thought. So too many people in this world have thought—until it was too late.

GEORGES   *(soberly)* Yes. That's right. We have never under-estimated them. They may catch me; according to you, and to others I know, they probably will. But I still have work to do, and too many Frenchmen and Slavs and Norwegians and Belgians and Dutch have died at this same job for any one of us to hesitate.

JEAN   Go.

GEORGES   Come over to us.

JEAN   At this late date, would any of you believe me? *(they look at one another)* Would they? *(Georges doesn't answer)* Go!

GEORGES   Come over to us.

JEAN   No.

GEORGES   No.

JEAN   *(turns, pauses)* Twenty-four hours.

GEORGES   I will remember you did that much.

INT. CORRIDOR   CLOSE   JEAN'S OFFICE DOOR

—favoring corridor as Jean approaches. He is sober, thoughtful. He puts hand on door, opens it, is about to enter, pauses, enters.

INT. OFFICE   CLOSE   FAVORING GERMAN ORDERLY

Jean has entered.

ORDERLY   The Colonel's compliments. In his office. At once.

INT. COLONEL'S OFFICE

Jean stands facing desk. The colonel stands looking out the window, his back to the room. He still does not like this, but he is still a servant of the German government. The Gestapo officer stands in front of the desk, facing Jean. A closed door in wall in b.g.

GESTAPO   Last night you met a man on the street. After you separated, the man was arrested. He is still being held. His replies tally with the registration of him which we already had: Jacques Villemon, wine-broker, of Rheims. Of course this man is not your brother.

JEAN   No.

GESTAPO   We thought not. Otherwise, you would have reported him. So he will be released. But meantime there is still the question of this Georges Mornet, an agent of our enemy's, somewhere in France. Since we cannot wait any longer for you to meet him and inform us, we have taken steps of our own—

The Gestapo turns, goes to the door, puts hand on the knob, turns and looks at Jean a moment, opens the door.

CLOSE THROUGH DOOR   A LONG CORRIDOR

—Mme Mornet seated in a chair at end of it, a German policewoman standing beside her. She is watching the door when it opens. She starts up. The policewoman presses her back. She struggles. She is dressed for traveling, a suitcase on floor beside chair.

MME MORNET   Jean! Don't tell him! Don't—

The door closes.

CLOSE   JEAN AND GESTAPO AT THE DOOR

—Jean poised to spring, the Gestapo with his hand on his holster.

GESTAPO   Stand back, Mornet. Other Frenchwomen as old as she have stood the trip to Germany. There will be other men and women, too; Belgian and Dutch and Norse and

Slav as well as of her tongue, to keep her company when she misses France.

CLOSE   JEAN, GESTAPO AND COLONEL AT DESK

The colonel still stands staring out the window. The Gestapo sits at the desk, a many-leaved dossier open before him. Jean stands at desk.

> **GESTAPO**   This Jacques Villemon is Georges Mornet?

> **JEAN**   I can take my mother home? She will not be disturbed again?

> **GESTAPO**   This Jacques Villemon is Georges Mornet?

> **COLONEL**   (*from window*) Yes. She will not be disturbed again.

> **JEAN**   (*to Gestapo*) Yes.

DISSOLVE TO:

JEAN'S GERMAN OFFICIAL CAR

—with soldier driver standing in front of the Mornet house.

INT. HALLWAY   CLOSE   JEAN AND CATHERINE

Catherine is frantic.

> **CATHERINE**   Die? Of course he'll die! When they have known for six months what he was doing, when all France, even they, know now what he has accomplished? They better destroy him while they can!

> **JEAN**   He knew that, too. He took that risk. We lost the war. He declined to accept the fact, and escaped. All right. But he was not content to stay there. He had to come back, to gamble his life against a trained police who had had all Europe to practice on before they even came here—not only his life, but his mother's too—

> **CATHERINE**   And you saved that, not she. She wouldn't have told. You told them.

> **JEAN**   Yes. He would have done the same, if he had been in my place and I in his.

CATHERINE So you think. But of course you would say so—you would have to justify it. He has sacrificed his own for France; do you think he would have spared yours?

JEAN I spared his mother's.

CATHERINE Then spare hers with mine. Spare hers and his both, with mine.

JEAN It's too late now. But even if it wasn't, how with— *(pauses, stares at her)* How with yours?

CATHERINE I'm married to him. I've got his child. Didn't your German friends tell you that?

INT. MME MORNET'S BEDROOM   CLOSE   BED

Mme Mornet in bed, Marthe beside her. Jean standing at bed. Marthe gives him a swift look, then keeps her eyes turned away.

MME MORNET *(opens her eyes)* Jean.

Jean takes her hand. It doesn't move, limp.

MME MORNET They'll shoot him.

JEAN They won't shoot him. They just want to stop him from what he was doing. They've done that. I'm going back right away. I'm going to take Coupe-tête with me.

MME MORNET *(closes her eyes)* They'll shoot him. All Frenchmen who are young and brave have to die. I'm cold, Marthe. Cover me.

Marthe passes Jean, gives him another quick, defiant and fearful look, draws more covers up over Mme Mornet.

JEAN *(to Marthe)* Did you hear? I'm going to take Coupe-tête with me.

MARTHE Take him! Get him shot, too!

Jean turns away.

DISSOLVE TO:

EXT. CAR IN MOTION   CLOSE   JEAN AND COUPE-TÊTE

—in back seat. Jean is grave. Coupe-tête looks calmly about.

COUPE-TÊTE I didn't know France was this big. No wonder it can hold so many of them. At this rate, there will be at least one apiece for all of us, the women and children, too.

DISSOLVE TO:

INT. JEAN'S ROOM   PARIS   CLOSE   COUPE-TÊTE AT A CUPBOARD

It is a shelf, before which hangs a cloth curtain. Coupe-tête is holding the curtain aside with one hand. On the shelf are packages of food. Coupe-tête takes one down, holds it in his other hand while he examines it—a small tin labeled: TRUFFLES.

COUPE-TÊTE Aha. Encore.

INT. EMILIE'S ROOM   CLOSE   JEAN AND EMILIE

—standing beside sewing table and lamp. Doriot asleep in his chair before the fire.

JEAN I have come to ask you to marry me.

EMILIE Why? I think I know, but I want to hear you say it.

JEAN Why do men always ask it? I—

EMILIE No. That's the lie.

JEAN Then I offer all the lie itself could offer if it were truth: our land is ours, my mother is a widow and will welcome you, there's only my brother and me, and I am the older—

EMILIE —and I am a waif, homeless, without a country, a nobody, and dishonored. But I'm a woman, too. Don't you know I'd rather have had the lie than an offer of outright purchase?

JEAN Yes. I began wrong. And it's too late now. There's no time now to tell you the lie. There's not time now to make you believe it—

EMILIE Isn't there?

Jean stares at her, takes a step toward her. She watches him. He stops.

JEAN Is there time yet?

EMILIE We have so little to purchase with, by your standards. Yet we have all the world to need to buy—

Jean moves again, puts his arms around her. She stops him again, her hands against his chest, her head back, watching him.

JEAN I don't even know your name. Your father just calls you daughter—

EMILIE Emilie. So you are ready to tell the lie, even.

JEAN Maybe it won't be a lie. You will be honored, loved by more than—

EMILIE Wait. Tell me another lie first. One that I would rather hear right now than the first one, even. *(she stares at him)* For France.

They stare at one another.

JEAN No. I cannot. I—

EMILIE Your actions can say that Jean Mornet was wrong, but Jean Mornet himself cannot say it.

JEAN I am what I have been; I am now what I will always be.

EMILIE But you can say the first lie now.

JEAN Maybe it never was a lie. Maybe from that first afternoon when you dropped the potatoes—Maybe when all this is over, a dream, a nightmare, and this poor unhappy France—

EMILIE No land is poor while there are brave men in it. No land is unhappy which still can hope.

ANOTHER ANGLE   JEAN AND EMILIE

—apart, facing one another.

EMILIE Tomorrow morning, then. As soon as you have had me re-registered as your wife. I won't tell Father until afterward. He will believe the second lie has been told, too. Go now. Coupe-tête must be hungry.

JEAN   If he still is now, he is not Coupe-tête.

He takes her hand, begins to raise it toward his lips. Before he can stop her, she raises his hand, kisses it, releases it, steps back.

EMILIE   That was not for me, either.

                                     DISSOLVE TO:

INT. JEAN'S ROOM   CLOSE   COUPE-TÊTE

—sitting on the floor, a stool between his knees for a table, two or three small tins of jellies, caviar, etc., open on the stool, a wine bottle on the floor. He has a towel tied around his neck like a napkin protecting his Sunday coat. He holds a shaving mug of wine in his hand. His mouth is full as he looks up at Jean standing over him.

JEAN   I just remarked that if you were still hungry, I didn't know you. We will go back home tomorrow.

COUPE-TÊTE   Tomorrow? I have hardly seen France yet. I haven't seen Paris at all.

JEAN   Then both will have to wait. We are going tomorrow night to take my wife home.

Coupe-tête sets the mug carefully on the floor, swallows, wipes his mouth on the edge of the towel.

COUPE-TÊTE   Jean Mornet's wife.

JEAN   Yes. Jean Mornet and his wife.

Coupe-tête rises quickly and quietly, pauses, takes up the wine bottle, examines the remaining wine, raises it toward his mouth.

COUPE-TÊTE   Then perhaps we had better get some sleep.

                                       DISSOLVE TO:

INT. CAR   NIGHT   CLOSE   EMILIE AND GEORGES

—traveling fast. Emilie and Georges in back seat. Georges

wears Jean's clothes, has been drugged. He rouses. Emilie passes bottle of ether or whatever it is under his nose. He sleeps again.

WIPE TO:

EXT. MORNET HOUSE   NIGHT

The car stopped in front of Mornet house. Three shadowy men emerge, lift Georges out. Emilie speaks rapidly and efficiently to the German soldier driver in German. We distinguish the one word: PARIS.

DRIVER   Ja, Frau Mornet.

The car exits. The group turns toward the house, carrying Georges.

INT. MORNET KITCHEN

—shades drawn, etc. Mme Mornet, Marthe, Catherine, as Emilie and Coupe-tête, Guezonnec, two others, enter, carrying Georges.

CATHERINE   Georges!

COUPE-TÊTE   *(panting)* Save it. *(to the men)* Over here.

CLOSE GROUP

Georges in chair.

EMILIE   *(to Catherine, harshly)* You're Catherine. He's just drugged. He's all right.

MME MORNET   Jean. Where is—

Her voice dies; she stares at Emilie.

EMILIE   *(to Mme Mornet, gentler)* You're his mother.

She approaches Mme Mornet, pauses, moves again, takes Mme Mornet's hand, kisses it.

EMILIE   He is where he would be. He has saved his soul, even if he won't admit it. *(she turns to Catherine again)* He's in that cell. Where would he be? How else would your husband be there in that chair? Didn't you realize that as soon as you saw him? His mother did.

CATHERINE   You lie. Georges didn't—

EMILIE   Don't worry. That's why he's drugged. He wouldn't have left that cell either, otherwise. But he can't stay here. Maybe they have already found out which one they have—

COUPE-TÊTE   And never a truer word. We are only waiting for His Reverence and the cart.

INT. COMMANDANT'S OFFICE, MAIRIE   CLOSE

Priest at desk, the young spectacled precise German lieutenant behind it. The lieutenant examines a paper.

LIEUTENANT   Permission to bury _____ Quinnoneaux, called "The Flea"—*(he looks up)* That's that idiot.

PRIEST   They can die, too. Perhaps they have souls, too.

LIEUTENANT   He will not know it, dead.

He signs the pass.

EXT. STREET   NIGHT

The Mornet cart moving along street. Priest and another man on seat, a cheap coffin in the cart.

EXT. MORNET FARMYARD   NIGHT

The cart halted inside the Mornet farmyard. Coupe-tête and the others open the coffin, help the idiot out. He is young, timorous, uncoordinated, clumsy. They lift Georges into the coffin, close the lid. The cart drives away, leaving priest, Coupe-tête, the idiot.

IDIOT   Did I do all right, Father? I wish to save Brittany, but I don't wish to die.

PRIEST   You did well. You will not die. Go with Coupe-tête and sleep.

The idiot kneels, the priest blesses him.

COUPE-TÊTE   *(to idiot)* Come, then, since you have saved Brittany.

Coupe-tête turns away. The idiot follows. Coupe-tête pauses, turns back to look at the priest.

    COUPE-TÊTE   Bless yourself, Father, if you can.

He and the idiot go on.

DISSOLVE TO:

EXT. ROAD   NIGHT

The cart halted by two German sentries with flashlights. They look into the cart. The driver hands down the pass. The German holds his light on it, hands the pass back to the driver, steps aside.

    SOLDIER   Pass on. To Quimper. With the body of Quinnoneaux, called "The Flea." Pass on.

DISSOLVE TO:

EXT.   DAWN   CLOSE   EMPTY COFFIN

—hidden in bushes.

DISSOLVE TO:

INT. COMMANDANT'S OFFICE

The German captain and the small lieutenant at desk, the priest before the desk, the idiot being held between two German soldiers, trembling and frightened.

    IDIOT   *(to priest)* Father! You promised me—

    PRIEST   Peace, son. You have done your duty. You will not suffer.

    LIEUTENANT   Yes, he has done his duty. That was all we wanted.

He speaks in German to the soldiers. They release the idiot. The idiot watches the priest.

    PRIEST   *(to idiot)* Go. You will not be harmed.

The idiot scuttles out. The lieutenant rises, barks an order in German to the soldiers. They fall in on either side of the priest. The lieutenant barks another order. The soldiers wheel stiffly to advance, the priest between them. The lieutenant barks another order. The soldiers and the priest begin to march. The priest's face is quite calm.

EXT. THE SQUARE

The whole village has gathered. The faces are grim, tense. A file of soldiers enters, the priest among them. A repressed sound goes up from the people, stops. The priest is marched into position against a wall. The soldiers leave him.

MED. CLOSE   PRIEST

Soldiers in b.g. The German captain in b.g.; the lieutenant in f.g. with paper.

> **LIEUTENANT** For assisting in the escape of the condemned French traitor and prisoner, Mornet, Guillaume Riom, Priest, is hereby sentenced to execution. Signed: _____, Commissioner of Police, Paris.

He folds paper, turns stiffly, approaches the priest. The repressed sound comes again from the people.

CLOSE   PRIEST AND LIEUTENANT   CAPTAIN IN B.G.

The captain gives an order in German. The soldiers half-present their rifles. The sound from the people ceases. The captain speaks in German to the lieutenant. The lieutenant answers, turns to the priest.

> **LIEUTENANT** *(watches priest's face)* You have German, eh?

> **PRIEST** Yes. The captain told you to beware. I tell you that also: Beware!

> **LIEUTENANT** Of what? Of sheep? We could have used you. For your advantage and that of these cattle, too, with whom you threaten us. We already have a better hostage for this Mornet in Paris now. But we do not want a hostage. We want Mornet. And he will return and we will get him. I was given this authority.

He takes out the paper, tears it and drops it. The scraps float toward the priest, who draws his gown aside as if to keep them from touching him. The lieutenant watches.

LIEUTENANT   So—*(he stares at the priest)* So.

He jerks his hand up suddenly. The captain speaks sharply in German. The lieutenant pays no attention.

LIEUTENANT   *(to the priest)* Heil Hitler!

PRIEST   I will tell you what one of your own priests once told your fuehrer: "God, not you, is my leader."

The lieutenant jerks out his pistol. Another sound from the watching people. The captain moves, speaks again in German.

LIEUTENANT   *(glares at priest)* Heil Hitler!

The priest spits in the German's face. The lieutenant shoots him. The priest falls. A sound from the people. The captain speaks sharp and loud; the soldiers aim rifles.

REVERSE ANGLE

The villagers, paused, the faces grim, threatening, unafraid.

                                        DISSOLVE TO:

EXT. BRETON COAST

—favoring the sea. A small sailboat standing away from the coast, bound for England.

                                        FADE OUT.

FADE IN

TITLE: July 14, 1942.

                                        DISSOLVE TO:

ARC DE TRIOMPHE, PARIS

An aeroplane bearing the cross of Lorraine. [Nungesser[9] flew a Spad through the arch in '20-'22, etc. I don't know whether the British F/Lt. took a Beaufighter through or not.]

                                        DISSOLVE TO:

9. Charles Nungesser (1892–1927) was a French flying ace during World War I.

CLOSE SHOT   JEANNENEY AND HERRIOT

A voice over scene reads the joint letter they wrote to the Vichy parliament.

> VOICE   . . . that liberty should ever perish from the land where it was born and spread to all the world . . .

DISSOLVE TO:

MAP OF FRENCH CHANNEL COAST

PAN TO:

A TOWN ON COAST

[Research for this by date.]

DISSOLVE THRU TO:

EXT.   CLOSE   COUPE-TÊTE   NIGHT

—gunfire, searchlights, etc. Coupe-tête crouching behind a corner as Commando men run past. Each time a group passes, Coupe-tête shouts.

> COUPE-TÊTE   Mornet! Georges Mornet!

The men run on. Coupe-tête looks after them. Another burst of firing comes. He crouches, peering out. Three men run past. Coupe-tête steps out to intercept them.

> COUPE-TÊTE   Georges Mornet! Est-ce que vous avez vu—

> SOLDIER   (in English) Get out of here, old man!

The three British soldiers run. Coupe-tête follows.

CLOSE

A German soldier whirls, tries to raise rifle. Three men fling themselves on him. All go down. A grenade bursts. After the flash, the soldier lies dead, Coupe-tête beside him, the three British soldiers bending over them. Coupe-tête opens his eyes. Another grenade bursts. The three men snatch Coupe-tête up, exit.

BEACH   CLOSE   COUPE-TÊTE   DAWN

Fire in b.g., shots, etc. Coupe-tête lying on beach, landing barges in b.g.; commandos with blackened faces enter, firing backward toward land. Several men bending over Coupe-tête. A British officer pours brandy from a flask into his mouth. Coupe-tête opens his eyes, takes the flask in his own hand, is about to drink again, pauses.

REVERSE ANGLE

Coupe-tête looking up at Georges. Georges's face is blackened, smudged with sweat, etc.

> **COUPE-TÊTE** It's a boy.

> **GEORGES** What?

> **COUPE-TÊTE** Your son. What else do you think I am doing here? Bah! They will never beat us, so long as Frenchmen continue to replace themselves after one visit home.

> **GEORGES** None of us had better be here long.

> **COUPE-TÊTE** Go then.

Georges looks quickly about, points, rises. Four men pick Coupe-tête up.

CLOSE BEHIND A HUMMOCK

The men put Coupe-tête down.

> **COUPE-TÊTE** Now a grenade—pistol—something.

> **GEORGES** What will you do with a grenade or a pistol?

> **COUPE-TÊTE** What did I do with them in 1914?

Georges gives him a grenade. The men exit. Coupe-tête crouches in his hole, listening. Sounds off scene. He turns over, grimacing, raises his head, peers out, pulls pin of grenade, throws it, ducks back. The explosion comes—a burst of machine gun fire. Coupe-tête raises his head cautiously, peers out.

A PARTY OF GERMAN SOLDIERS ON BEACH   COUPE-TÊTE'S ANGLE

—looking this way and that. They decide on a direction, exit.

CLOSE   COUPE-TÊTE

He sinks back in his hole. His hand fumbles at his pocket. He takes out the officer's flask, makes himself comfortable, drinks.

DISSOLVE TO:

MONTAGE

Titles: SEPTEMBER OCTOBER NOVEMBER

—DISSOLVING one into another to:

1943

DISSOLVE TO:

INT. THE RUINED TOWER-CAVE NIGHT

Coupe-tête and all the other faces which we know, and many more until the cave is crowded. Guezonnec is the leader.

> **GUEZONNEC**   They will tell us when. The word will come. Then we must light beacons for them—beacons to lead them.

> **A MAN**   We have no beacons.

> **GUEZONNEC**   Yes. We have. We have—

DISSOLVE TO:

FULL SHOT AERODROME RUNWAY ENGLAND TWILIGHT

Bombers are taking off, one after another.

INT. OPERATIONS OFFICE A SQUADRON OF FRENCH PILOTS

De Gaulle and Georges and squadron commander, adjutant, etc., about loudspeaker.

> **RADIO**   Badger to Corridor. Over.

> **RADIO**   Corridor to Badger. Good hunting. Over.

> **COMMANDANT**   They are leaving the coast now. Soon they will be over France—

> **GEORGES**   Over Germany, sir.

> **COMMANDANT**   Yes. Over Germany. But not forever.

> **GEORGES**   Not for long.

COMMANDANT Yes. Not for long.

INT. MORNET KITCHEN

Coupe-tête peering out window. Marthe, Mme Mornet, and
Emilie knotting bundles of what they can carry. Catherine holding the child. All are dressed to leave the house. A faint distant
light appears beyond the window. Coupe-tête turns quickly.
Emilie stops, glances up at him.

COUPE-TÊTE Yes. It is time.

He hurries out. Emilie follows. The others gather up bundles
and exit.

EXT. STABLE   CLOSE   COUPE-TÊTE AND EMILIE   NIGHT

—as they set fire to the stable, hay, etc.

CLOSE   MME MORNET, CATHERINE WITH CHILD, MARTHE

—with bundles, favoring stable as it begins to blaze. Emile and
Coupe-tête enter and Coupe-tête takes some of the bundles.
They exit. Other faint fires begin to spring up, shouts, shots in
distance.

CLOSE   GROUP

—all on a hill, favoring the countryside, fires blazing about it,
faint shouts, shots.

COUPE-TÊTE Who said there would not be beacons?

INT. COCKPIT OF A BOMBER IN FLIGHT OVER FRANCE

The dark countryside is spotted with fires. Others spring up as
the pilot speaks into mike.

PILOT *(into mike)* Fires. They are springing up everywhere.

INT. SQUADRON OPERATION OFFICE

De Gaulle and others at loudspeaker.

RADIO They are lighting the way for us.

CLOSE   LETTERS ON A WALL

—name of a factory making German munitions. Air raid sirens begin, A.A. fire, etc.

DISSOLVE THRU TO:

INT. FACTORY CLOSE JEAN

—favoring a long interior, half-finished guns, etc.; as the French workers pause, an alarm bell ringing, sirens from outside, gunfire coming nearer as the raiders approach, the faces showing exultation. German soldier-guards excited, alarmed. Jean begins to sing the Marseillaise. Other voices take it up. The bombs begin, more voices singing.

OPERATIONS OFFICE

De Gaulle, Georges, others listening to the radio.

RADIO More of them! More of them! You can almost hear them, like voices singing! All Europe is blazing, blazing . . .

FADE OUT.

THE END

V

The De Gaulle Story
Revised Screenplay

FADE IN

CLOSE SHOT   SIGN IN A HOUSE WINDOW

The sign has a faintly homemade look:

> CARNOT
> Notary

DRAW BACK TO:

EXT. FRONT OF A COTTAGE   FULL SHOT

—sign in the window, a narrow stoop and a goose sitting on the stoop as a woman about fifty, fat, her head tied up in a cloth, wearing an apron and sabots, comes around the house carrying a broom. She waves the broom at the goose, shouts—

WOMAN   Get out of here! Scat!

The goose leaps off the stoop, half flying, exits. The woman sweeps the stoop off, shakes the broom after the goose, turns and goes back around the house. DISSOLVE through wall to:

INT. PARLOR-OFFICE   CLOSE   CARNOT

—seated at table, papers spread before him, holding a paper in his hands and reading from it. He is about fifty, small, wry, with a Voltairean-lawyer face. He wears a black frock coat, glasses on a black ribbon. Opposite him sits another notary, also in a black frock coat, glasses with black ribbon. He is about the same age but fat, sits listening and staring profoundly out of scene.

In b.g. Mme Mornet, the mayor and Senator Coudron sit in chairs, listening quietly. Mme Mornet is sixty, has a firm, intelligent face, is dressed in well-to-do middle-class widow's street clothes, hat, etc. The mayor wears a frock coat, is pompous, principal man in the village, etc., but at the moment is a little

213

overshadowed by the senator, the big man, who is the mayor raised to nth power.

> **CARNOT**   (*reads from paper*) [Will ask M. Berger for general wording, etc., of the contract of marriage between Georges Mornet and Catherine Guerlon; Carnot reads the legal preamble, says:]
> Item—

EXT. HOUSE   CLOSE   GOOSE

—standing beside house, beneath an open window. Through the window Carnot's voice can be heard as he enumerates the silver: spoons, bowls, platters, etc.

> **CARNOT**   Item—

His voice enumerates the linen, napkins, cloths, etc., finishes the contract.

> **CARNOT**   This day Anno Domini __th May, 1940. [The day before Holland was invaded]

INT. PARLOR-OFFICE   FULL GROUP

—as Carnot lays the paper on desk, looks up.

> **CARNOT**   Ladies and gentlemen?

> **MAYOR**   (*to Mme Mornet*) You are to give the silver, I, the linen.

> **MME MORNET**   Yes.

> **SENATOR**   By mutual agreement: so stated.

> **MAYOR**   It was described as *new* linen.

> **SENATOR**   Silver improves with use.

> **SECOND NOTARY**   If the Senator can call becoming lighter in weight each infinitesimal time a morsel of food is cut, an improvement.

> **CARNOT**   The same thing happens to a napkin each time it is thrust into a shirt collar.

> **SECOND NOTARY**   But the depreciation is only half. Ladies don't have shirt collars.

CARNOT But they all eat.

SECOND NOTARY Good. Then how better enhance Madame's awareness of her own generosity and affection than the knowledge that each bite of food in her son's house has precious metal in its sauce?

CARNOT It'll all belong to the children, anyway. *(looks about)* Well, ladies and gentlemen?

SENATOR Come, then.

He rises, claps the mayor on the shoulder.

SENATOR It will belong to the children. Let it be new linen then.

All watch the mayor. He shrugs, rises, all rise.

MAYOR *(to Mme Mornet)* Let it be so, then.

He and Mme Mornet shake hands.

EXT. FRONT DOOR   GROUP

As Mme Mornet, mayor and the senator emerge from the door, the goose is just flapping frantically off the stoop again, Mme Carnot, the fat woman, just coming around the house with the broom, shaking the broom at the goose.

MME CARNOT Will you scat out of here? Get! *(to the others)* Good morning, Madame—Senator—Your Honor. *(to Mme Mornet)* It's arranged, then?

MME MORNET Yes. At three this afternoon. You will be there.

MME CARNOT This afternoon? I had hoped it would be either tomorrow, or Monday. Then Carnot could make one shirt do for Sunday, too.

SENATOR Bah, Madame. The Notary Carnot can certainly have a fresh shirt for a wedding.

MME CARNOT Yes, Senator—provided the Notary Carnot's wife launders it for him. Till this afternoon, then.

They go on. When they exit, the goose is revealed at the corner of the house, waiting to return to the stoop. Mme Carnot flings the broom at it.

    MME CARNOT Scat! Are you the cousin of a senator or the daughter of a mayor, too, perhaps, to spend the whole morning listening to talk?

DISSOLVE TO:

INT. PARLOR, MORNET HOUSE   CLOSE   COUPE-TÊTE

—on hands and knees, waxing floor. He wears smock, is in stocking feet. He is a peasant, about sixty, tough, crabbed, bibulous, saturnine and shrewd. He farms the Mornet land while the sons are absent, or probably since Mornet's death and his widow's takeover.

DRAW BACK TO:

MED. FULL   ROOM

Coupe-tête on floor, Marthe at table, wiping silver, etc. The room is being decorated for the ceremony of signing the wedding contract. Marthe is Coupe-tête's wife, sixty, a peasant, too, in cap and apron and carpet slippers. She cooks for the Mornets, is half servant, half companion, independent yet faithful to the family.

    COUPE-TÊTE Friday. Saturday. Sunday. Monday. Then the wedding. Then they will return to the war again. Then you can wax the floors again.

    MARTHE *I* can?

    COUPE-TÊTE Yes. You. I'll be planting corn then. Or something of more value than rubbing wax on a plank.

    MARTHE At neither of which you will ever hurt yourself. Well, it will be over soon, and Georges can come back home where he belongs and help you. Perhaps the two of you together can do the work of one industrious man.

    COUPE-TÊTE Hah. What Georges should be planting after next Tuesday, he should need no help at. If he does, then Catherine—

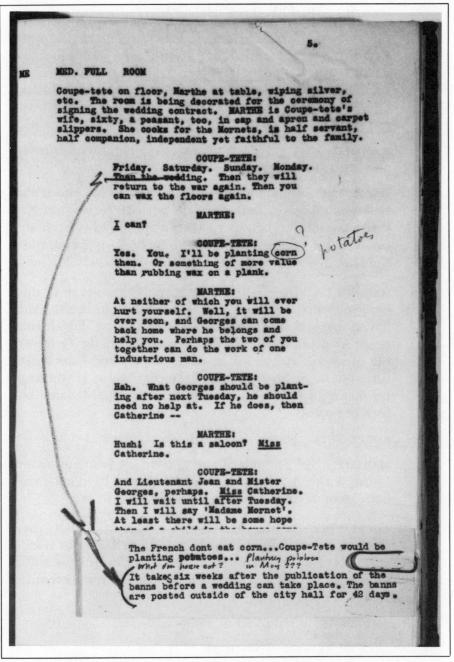

5.

ME   MED. FULL ROOM

Coupe-tete on floor, Marthe at table, wiping silver,
etc. The room is being decorated for the ceremony of
signing the wedding contract. MARTHE is Coupe-tete's
wife, sixty, a peasant, too, in cap and apron and carpet
slippers. She cooks for the Mornets, is half servant,
half companion, independent yet faithful to the family.

                    COUPE-TETE:
          Friday. Saturday. Sunday. Monday.
          Then the wedding. Then they will
          return to the war again. Then you
          can wax the floors again.

                    MARTHE:
          I can?

                    COUPE-TETE:
          Yes. You. I'll be planting corn
          then. Or something of more value
          than rubbing wax on a plank.

                    MARTHE:
          At neither of which you will ever
          hurt yourself. Well, it will be
          over soon, and Georges can come
          back home where he belongs and
          help you. Perhaps the two of you
          together can do the work of one
          industrious man.

                    COUPE-TETE:
          Hah. What Georges should be plant-
          ing after next Tuesday, he should
          need no help at. If he does, then
          Catherine --

                    MARTHE:
          Hush! Is this a saloon? Miss
          Catherine.

                    COUPE-TETE:
          And Lieutenant Jean and Mister
          Georges, perhaps. Miss Catherine.
          I will wait until after Tuesday.
          Then I will say 'Madame Mornet'.
          At least there will be some hope

          The French dont eat corn...Coupe-Tete would be
          planting pebatoes... *Planting potatoes*
          What dm house eat?   in May ???
          It takes six weeks after the publication of the
          banns before a wedding can take place. The banns
          are posted outside of the city hall for 42 days.

13. Page from copy of "The De Gaulle Story" containing Robert Buckner's
notations regarding revision and filming (note the Faulkner rejoinder on
this page)

MARTHE   Hush! Is this a saloon? *Miss* Catherine.

COUPE-TÊTE   And Lieutenant Jean and Mister Georges, perhaps. *Miss* Catherine. I will wait until after Tuesday. Then I will say "Madame Mornet." At least there will be some hope then of a child in the house someday, which is more than Mister Georges's brother, the Lieutenant Jean, can say.

MARTHE   Jean will marry an admiral's daughter. It's probably already arranged.

COUPE-TÊTE   When? When he has become old enough to be his children's grandfather? Or perhaps he is waiting to find an admiral's daughter who can and will wax his floors for him. He will be old enough to be his own grandfather then.

MARTHE   And you will still be alive, because even in that time you will have done nothing to injure your health. And if you are still alive, you will still be talking. Finish that floor. At three this afternoon not only Senator Coudron but the whole village will be here, not to witness the signatures but to see how Madame keeps her house. If you have no shame of your own, at least don't shame Madame before her cousin.

COUPE-TÊTE   Senator Coudron is a politician. I doubt—

MARTHE   Yes! Enough of one to have got Jean appointed to the Naval Academy. Enough of one to have got them both leave to come home so Georges could marry.

COUPE-TÊTE   It was not Senator Coudron that gave Georges permission to come home. It was a piece of Boche shrapnel. But whether or no, Senator Coudron is still a politician. I doubt if a politician could even recognize shame, let alone feel it—

He stops, looks up out of scene.

ANOTHER ANGLE   FAVORING DOOR

Mme Mornet stands in the door.

MME MORNET   *(to Marthe)* What makes you think it will be over soon?

MARTHE   The Boche has gone South, then East, and now North. There is only the West left, and on the West is our Maginot Line, that cost us three thousand francs.

COUPE-TÊTE   Three thousand francs! That might pay for the flags on it. It cost five hundred billion.

MARTHE   *(pauses)* Five hundred billion? For a fort? We could have bribed all Europe to leave us alone for five hundred billion francs.

COUPE-TÊTE   Five hundred billion francs is no longer a bribe among politicians. It is just a test, to see if the bribe is really vulnerable—

MME MORNET   *(enters)* Hush. *(to Marthe)* Where are Jean and Georges?

MARTHE   At the cafe.

COUPE-TÊTE   Hah. If Georges is at the cafe now, perhaps he will need help—

MARTHE   But not from you, or his affairs will be in no better shape than that floor is. Didn't you hear Madame? Or can you hear nothing but your own clacking?

                                                        DISSOLVE TO:

EXT. SMALL GARDEN   CLOSE   GEORGES AND CATHERINE

A small garden, middle-class but well-to-do. Flowers, small sundial, terra-cotta fauns, statuary, etc., an arbor. Georges is twenty-five, merry, carefree, in careless countrified civilian clothes, farm clothes, almost. Catherine is about twenty, dressed as the mayor's daughter in a small Breton town or village would dress.

They are kissing. Catherine breaks, pushes herself back. Georges still holds her. Catherine is disturbed a little. Georges begins to draw her face up again. She resists.

CATHERINE   No. No.

GEORGES   Yes. Yes.

CATHERINE   We should wait until after the papers are signed this afternoon and the banns are called tomorrow.

GEORGES   All right. I'm waiting. I came all the way from the front to wait.

He draws her face up. She struggles. He stops, hold her.

GEORGES   You are the berries in my pie.

CATHERINE   What is pie?

GEORGES   That's what they say in America. It's tart. Only you're not tart. Yes, you are. You're tart and sweet both.

He draws her face up. She resists. He kisses her. She stops resisting for a moment, then breaks free.

CATHERINE   Let me go. Let me go.

She breaks away, except her hands. He still holds them. He is disturbed, too.

GEORGES   You're wrong about just the papers and the banns, too. We'd better wait until after Wednesday.

CATHERINE   We're going to.

She wrenches her hands free, turns, beginning to run.

CATHERINE   Go now. Go on.

She runs out. Georges looks after her, turns to exit.

DISSOLVE TO:

INT. CAFE   CLOSE AT BAR

Jean at bar, patron behind it, five or six villagers, older men, gathered deferentially about Jean. He is thirty-five, wears a city civilian suit, looks like a city man, but with the navy stamp on him, the professional, career military man. He is cold as compared to Georges, reserved. He and the others all hold glasses.

PATRON   (*raises his glass*) Gentlemen.

The others raise their glasses. Jean follows suit. We can see that he does it merely out of courtesy, that he feels he no longer has much in common with these people save the geography of his birthplace, home, etc.

PATRON It will be a land victory, as in 1914. But this time, Gamelin will whip them in a month. Thus the gentlemen of the navy, like the Lieutenant here, will have been robbed of glory, not alone by their own strength but by that of the army, too. So we will drink not to glory, but to the peace which will follow: that peace which is today being exemplified here in Saint Odile by a marriage contract between two of our first families—that family whose chief is Lieutenant Mornet and which is honored by the kinship and patronage, too, of Senator Coudron, and that family whose head is His Honor the Mayor himself—

The patron pauses, looks out of scene. The others turn heads.

CLOSE GROUP

—favoring door as Georges enters, approaches.

PATRON *(to Georges)* In a moment. You are only the bridegroom. Your time will come later. *(raises glass again)* To the families Mornet and Guerlon.

A MAN And Senator Coudron.

PATRON Certainly. Senator Coudron.

All drink. Jean sets his glass on bar, starts to turn.

JEAN Thanks, gentlemen.

MAN The honor is ours, Lieutenant.

PATRON The honor is Saint Odile's. In the last analysis, what are Lieutenant Mornet and Senator Coudron, either, but citizens also? Eh, Lieutenant?

JEAN Yes. Thanks again.

CLOSE JEAN

—pauses as he passes Georges.

JEAN Coming home now?

He goes on without waiting for an answer. Georges follows.

EXT. STREET BEFORE CAFE   CLOSE

—as Jean emerges, Georges following.

>   GEORGES   I'm not coming home now. (*Jean pauses, looks back*) As Carnac said, I'm just the bridegroom. Nobody wants me around until next Wednesday.

>   JEAN   Uncle Coudron will expect you. He's going back to Rennes after the contract is signed.

Jean turns, walks again toward Camera. Georges watches him, moves.

>   GEORGES   All right . . . admiral.

>   JEAN   (*pauses*) What?

>   GEORGES   Nothing.

Jean turns on, Georges follows toward Camera.

>   WIPE TO:

INT. JEAN AND GEORGES'S BEDROOM   MED. CLOSE

It contains a single big, old-fashioned bed. Jean and Georges are dressing in their uniforms, Georges at mirror, knotting his tie, Jean watching him. Georges accidentally knocks over the chair on which Jean's uniform coat hangs, catches it before it falls, sets it up again, brushes off the coat with exaggerated care, clowning a little; becomes sober again, watching Jean in mirror.

>   GEORGES   Thanks, anyway.

>   JEAN   For what?

>   GEORGES   For not wearing that uniform for a while, at least. At least for a while I don't have to salute and say "sir."

>   JEAN   I thought we settled that last night—at least until after your wedding.

>   GEORGES   Uncle Coudron settled it fourteen years ago, on the day he got you appointed to the naval academy. No. It was settled three years ago when I got drafted.

JEAN And you will have to keep on saying "sir" to uniforms for a while longer yet, until France is out of danger.

GEORGES Yes. And I still won't like it.

JEAN Why?

GEORGES I'm in love.

Jean turns and looks at Georges a moment. Georges's face is grave, too.

JEAN So you will let someone else, anyone else, defend the security in which you can spend your time being in love.

GEORGES No. I'll defend it. Thank God there are a lot more young men in France and Europe who don't want to say "sir" or "heil" to a uniform, but who want to be in love. Because peace will have to come from them—not from the professional soldiers. Men with aptitude and skill win the brilliant victories, but it's men like me, young enough to have reason enough to hate war enough, who will finally put an end to warfare.

JEAN So you think. Without any proof in history.

GEORGES There has been proof in history, implied in the fact that at one time all men are young and want to love in peace and leave peace after them for their children to love in. Only, each time they have been betrayed, by the false reasoning of old men whose hearts are dead.

JEAN Who, according to you, were at one time themselves young men who wanted only to love in peace. What changed them?

GEORGES They were betrayed in their turn.

JEAN As these young men whom you represent will be.

GEORGES But each time, there are fewer of them.

JEAN There still seems to be enough.

GEORGES Yes. But in 1918 they had destroyed so many

young men that they were aghast. This time, before this is over, they will have destroyed so many that even they will be afraid.

Jean stares at Georges a moment. He turns toward the chair where his coat hangs.

JEAN   I hope all that is some comfort to you.

GEORGES   To more than just me.

He turns as Jean reaches the chair and prepares to take up the coat. Georges takes up the coat first, holds it for Jean to put it on. Jean pauses, looks at Georges.

GEORGES   You are still the head of the family, even if you are an officer.

JEAN   Thanks.

He puts the coat on while Georges holds it.

WIPE TO:

INT. PARLOR   FULL SHOT

The two notaries and their clerks are at the signing table with the papers. They look like four undertakers. The refreshment table is set with wine, decanters, glasses, plates of cakes, etc. The relations of the two families sit in chairs along the wall, dressed in their best.

CLOSE GROUP

Mme Mornet and the senator seated on a sofa, mayor in a chair beside the sofa. Mme Mornet wears her best dress, black silk, lace at cuffs, etc. The senator and mayor are dressed as before. Behind them in b.g. is the legal table, the fat notary seated at it, his clerk and Carnot's clerk, also in best clothes, standing. Carnot has just approached the sofa from behind. Jean, in uniform, stands beside the sofa.

CARNOT   Madame. Your Honor.

They rise.

SENATOR   (to Jean) Your arm to your mother, sir. I will attend the mayor.

Jean offers Mme Mornet his arm. They approach the legal table, mayor and senator following.

CLOSE GROUP AT TABLE

The contract is signed and witnessed.

DISSOLVE TO:

INT. KITCHEN

Marthe, in fresh cap and apron, with tray, stops and stares at Georges. He sits with his uniform coat off at the table, eating with his hands, his mouth full as he talks, Marthe staring at him with cold disapproval.

> **GEORGES** *(mouth full)* So someone missed me in there, after all.

> **MARTHE** You?

> **GEORGES** Oh. I thought maybe you had come to bring me a glass of wine.

> **MARTHE** Wine? You?

She starts out, pauses, turns, crosses rapidly to cupboard, takes out a crude pitcher, sets it on table before Georges, turns to exit.

> **GEORGES** What's that?

> **MARTHE** Cider.

She exits. Georges looks after her, turns and takes up the pitcher, shrugs, drinks from it.

WIPE TO:

INT. DINING ROOM GROUP SHOT

All at table with wine glasses. The senator holds his glass up.

> **SENATOR** . . . that, threatened by assassins and paranoiacs, we can still find not only the inclination but the security, too, in which to form an alliance between two families which exemplify all that is most durable and solid in France and the French people—

DISSOLVE TO:

EXT. FRONT OF MAYOR'S HOUSE   FULL SHOT   EVENING

—as Jean enters scene, walking stiffly erect in his uniform, and approaches door and knocks. The door opens, a servant appears.

WIPE TO:

INT. PARLOR   CLOSE   JEAN AND CATHERINE

—something like the Mornet parlor: solid, well-to-do, yet provincial.

CATHERINE   Lieutenant. . . .

JEAN   I was Jean once, as I remember.

CATHERINE   I was a child then.

JEAN   But I am still Jean. More so than ever now. In our father's place, I welcome into our family my brother's wife.

DISSOLVE TO:

INT. KITCHEN   CLOSE GROUP   EVENING

Jean, Georges, Mme Mornet at supper; Coupe-tête in a chair in b.g., Marthe moving back and forth as she serves them. They have just finished.

COUPE-TÊTE   So we drank the wine. We signed the papers. At last Catherine—

MARTHE   *Miss* Catherine.

COUPE-TÊTE   Miss Catherine. Yesterday she wore diapers. Someone changed them, too.

MARTHE   Hush!

GEORGES   Not you, though.

MARTHE   Hush! For shame! Is this what the army taught you?

GEORGES   It taught the English something about such facts, too. They have a song about it. (*sings, loud, off-key*) We'll hang our washing on the Siegfried Line—(*he rises; to*

Mme Mornet) We're going to the cafe for a while. We won't
be late.

DISSOLVE TO:

INT. CAFE   BAR IN B.G.

Proprietor and his wife behind the bar, a few men at the bar,
tables about, men sitting at tables, drinking and smoking. In
f.g. and in principal place is a table with a card game in progress. At this table sits the mayor. His opponent is another oldish
man, prosperous looking also. A few men watch the game,
respectfully; these are the village big-wigs, playing, two or three
other important ones sitting in chairs to watch.

CLOSE   AT TABLE

—as Jean and Georges approach it. The mayor looks up, card
poised to play in his hand.

> **MAYOR** *(to Georges)* Not on duty tonight, eh? Well, this is
> no time for a soldier to be dangling around a petticoat or in
> a cafe either.

> **JEAN** Maybe a wife will give him more incentive to fight.

> **MAYOR** He shouldn't need any more. The example of his
> forefathers should be enough. But then, you might as well
> be here as at the front. Squatting in a concrete trench, bah!
> Attack! Attack! *(he turns back to the table)* Stand aside, will
> you? You are in the light.

Jean and Georges move away.

CLOSE AT BAR

Georges, another young soldier, three older civilians, the patron facing them behind the bar, waiting for the order.

> **GEORGES** Can we choose it, too? *(the patron watches him)*
> Isn't this one on the house?

The patron shrugs, sets out bottle and glasses, begins to fill
them.

> **SOLDIER** *(to Georges)* I thought you'd be buying drinks
> today.

GEORGES   No. Not until Tuesday.

PATRON   And maybe not then, eh?

FIRST MAN   Any wife is worth a drink.

SECOND MAN   Yes. One.

GEORGES   I am here to be married: not to discuss it.

SOLDIER   Discussing marriage is better than discussing war, though.

SECOND MAN   Did you expect to discuss war here?

SOLDIER   Why not? We spend our time in the lines talking about home: why shouldn't we expect to spend convalescent leave talking about the war?

GEORGES   That's right. I expected to have to give a complete résumé of the general staff's whole strategy by this time.

A NEW VOICE   Which could be put into a nutshell.

ANOTHER ANGLE

—favoring two more men seated at a table. One has just spoken.

SOLDIER   A nutshell?

MAN AT TABLE   Yes. Squat.

GEORGES   Not a nutshell. At least a nutshell has to be cracked.

FIRST MAN   *(to Georges)* Just what do you mean by that?

SECOND MAN   That the Boche hasn't anything to crack our line with, just as we haven't anything to crack his.

MAN AT TABLE   And that we'll squat behind it until it rots and falls down. And then run the Boche back to where he came from by making faces at him.

GEORGES   And what would you do?

SOLDIER   Here, here. I thought we didn't have to discuss the war.

GEORGES   Who is? If anybody is talking about the Maginot Line? Who ever called that war?

SECOND MAN   Do you really believe that the Germans or anybody else can break the Maginot Line?

GEORGES   I don't know. I don't imagine they know either. Or care.

MED. FULL   FAVORING BAR

Two or three tables, men at them listening.

GEORGES   They won't have to crack it. They will go around it. Colonel De Gaulle says so. He said it in a book, told exactly how to do it—

CLOSE   GEORGES AND OTHERS AT BAR

Georges has turned, his elbows on the bar, relaxed and easy.

FIRST MAN   And just who is this Colonel De Gaulle?

GEORGES   He commanded the tank school. Where I was trained. He told how to do it in a book three years ago. But the generals didn't like it. So they sent him to Syria, where the noise wouldn't disturb them. He's back in France now. They needed him bad enough to send for him. But not bad enough to listen to him. That will have to wait until later.

FIRST MAN   When will that be?

GEORGES   When we wake up one morning and find out that, as far as keeping an enemy out of France, the Maginot Line might just as well be soap—

A loud crash off scene.

FULL SHOT

Mayor standing beside his overturned chair, facing Georges across the room, others all watching.

MAYOR   Soap? The Maginot Line that took five hundred billion francs out of the pockets of every man, woman and child in France? That has held the enemy out of France for eight months, while Poland and all Scandanavia fell? Soap?

GEORGES   Yes, sir. Better if it was soap. Because then our troops and the Germans, too, could—

Jean enters quickly, takes Georges's arm.

JEAN   Hush, now. Come on.

CLOSE   JEAN AND GEORGES

—face mayor, others gather about them.

GEORGES   I don't know what it was I did or said, but I'll apologize for it. But I won't apologize for anything Colonel De Gaulle said, or for supporting what he said. Because what he said is true—

JEAN   Hush, I tell you! *(to mayor)* I'll take him on home—

A VOICE IN B.G.   Sssssssssst.

All pause. The mayor turns, looks off scene.

MAYOR'S ANGLE   SOLDIER

MAYOR   Did you do that?

SOLDIER   Why not?

MAYOR   Do you call the Maginot Line soap, too?

ANOTHER VOICE   Sssssssssst.

MAYOR   *(turns his head slowly)* Will that gentleman come forward?

The man who was sitting at the table comes forward, stares defiantly at mayor. Others all watch.

MAYOR   Mr. Kereon. Perhaps you call the Maginot Line soap?

KEREON   And fatheads, those who keep our army sitting inactive behind it. The best army in Europe. If we just had generals—

MAYOR   Generals? Gamelin! Weygand! Pétain, who beat them at Verdun—

A MAN BEHIND THE MAYOR   Bah!

The mayor turns, looks at the man.

MAYOR Did you speak, sir?

MAN Yes. Bah!

MAYOR Bah!

ANOTHER ANGLE

—favoring a carter, a big man, slightly drunk.

CARTER Pétain didn't beat them at Verdun! We did. I was there. The French soldier beat them. The unknown French soldier—

VOICE The unknown soldier!

GEORGES That's Colonel De Gaulle. If there ever was an unknown French soldier—

JEAN Hush, fool! Hush!

A VOICE Attack! Attack! To hell with this squatting in a—

A VOICE Gamelin says—

A VOICE To hell with Gamelin—

A VOICE Treason! Treason!

A VOICE Attack! Attack! Attack!

EXT. STREET BEFORE CAFE   NIGHT

A muffled uproar of voices comes through the wall. A gendarme enters on bicycle, stops, dismounts, listens to the uproar, leads the bicycle to the wall and leans it up; pauses to see that it is not going to fall, turns and enters the cafe without haste, the uproar growing loud as he opens the door, fades when he shuts it after him.

INT. CAFE   GENDARME, GEORGES, JEAN, THE SOLDIER, THE MAYOR
OTHERS IN B.G.

GENDARME *(to mayor)* Your Honor. *(to Jean)* Lieutenant. *(shakes hands with Jean, looks about at the others)* Now what? *(to Georges and the soldier)* So this is how you recover from wounds: by badgering civilians.

MAYOR Badgering civilians? Defeatism! Communism!

GENDARME *(to mayor)* Now then. Your Honor.

He approaches Georges and the soldier, leans and sniffs at them, smells nothing apparently, moves, sniffs, pauses at the carter.

GENDARME So it's you I smell. You are big enough to have made all the noise alone. *(to Georges)* Have you done?

GEORGES I haven't even started. I—

JEAN Yes. We're going home now. *(puts his hand on Georges's arm)* Come on.

GEORGES *(flings Jean's hand off)* I can walk alone, even if I had no better sense than to mention Colonel De Gaulle.

He exits. Jean looks after him, pauses, turns back to mayor.

JEAN He will apologize tomorrow.

MAYOR Apologize? To me? Why should he apologize to an old fogy who is foolish enough to believe that five hundred billion francs can buy a little more than soap?

JEAN *(bows slightly)* Yes. Goodnight, sir. Gentlemen.

He exits.

GENDARME Now then. Any of the rest of you who are unable to let this war stay on the Western Front. . . .

EXT. STREET   MED SHOT   GEORGES AND JEAN   NIGHT

Georges's face is furious, seething. He glances back, sees Jean beside him, crosses the street to the opposite side. Jean hesitates, follows him. Georges looks back, sees Jean, crosses street to opposite side again. Jean watches him, shrugs slightly, goes on. They walk up the street on opposite sides, Georges striding angrily ahead.

WIPE TO:

EXT. FRONT DOOR OF MORNET HOUSE   NIGHT

Georges enters, striding angrily toward door. Jean follows. Georges opens the door.

INT. HALL   MED. CLOSE

—as Georges enters, Jean following. Mme Mornet in her bed-room door. She wears a dressing gown, stands in the door as Georges crosses the hall, begins to mount the stairs, Jean following. Mme Mornet comes out. Jean sees her, stops. Georges strides up the stairs.

MME MORNET   What is it?

JEAN   Nothing. It will be all right tomorrow. Goodnight.

He stoops, kisses Mme Mornet on cheek, follows Georges up the stairs. Mme Mornet stands watching them.

DISSOLVE TO:

INT. BEDROOM   CLOSE

Georges in bed, covered, his face toward wall. Jean enters, in sleeping suit, stops, looks at Georges a moment, gets into bed, is pulling covers up, stops, raises onto his elbow, leans and looks at Georges.

JEAN   Georges.

Georges doesn't answer. Jean puts hand on Georges's shoulder. Georges flings the hand off without turning.

GEORGES   Let me alone!

FADE OUT.

FADE IN

MONTAGE

—over sound of bombs and gunfire, on the Saturday morning when the Germans broke through the Dutch frontier, tanks in action, the bombing of Rotterdam, parachute troops landing, etc.

DISSOLVE TO:

INT. BEDROOM   JEAN AND GEORGES   MORNING

—dressing.

JEAN   You'll have to apologize to him, you know.

GEORGES For what? For telling him the truth? I didn't invent it. Even Colonel De Gaulle didn't invent it. He just stated it—with nobody to listen and believe him, too, like me last night.

JEAN Then you should have taken this De Gaulle for an example and kept your mouth shut. But since you didn't, you'll have to apologize. He's Catherine's father.

GEORGES That's something he'll have to apologize for; I can't.

DISSOLVE TO:

CLOSE SHOT   CHURCH SPIRE AGAINST SKY

Bell ringing peacefully.

FULL SHOT   PROCESSION

—approaching church, priest leading, choirboys carrying Host, etc., girls in white, flowers, etc. Sound of bells OVER SCENE.

EXT. ENTRANCE TO CHURCH

The villagers are gathered, watching the procession pass— women, children, older men.

CLOSE SHOT   MME MORNET, JEAN AND GEORGES

—as the mayor passes them, refuses to speak, drags Catherine on into the church.

INT. CHURCH

The church is old, not large, and on the plain side as to pews, furnishings, etc. But some of the religious furniture is rich, though meager: the candlesticks, etc., and altar ornaments. The villagers sit in the pews; the choir is singing.

FULL SHOT

—of priest as he comes to podium. The singing ceases. The people in the pews kneel. The priest speaks a short brief prayer in Latin, makes sign with his hand; the people rise and sit back in the pews. The priest is about fifty, a peasant type by birth, but his face is thin, ascetic, intelligent, wise, yet still strong.

PRIEST In the beginning was the earth. It and all within it were for man's use and comfort. There was enough for all.

CLOSE SHOT   MAYOR'S PEW   MAYOR, CATHERINE AND ADJACENT FACES IN OTHER PEWS

PRIEST'S VOICE But he was not content, even when there were but few of him, even when what he knew as his nation was just a collection of caves in a single hill, with a little fire to lift its puny hand between him and the darkness and the unknown.

CLOSE SHOT   MORNET PEW   MME MORNET, JEAN, GEORGES AND ADJACENT FACES

Mme Mornet and Jean listen attentively. Jean is grave. Georges has an expression of sardonic contempt on his face. The voice continues:

PRIEST'S VOICE Now the boundaries of what he boasts of as his nations interlock one with another across all the earth. Now he claims the air above and the seas which surround him. And still the young men of his nations face each other across these barriers, with guns in their hands which have been blessed and dedicated to patriotism and love of home, for the purpose of destroying one another in the name of ultimate peace.

MED. LONG SHOT   AISLE OF CHURCH   PRIEST IN B.G.

—facing his audience.

PRIEST *(continuing)* We have deposed Him. We have set up in His place rapacity and greed and power and vainglory, naming them in outrageous travesty of what He preached: love of man for man, of land and home, living space. So is it any wonder, then, with the blood of women and children, of Slav and Magyar and Jew, crying up to Him, that He has said, "So be it, then. If this is what must be, so be it, until all this blood-soaked Europe cries aloud against those who made it flow, their nights are filled with the eyes of their victims as the sky's night is with its stars, until there is no place on earth or beneath it where they can forget that choired indictment, as I Myself will not forget it!"

The priest ceases, stands motionless.

MED. LONG SHOT   ANOTHER ANGLE

Priest facing audience.

    PRIEST   *(quietly now)* We must endure. Rapacity cannot be bribed. Lust and satiety are not drugs but habits. If France were nothing, it would not have existed. To remain France, it will have to endure. If it still is France, it will endure.

He raises his hand. The villagers kneel; the priest pronounces benediction, makes sign of cross, turns as choir rises and begins to sing.

                        DISSOLVE TO:

EXT. CHURCH   CLOSE   MME MORNET, JEAN AND GEORGES

—as mayor passes them again, refuses to speak; drags Catherine on after him.

EXT. BULLETIN BOARD   CLOSE   MAYOR AND CATHERINE

Georges and Catherine's banns have been posted on the board. The mayor jerks the notice from the board, crumples and flings it away, drags Catherine on.

CLOSE SHOT   MME MORNET, JEAN AND GEORGES

Mme Mornet looks at Jean and Georges grimly.

    MME MORNET   Now then . . .

                        DISSOLVE TO:

INT. CATHERINE'S BEDROOM   CLOSE SHOT   CATHERINE

—lying face-down on bed, crying, head in pillow. A woman servant enters, middle-aged, approaches bed, stands looking down at Catherine. Catherine turns her head, looks at maid, buries face again.

    CATHERINE   Go away. Let me alone.

The woman exits.

INT. MAYOR'S PARLOR   CLOSE   MAYOR

—reading newspaper, grim. The servant woman enters. The mayor lowers paper, turns his head.

MAYOR   Now what?

SERVANT   All that food. For three extra. Apparently there will not only be no extra ones, but Catherine herself—

MAYOR   I eat, don't I? You eat.

SERVANT   But not all that food.

MAYOR   Use it for soap, then. *(he turns back to paper)*

SERVANT   Soap?

MAYOR   Yes. I understand that's how France is converting all her other assets.

The servant exits.

INT. KITCHEN   CLOSE   STOVE

The servant woman removes half-cooked food from it, puts it away.

DISSOLVE TO:

EXT. STREET   CLOSE TRUCKING SHOT

Mme Mornet striding grimly, Jean and Georges following. Jean is grim, too. Georges looks like a small boy caught in mischief, cowed a little but still trying to carry the matter off.

INT. MAYOR'S PARLOR   CLOSE   MAYOR

—standing; Mme Mornet, Jean and Georges have just entered.

MME MORNET   He has come to apologize. *(to Georges)* Come.

GEORGES   I apologize. But not for what I said. Colonel De Gaulle . . .

MME MORNET   That will do. Just apologize. That'll be enough.

GEORGES   I apologize.

DISSOLVE TO:

INT. KITCHEN

The servant woman putting the dinner back into the stove.

DISSOLVE TO:

EXT. GARDEN   CLOSE   GEORGES AND CATHERINE

—kissing.

DISSOLVE TO:

INT. DINING ROOM   CLOSE GROUP   FAVORING MAYOR

All at table, finishing dinner. The table is decorated, betrothal meal, etc. The servant woman setting a bottle before the mayor. The mayor looks at it.

MAYOR   No, no. The other one.

The servant takes up bottle, exits.

ANOTHER ANGLE   GROUP   AT TABLE

The servant enters, passes about table, pouring champagne. The mayor rises, holds up his glass.

MAYOR   For several years now we have been looking forward to this union between our two families—

GEORGES   Hear, hear.

CATHERINE   *(to Georges)* Shhh!

CLOSE   GEORGES'S AND CATHERINE'S HANDS

—clasped below edge of table.

MAYOR'S VOICE   —though for a while it looked like the event would be indefinitely deferred by my son-in-law's previous commitment to a condition or at least a location which he has been pleased to refer to as soap—

CLOSE   MAYOR   FAVORING OTHERS

MAYOR   But never mind about that. We are all young once, with notions to express which later we, too, will regard as folly, and with a free country about us in which we can express even folly—

GEORGES It was Colonel De Gaulle who spoke the folly first; not me—

CATHERINE Hush! Shhh!

JEAN *(tense, not loud)* Georges!

The mayor stops. Georges turns innocently to Jean.

GEORGES Pardon? Did you say something?

MME MORNET No. *(to mayor)* Go on, Philippe.

MAYOR It appears that your son has something of more importance than mine to say. *(to Georges)* You were saying, sir?

CATHERINE Papa!

GEORGES No, sir. I just said that Colonel De Gaulle—

JEAN *(to Georges)* Will you hush!

GEORGES I'm still trying to. I even thought for a while that I had—

MME MORNET Both of you hush. Philippe! Georges!

MAYOR *(to Georges)* Come, sir. Continue. The Maginot Line, that has held the enemy out of France for eight months—

GEORGES Colonel De Gaulle never said it hadn't. But it has an end, that can be turned. By a mechanized attack. And he said that only a mobile mechanized force can stop a mechanized attack—not the best entrenched infantry in the world. So, for all the good the Maginot Line will do us when the attack really comes, it might as well be soap—

CATHERINE Georges! Papa!

MAYOR The Maginot Line? That cost France five hundred billion francs?

GEORGES Marthe says it cost three thousand. That's better still, because when the government finally turns it into a national curiosity for tourists, it won't take so long at two francs a look to pay—

A sudden uproar out of scene. SOUND of feet, voices, the loud voice of the woman servant. All about the table stop, look toward the door as it bursts open. The servant enters, backward, swept into the room by the men she is trying to keep out of it, her voice still raised.

CLOSE SHOT THE DOOR

—as maid enters backward, the constable shoving her aside, a stranger, a messenger following him, other villagers stopping still, respectful of the mayor's house, at the door.

MAID You can't come in! His Honor is eating. Eating, I tell you!

CONSTABLE Eating? Eating? This is no time for eating.

FULL SHOT ROOM

—as the constable enters, followed by the messenger. The other villagers stop at the door, looking into the room as the constable hurries forward.

CLOSE SHOT

Mayor standing, facing constable, others in b.g. The constable is bursting with excitement.

CONSTABLE The Germans crossed the Dutch frontier this morning! The French and British are rushing to join the Belgians—

CLOSE FAVORING JEAN AND GEORGES CATHERINE AND MME MORNET IN B.G.

GEORGES It has begun!

CONSTABLE (to Georges and Jean) And you, too. All soldiers and sailors are ordered to report.

GEORGES (shoves constable aside) He was right! Colonel De Gaulle was right! They are going around it!

CONSTABLE Of course they will go around it! We will join the Belgians and hurl the whole German army into the North Sea!

EXT. STREET   AT MAYOR'S DOOR

Georges, then Jean, come out and hurry up the street. The constable and others come out. People begin to appear at other doors along the street.

GROUP SHOT

Constable, surrounded by anxious villagers, as they show reaction to the news which they have been expecting and dreading for so long.

> **CONSTABLE** It has come. Holland has been invaded. Gamelin and Gort are rushing to join the Belgian king—

EXT. MORNET HOUSE

Side view of cart, Coupe-tête at rear end of it, writing something on the tailgate. Catherine enters, running, worried, pauses, goes on toward house, running.

INT. JEAN AND GEORGES'S BEDROOM

Georges dressing, gathering up pack, etc. Mme Mornet is worried, concerned, but helping him competently.

> **MME MORNET** You still have another week of convalescent leave. You can't—couldn't . . .
>
> **GEORGES** How can I, now? How can any of us?
>
> **MME MORNET** Yes. Wait.

She takes socks from bed, thrusts them into pack.

INT. LOWER HALL   CLOSE   GEORGES AND CATHERINE

—embracing.

> **GEORGES** It's too bad they couldn't have waited another two days. No, I don't mean that. Because maybe I couldn't have left at all then. So, instead of being the intended bride of a soldier, you would have been the wife of a deserter; maybe even the widow . . .
>
> **CATHERINE** Hush! Hush! Don't say it!
>
> **GEORGES** I'll be inside a tank. Shells just bounce off tanks.

Or maybe your father and Michel Kereon are right, and General Gamelin will have whipped them before we can even get there. So it's not goodbye, then. Just—to the return.

CATHERINE To the return.

They kiss. Georges releases her. She clings to him. He pulls her arms away, turns, exits. Catherine looks after him, pauses, looks out of scene.

ANOTHER ANGLE   CATHERINE AND JEAN

JEAN This is too bad. Fatherland is too loose a word. It means too much, and too little. It's not enough.

CATHERINE What do you mean?

JEAN Not enough for Georges. For me, yes. My course of conduct is fixed. I am used to it. Any aberration from it I can make already has a name, even: treason.

CATHERINE Georges is a soldier, too.

JEAN Georges is a farmer. He is a soldier only by the force of circumstance. Fatherland will not be enough.

CATHERINE Yes. It will be. It will be. You are the one to worry—not Georges.

JEAN I?

CATHERINE Yes. I'm not afraid for the man who can commit only what people call cowardice; I am afraid for the man who believes that all he can be guilty of is what the people above him will call treason.

Catherine turns, exits hurriedly. Jean looks thoughtfully after her.

GEORGES (*off scene*) Jean! Come on. Coupe-tête has to come back and milk.

Jean rouses, follows.

MED. CLOSE   GROUP   AT WAGON

Jean embraces Mme Mornet, kisses her, mounts to wagon seat

where Georges and Coupe-tête already sit. The wagon moves. Catherine enters, stands beside Mme Mornet. They look after the wagon as it exits.

CLOSE WAGON IN MOTION

—as it turns and the back end of the wagon comes into view. Across it in chalk, crudely printed:

DOWN WITH THE WAR

Two or three lines have been drawn through the words; beneath them Coupe-tête has written:

DOWN WITH HITLER

The wagon grows smaller in—

FADE OUT.

FADE IN

MAP OF WESTERN EUROPE

Holland is blacked out. The black crosses the Belgian frontier and moves on toward France as we watch it, as the front advanced during May. A radio voice in b.g. repeats bulletins of the battle during the time, highlights, etc. The black halts as we PAN to SEDAN on map. The black bulges, breaks through, spreads, the voice continues over—

DISSOLVE TO:

EXT. A BIG CAFE PARIS STREET

People passing, showing little anxiety. The street scene is almost as usual, save for absence of soldiers, etc. CAMERA MOVES FORWARD to:

FULL SHOT CAFE TERRACE

People at tables, drinking, talking, waiters moving about, scene almost normal, as if the people were hardly listening to the radio voice in b.g.

RADIO The enemy have opened a breach in our lines, but we have stopped them. We will stop others. General Weygand has been recalled from the East and is now in command. He promises victory if we can hold them one month. Meanwhile, do not be alarmed. They will not pass the Somme.

DISSOLVE TO:

[NOTE TO M. DIAMANT-BERGER: The following is an imaginary scene, now rewritten to correct inaccuracies. Is there any objection to it as an imaginary incident? This is the scene in which De Gaulle was given the tank command by means of which he fought the battle of Laon. It was invented in accordance to a comment of M. Berger to the effect that we show how, at a conference of the staff some years before, Col. De Gaulle had made a plea for tanks and had been ignored. This plea and its occasion is established in this scene. We have used M. Reynaud as the principal power which finally gave De Gaulle his tank command for which he had asked and been heretofore denied. Is there an objection to giving Reynaud this role?]

FULL SHOT   CHAMBER OF DEPUTIES

The scene is orderly, though tense. There is no panic nor violence.

TRUCK TO:

MED. CLOSE   REYNAUD

—standing, the cabinet grouped behind him, facing the Chamber. He is quite calm.

REYNAUD   Gentlemen. If you please.

CLOSE   FAVORING FACES OF DEPUTIES

They are fairly calm, anxious but not yet alarmed, more antagonistic than panicky.

A DEPUTY   De Gaulle? Who is De Gaulle?

REYNAUD   You may well ask that. That's a question that the Marshal and General Weygand either could answer. And there are some among you now who could answer—

PAN to another Deputy.

DEPUTY   Yes, I was there.

REYNAUD Yes, Mr. _____ was there, a member of the National Defense council, not only on that day in 1934 when I proposed a law to create a panzer division like that whose weight our forces are still feeling, but on that day in 1929, eleven years ago, when with my support Colonel De Gaulle advocated the same thing.

DEPUTY That is true.

REYNAUD —that the 3000 tanks which we then had be grouped in one armored command, against such a day as France is now suffering: to be used as the Germans themselves are using tanks across the Somme. And Mr. _____ will also remember what response he got from those in whose hands the security of France lay—*(pauses)*—and still lies.

A VOICE Treason!

Reynaud pauses, looks about.

CLOSE SHOT   FIRST FACE

PAN to others, all watching Reynaud, quietly and intently now.

CLOSE SHOT   REYNAUD

REYNAUD Will that gentleman stand? *(he looks about, waits; no one rises)* The French people put this portfolio in my hands. They need only ask to have it back.

ANOTHER ANGLE

—Reynaud in f.g., three-quarters, the faces watching him.

REYNAUD Colonel De Gaulle: an obscure dreamer, servant of an illusion—little better than a poet, in fact. Why should you know him? Why should anyone in France have heard of the man whom the marshals and generals of France rejected and ignored—

FULL SHOT   THE SEA OF FACES

—filling the Chamber.

VOICE No! No!

VOICE A nonentity! An unknown!

VOICE Let our experienced generals—

CLOSE SHOT REYNAUD

—facing them.

REYNAUD Make him a general then. Give him all the tanks, all of them—

FULL SHOT THE FACES

CLOSE SHOT A DEPUTY AND REYNAUD

DEPUTY No! No!

REYNAUD I say yes!

DEPUTY We are France!

CLOSE SHOT REYNAUD

REYNAUD Be it. I am the French people.

DISSOLVE TO:

CLOSE SHOT MAP

SOUND of battle in b.g. The black of the German advance spreads toward Laon, pauses, begins to bulge on either side as the German advance is temporarily stopped. Sound of battle grows louder over—

DISSOLVE TO:

MED. TRUCKING SHOT A MOVING TANK

The tank stops beside a French soldier, dirty and unshaven, sitting in the shelter of a fallen wall of a bombed house, eating a piece of bread. The soldier looks up for a moment, then away again, still eating. The hatch opens; Georges stands up in it, looks down at soldier.

GEORGES Don't let us disturb you.

SOLDIER Then take that tin can somewhere else, before a Boche comes along and decides to bomb it.

GEORGES We intend to. Where's Brigade H.Q.?

SOLDIER *(bites bread)* In Belgium, the last time I saw it. Will the General himself do?

The tank sergeant stands up in hatch beside Georges.

SERGEANT Now what?

GEORGES *(to soldier)* Whoever saw a brigade commander in a battle?

SOLDIER You will when you see De Gaulle. He was fighting one of your baby carriages himself until he took a direct hit on it about an hour ago.

GEORGES Who? Colonel De Gaulle? *(he begins to climb down)*

SOLDIER General De Gaulle.

The sergeant and a third man get out of tank.

SERGEANT Which way?

The soldier points over his shoulder with the bread, bites it again.

SOLDIER That way. Just look around until you find a man that looks like he was weaned on a shoelace. That's De Gaulle.

MED. SHOT   A TANK

—which has been disabled by a shell. Beside it a command car.

MED. CLOSE SHOT

The sergeant, Georges, and the third man at attention facing De Gaulle. De Gaulle wears a tank helmet, a leather coat, greasy khaki pants, no insignia. He is listening into earphones. His face is unshaven, strained. In b.g. two or three aides, radio corporal and radiomen, etc. De Gaulle listens to the progress of the battle all during scene.

DE GAULLE *(to sergeant)* I expected you last night. What happened?

CLOSE SHOT

—sergeant, Georges and third man beside him.

SERGEANT   We ran into the battle yesterday afternoon and were scattered. The last order from the Commandant was to disengage and keep radio silence and report to head-quarters as we were able.

DE GAULLE   That took you until now?

SERGEANT   We ran into the battle again this morning, sir.

DE GAULLE   Ah.

PAN to Georges's face, De Gaulle's angle; then to third man. PAN BACK to Georges's face.

DE GAULLE   *(to Georges)* You were at the tank school. What is your name?

GEORGES   Mornet, sir.

DE GAULLE   Yes. Mornet.

PAN to sergeant.

DE GAULLE   Your tank is all right?

SERGEANT   It's all right, sir.

DE GAULLE   Grenier!

The aide enters.

DE GAULLE   Pack up. Move back to _____ village and set up again.

FULL SHOT

The tank beside the fallen wall. The runner at attention, hiding the piece of bread against his leg as De Gaulle, followed by sergeant, Georges and the third man, enters.

DE GAULLE   *(to runner)* What are you doing here?

RUNNER   Taking cover, sir.

DE GAULLE   If you don't hurry, they are going to leave you.

De Gaulle goes on to tank. The runner breaks off as Georges passes him.

GEORGES Run! They were already serving dessert when we left.

De Gaulle and the other three enter the tank.

DISSOLVE TO:

THE MAP

The black moves down the Somme toward Abbeville. SOUND of battle, bombs, gunfire. A radio voice in b.g., a little more anxious.

RADIO The Belgian army has surrendered. The King has returned to his palace in Brussels as a voluntary prisoner of war, to share the fate of his people, he states. The British and a scattering of French troops have reached Dunkirk. The __th Army under General Prioux[1] was last reported fighting a heavy action in the North to protect the evacuation. It is feared that General Prioux and the remnants of his forces are now prisoners of the enemy. Our tanks are engaged in front of Abbeville—

DISSOLVE TO:

CLOSE SHOT   THE TANK IN MOTION   BATTLE SOUND IN B.G.

De Gaulle stands up in the hatch, looking back toward the battle. SOUND of a bomber as it dives on the tank, zooms away. De Gaulle pays no attention to it. SOUND of aeroplane beginning third dive at tank. Georges rises beside De Gaulle, grasps him by belt and tries to pull him down.

GEORGES For God's sake, General!

DE GAULLE All right. Perhaps I will always be too tall for French tanks.

DISSOLVE TO:

INT. FARMHOUSE   PARLOR

—dismantled, evacuated by family. De Gaulle's field h.q., packing box for desk, camp chair, telephone, etc.

1. General Rene Prioux's armored cavalry corps temporarily checked the German advance on May 12–13, 1940, but was forced to retreat on May 15.

GROUP

De Gaulle, unshaven, tired, dirty. Grenier, his aide, stands behind the desk. Between them stands the staff officer from Paris,
in noticeable contrast to the battle-stained De Gaulle and
Grenier.

STAFF OFFICER   From the Commander-in-Chief, General.

He produces papers, extends them.

STAFF OFFICER   And a note from the Premier.

DE GAULLE   Thanks. *(takes the papers)* You haven't dined, of
course.

STAFF OFFICER   Thanks.

DE GAULLE   *(begins to open paper)* Grenier—

GRENIER   *(raises voice)* Grignon!

Batman enters.

GRENIER   *(to batman)* Show Captain Latour-Brix to my
room. Find him a clean towel, if you can.

STAFF OFFICER   Thanks. *(he follows batman out)*

INSERT   LETTER IN DE GAULLE'S HANDS

General:
    Relinquish your command, as the accompanying from
the General instructs you, and return to Paris to receive the
thanks of the Republic which has a still further demand to
make upon him who has already served it well.

REYNAUD

CLOSE SHOT   DESK

—De Gaulle seated at desk, his hand on the telephone, Grenier
standing beside him, holding the phone down.

GRENIER   It's an order.

DE GAULLE   I am fighting a battle. I have not even won it
yet. Yet I am to quit it and return to Paris, to receive my
reward.

GRENIER *(holds phone)* It's an order. In writing. From the Premier.

DISSOLVE TO:

INT. COUNCIL ROOM   WAR MINISTRY   FULL SHOT

—Council seated around table. Reynaud standing.

REYNAUD —needs no introduction to any Frenchman. His credentials are his record; his references are the German army at Laon and again at Abbeville—

CLOSE SHOT   DE GAULLE

—seated at Reynaud's left. He now wears clean uniform, two stars of brigadier general.

REYNAUD The Under-Secretary for War—Brigadier General De Gaulle.

CLOSE SHOT   FIRST FACE

—anxious, grave, waiting to see what the reaction will be. PAN to other faces in turn, same expression, showing how some favor Reynaud, are his yes-men, others not decided, others opposed. PAN to Pétain, who appears bored, indifferent. PAN to Weygand, who is grim, anxious, yet he is Pétain's man.

A man out of scene begins to applaud, others take it up until all join in save Pétain and Weygand. Pétain seems to shrug the whole matter off. Weygand seems grim and anxious, yet he suits his behavior to his superior.

INSERT   MAP OF FRANCE

—showing battle line as of June 8. The Somme has been crossed, the black covers all of the Low Countries, is spreading across Normandy.

GROUP SHOT AT TABLE   REYNAUD, DE GAULLE, PÉTAIN, WEYGAND

—other members of war council in b.g. The map is spread on the table. The adherents of Pétain and Weygand are reserved, inscrutable. The others are anxious, watching. The babble of voices from within the Chamber of Deputies continues. De Gaulle is grave, quiet. Weygand is grim, looking at map. Pétain is almost doddering, contemptuous, old. Reynaud watches Weygand.

WEYGAND   We will continue to retreat.

DE GAULLE   To where? The purpose of a retreat is to establish a tenable position. When it stops doing that, it ceases to be a retreat.

PÉTAIN   Does Brigadier General the Under-Secretary wish to give General Weygand a lesson in strategy, or merely in hope?

REYNAUD   Come, come, Marshal. General De Gaulle merely wants you to answer the question we are all asking now: retreat to where? Where will our new line be established?

PÉTAIN   Let the map of France answer him. That, and the condition of the French people.

Reynaud looks at Pétain a moment, rises.

CLOSE SHOT   LOUDSPEAKER ON WALL

Reynaud enters, turns switch. Out of loudspeaker comes the babble of voices from the Chamber.

VOICES   Attack! Attack! We have generals; what are they doing?

FULL GROUP SHOT   WAR COUNCIL ABOUT THE TABLE

—favoring Reynaud standing at loudspeaker. Reynaud switches it off.

REYNAUD   Does that sound like there is anything wrong with the condition of the French people?

A civilian begins to applaud, ceases as if aghast, another starts, others take it up, until only the army officers remain still. Pétain rises.

MED. CLOSE

Pétain standing above others, his face still contemptuous. The applause begins to die away. Pétain waits until it stops, Weygand still grimly down-looking beside him.

PÉTAIN Applaud then. Louder. So that the enemy can hear it and perhaps mistake it for gunfire.

EMPTY COUNCIL ROOM   CLOSE SHOT   REYNAUD AND DE GAULLE

Conference is over.

REYNAUD To London. See Mr. Churchill. Take all the time you need. Do not worry about us here. I myself will hold Paris single-handed until you return. The twilight of France is not to follow so short an afternoon.

INT. AEROPLANE IN FLIGHT   CLOSE SHOT   DE GAULLE AND GEN.
SPEARS

SPEARS You speak no English, General?

DE GAULLE No.

SPEARS No matter. Mr. Churchill can hear and understand all men who love freedom and believe in courage.

EXT. 10 DOWNING STREET, LONDON

De Gaulle and Spears enter; sentry presents arms.

INT. CHURCHILL'S OFFICE   CLOSE SHOT

—a plump, thick hand in white cuff and black sleeve, holding a burning cigar, lying on table in f.g. De Gaulle standing facing CAMERA across the table.

CHURCHILL'S VOICE Welcome to England, General. Welcome to all that England has, as are all who stand as England stands in these dark days when all who still love liberty and freedom must league together.

DISSOLVE TO:

MONTAGE

"French government will move from Paris" as De Gaulle in London hears it.

[M. Berger: Imaginary, poetic license here, for its dramatic and poetic value.]

CLOSE SHOT   FACE OF FRENCH PARLIAMENT BLDG.

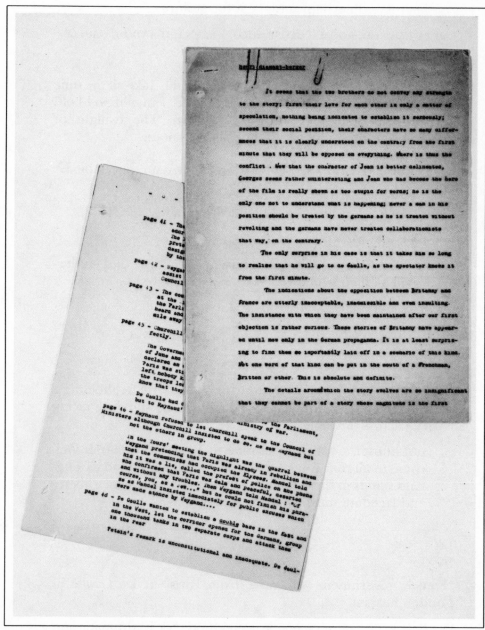

14. Henri Diamant-Berger's critique of Faulkner's screenplay

The words engraved across front, beneath drooping French flag:

LIBERTE   EGALITE   FRATERNITE

DISSOLVE TO:

EXT. STREET BEFORE BUILDING

—almost deserted. De Gaulle and aide looking about. They enter.

WIPE TO:

INT. MARBLE CORRIDOR

—empty, hollow echo of footsteps as De Gaulle and aide enter, alone, dwarfed by it and its solitude. De Gaulle and aide go on; a solitary servant emerges.

DE GAULLE   *(to servant)* They have gone?

SERVANT   Yes, sir. Last night.

AIDE   We are too late.

DE GAULLE   No. Never. We are not too late.

He turns, advances TOWARD CAMERA, aide following.

DISSOLVE TO:

MAP OF FRANCE

—showing the black front of the German advance on June 11. PAN to TOURS on map.

DISSOLVE TO:

INT. OFFICE   CLOSE   REYNAUD

On wall behind him, Churchill's shadow: cigar, etc. Reynaud's face is cold, adamant.

CHURCHILL'S VOICE   Let me speak to them myself.

REYNAUD   No. You have come from London to offer France your support—

CHURCHILL'S VOICE   Not mine, England's.

REYNAUD *(bows)* You can do no more. Don't insist. I pray. Your presence will be enough. You will excuse me?

Reynaud turns, walks.

WIPE TO:

INT. COUNCIL ROOM   GROUP ABOUT TABLE

Reynaud, Mandel, Pétain and others present at this council.

REYNAUD I have requested General Weygand to be present, to make a report as commander of the army. General Weygand?

PAN SHOTS of the various faces. PAN TO:

WEYGAND

—holding a paper open.

WEYGAND . . . and therefore, in the judgment of the General Staff, nothing remains but to ask the German High Command for an armistice.

He folds the paper, deliberately, lays it on the table.

A MEMBER Why?

WEYGAND Why? The front is now at _____. Paris is in rebellion. The Communists have occupied the Elysees—*(a sound off scene)*

CLOSE SHOT   MANDEL

He has risen.

MANDEL Mr. Premier. With your permission.

He picks up telephone. [Could it have been on the table?]

MANDEL *(into phone)* Yes . . . Thank you. *(puts phone down)*

GROUP AT TABLE   MANDEL STANDING

MANDEL *(to Weygand)* I have spoken with the Prefect of Police himself. Paris is calm and peaceful. There is no trouble of any sort. Your statement is a lie.

WEYGAND Of course, you, as a Jew—

VOICE Shhhhhhh.

VOICE Shame!

REYNAUD Gentlemen!

MANDEL *(to Weygand)* I request an apology, General.

WEYGAND *(after a moment)* I offer it.

Mandel sits down.

ANOTHER ANGLE

REYNAUD Yesterday I telephoned to President Roosevelt in America, asking for any help that can reach us quickly. I will telephone him again today—

De Gaulle rises.

REYNAUD *(to De Gaulle)* General?

CLOSE SHOT   REYNAUD   FAVORING DE GAULLE   OTHERS IN B.G.

DE GAULLE Let us help ourselves first, before we ask for help. One of our armies is still intact. The others are still serviceable forces—

PÉTAIN Bah!

DE GAULLE And there is England, as Mr. Churchill has assured me. And a commander-in-chief who was a pupil of Marshal Foch—

CLOSE

Weygand grim, Pétain beside him, fretted, contemptuous, apparently annoyed even.

PÉTAIN And what will we do with these forces?

SHOT   FAVORING DE GAULLE

DE GAULLE Establish a double base, one in the East, based on that end of the Maginot Line which has never been broken, the other in Brittany, where we can draw from England just across the Channel. Form a corridor through which the enemy will have to pass, so that he will have to offer us two flanks—

REYNAUD *(to Weygand)* Well, General?

WEYGAND The intact army which General De Gaulle speaks of is already isolated. The others are no longer armies. We have lost this war.

DE GAULLE We have not lost the war. We have merely lost a battle.

SHOT   FAVORING PÉTAIN

PÉTAIN Is the new general advising us as a soldier, or as the Under-Secretary of War?

REYNAUD In either case, he has the right to speak here. As the one, he was requested to speak; as the other, the right to speak is inherent in his office.

PÉTAIN Granted. It is his advice that I mean. In the one case, he is a junior, and is insubordinate until the Commander-in-Chief asks his advice. In the other, he is a civilian, and his advice is incompetent.

De Gaulle sits down.

SHOT   FAVORING REYNAUD

—as he looks about at the faces.

REYNAUD *(to Weygand)* That is your best advice, General?

WEYGAND It is, sir.

REYNAUD Then it remains only for me to request of Mr. Churchill that England release France from the obligation between the two countries that neither shall ask for a separate armistice.

WIPE TO:

INT. OFFICE   CLOSE   CHURCHILL'S HAND

—with cigar resting on a desk, Reynaud facing desk. The hand slowly crushes the cigar, drops it.

CHURCHILL'S VOICE England answers, "No," Mr. Reynaud. Never!

DISSOLVE TO:

COUNCIL ROOM   FAVORING REYNAUD

—standing at head of table.

> **REYNAUD** The Government will move to Bordeaux. Our retreat will continue. Meanwhile, I will make one more plea to the President of the United States.

WIPE TO:

REYNAUD'S OFFICE   CLOSE   REYNAUD AND DE GAULLE

De Gaulle leans over desk, talks urgently, rapidly; Reynaud listens.

> **REYNAUD** We can resist from Africa, where we have an intact establishment.

> **DE GAULLE** With the whole continent of Europe dividing us from our own ally? No. If we must relinquish in the East, if we must concentrate anywhere, let it be in Brittany, where we will have only the Channel between us. Not Bordeaux! Countermand the move.

> **REYNAUD** No! We will move to Bordeaux tonight.

De Gaulle stands up slowly.

> **DE GAULLE** That is definite?

> **REYNAUD** Yes.

De Gaulle bows, turns quietly, walks toward CAMERA, his face grave.

DISSOLVE TO:

MAP OF FRANCE

The black of the German advance spreads as of June 13-14th.

DISSOLVE TO:

CLOSE SHOT   PILOT'S FACE

—in aeroplane in flight. It is Jean, looking backward constantly from side to side, as he twists and turns.

FULL SHOT   AEROPLANE

—with French markings, in flight, chased by Germans. The

whole sky seems full of Germans; they are almost in each other's way. The French plane turns and twists, shoots down one enemy as it draws further and further away. There are so many Germans that they cannot even bring their guns to bear on it for fear of shooting at one another.

DISSOLVE TO:

EXT. BATTLEFIELD

—crashed French aeroplanes, battered French tanks—all the refuse and flotsam of the retreating and routed French forces; German troops, tanks, etc., still advancing.

CLOSE GROUP SHOT

—a party of stained and bedraggled French captives under guard of two German soldiers. Again we get the sense of there being so many Germans, victors, that they are in one another's way. Georges is among the captives.

TRUCKING SHOT

—as the prisoners march on, Georges and another soldier, their faces watchful and wary.

GEORGES   *(from side of his mouth)* Now?

The other man glances sideways, not moving his head as they tramp on.

MAN   All right.

Georges and the man leap toward CAMERA.

GROUP SHOT

—as the men overpower the two guards, knock them down, run.

CLOSE SHOT

Guard on the ground fires his rifle, yells.

GROUP SHOT   A GERMAN OFFICER AND A FEW MEN

The officer shouts, the men begin to run across scene, stopping and firing, running again.

LONG SHOT

Georges and other prisoners running across a field toward woods; in f.g. two German soldiers firing at them, sound of machine gun in b.g. The prisoners reach the woods, enter it.

DISSOLVE TO:

MAP OF FRANCE

CAMERA STOPS ON BORDEAUX. Babble of voices over—

DISSOLVE TO:

INT. COUNCIL ROOM   FULL SHOT AT TABLE

—cabinet around it, Reynaud presiding, De Gaulle, Pétain, Weygand, others, etc. Babble of anxious voices from the members.

REYNAUD   Gentlemen! Gentlemen!

The noise ceases.

WEYGAND   We must ask for an armistice.

DE GAULLE   In whose name?

WEYGAND   In the name of the Army.   Of France.

DE GAULLE   Of neither. *(to Reynaud)* You are France yet. Give the order for Africa. We have time yet. We have an intact establishment already there. The fleet and transports are at Toulon—

The uproar begins again.

VOICES   No! No! An armistice!

VOICES   Yes! Yes! No armistice! We are not whipped.

The uproar grows louder in—

WIPE TO:

CLOSE SHOT   REYNAUD AND DE GAULLE

—alone. Reynaud is grave, troubled for the first time.

REYNAUD   All right. To London then. I will try to hold them until you have seen Mr. Churchill.

DISSOLVE TO:

DE GAULLE   AT TELEPHONE

CHURCHILL'S VOICE IN PHONE   A Union between France and England—

DISSOLVE TO:

SHADOW OF CHURCHILL

—holding phone on wall.

CHURCHILL'S VOICE   —for now and for all time. One people, with one victory to strive for and one glory to gain—

DISSOLVE TO:

CLOSE SHOT   REYNAUD'S HAND HOLDING TELEGRAM

MR. CHURCHILL OFFERS UNION BETWEEN FRANCE AND BRITAIN TO CONTINUE THE WAR

DE GAULLE

Babble of voices begins in b.g.

VOICES   Yes. Yes.

VOICES   No. No. Against. Against.

LAST VOICE   Against.

DISSOLVE TO:

[NOTE in re. M. Berger's note on p. 54. This radio broadcast is imaginary, could have been unofficial, could have come on the operations beam on which the aircraft was flying. Could have been gossip, relayed by English dispatcher. It economizes space of film. It implies that he had gone to England more or less unofficially, on Reynaud's private say-so, and, having violated his office by doing so, was liable to arrest, having been disclaimed by his own government, etc.]

INT. AEROPLANE IN FLIGHT   CLOSE SHOT   DE GAULLE AND SPEARS

—other British diplomats, listening to radio broadcast.

RADIO   Mr. Reynaud has resigned as Premier of France. President Lebrun has appointed Marshal Pétain to form a new cabinet, for the purpose of asking armistice terms of the German government. General De Gaulle has been declared a traitor to his country and will be arrested on sight.

DISSOLVE TO:

EXT. AN AIRFIELD   FULL SHOT   NIGHT

—the backs of a group of men, mostly soldiers, standing without order. In b.g. facing them a transport, engines idling, door open; standing before door is De Gaulle, and members of the British mission. An aide stands beside De Gaulle, holding a clumsy military-type gasoline torch which makes a murky flickering light, the whole atmosphere to indicate that De Gaulle is departing almost secretly to save himself from arrest.

CLOSE SHOT   A FACE IN THE GROUP

—a soldier, unshaven, tired and strained-looking, anxious. CAMERA PANS to other faces resembling it: of soldiers who have escaped from the routed French forces. PAN to another face, then to Georges, staring anxiously at De Gaulle.

MED. CLOSE SHOT   DE GAULLE

—facing group as he recognizes Georges.

> **DE GAULLE**   I cannot take you all. I will take none of you now. There is work here in France for you to do. We have lost a battle, not the war. I am going to England, to prepare for all Frenchmen who still will fight, to come to me against the day when we can drive the enemy out again. Be of good courage, and remember: France has lost a battle, but France itself is not lost. Never!

He salutes, turns and enters plane, others follow. SOUND of engines grows loud into:

DISSOLVE TO:

INT. PLANE IN FLIGHT   CLOSE ON DE GAULLE AND SPEARS

De Gaulle and Spears are looking back and down through windows. They turn.

> **SPEARS**   Farewell to France, then.

DE GAULLE It is not farewell.

SPEARS You are right. I stand corrected, and I ask your pardon. Ah—

He takes out cigarette case, leans across aisle and offers it. De Gaulle looks down, takes cigarette.

DE GAULLE Thanks.

Spears takes out lighter, snaps it on, offers the lighter. De Gaulle leans toward it. Spears draws the lighter back slightly.

SPEARS To the day when you return.

DE GAULLE *(raises cigarette for an instant, as if he and Spears were drinking a toast)* To the day.

DISSOLVE TO:

INT. AN AIR SQUADRON OPERATIONS OFFICE

A blackboard with scrawled operations orders, names, etc. The request for armistice has been made, the French forces have ceased fighting. This is the present base to which this navy air squadron has retreated on the day the armistice was asked.

[I will consult Mr. Berger about this scene for authenticity.] It is Jean's navy air squadron, based temporarily on land to help halt the Germans. The armistice has been signed; three of the members refuse to accept the armistice, and depart. If possible, the squadron commander allows them to depart in peace, first stripping them of rank, to which one of them also adds his medal for valor, declining to wear it until France, who gave it to him, has expiated her own cowardice and treason, etc.

FADE OUT.

FADE IN

CLOSE SHOT   A GROUP OF PEOPLE ABOUT A RADIO

RADIO I, General De Gaulle, speaking from London, invite the French officers and soldiers, with their arms or without their arms, I invite the engineers and the workers skilled in the manufacture of armaments—

INT. CAFE   FULL SHOT

—favoring entrance from street. The patron is cleaning glasses behind the bar; a few villagers sit quietly about.

RADIO   In the face of the confusion of French arms, in the face of the disintegration of a government—

The door opens quickly; a villager, a man, enters. The radio voice cuts off abruptly; another voice begins, very loud as two German soldiers enter and approach the bar.

RADIO   Faced with the desperate situation of the lost war and the general collapse of the French people—

The two Germans look about at the men, stop at the bar. One of them points out a bottle. The patron puts glasses on the bar and fills them.

RADIO   —I, therefore, Pétain, Marshal of France, took power into my own hands to obtain an honorable armistice from the enemy.

ANOTHER ANGLE

Germans drink.

RADIO   There were only two alternatives in the face of the conditions imposed by the enemy: accept them and remain in Bordeaux, or refuse them and take refuge in Africa, far from our land and our people who could not depart for safety, as we, the government, could—

The Germans set the glasses down, look about again at the quiet men, turn and tramp to the door and go out. The man who entered first turns and follows them, shuts the door.

RADIO   I recognize that the fate of the French people will be harsh and hard. But I, your leader, Pétain, Marshal of France—

The radio voice cuts sharply off. The second voice, De Gaulle's, begins. The patron takes the two glasses the Germans used, throws them onto the floor, where they break. The other men do not move.

RADIO I, General De Gaulle, Franch soldier and chief, assume the right to call upon all of you. Soldiers of France, wherever you may be, arise.

DISSOLVE TO:

CLOSE SHOT   WOODS

Georges stooping over the body of a dead German soldier. He is unshaven, wears portions of his uniform, with other mismatched and dirty and misfit civilian garments. He is harried looking, strained. Georges drags the body out of scene.

CLOSE SHOT

Georges hides the body in a clump of bushes, exits hurriedly and cautiously.

DISSOLVE TO:

INT. STABLE   CLOSE SHOT   GEORGES AND COUPE-TÊTE

Coupe-tête has been pitching hay. He pauses with hayfork.

COUPE-TÊTE So you killed him. If you wish to hang, why just one?

GEORGES All right, all right. Who's here?

COUPE-TÊTE One too many now.

GEORGES Don't worry about that, either. I just want to get something to eat and to get rid of this—*(indicates uniform)* Then I'll be gone, too—to England where there is still one Frenchman who will fight.

COUPE-TÊTE Good. Do that. But not until I get back. You stay right here now, until I return.

CLOSE SHOT   COUPE-TÊTE IN THE WOODS

—as he tumbles the dead German into a shallow grave and begins to cover it. He smooths the earth over the grave and removes digging traces with leaves, brush, etc.

INT. STABLE   CLOSE SHOT   COUPE-TÊTE

—as he stands looking about the stable, finds Georges is gone, turns and exits.

INT. HALL   CLOSE SHOT   CATHERINE AND GEORGES

—in one another's arms, kissing. Coupe-tête pauses in the door, looking at them with grim displeasure. Georges raises his head, sees Coupe-tête. He and Catherine break apart.

CLOSE SHOT   CATHERINE, GEORGES AND COUPE-TÊTE

> **COUPE-TÊTE**   So this is what you call concealment.
>
> **CATHERINE**   He must wait on the others.
>
> **COUPE-TÊTE**   What others?
>
> **CATHERINE**   Armand Micoux—
>
> **COUPE-TÊTE**   Paroled. To the priest. On good behavior.
>
> **CATHERINE**   Guillaume Hoel.
>
> **COUPE-TÊTE**   Paroled. To the priest. On good behavior.

CLOSE ALL   FAVORING THE OPPOSITE DOOR

—as it opens and Marthe enters and stops, still holding the door. Her face is grim, like Coupe-tête's, but it is troubled and anxious where Coupe-tête conceals his anxiety, which is greater.

> **MARTHE**   *(to Georges)* His Reverence is here. And Madame would probably like a little moment with you, too, if you are done killing Germans in her back yard.
>
> **COUPE-TÊTE**   Peace, woman.
>
> **MARTHE**   Let him think of peace when next he comes stealing into his own home like a murderer.
>
> **COUPE-TÊTE**   Let them think of peace who force a man to become a murderer to enter his own house.

INT. KITCHEN   MED. SHOT

—priest, others in b.g., as Georges bends one knee quickly before him, then stands again.

> **GEORGES**   I would do it again. I have not surrendered.
>
> **COUPE-TÊTE**   He in the woods received no sacrament, either. Perhaps we both need absolution.

PRIEST Seek it where all Frenchmen must, and find it where all Frenchmen will: in the freeing of France.

MME MORNET *(to Georges)* Come. Eat.

MED. CLOSE   AT TABLE

—Georges sitting. Mme Mornet standing beside him, Marthe setting a bowl before him, others in b.g.

GEORGES It's hot. I haven't seen hot food in—

COUPE-TÊTE Eat it, then, as your mother told you. You will need it. You will need enough for you and Micoux and Hoel, all three, after that Boche sergeant calls the roll to-night and finds himself one swine short.

Georges eats ravenously.

DISSOLVE TO:

A WALL AT A CORNER   NIGHT

Four men crouching against the wall. Sound of tramping soldiers increases. A patrol passes, the tramp of feet dies away. The four men rise and steal on.

A HILL   CLOSE   COUPE-TÊTE, GEORGES, MICOUX AND HOEL
NIGHT

GEORGES *(to Coupe-tête)* You'd better go back now.

COUPE-TÊTE I just hope you don't go faster any slower.

GEORGES Don't worry about that. And we'll come back, too. The General and all of us. Don't you worry about that, either.

COUPE-TÊTE Get there first. Then talk about coming back. Go on. I'll take care of the land and of your mother, and of your wife, too, if you ever stay in a home long enough again to get one. Go on!

The three go on, vanish into the darkness. Coupe-tête turns.

INT. KITCHEN   GROUP   PRIEST, MME MORNET, CATHERINE,
MARTHE

—as Coupe-tête enters.

MME MORNET Well?

COUPE-TÊTE Three missing from the village tomorrow morning, two of whom are known, for whom His Reverence has given parole. And that Boche lying in the woods for the first stray dog to dig up.

PRIEST There is God.

COUPE-TÊTE Where?

CATHERINE If there is a Frenchman left who is willing to fight for France, we who can't fight can at least suffer to help him.

COUPE-TÊTE A Frenchman, bah! A Frenchman thinks first of his stove, then of his bed, and then of beautiful France. But if there can still be found one who still thinks of France and thinks well enough of it to fight for it, I suppose we of Brittany can still help him.

MARTHE Peace, fool! Are you deaf even to your own clacking?

FADE OUT.

FADE IN

EXT. STREET NIGHT CLOSE SHOT MEN'S FACES

The street is filled with shadowy men standing in the rain. They are Frenchmen who have escaped from France and reached England. They are all staring past Camera as though waiting. They are grave, a little anxious, patient.

REVERSE ANGLE HEADS SILHOUETTED FAVORING AN OPEN DOOR

—lighted from inside; against the door De Gaulle and an aide stand.

AIDE The General speaks no English. He asks, what do you wish?

A VOICE We are not English! We are Frenchmen!

DE GAULLE Frenchmen?

He steps forward.

FULL SHOT   DE GAULLE AND AIDE

—on stoop, the men in the street below, looking up at him.

DE GAULLE   Welcome to England then.

A VOICE   Welcome to France again!

DE GAULLE   Yes. Welcome again to France.

DISSOLVE TO:

INT. HUGE WAREHOUSE   FULL SHOT

—barren, filled with army cots, semi-military. Long row of cots, a Frenchman standing rigidly at attention before each cot like soldiers on parade. De Gaulle and aide in f.g. facing first man.

MAN   Ledoux.

DE GAULLE   *(shakes hands)* Ledoux. Welcome.

He moves on to next man; first man stares rigidly ahead.

NEXT MAN   Pelletier.

DE GAULLE   *(shakes hands)* Pelletier. Welcome.

He moves on to next man.

CLOSE   DE GAULLE   (FAVORING GEORGES AT ATTENTION)

DE GAULLE   Mornet. I saw you last that night at Bordeaux. Did the others escape?

GEORGES   A few, General.

DE GAULLE   I hope they will come to me.

GEORGES   They will, General. All France is coming to you.

De Gaulle moves on.

NEXT MAN   Masson.

DE GAULLE   *(shakes hands)* Masson. Welcome.

DISSOLVE TO:

INT. B.B.C. BROADCASTING ROOM   CLOSE SHOT   DE GAULLE AT MIKE

—operators, aides, Georges—now something between a sergeant and De Gaulle's orderly—beside him with notes, etc.

DE GAULLE Marshal Pétain, it is a French soldier who speaks to you. I heard your voice, which I know well from the old times when I was one of your subordinate officers. . . . You declared that there were only two alternatives imposed by the enemy: accept his terms and remain in France, or refuse them and take refuge in the empire to continue the war. You chose to stay in France. You, who were head of our military organization after 1918, who were Generalissimo up to 1932. We didn't need you, Marshal, to obtain and accept conditions of slavery. We didn't need the conqueror of Verdun to do this. . . .

You call upon France—a France surrendered, pillaged, enslaved—to go back to work; to build anew and rise from her ruins. But by what means, in the name of what, do you expect her to rise again? France will rise again. Throughout the Empire, throughout the world, French forces are forming and organizing. The day will come when our arms will join those of our allies. Then indeed we shall remake France.

He stops speaking, turns away from microphone. The operators cut switches, etc., go through routine of ending broadcast efficiently. Georges gathers up papers, etc.

CLOSE SHOT

An official holds the door open for De Gaulle to go out, Georges following.

DE GAULLE (pauses) Yes?

OFFICIAL Lord Halifax asks to see you, sir. He is waiting in your office.

DE GAULLE Thank you.

He exits, Georges follows.

INT. OFFICE   CLOSE SHOT   DE GAULLE AND HALIFAX

—seated at desk, aides, etc., in b.g.

HALIFAX   These men came to England for refuge after Narvik and after Dunkirk—

DE GAULLE   They were Frenchmen.

HALIFAX   Who had no country to return to. Yet you will permit these agents of Vichy to see them and demand that they return and assume allegiance to that government which has declared you a traitor and betrayed your native land.

DE GAULLE   Yes. Because those who accept Free France must do it of their own will and desire. I am not a politician and I don't want to be. I don't want to be even the commander of the French armed forces. I want to be the Chief of all Frenchmen who want to be free. For how can you command a man by force to risk his life in the name of freedom? In that case, that for which he suffers has already made him a slave. You can only lead him. And only he who loves freedom so well that he is willing to die for it at need.

HALIFAX   *(pauses)* I see. *(pauses again, rises)*

CLOSE   DE GAULLE

—standing, facing Halifax, standing.

HALIFAX   I am not a military man, and this will be clumsily done. But perhaps you can accept the will. *(salutes De Gaulle, turns)* Shall we have it over with, then?

DISSOLVE TO:

EXT.   MED. CLOSE   DE GAULLE, AIDES, THREE VICHY AGENTS

The agents are civilians, watchful, ill-at-ease.

DE GAULLE   *(to Vichy men)* Some of them are absent. They are at sea in British destroyers and trawlers, or at the airfields. But you can give your message to the ones who are here.

ANOTHER ANGLE   CLOSE ON DE GAULLE

—favoring a large courtyard outside a barracks. A small crowd of men faces him. They are Frenchmen, some in army and navy uniforms, some in misfit civvies, some in a mixture of both, some with crutches, sticks, bandages and slings, etc. They watch him quiet, curious, puzzled.

DE GAULLE These gentlemen are from Vichy. They have something to say to you. You are free men. Answer them as you desire.

MED. CLOSE GROUP

—as De Gaulle turns and walks out. The others look after him, the three Vichy men nervously. The Vichy spokesman steps forward, speaks. Georges and others stare rigidly ahead.

SPOKESMAN I come to you from the French government, that government to which your oath of allegiance and faithful service was transferred at the instant when it came into legal being in France's hour of darkness—

DISSOLVE TO:

INT. OFFICE CLOSE SHOT

—De Gaulle seated at desk, Georges standing facing him.

DE GAULLE Well?

GEORGES One man. Will you talk to him?

DE GAULLE He's a sailor.

CLOSE SHOT FAVORING GEORGES

—as he remembers how his own brother went for Vichy.

GEORGES Yes.

DE GAULLE Tell me. Why have so few sailors left France for us?

CLOSE SHOT BOTH

GEORGES (*harshly*) They are fascists. Because their officers order them to be.

DE GAULLE Because their officers order them. Stop at that. Yes, a soldier's wife and mother is his land, his government; a sailor's is his ship, no matter what flag it flies. Let him come in.

Georges exits.

ANOTHER ANGLE   DE GAULLE   AT DESK

—the sailor facing him. He is about twenty-five. His face is watchful, defiant.

    DE GAULLE   You wish to return to France?

    SAILOR   I have a wife. We have been married only a year. I have a child I haven't even seen. I. . . . *(pauses, stares at De Gaulle, watchful, defiant)*

    DE GAULLE   You were at Narvik. You did well there, I have been told.

    SAILOR   I did what all did. What I would do again if—*(he stops abruptly, watches De Gaulle)*

    DE GAULLE   *(finishes sentence for him)* If France could be so served again. *(the sailor stares at him, watchful, defiant)* Go then. You are free.

The sailor stares at him a moment, turns and exits. De Gaulle looks after him, grave and stern.

DISSOLVE TO:

INT. DE GAULLE'S OFFICE   CLOSE   DE GAULLE

—seated. Georges is placing pins in map on the wall. This scene will show the progress of the Free French movement up to date of Catroux's arrival in London—will reveal something of De Gaulle's future plans, or whatever is historically accurate to give us a time-lapse to Catroux's arrival. A voice speaks off scene, in adjoining room; De Gaulle and Georges pause, look out.

    VOICE   General Catroux.

INT. ANTEROOM   CLOSE   FRENCH MAJOR

—standing at salute behind the desk from which he has risen, facing door as Catroux, who has just entered, glances about, advances toward the desk. Catroux is travel-stained, looks tense, impatient, hurried.

CATROUX Morning. Where's De Gaulle?

MAJOR We have been expecting you, sir, ever since we heard how you, too, refused to accept the armistice and escaped, across the Pacific and across America, too—

CATROUX All right, all right. Where's De Gaulle? I will report to him.

MAJOR Report, sir? An army-group commander, reporting for duty to a brigadier?

CATROUX Eh? Oh. *(he approaches desk swiftly)* Your knife.

the major stares at him, puzzled. Catroux looks at desk, swiftly takes up paper knife, rips three of his five stars from his sleeve, flings knife and stars onto desk.

CATROUX Well, man? Where is he?

MED. CLOSE   INT. OFFICE

De Gaulle and aide risen, Georges turned from map as Catroux enters, pauses, looks quickly about.

CATROUX De Gaulle? *(sees De Gaulle)* Ah. *(he salutes)* Catroux reporting for duty.

DE GAULLE *(moves quickly forward)* Catroux is welcome.

DISSOLVE TO:

EXT. ALDERSHOT PARADE GROUND   MED. FULL SHOT   REVIEWING STAND

—De Gaulle, aides, British staff, King and officers; flags, French band playing (some well-known military tune for marching). Reviewers at salute.

REVERSE ANGLE   FROM STAND

—of Free France in first official parade. All the old men wear uniforms now. They march according to their old corps, regiments, and battalions. We will show Tirailleurs, Air Force, Chasseurs, etc., with their old battle flags, marching proudly now, stiffly eyes right as they pass the reviewing stand, etc. The last unit passes. PAN with it. It is a mixture of army and navy uniforms, misfit refugee civvies, and sometimes both together. The men have been wounded, on crutches, sticks, with slings and bandages. They look spent, gaunt, weak, yet happy, exalted, marching as stiff and smart as any, or trying to, helping one another. Georges is in command, gives the eyes right as they pass, then eyes front again as they pass on. Music dies away.

CLOSE   DE GAULLE

—favoring line of mismatched wounded men at attention. De Gaulle speaking to first man. Georges follows De Gaulle.

FIRST MAN   Fayol, General.

DE GAULLE   Fayol. Welcome.

TRUCK with De Gaulle to next man. Georges follows.

MAN   Dal, General.

DE GAULLE   Dal. Welcome.

TRUCK with De Gaulle to next man. Georges follows.

DE GAULLE   I saw you that morning at Chalandry. You behaved well. It goes?

MAN   It goes, General.

DE GAULLE   Good. *(he is about to pass on, looks at next man, stops; the man is on a crutch, is gaunt and weak)* Chalandry also. I thought you were dead. What brought you back?

WOUNDED MAN   *(weakly)* France, General.

FIRST MAN   Someone whispered "De Gaulle" in his ear.

GEORGES   Silence in ranks, there!

DE GAULLE *(without turning, to Georges)* That will do, Sergeant. *(to first man)* Does that raise the dead in France?

FIRST MAN   It does better than that. It raises the living in France.

DE GAULLE   Let's hope it will do so.

He moves on, pauses, stops dead, staring at him.

CLOSE FAVORING THE MAN

It is the sailor who decided to go back to France with the Vichy agents. He looks haggard, desperate, grim. He is unshaven, muddy, a long unhealed recent wound across his forehead. He stares at De Gaulle, smoldering and fierce.

DE GAULLE You have come back.

SAILOR I—I—

DE GAULLE To France.

The sailor stares fiercely at De Gaulle, represses some fierce reaction.

SAILOR To France.

De Gaulle passes on.

DISSOLVE TO:

INT. DE GAULLE'S HOME DEN OR SMALL SITTING ROOM
EVENING

De Gaulle reading, Mme De Gaulle sewing.

MED. CLOSE FAVORING DOOR

—as it opens and Georges enters. De Gaulle looks up.

GEORGES He's here, sir.

DE GAULLE Yes. All right.

He lays book (papers probably) down and rises. Mme De Gaulle looks up.

DE GAULLE (*to Madame*) I'll go on to the studio from here. I speak at midnight.

MME DE GAULLE Nazis don't sleep at midnight, either.

DE GAULLE Perhaps not. But neither do the people Nazis rule.

He turns to exit, Georges holding the door.

INT. OFFICE-DEN CLOSE DE GAULLE AND THE SAILOR

SAILOR Yes. I found them. I found the grave. There are

three now: one for her shame and my dishonor, one for the beast that did it, and one for another beast to keep the first one company into hell. He gave me this before he died. (*touches wound on his head*) Fool, to think a bullet could stop grief and rage. So I am back.

DE GAULLE   Why?

SAILOR   Just another young woman of the people, wife to a common sailor and mother of his son—nobody. You'd think we would have been too small for them to trouble. Too small to have made them fear.

DE GAULLE   Why?

SAILOR   (*pauses*) Why? For vengeance. To kill them.

DE GAULLE   That's not enough. It's good but not enough.

CLOSE   FAVORING THE SAILOR

—as he stares at De Gaulle.

    DE GAULLE   Not just for vengeance: for liberty and freedom.

He puts his hands on the sailor's shoulders. The sailor stares at De Gaulle. His face breaks. He strives against it, staring at De Gaulle. It goes completely. The sailor stares at De Gaulle, tears running down his cheeks.

    DE GAULLE   For liberty and freedom. For peace.

    SAILOR   For peace. Where all the little people—all the little people—

DISSOLVE TO:

INT. BARRACKS   MED. CLOSE

Five or six cots, the sailor in one, his back to the others, his eyes closed. Georges, the wounded man, two others going to bed. Window open in b.g., moon shining, air raid in distance. A man is helping the wounded man off with his clothes.

    WOUNDED MAN   He remembered me.

    GEORGES   He remembers all of us. He says all men who love freedom have only one face to remember.

FIRST MAN   Besides, there are not enough of us yet to start forgetting.

WOUNDED MAN   But there will be soon.

FIRST MAN   Yes. If he just keeps on calling the dead back to life like he did you.

GEORGES   And he will remember their faces, too.

INT. B.B.C. STUDIO   CLOSE SHOT   DE GAULLE AT MICROPHONE

DE GAULLE   All of you whose sons and fathers and husbands and brothers have died, grieve for them but do not despair. All of you whose sons and fathers and brothers and husbands have merely vanished from the places that once knew them—

DISSOLVE TO:

FIVE OR SIX FRENCH PEOPLE

—crouching, tense, listening, watchful. De Gaulle's voice cuts short off. Tramp of army feet increases, the shadow of a patrol, rifles slanted, legs tramping in unison, passes across, disappears, the tramp of feet dies away. The voice comes on again, the people quiet, listening.

VOICE   —do not even grieve. Because they have come to me. They come to me here daily, and our battalions and regiments live again. They are with me today, and they tell you in my voice to believe and hope, for even you who for a little while yet the enemies of France continue to hold, you also are not alone and are not forgotten.

FADE OUT.

FADE IN

Jean was wounded at the affair of Oran. He is still in the navy. He has been given a job by the Vichy government, in France.

[NOTE: In this case, will he have the use of a German official car and driver?]

EXT. VILLAGE SQUARE BEFORE THE CAFE

Opposite is the mayor's office and city hall, a German flag over the door. In the square is the bronze poilu commemorating the village men who died in 1914–1918.

CLOSE   ON A GROUP OF VILLAGERS, MEN

—before the cafe as a German military car, Nazi pennon, etc., a German soldier driving it and Jean in back seat, rushes past. The men look after it, astonished.

> **VOICE**   It's Jean Mornet.

> **ANOTHER**   What?

> **THIRD**   Yes. Jean Mornet. Jean Mornet.

DISSOLVE TO:

FULL SHOT   THE MORNET HOME

The car is halted in front of it.

INT. MORNET KITCHEN   JEAN, COUPE-TÊTE AND MARTHE

Jean shows recent illness, walks with a stick, etc. He has just arrived.

> **COUPE-TÊTE**   You were at Oran? Then what are you doing here?

> **JEAN**   Where would you expect me to be?

> **COUPE-TÊTE**   Where your brother is. Where any Frenchman should be now who was present at Oran.

> **JEAN**   What do you think happened at Oran?

> **COUPE-TÊTE**   Evidently I don't know. The official radio told us, but the official radio also said that England would be conquered too, in one week. That was two months ago. All we know is, someone fought at Oran for France. And if anyone fought anywhere for France, he fought Germans. So if a Mornet was at Oran, he wouldn't be coming here to Saint Odile except to hide while he got his breath to run again, as your brother did.

> **MARTHE**   Hush! Here comes Madame!

Jean turns as Mme Mornet enters, hurries to him, embraces him.

MME MORNET Jean! You've been hurt!

JEAN It's nothing. It's all right now.

CLOSE GROUP

Mme Mornet and Jean seated, Coupe-tête and Marthe standing.

JEAN They caught us without warning, bottled in the harbor without steam up to fight and no sea-room to fight in, if we had had the steam. But no matter. Maybe they had to, or believed they had do. But we are not England, with an intact government and a home army and an island to protect us. We are France, already partly occupied, our capital lost and already under terms to the enemy because the people and the army they composed and the government they supported collapsed—

COUPE-TÊTE Not the people. Not the army. The generals and the politicians.

MME MORNET Coupe-tête.

JEAN It's done now. Why, doesn't matter. What does matter is that we hold together what is still left of France to be a bargaining factor when the day comes—

COUPE-TÊTE Guns will do that. Just as in 1918 . . .

MME MORNET Hush!

JEAN Let him finish. Then let him look about him and see what is happening to the people who believe and act as he sounds like he believes.

MME MORNET Not all of them.

JEAN I know what you mean, Georges. I have already heard—

COUPE-TÊTE Yes. Not all of them. Not any of the young, the strong, and the brave—

MARTHE Hush! Hush!

COUPE-TÊTE This Hitler. This nothing. This little pinch of rotten dirt in the face of God—

MARTHE   Will you hush?

MME MORNET   *(to Coupe-tête)* Hush, now. *(to Jean)* Now tell me. I want to understand it if I can.

JEAN   We lost the war, the army did. We risked one battle, and we lost it. Or the army did. Our navy still exists. There is only the navy left to keep what still remains of France. To do that, the navy must observe the terms of the armistice entered into by the French government. I have been designated by the navy, of which I am still a member, to a shore job.

COUPE-TÊTE   As a German policeman.

MME MORNET   *(to Coupe-tête; still watching Jean)* Hush! Yes?

JEAN   *(after a moment)* I see. You, too.

MME MORNET   Better to perish as Frenchmen than to survive by surrendering all that made us French.

JEAN   You're old, a woman; you don't understand.

MME MORNET   Perhaps not, I only know that your brother knew exactly what he must do, and did it without the thought ever occurring to him to stop and give anybody a reason for it. And that your and his father died in 1917 without having to give anyone a reason why he did that. And that if he had had the choice between dying then and living to see what we can see today, he would have chosen to die.

Jean rises. Mme Mornet rises. Coupe-tête and Marthe watch.

JEAN   I must go. I just came. Had you rather I didn't come back—

MME MORNET   *(moves quickly to him)* You are my son, too. *(embraces him)* Come back when you will, whenever they will let—*(stops short, embraces him)* Take care of yourself. Take care.

JEAN   I'll be all right. They are—*(stops—to Coupe-tête)* Maybe I don't like this, either. If Oran hadn't happened, maybe I wouldn't be doing this. Let them who shot my old job out from under me find me a new one.

COUPE-TÊTE They will. As they have found your brother one.

MME MORNET *(to Coupe-tête)* Hush!

COUPE-TÊTE Madame.

DISSOLVE TO:

EXT. VILLAGE STREET

The car rushes through it; men and women turn to look after it.

CLOSE SHOT

The car stopped before the mayor's house, faces peering out from beneath lifted curtains in the adjacent windows as Jean gets out of the car, pauses, sees the faces for a second before the curtains drop and the faces are jerked away. Jean goes toward the door, limping on his stick.

CLOSE SHOT   JEAN AT DOOR

It opens. The mayor's woman servant looks out, fearful, shrinking. She is afraid of Jean, the German car, etc. She disapproves of Jean in his present capacity. He is now an enemy. Jean enters.

INT. LIVING ROOM   CLOSE SHOT   JEAN

—standing, favoring the door as it opens and the mayor enters. He is uncertain. In his official position, he is forced by the German commander to collaborate. He must accept daily the German's contempt of him as a conquered Frenchman. Because of his position as official head of the village, he feels his duty is to protect his people and their property. Also, he wants to protect his own property. But he is aware of the unrest among his people, of their hatred toward the invaders, so he is not sure which side to definitely commit himself to. He is the pompous martinet he once was only on the surface. He is definitely worried, troubled.

He pauses in the door.

MAYOR Lieutenant.

He crosses quickly, shakes Jean's hand.

MAYOR   Someone official, at last. So far they have given us nothing, nothing: no word, no contact—only the German garrison and the official radio. As if I could know what to do, what they wished. Young men escaping each night to England, the Germans taking hostages from among us in reprisal . . .

JEAN   I am on duty from the navy.

MAYOR   Then you bring me no instructions at all?

JEAN   No. I stopped for a moment to speak to Catherine, with your permission.

MAYOR   Oh. Yes. I see.

The mayor turns, crosses to door, goes out, closes the door. Jean watches the door. It opens, the servant comes in just far enough to see Jean.

SERVANT   Miss Catherine is not at home.

The servant closes the door. Jean turns, walks toward Camera.

EXT. STREET   CLOSE ON CAR

—as Jean approaches, gets into it. The car moves; faces appear again beneath the lifted shades.

EXT. A ROAD

A small, dirty boy at roadside, watches the car as it approaches; SOUND of car increases. The boy stoops into weeds as the car passes. The boy rises, flings something at it, ducks down again. The car goes on. PAN to the object the boy threw; a dead cat lying in the road.

FADE OUT.

FADE IN

Jean, still on duty from the navy and still under Vichy authority, is a member of the Vichy Gestapo, under unofficial German supervision. He uses his position and authority to deflect some of the food requisitioned by the Germans from Vichy under the armistice terms, and sends it to his mother. He doesn't boast openly about what he is doing, but he does not try to conceal it.

He simply orders certain packages to be sent to his mother, knowing that the Germans probably are aware of it, or can find it out easily enough. To conceal what he is doing, he would have to juggle records, bribe people, either of which would be a violation of his character and of his navy oath, to which he is remaining faithful rather than to Vichy. [Does this correct the matter criticized by M. Berger re. Page 87?]

INT. OFFICE   CLOSE SHOT

Jean seated at desk with papers, etc. A clerk enters with other papers. [Will ask M. Berger if this is a soldier or a civilian, possibly a transplanted German clerk or perhaps a woman, French or German.] The clerk lays the papers before Jean, waits. Jean examines the papers.

JEAN   You have checked them?

CLERK   Three boxes, sir.

JEAN   To Madame G. Mornet, Saint Odile, Ile-et-Vilaine.

CLERK   To Madame G. Mornet, Saint Odile, Ile-et-Vilaine.

JEAN   Tonight. With priority.

CLERK   Tonight. With priority.

JEAN   Thank you.

The clerk exits. Jean looks out of scene until the sound of a door being closed comes. Then he takes up the paper, tears it, burns the pieces carefully over an ash tray, mashes the ash to dust, is emptying the ashes into a wastebasket, pauses, looks up.

CLOSE   JEAN AT DESK

—favoring a door, open, a German orderly in the door. The orderly enters, clicks heels stiffly, though even in this he contrives to show contempt or at least disregard for Jean, the Frenchman, and as far as the German is concerned, a traitor or at least a weakling.

ORDERLY   The Colonel's compliments. At once.

The orderly exits without waiting for an answer. Without haste, Jean finishes emptying the ash into the wastebasket, puts the tray back on the desk, rises.

CLOSE SHOT

Jean approaches a corridor door. The door opens before he can touch it. Through the door can be seen a slightly more luxurious office, French in style and furnishings—an atmosphere rich and somehow faintly decadent. A hat-rack or -tree just inside door, a German military overcoat and sword and a helmet in grim paradox to the room. A broad desk at the far end, the German colonel seated behind it. He is Prussian, typical almost, though his face is shrewder, a little more scholarly. But he is hard. He is a soldier first, officer caste, etc. Jean enters. The orderly shuts the door behind him.

CLOSE SHOT   AT DESK

Jean approaches it. The colonel is writing. He does not look up.

    COLONEL   Sit down.

Jean sits in a chair at end of desk. The colonel pushes a box toward him with one hand, without looking up.

    COLONEL   Cigarette. Excuse me a moment.

    JEAN   Thanks.

He doesn't take the cigarette. He sits quietly. The colonel signs the paper, blots it, pushes it aside, looks up, takes a cigarette from the box, looks at Jean, takes up the box and offers it again. Jean doesn't take one.

    JEAN   Thanks.

The colonel puts the box down, takes up a lighter and lights his cigarette, puts the lighter down.

    COLONEL   You have been sending food home to your mother. Of course you have known all the time that we have known that all the time.

    JEAN   You could have stopped it.

    COLONEL   I could have stopped it. I was instructed not to.

ANOTHER ANGLE

    COLONEL   We expected you to send food home. I was surprised to find you content with so little.

JEAN Then what do you want me to do about it?

COLONEL Nothing. Continue to send it, which of course you will do. Send enough of it. If you did not have enough love of family to grieve when they suffer, and the courage to do something to rectify it, do you think you would be of any value to us? When we need rascals and poltroons capable of any act, who can be bought for almost any price, we do not need to search for them among the people we conquer: we breed our own.

JEAN Just what do you want me to do?

COLONEL There is an Underground in France. That's natural. It happens each time. We anticipate it by now. If it did not occur, we would begin to doubt human nature, and therefore ourselves. To combat it would require another army, a larger army even than was required to capture the country. So we use the people themselves, the ones among them who are intelligent enough—

CLOSE   JEAN STANDING

—the colonel still sitting.

JEAN You use your conquered "friends."

COLONEL Success has no friends. It has sycophants.

JEAN I am not a spy. I am a Navy officer, under orders from my superior—

COLONEL Until your superior orders otherwise.

Jean stares at the colonel. The colonel watches Jean. Then the colonel bends down, pulls out drawer, produces brandy bottle, sets it beside glasses on tray on the desk.

COLONEL Drink?

JEAN No, thanks. Was that all you wanted now?

COLONEL Yes. Think it over.

JEAN I have. I am a traitor perhaps, but no spy.

COLONEL I am afraid you will discover you have gone too

far to have much choice—which will be a misfortune for you, and a grief to them who love you. Someday you are going to have to obey your conscience. Then in the next moment you are going to lose your life trying to rectify the act.

DISSOLVE TO:

EXT. STREET   CLOSE SHOT

—a burst paper sack, scattered potatoes on the cobbled pavement, a girl's hands gathering them. Feet of passers as they step around the potatoes. One pair of feet stop.

CLOSE   JEAN STANDING

—Emilie kneeling, gathering up the potatoes. She is about twenty, looks poor, hungry, thin, that is. Jean stoops, begins to help gather up the potatoes. She becomes aware of him, starts as though she believed he was about to steal some of them, sees him, recognizes him.

> **EMILIE**   Thank you, Mr. Mornet.

Jean pauses, surprised, looks at her. She watches him.

> **JEAN**   How did you—*(begins to recognize her)*

> **EMILIE**   Yes. On the stairs. We live on the floor beneath you. You are the lonely man.

> **JEAN**   We?

> **EMILIE**   My father and I.

> **JEAN**   Oh. Then we can walk home together, if you are going that way.

> **EMILIE**   Yes.

They finish gathering up the potatoes. The burst sack will not hold them.

> **JEAN**   Wait.

He begins to take off his overcoat.

> **EMILIE**   No, no. They're dirty. They'll soil it. My shawl—

JEAN *(removes overcoat)* I doubt if any food can soil a Frenchman's clothes any more.

EMILIE That depends on what that Frenchman has paid for it.

Jean pauses, stops, holding the coat, looking at her.

ANOTHER ANGLE

Emilie folds the potatoes rapidly into her shawl, Jean still watching her, holding his coat.

EMILIE *(rises)* There. Come along.

JEAN Won't you let me carry it?

EMILIE It's not heavy.

CLOSE   BOTH

—walking along street past cafe. (Café de la Paix, or other, tables filled with German officers, etc.) French people passing, depressed, sullen. Emilie's face is calm, Jean's grave, thoughtful.

JEAN So you really do know who I am.

EMILIE Yes.

CLOSE   JEAN AND EMILIE

—at a door, entrance to tenement, apartment, etc. Jean opens the door for Emilie to enter.

JEAN Then there are other French people in Paris who know it, too.

EMILIE Yes.

She enters. Jean follows.

INT. STAIRCASE   CLOSE SHOT   JEAN AND EMILIE

—dim and dingy. Jean and Emilie at landing, door behind them.

EMILIE Thank you.

JEAN For what little I did.

He raises his hat, turns, mounts the stairs. Emilie looks after him.

EMILIE   Mr. Mornet.

Jean stops, turns, looks back.

EMILIE   Come and eat them with us.

CLOSE   JEAN AND EMILIE

—on landing again.

JEAN   Why did you say I am lonely?

EMILIE   I told you we live just under you. I can hear your feet at night. Too late at night.

JEAN   Is that loneliness?

EMILIE   No. It's more.

JEAN   More?

EMILIE   It's worse.

She turns toward the door. Jean takes hold of knob to open it. She turns, stops him for a moment.

EMILIE   *(rapidly)* I won't tell Father who you are. You will excuse him—us.

Jean bows, opens door. Emilie enters. He follows.

INT. ROOM   CLOSE   MOELLENS

—asleep in an armchair before small weak meager fire in the grate. The room is sparsely and poorly furnished, such as refugees without money would live in, rented. Moellens is old, sixty, looks weak, nervous, prematurely old, ill almost. Emilie approaches, Jean following, and stops at chair, looking down at Moellens.

EMILIE   Father.

Moellens starts, wakes, looks up, sees Emilie, then Jean.

EMILIE   This is Mr. Mornet, Father.

MOELLENS   He has had to leave his home, too?

JEAN Yes.

MOELLENS He is welcome, then.

CLOSE   SUPPER TABLE

It is a makeshift table, set with mismatched china, etc. It bears the single dish of potatoes and a loaf of poor bread, which would have been the Moellens' meal, also two or three things which Jean has evidently brought from his room—obvious luxuries which he had from the Germans. There is a bottle of wine. The only wine glass is at Jean's place. Moellens has a chipped mug. Emilie is not drinking any of the wine. Moellens is pouring the last of the wine into his and Jean's glasses. He is quite shaky. He sets the bottle down and raises his mug.

> **MOELLENS** Let us drink to the guest, whose kindness supplied us with these luxuries, as well as the wine we toast him in. Though the very possession of such delicacies as these would nowadays mark any man but a Breton—or a Belgian. *(he pauses, his face darkens for a moment, recovers)* But if he were not a true man, Frenchman or not, he would not be here. *(raises mug)* To the Day. When Breton and Belgian and all the dispossessed can return. Confusion to them who robbed our nations of honor and our peoples of peace.
>
> **EMILIE** *(quickly yet firmly)* Father!
>
> **MOELLENS** *(recovers)* Yes, my dear. *(raises mug again)* We will drink to our guest, then. That will be better. *(bows to Jean)* With gratitude.

Jean bows. Moellens drinks. Emilie rises, takes up a dish.

> **EMILIE** *(to Moellens)* Go back to your chair at the fire, while I clear the table.
>
> **MOELLENS** Yes, my dear. *(raises his mug again to Jean)* Come then. The toast has been declared. We will not need to repeat it. To the Day.

Jean raises his glass. They drink. Emilie picks up another dish, exits with them.

MOELLENS —The suffering they caused, the blood they have shed, the very earth itself will take care of—the earth which drank it, the air which heard the grief, the sun which watched—all these will weigh and indict them and set the punishment and carry the sentence out.

ANOTHER ANGLE

MOELLENS But the other crimes, little crimes in the sense that neither their commission nor omission could have advanced or retarded their aims one jot: the music they banned and scattered, the books they burned and destroyed, the pictures they stole—I was a musician. I played at the Royal Opera in Brussels. I have played command performances, not only before our king but at the Hague and in London—Yes, there will be a particular providence, a small, petty, even vengeful one, which will have charge of the punishing for that, so that the greater one, the God who is God—

Emilie enters quickly, pauses, anxious.

MOELLENS —will have nothing else to do but listen to the blood they shed and the suffering and the grief and the dishonor and the shame—the shame—

Emilie steps quickly up, touches his shoulder. Jean is watching her. She looks up at him, looks away.

EMILIE *(quietly and firmly)* Father.

MOELLENS Yes? Yes?

EMILIE Go to your chair. It's getting cool.

MOELLENS Yes, my dear. *(Emilie helps him up)*

CLOSE

Moellens seated again. Emilie spreads shawl about his shoulders. Jean in b.g.

MOELLENS He is a true man, a Frenchman, or he would not be here, in this room. It is coming. All Europe will rise against them: one family, one blood, one suffering, for all of us, one grief, one dishonor—

EMILIE Yes. Don't talk any more now.

MOELLENS Bah! I don't need to talk to tell him. He knows it. Isn't he a Frenchman? It is all one suffering: Frenchman, Slav, Norse, all.

EMILIE Yes. Yes. No more now.

She tucks the shawl in, rises, turns. Jean is watching her, sober and thoughtful. She looks at him for a moment, grave, lowers her head a little and passes him, exits.

CLOSE   EMILIE AND JEAN

JEAN You knew who I was. And you knew that—*(indicates the old man's position with a slight movement of his head)*—was going to happen. Why did you let me come?

EMILIE Because you are not a spy. You may be a—*(catches herself, watching him)*

JEAN Traitor? *(she doesn't answer)* There is an Underground. I know that. They do, too. But not from me.

EMILIE Yes. It exists. Stronger than you think. It will be stronger still, as we learn better how to be Underground. We were free too long. But soon all Frenchmen will belong to it. They will have to. Or it will be too late.

JEAN Too late?

EMILIE Wait.

She exits, returns, hands him a paper. He unfolds it.

CLOSE SHOT

The list of proscribed Frenchmen compiled by the Underground. Among other names, PAN to:

Naval Lieutenant Mornet, Jean

CLOSE   JEAN AND EMILIE

JEAN So you knew I was not a spy.

EMILIE Spies are fearful and gregarious. You are just lonely and not afraid.

JEAN   Oh. How did you learn so much about men? You were married?

EMILIE   No. I was engaged. He was in Fort Emael.

JEAN   I see. He is dead?

EMILIE   I don't know. He would probably hope so.

JEAN   I see. There was something else, something your father almost said. About dishonor. *(Emilie watches him, faces him)* May I ask about that?

EMILIE   No. Don't ask about that.

JEAN   Yes. Goodnight. *(he turns, exits)*

DISSOLVE TO:

LANDING   CLOSE   JEAN

—sets several parcels of food on floor before the door, knocks on the door, exits.

INT. JEAN'S BEDROOM   CLOSE AT DOOR

—as it opens and Jean enters, shuts door, stands for a moment, grave, thoughtful, rouses, removes his coat, pauses as a knock sounds at door. Jean puts the coat back on, opens the door. Emilie stands there holding the parcels.

EMILIE   Thank you. I accepted at supper because he needed decent food. He would forgive me for that once, but not again.

JEAN   Tell him that every bite he takes is one bite less for them to get—

Emilie stands looking at him quietly until he ceases. He takes the parcels from her. She begins to turn away.

EMILIE   Goodnight.

She exits. Jean closes the door.

FADE OUT.

FADE IN

THE VILLAGE

Michel Kereon, a native, moved to Paris years ago and went to work in a French factory. After the fall of France, the Germans converted the factory into a munitions plant. Kereon reappears in the village. He tells the villagers that he has quit, will make no more guns for the enemy, etc. If the Germans catch him, they will send him back. [Will consult M. Berger as to just how Kereon can return to the village and remain there: in hiding, or forged papers, or what means.]

Kereon and a few of the villagers, led by Coupe-tête, have a meeting place in an old tower dungeon. This is an Underground cell in embryo. That is, at this time there is no connected Underground. This cell of discussion and possible active resistance was just spontaneous with this village. They do not have any way of knowing that this same impulse is probably beginning all over France. They just meet secretly here to listen to a hidden radio and to talk. Kereon tells them something of what is going on in Paris and the rest of France: of the resistance of individuals, the suffering, the deeds, etc.

When the food sent by Jean arrives, Mme Mornet divides it out among the needy villagers, for the women and children. It is luxuries; only the city people are suffering yet for food. The country people have their crops, gardens, etc. Guezonnec, a villager, is a grim, fanatic man. The whole village knows where the food comes from, but it remains for Guezonnec to decide that the food is sent by a traitor to France and is therefore tainted and must not be eaten by true Frenchmen. He takes three companions, persuades them likewise. They break into the station, take a box of the food and burn it.

Coupe-tête and the others are shocked at this—at the folly of destroying the food, and the folly of incurring reprisals from the German village garrison for such a trivial matter. Kereon agrees; if they wish to do something, do something worthwhile. Now they notice something in Kereon's manner. A man wishes to know, do what, for instance? Kereon tells them of what he intends to do, what he has really come home to do—to wreck a train of munitions going to the coast to install fortifications, etc.

He tells how he will have a signal which train it will be. This was arranged before he left the factory, and is why he left. He is waiting now for the signal to come to him. We will show here how at this point such deeds are being done, by men who will die in the act without glory or recognition, because so far there is no way in which they can communicate with one another. [Will ask M. Berger just how much intercommunication, secret newspapers, etc., existed at this time: spring-summer, 1941.] Kereon now gets plenty of volunteers to help him sabotage the train.

The German garrison commander in the village knew about the food, of course. He neither knew nor cared who sent it. But it came officially, and he would see each time that Mme Mornet got it. When the box was burned, to him it was a simple case of insubordination, unrest in the village which it was his duty to keep quiet. He looks through his list to pick out a hostage, to arrest and thus force the real culprit to confess. He discovers Kereon on his list. Kereon is now ambiguous. The German learns that Kereon has deserted from the factory, sends out to arrest him. Kereon is warned in time, hides. Another villager is arrested.

The hostage is an old man. He will not live through much hardship, etc. There is a meeting in the dungeon. They want to know what Guezonnec is going to do about it. Guezonnec is still grim, defiant. He says, let Kereon surrender; all they will do to Kereon is send him back to his job. Coupe-tête and others repeat that Kereon must see to wrecking the train. Guezonnec says that when he sacrifices himself, it will be to accomplish something, not just to pay for burning a box of food.

Kereon gets his signal when the train will pass. With his party of villagers, he prepares to wreck it. [Will consult M. Berger as to just how much order, what equipment, etc., they would have, or if they would use whatever means they could find themselves.] Coupe-tête, Guezonnec and Kereon go to the railway and place the obstruction or dynamite. Kereon wishes to do it alone, but Guezonnec is still grimly determined to show his mettle. He insists on going. Coupe-tête goes along, too. He says to see that the job is done right but actually to control the situation, supervise Guezonnec's fanaticism, etc.

They place the obstruction, the train is wrecked. From their hiding place, Coupe-tête, Kereon and Guezonnec catch a glimpse of two men, whom they take to be tramps or someone escaping in the wreck. They realize that if the two men are found near the wreckage, the Germans will arrest them. They creep up to get the men away, help them if injured, find two Frenchmen in rough clothes. Coupe-tête recognizes one of them as Georges. He and Kereon and Guezonnec carry them from the scene, manage to get a cart and carry Georges and his companion away before the Germans find them.

When Georges comes to, he is in his mother's house. He learns how he got there, what happened, and that his companion died and Coupe-tête and the others buried him. Georges tries to get up and leave at once, though injured. He tells Coupe-tête and his mother and Catherine that he should not be there, must not stay. They restrain him because of his injury. Finally he tells them that he and his companion were agents from De Gaulle, to help the Underground organize, that they both took an oath never to try to see their families or even let them know that they were in France. He must go; he will go. The women try to soothe him but in vain until Coupe-tête tells him how the whole countryside is being watched by the Germans to catch the saboteurs. So Georges must remain hidden until he can escape.

Men are arrested in all the villages in the district as the Germans hunt the saboteurs. Two are arrested in the Mornet village, making three which are being held. They are to be shot. Kereon goes forward and surrenders himself, believing that this will save the others. The village learns that Kereon has a skilled job, is too valuable to shoot, and will be sent back to his old factory. This is Guezonnec's chance to make good his words. He goes forward, claims sole responsibility for the wreck, believing this will save the other lives. It does not. He and the others are taken away to the capital city in the district for trial and execution.

Now all the men in the district who are trustworthy come to the dungeon to speak to Georges, the authentic De Gaulle man, and listen to him. They only want to know what to do. They have experienced suffering and slavery, seen the enemy's bloody retaliation; they only want someone who knows to tell them they are not forgotten and how to give their lives. Georges talks to them. He tells them what has happened and is happening outside in the world, about how the old French empire is gradually coming over to the one man who promises Frenchmen freedom. He tells them he is on a mission now to visit the people in France who feel as they do, and give them hope and courage. He tells them that Charles De Gaulle in London will keep in touch with them and advise them, and to believe always in France and liberty. They depart.

GEORGES, THE PRIEST, MME MORNET, CATHERINE, COUPE-TÊTE, MARTHE

—are alone. Georges says he must go now. He has already stayed too long. He shouldn't have come at all, has lost that much time in his work. He will not return again until France is free and he can return to peace and freedom and to all that liberty means.

   PRIEST Why do you wait until then?

All react as they comprehend what he means.

   PRIEST Your banns have already been posted, except for that day when your father in his anger tore the notice down. But I imagine Coupe-tête can rectify that.

Coupe-tête reacts as he understands the implication.

   PRIEST So far you and other young Frenchmen like you have had incentive only to risk your lives. There is no question of courage. All men who wish to be free must have courage. You need more than the incentive to die if necessary. You must need to live, as well. To live, and to return.

   GEORGES I will come back. With men and guns.

   PRIEST For still more blood and destruction and death. You must have incentive for more than that: for peace, contentment. So why do you wait?

   GEORGES Now? When I may be dead next month, next week, maybe tomorrow?

PRIEST Look at her. Does she look afraid?

Catherine and Georges look at one another.

PRIEST A man is almost impossible to destroy, when he has enough incentive to stay alive. *(he takes their hands, joins them)*

GEORGES There is France.

PRIEST There is no harm to France in your love.

DISSOLVE TO:

Coupe-tête posts again the final notice required for Georges and Catherine's marriage, to make the marriage legal. He does it in such a way that the Germans will think it is an old notice, without significance now.

THE DUNGEON   NIGHT

Smoky torches, the Mornet household, Catherine, villagers, others who have been coming to listen to instructions from Georges. The village clerk performs the legal ceremony, proud to be acting again as a free Frenchman. Then the priest performs the religious one.

CLOSE   KNEELING MEN AND WOMEN

—favoring Catherine and Georges kneeling before priest. A round stone slab has been dressed with altar vestments, candles, etc. Mme Mornet, Marthe, Coupe-tête in b.g.

PRIEST —in sickness and in health, in sorrow and joy, until death. Whom God hath joined, let no man put asunder.

He makes sign of cross. Georges rises, helps Catherine up. All rise. Georges turns to face them.

GEORGES The General said we have been free too long in France; we didn't know how to be secret and be strong. But we are learning. There are many more like me, that he has sent, to go among all the villages and towns as I have come here, to bring his message. He says, "Be secret and be strong, and wait and hope, and above all, work."

COUPE-TÊTE *(advances)* But first, of course, is to salute the bride.

INT. HOUSE NIGHT

Coupe-tête stooping before a closed door, cautiously hanging onto the knob a string to which is tied bottles, tin cans, an old shoe, etc., which clash and jangle together as he loops them cautiously about the knob. Marthe enters behind him, pauses. She wears her nightgown, shawl over her shoulders, her hair in papers.

MARTHE *(whispers)* What are you doing?

Coupe-tête starts, catches himself, merely looks back as he ties the cord.

COUPE-TÊTE I intend to remind him tomorrow he was a free man once, even if he doesn't know it yet.

He rises, pulls the string slightly, releases it. The bottles and cans clash faintly.

MARTHE Hush! Hush! Will you wake the whole house?

COUPE-TÊTE If some in the house need to be waked at this moment, so much the better for France, according to His Reverence. But I am not one.

He turns. Before Marthe can move, he embraces her. She struggles.

MARTHE Let go, you old fool! You, gray as an old badger, and not two teeth in your head that meet one another!

COUPE-TÊTE *(embracing her)* A man's teeth and hair have nothing to do with the condition of his heart nor the strength of his sap.

He draws her to him. She struggles, slapping at him. He holds her face, kisses her. She stops, clasps him a moment, turns her cheek to his, patting his back.

MARTHE My old man.

DISSOLVE TO:

Guezonnec has given his life, indirectly because of the food, because of its taint as having come from a traitor to France, in the estimation of the villagers.

A scene in the dungeon, Coupe-tête and the others. The food is food; their women and children shall still have the benefit of it. But they have now established themselves as people of resource and courage, who will fight the oppressors. They will continue to do so. They will act now as Guezonnec would have liked them to.

DISSOLVE TO:

INT. RAILROAD OFFICE

The agent asleep on the cot. A shadowy man enters, stops, leans over the cot. The agent wakes, turns, raises his head.

    MAN'S VOICE   Go back to sleep.

The agent turns back in cot, pulls cover up over his head. The shadowy man takes a rope from under his smock and binds the agent rapidly into the cot, winding the rope about the cot and tying it. Then he goes to the chair, takes up agent's pants, puts hand into pocket, withdraws his hand, puts the pants back on the chair and exits.

INT. FREIGHT SHED   CLOSE

A packing box like the other one. Four shadowy men busy about it, hurried, yet quiet. They pry a board up, remove the contents, which are various packages of food, and replace them with trash, refuse: whatever a Frenchman would admit to be refuse, rocks, pieces of wood, etc. They replace the prised-up board, load the packages of food into sacks, and steal out.

INT. OFFICE

The agent in cot, head covered. The rope is gone now; a package containing food lies on the cot with the agent. Faint sound of feet; the feet cease, die away. The agent uncovers his head, listens, looks cautiously after the feet, takes the package and draws it beneath the covers with him.

EXT. STREET   MED. CLOSE   COTTAGE

Two men, one carrying a sack, pause at the door. One takes a package of food from the sack, sets it before the door, knocks lightly on the door. The men go on. The door opens a crack, someone looks out, stoops, picks up the package and withdraws. The door closes.

INT. A COTTAGE   CLOSE

—shades drawn closely. Coupe-tête sitting at the end of a table. The table bears a candle in an empty bottle, and different kinds of food: luxuries, jellies, pâté, a whole roast fowl, a bottle of wine. The plates and cutlery are the poorest kind. Coupe-tête sits motionless, a napkin tucked inside his collar, staring grimly at CAMERA.

REVERSE ANGLE   TABLE

A woman in nightdress sitting at it; two children in nightgowns, who have obviously just been waked up and hauled out of bed; opposite Coupe-tête a man, dressed, too, bent over his plate, knife in one hand, the blade of the knife loaded with food. He is about to put it into his mouth, finds Coupe-tête staring at him, pauses. The woman and children pause, too, look from one to the other.

> **COUPE-TÊTE**   Do you know what that is you are shoveling into your maw like so much sawdust?

> **MAN**   No.

> **COUPE-TÊTE**   It's caviar.

> **MAN**   Is it?

He starts to put knife into his mouth again, finds Coupe-tête watching him, stops again.

> **COUPE-TÊTE**   Bah!

CLOSE   ALL

Coupe-tête spreads caviar on a piece of bread, hands it to the woman, who passes it to next child, who passes it to next, who passes it to the man, all watching the bread, as the man sits holding it. Then all look at Coupe-tête again as he spreads another piece of bread, passes it to woman, who passes it to next child, who passes it to the next, all watching that piece, too, then all watching Coupe-tête as he spreads the next piece and passes that. Coupe-tête spreads another piece, hands it to the woman. The man, the two children and the woman glance at one another secretly, start to eat.

COUPE-TÊTE Wait. *(all stop)* Who sent you this?

FIRST CHILD Mister Jean Mornet.

COUPE-TÊTE Hitler sent it. By the hand of Michel Kereon and Louis Guezonnec.

ANOTHER ANGLE

Coupe-tête with wineglass raised; the man, the woman, the two children holding up their pieces of bread.

COUPE-TÊTE Michel Kereon and Louis Guezonnec.

The man, woman and the children cross themselves, raise the bread again.

CHILDREN Michel Kereon and Louis Guezonnec.

FADE OUT.

FADE IN

Jean is engaged in his police work. The Germans have learned of De Gaulle agents working in France. They have learned that Georges is one of them, is a sort of bodyguard-secretary to an important one.

One day the German colonel sends for Jean. He gives Jean a mission to a certain munitions plant. The colonel is courteous as always. Jean has so far got along quite well with him, since the German is also a military man primarily, forthright in his dealings with another military man. Now Jean realizes that the colonel is not telling him all the truth about this mission, and that the colonel himself is ill-at-ease a little, as if he did not like something about it, regretted having to be mixed up in it but was following his own orders.

But Jean's relations with the colonel have been all right; they have come to trust one another, rely upon one another's integ-

11/19/42
120.

FADE IN

Jean is engaged in his police work. The Germans have
learned of De Gaulle agents working in France. They
have learned that Georges is one of them, is a sort
of bodyguard-secretary to an important one.

One day the German colonel sends for Jean. He gives
Jean a mission to a certain munitions plant. The
colonel is courteous as always. Jean has so far got
along quite well with him, since the German is also
a military man primarily, forthright in his dealings
with another military man. Now Jean realizes that
the colonel is not telling him all the truth about
this mission, and that the colonel himself is ill-at-
ease a little, as if he did not like something about
it, regretted having to be mixed up in it but was following his own orders.

But Jean's relations with the colonel have been all
right; they have come to trust one another, rely upon
one another's integrity and decent behavior, etc.
Jean accepts the mission, does not press the colonel
for the true reason. He is given unusual carte-blanche
to go through the factory. A German civilian whom Jean
knows is a Gestapo agent goes with him. The Gestapo is
polite, obsequious. Jean realizes that the Gestapo
knows the true reason, too. (If the factory is being
run by Frenchmen, will consult M. Berger as to what
their reactions to Jean, whom they will know, perhaps
by name or at least they will know the Gestapo and
therefore will assume Jean's status.)

When Jean starts through the factory, the Gestapo agent
politely excuses himself, so that Jean realizes he is
probably being spied on. Jean goes on with his inspection, still not knowing what it is all about. He sees
Kereon, recognizes him, stops at the bench where Kereon
is working. Kereon turns, recognizes Jean, shows surprise, quickly hides his reaction.

                    JEAN:
          You here? I thought --

                    KEREON:
          Yes. That's as surprising as to find
          a Mornet here, isn't it? But times
          and Frenchmen, too, have changed since
          May a year ago. But maybe the French-
          man who changed was the wise one --
          Lieutenant Mornet?

                              (CONTINUED)

15. First page of Faulkner's last known revision of "The De Gaulle Story"

rity and decent behavior, etc. Jean accepts the mission, does not press the colonel for the true reason. He is given unusual carte-blanche to go through the factory. A German civilian whom Jean knows is a Gestapo agent goes with him. The Gestapo is polite, obsequious. Jean realizes that the Gestapo knows the true reason, too. [If the factory is being run by Frenchmen, will consult M. Berger as to what their reactions to Jean, whom they will know, perhaps by name, or at least they will know the Gestapo and therefore will assume Jean's status.]

When Jean starts through the factory, the Gestapo agent politely excuses himself, so that Jean realizes he is probably being spied on. Jean goes on with his inspection, still not knowing what it is all about. He sees Kereon, recognizes him, stops at the bench where Kereon is working. Kereon turns, recognizes Jean, shows surprise, quickly hides his reaction.

JEAN You here? I thought—

KEREON Yes. That's as surprising as to find a Mornet here, isn't it? But times and Frenchmen, too, have changed since May a year ago. But maybe the Frenchman who changed was the wise one—Lieutenant Mornet?

JEAN Yes. *(he starts to go on)* I suppose there's no message I could send home for you, since you can go there yourself if you like.

KEREON No. Wait.

Jean pauses.

KEREON AND JEAN AT BENCH

Kereon's hand fumbling in his pocket while he talks.

KEREON Yes, I can go home whenever I like—by surrendering my food card. Or I could. It was because of that food you send your mother.

JEAN The food.

KEREON She would divide it among the women and children. But Guezonnec thought even the women and children shouldn't eat it. So he took a box of it from the station and burned it. I was there at the time, so when they looked over the list to choose a hostage to put the squeeze on Guezonnec, they found my name. So I'm back again.

JEAN You mean Guezonnec—

KEREON Guezonnec is dead.

JEAN Dead? For burning food?

KEREON It was a little more than that.

His hand comes out of the pocket and goes to the bench and fumbles on the bench as though it were writing something. He still looks at Jean.

KEREON But we are still grateful to your mother; so we want to take every opportunity to thank her because she kept none of it for herself but put every mouthful into the hand—

His hand moves across the bench.

KEREON (*accents slightly*)—the *hand* can see us; maybe can hear, too. The *hand*—

Jean is watching him, puzzled, begins to comprehend, looks down toward bench.

CLOSE   KEREON'S HAND

—holding a short piece of chalk. It has written on the bench:

OUT QUICK 1 O'CLOCK

The hand goes back, erases the words, scrawls:

GO GO MOTHER

The hand returns, erases that quickly.

CLOSE   JEAN AND KEREON

KEREON I ate some of it, too, German food or not; so I want to thank her *quick* before *one o'clock* we quit and *out of here go go*—

He turns quickly and pulls lever starting lathe as the Gestapo enters, stops deferentially behind Jean.

GESTAPO You are finished here, Lieutenant?

JEAN Yes.

He looks at Kereon's back a moment longer, turns and exits. The Gestapo looks after him. Then the Gestapo's manner changes. He turns, signals out of scene peremptorily.

LONG INTERIOR SHOT   FACTORY

Men at machines, French workers. Two German soldiers with sidearms tramp stiffly toward Camera. Above, against wall in b.g. a big clock, the hands at two minutes before one. The hand moves on toward one minute before one.

LONG INTERIOR SHOT   LABORERS AT MACHINES

Jean in f.g. as he looks at them. He is grave, thoughtful. He walks on.

CLOSE   JEAN AT A BIG DOOR

A porter opens it. Jean pauses, looks back, his face puzzled, concentrated. He exits; the porter closes the door.

CLOSE   BIG CLOCK ON WALL

The hand at one past one, moves on.

CLOSE   BENCH

Kereon working, the Gestapo and the two soldiers behind him.

GESTAPO Mornet.

Kereon doesn't turn. The Gestapo touches his shoulder.

GESTAPO Mornet.

Kereon turns.

KEREON My name is Kereon.

The Gestapo speaks to the soldiers in German, turns. The soldiers fall in on either side of Kereon. The Gestapo walks on; Kereon and the soldiers follow.

CLOSE   CLOCK FACE

The hands at three past one. Voices in b.g. begin to sing Marseillaise; other voices take it up.

CLOSE GESTAPO, TWO SOLDIERS WITH KEREON

—favoring factory room, row of unfinished tanks; the conscripted French laborers have stopped work, look toward Gestapo's group, singing. Kereon singing, too. A soldier strikes him down. Gestapo shouts in German. An alarm bell rings; more voices join the singing. In b.g. other German soldiers run in.

CLOSE LIGHT MASTER SWITCH

A German soldier pulls it. Lights go out; singing continues. A Frenchman enters, knocks soldier away, closes switch again. Lights come on. Soldier rises to approach the German. The singing is very loud. Sound of anti-aircraft fire and sirens begin in distance, grow louder. First bomb explodes. Debris falls on the group at light switch.

CLOSE JEAN

—crouching behind a low wall of an outdoors cafe. Chairs and tables are overturned where patrons have scattered. Air raid sirens going. A.A. fire, bombs bursting in b.g. as Jean stares out of scene. The singing can still be heard, many voices, faint.

DISSOLVE TO:

INT. GERMAN COLONEL'S OFFICE, PARIS

Jean stands facing desk. Colonel seated at desk. A Gestapo officer seated at end of desk. The Gestapo officer is youngish, about thirty-five. The colonel ranks him, but the Gestapo has the support of Himmler and the police, the Nazi party, etc.

COLONEL Sit down.

JEAN Thanks. I'll stand.

GESTAPO Lieutenant Mornet. I cannot believe that you really hoped to deceive anyone that the man Kereon—

The colonel speaks to the Gestapo in German. The Gestapo hushes.

COLONEL *(to Jean)* Sit down, Mornet.

JEAN Thanks, Colonel. It shouldn't take you that long to explain to me why I was sent to that factory. In fact, I think I know—

COLONEL Yes. Your brother is in France, as an accredited agent of General De Gaulle in London.

JEAN I see. And I was sent to the factory to recognize and betray him.

COLONEL Yes. I'm sorry. I—

The Gestapo speaks to the colonel in German. The colonel stops, shrugs, relinquishes to the Gestapo, who turns to face Jean.

GESTAPO Lieutenant Mornet. If you please. I will not bore you with explanation of what was a necessity. Your brother is one of these London agents, somewhere in France, agitating. We know that he or someone has been among the workers in that factory. It was just possible that he was still among them. You convinced an underling that the man Kereon—

The colonel speaks again to the Gestapo in German.

GESTAPO *(to Jean)* Your pardon, please. An underling was convinced that the man Kereon was your brother. That is beyond testing now, because the underling and the man Kereon are both dead. So someone in that factory knew that the bombing was coming, and if that man was your brother and he was still there, it is too bad for him. And if you recognized him there, and he did not die, too, it will be bad for you because there will be other opportunities—

The colonel speaks a sharp command to the Gestapo. The Gestapo ceases. The colonel rises swiftly, speaks another German command to the Gestapo, who rises, also, stands to attention. The colonel looks at the Gestapo a moment, turns to Jean.

COLONEL Will you accept an apology?

JEAN Thank you. Is that all?

COLONEL Yes. *(Jean starts to turn)* Mornet. *(Jean pauses)* Take care.

JEAN Thanks.

He turns, exits.

EXT. STREET   CLOSE   DOORWAY

—to the apartment building where Jean lives. Emilie approaches from street, carrying market basket. As she reaches the door, Jean steps out. He is carrying a package.

JEAN It's German food again. But I thought that perhaps one time more—

EMILIE *(watches him a moment)* Come in.

DISSOLVE TO:

INT. MOELLENS' ROOM   CLOSE   MOELLENS

—asleep in his chair before the fire, Emilie in a chair beside lamp on table, sewing. Jean in another chair.

JEAN They all knew the bombs were coming. They even knew the hour. They could have got out just by telling the guards. But they didn't. They sang instead—*(he pauses, muses, rouses again)* At first I didn't understand why they sent me there.

EMILIE They thought perhaps your brother was there. They intended for you to identify him.

JEAN You knew it, too? That my brother is in France?

EMILIE *(quietly)* Yes. We all know it. General De Gaulle sent him to us.

JEAN We? Us?

EMILIE If you try to force someone to do as you want them to do, and they resist you and keep on resisting until the only thing left for you to do is to kill them, they have beat you. And if you do kill them, they have beat you forever because then they have escaped from you. It's like those little ants in the jungle that nothing can stand against—not the biggest and fiercest and the most powerful—nothing. You can kill them by the millions just by stepping on them, but they keep on coming because they are so little. That's the mistake they made. They tried to force the little people. And there are too many little people. There are so many of them because they are so small. All they have to threaten us with is death. And little people are not afraid to die. The little people and the very great. Because there is something of the little people in the very great: as if all the little people who had been trodden and crushed had condensed into one great one who knew and remembered all their suffering. And the little ones themselves are never afraid as long as they believe that the other little ants coming behind them will finally eat the elephant.

ANOTHER ANGLE

EMILIE This happened in your village; you see how well we keep in touch with one another, now that we have learned how. It was the food again, that you send your mother, after the man named Guezonnec burned the box that Kereon was taken for. It was your mother's old farmer—what's his name—

JEAN Coupe-tête.

EMILIE Coupe-tête. After that, to purify it so they could eat it, Coupe-tête and a few others would steal it, enter the station at night and pry the box open and take the food out and put rocks into the box and close it again. Then the next morning the German commander would send your mother word that the box had come, and for her to send and get it. They wouldn't deliver it, so Coupe-tête would have to come for it. It was too heavy for him to handle alone, so he would have to have help. But everybody knew the box had nothing in it now but rocks; they had eaten the food the night before. So Coupe-tête couldn't get anyone to help him. Each time he would have to pay someone with another of his and Kereon's Germans to help him load the box into the cart.

JEAN So you do know.

EMILIE We do know. Every day there are more of us who know. Because we are the little people, you see. We are neither generals nor statesmen nor politicians. We are just

the little people and there are too many of us. Too much of
individual grief and suffering—*(she pauses an instant, looks
at Jean)*—and dishonor and shame, until, since we are little
people, the suffering and grief and dishonor and shame
belong to all of us and we can resist—

ANOTHER ANGLE

Emilie has put the sewing on the table. She sits with her hands
in her lap, looking ahead. Her face is calm.

EMILIE   We were living in a little village outside of Meche-
len. We had no warning. No more warning, that is, than all
Europe should have had. But no matter. They came suddenly. Father was in Brussels then, and my brother and I
were in the house alone, when suddenly they were there—
three of them—three young men. It didn't matter who or
which three, just as to them I was a young woman and that
didn't matter who or which one; just female and of an
inferior race created for the spoiling that could make war
and the risk of sudden death bearable. Then it was over,
and they were gone, and at least I was still alive—

JEAN   Your brother?

EMILIE   He died. Quickly. And I was still alive, and I hated
it on my father's account—an old man, just a musician, too
old and unimportant even for them to destroy. But after
we reached Paris, and they overtook us again, and it was no
use to flee again because now nothing remained that we
could be despoiled of, another musician, a Frenchman, a
young man who knew Father, would come to see us. And
one night he brought a book, an American book written by
a Mr. Hemingway. He would read it to us at night and
translate it. It told about a young girl to whom that had
happened also, and about an older woman who was very
wise about people anyway, who said how, if you refused to
accept something, it could not happen to you. And I was
comforted because Jan—my brother—had died quickly beforehand, and Willem, to whom I was to be married, had
been in Fort Eben Emael and he would not have to hate
that, too, at least. So there was only Father, and he believes,

too, that some day the ants are going to eat the elephant. . . .

CLOSE   JEAN AND EMILIE

—standing, Jean holding Emilie's hand to his lips. Emilie withdraws her hand.

JEAN   So they sent me there today to find Georges. They knew I would have reported him.

EMILIE   No. They wanted to see whether you would or not. And you would have, knowing he was an agent of General De Gaulle.

JEAN   I have an oath.

EMILIE   To them, who keep none?

JEAN   To myself. I must do what I have to do, what I think is right to do, for what remains of my poor country.

EMILIE   France is not poor now. Every day all outraged Europe—

JEAN   *(quickly)* I must go. Goodnight.

He turns toward door. She watches him.

EMILIE   Mr. Mornet.

He pauses, looks back.

EMILIE   Come to us.

JEAN   *(harshly)* No. *(quieter)* It's too late now. What man or woman of what you call the true France would believe anyone now who changed to them this late? Goodnight.

He turns, advances toward CAMERA into—

FADE OUT.

FADE IN

MONTAGE

U.S. declares war on Germany. A secret newspaper which circulates among the French Underground. Perhaps a shot of small, clumsy hand-press running off the papers. A DISSOLVE through it to—

A FEW PEOPLE IN UNDERGROUND CELL

—crouched about a secret radio, showing joyful reaction as a Free French voice tells the news and its implications of new hope and guarantee to enslaved Europe.

DISSOLVE TO:

EXT. HOTEL CRILLON

[I think M. Berger said this is Nazi Gestapo headquarters in Paris.] Nazi flag over it.

CLOSE SHOT   CRILLON

DISSOLVE TO:

INT. BASEMENT

The first general congress of the Underground cells from all of France is held. Delegates are elected formally to go to De Gaulle in London and present the alliance of the whole Underground. Georges is chairman, or at least De Gaulle's official representative.

DISSOLVE TO:

EXT. BUSY STREET   CLOSE   JEAN

Rue de la Paix, perhaps, cafe in b.g. German officers, street thronged with French civilians and German soldiers. Jean walking, somber and grave. He stops, looks out of scene, shows astonishment.

REVERSE ANGLE

Georges, walking in crowd, looks up, sees Jean and recognizes him.

INT. A BASEMENT

—known to Georges and his confederates.

CLOSE   JEAN AND GEORGES

    GEORGES Don't worry. You're safe here; this is my rathole. The question is, am I?

JEAN Yes. For twenty-four hours. Give me your word that you will leave France and never come back.

GEORGES Or you'll report me. Go. Say it. I know you will, but I want to hear you say it.

JEAN I have an oath. I intend to keep it.

GEORGES To who? As what? As a French traitor?

JEAN To myself.

GEORGES Yes. That damned oath you took the day you entered the Naval Academy. When true France no longer has a navy.

JEAN The French navy no longer has a country, you mean. But never mind that. I'll give you twenty-four hours to get out of France.

GEORGES Not any more. Once I had to. But I have come back. And some day soon you and those who forced or persuaded you—

JEAN No man forced or persuaded me. I chose.

GEORGES All right, all right. —will have to get out of France, too, those who can. And they won't come back.

JEAN But that's not yet. Go. I'm being watched, too. They probably saw us meet; they have probably followed us here—

GEORGES In which case, you won't even have to report me. They'll find me all right with just a piece of rubber. . . .*(he stops—continues)* Of course. You'll tell them first; put yourself in solid for—No, I don't mean that. God, what a time, when brother and brother—*(recovers)* No, I won't go. Tell them, or let them beat it out of you or me, either, with the rubber hose. They can't hurt us now. The United States is in this now, and all France is ready. All France is waiting. I don't need to stay any longer, actually. There's nothing anybody needs to do any more. We don't even need a martyr to help our cause. But I think I'll stay, just to see what martyrdom is like.

He rises; Jean rises, too.

> **GEORGES** No, that's not true, either. I'm going to stay for the fun of it. Because I don't think you and your fine Gestapo can catch me.

> **JEAN** So you think. So a lot of men have thought. So too many people in this world have thought—until it was too late.

> **GEORGES** *(soberly)* Yes. That's right. We have never underestimated them. They may catch me; according to you, and to others I know, they probably will. But I still have work to do, and too many Frenchmen and Slavs and Norwegians and Belgians and Dutch have died at this same job for any one of us to hesitate.

> **JEAN** Go.

> **GEORGES** Come over to us.

> **JEAN** At this late date, would any of you believe me? *(they look at one another)* Would they? *(Georges doesn't answer)* Go!

> **GEORGES** Come over to us.

> **JEAN** No.

> **GEORGES** No.

> **JEAN** *(turns—pauses)* Twenty-four hours.

> **GEORGES** I will remember you did that much.

INT. CORRIDOR   CLOSE   JEAN'S OFFICE DOOR

—favoring corridor as Jean approaches. He is sober, thoughtful. He puts hand on door, opens it, is about to enter, pauses, enters.

INT. OFFICE   CLOSE   FAVORING GERMAN ORDERLY

Jean has entered.

> **ORDERLY** The Colonel's compliments. In his office. At once.

INT. COLONEL'S OFFICE

Jean stands facing desk. The colonel stands looking out the window, his back to the room. He still does not like this, but he is still a servant of the German government. The Gestapo officer stands in front of the desk, facing Jean. A closed door in wall in b.g.

GESTAPO Last night you met a man on the street. After you separated, the man was arrested. He is still being held. His replies tally with the registration of him which we already had: Jacques Villemon, wine-broker, of Rheims. Of course this man is not your brother.

JEAN No.

GESTAPO We thought not. Otherwise, you would have reported him. So he will be released. But meantime there is still the question of this Georges Mornet, an agent of our enemy's, somewhere in France. Since we cannot wait any longer for you to meet him and inform us, we have taken steps of our own—

The Gestapo turns, goes to the door, puts hand on the knob, turns and looks at Jean a moment, opens the door.

CLOSE THROUGH DOOR   A LONG CORRIDOR

Mme Mornet seated in a chair at end of it, a German policewoman standing beside her. She is watching the door when it opens. She starts up. The policewoman presses her back. She struggles. She is dressed for traveling, a suitcase on floor beside chair.

MME MORNET Jean! Don't tell him! Don't—

The door closes.

CLOSE   JEAN AND GESTAPO AT THE DOOR

Jean poised to spring, the Gestapo with his hand on his holster.

GESTAPO Stand back, Mornet. Other Frenchwomen as old as she have stood the trip to Germany. There will be other men and women, too; Belgian and Dutch and Norse and Slav as well as of her own tongue, to keep her company when she misses France.

CLOSE JEAN, GESTAPO AND COLONEL AT DESK

The colonel still stands staring out the window. The Gestapo sits at the desk, a many-leaved dossier open before him. Jean stands at desk.

GESTAPO This Jacques Villemon is Georges Mornet?

JEAN I can take my mother home? She will not be disturbed again?

GESTAPO This Jacques Villemon is Georges Mornet?

COLONEL *(from window)* Yes. She will not be disturbed again.

JEAN *(to Gestapo)* Yes.

DISSOLVE TO:

JEAN'S GERMAN OFFICIAL CAR

—with soldier driver standing in front of the Mornet house.

INT. HALLWAY CLOSE JEAN AND CATHERINE

Catherine is frantic.

CATHERINE Die? Of course he'll die! When they have known for six months what he was doing, when all France, even they, know now what he has accomplished? They better destroy him while they can.

JEAN He knew that, too. He took that risk. We lost the war. He declined to accept the fact, and escaped. All right. But he was not content to stay there. He had to come back, to gamble his life against a trained police who had had all Europe to practice on before they even came here—not only his life, but his mother's, too—

CATHERINE And you saved that, not she. She wouldn't have told. You told them.

JEAN Yes. He would have done the same, if he had been in my place and I in his.

CATHERINE So you think. But of course you would say

so—you would have to justify it. He has sacrificed his own for France; do you think he would have spared yours?

JEAN I spared his mother's.

CATHERINE Then spare hers with mine. Spare hers and his both, with mine.

JEAN It's too late now, but even if it wasn't, how with— *(pauses—stares at her)* How with yours?

CATHERINE I'm married to him. I've got his child. Didn't your German friends tell you that?

INT. MME MORNET'S BEDROOM   CLOSE   BED

Mme Mornet in bed, Marthe beside her. Jean standing at bed. Marthe gives him a swift look, then keeps her eyes turned away.

MME MORNET *(opens her eyes)* Jean.

Jean takes her hand. It doesn't move, limp.

MME MORNET They'll shoot him.

JEAN They won't shoot him. They just want to stop him from what he was doing. They've done that. I'm going back right away. I'm going to take Coupe-tête with me.

MME MORNET *(closes her eyes)* They'll shoot him. All Frenchmen who are young and brave have to die. I'm cold, Marthe. Cover me.

Marthe passes Jean, gives him another quick, defiant and fearful look, draws more covers up over Mme Mornet.

JEAN *(to Marthe)* Did you hear? I'm going to take Coupe-tête with me.

MARTHE Take him! Get him shot, too!

Jean turns away.

DISSOLVE TO:

EXT. CAR IN MOTION   CLOSE   JEAN AND COUPE-TÊTE

—in back seat. Jean is grave. Coupe-tête looks calmly about.

COUPE-TÊTE I didn't know France was this big. No wonder it can hold so many of them. At this rate, there will be at least one apiece for all of us, the women and children, too.

DISSOLVE TO:

INT. JEAN'S ROOM   PARIS   CLOSE   COUPE-TÊTE AT A CUPBOARD

It is a shelf, before which hangs a cloth curtain. Coupe-tête is holding the curtain aside with one hand. On the shelf are packages of food. Coupe-tête takes one down, holds it in his other hand while he examines it—a small tin labeled: TRUFFLES.

COUPE-TÊTE   Aha. Encore.

INT. EMILIE'S ROOM   CLOSE   JEAN AND EMILIE

—standing beside sewing table and lamp. Moellens asleep in his chair before the fire.

JEAN   I have come to ask you to marry me.

EMILIE   Why? I think I know, but I want to hear you say it.

JEAN   Why do men always ask it? I—

EMILIE   No. That's the lie.

JEAN   Then I offer all the lie itself could offer if it were truth: our land is ours, my mother is a widow and will welcome you, there's only my brother and me, and I am the older—

EMILIE   —and I am a waif, homeless, without a country, a nobody, and dishonored. But I'm a woman, too. Don't you know I'd rather have had the lie than an offer of outright purchase?

JEAN   Yes, I began wrong. And it's too late now. There's no time now to tell you the lie. There's not time now to make you believe it—

EMILIE   Isn't there?

Jean stares at her, takes a step toward her. She watches him. He stops.

JEAN   Is there time yet?

EMILIE We have so little to purchase with, by your standards. Yet we have all the world to need to buy—

Jean moves again, puts his arms around her. She stops him again, her hands against his chest, her head back, watching him.

JEAN I don't even know your name. Your father just calls you daughter—

EMILIE Emilie. So you are ready to tell the lie, even.

JEAN Maybe it won't be a lie. You will be honored, loved by more than—

EMILIE Wait. Tell me another lie first. One that I would rather hear right now than the first one, even. *(she stares at him)* For France.

They stare at one another.

JEAN No. I cannot. I—

EMILIE Your actions can say that Jean Mornet was wrong, but Jean Mornet himself cannot say it.

JEAN I am what I have been; I am now what I will always be.

EMILIE But you can say the first lie now.

JEAN Maybe it never was a lie. Maybe from that first afternoon when you dropped the potatoes—Maybe when all this is over, a dream, a nightmare, and this poor unhappy France—

EMILIE No land is poor while there are brave men in it. No land is unhappy which still can hope.

ANOTHER ANGLE JEAN AND EMILIE

—apart, facing one another.

EMILIE Tomorrow morning, then. As soon as you have had me re-registered as your wife. I won't tell Father until afterward. He will believe the second lie has been told, too. Go now. Coupe-tête must be hungry.

JEAN If he still is now, he is not Coupe-tête.

He takes her hand, begins to raise it toward his lips. Before he can stop her, she raises his hand, kisses it, releases it, steps back.

EMILIE That was not for me, either.

DISSOLVE TO:

INT. JEAN'S ROOM   CLOSE   COUPE-TÊTE

—sitting on the floor, a stool between his knees for a table, two or three small tins of jellies, caviar, etc., open on the stool, a wine bottle on the floor. He has a towel tied around his neck like a napkin protecting his Sunday coat. He holds a shaving mug of wine in his hand. His mouth is full as he looks up at Jean standing over him.

JEAN I just remarked that if you were still hungry, I didn't know you. We will go back home tomorrow.

COUPE-TÊTE Tomorrow? I have hardly seen France yet. I haven't seen Paris at all.

JEAN Then both will have to wait. We are going tomorrow night to take my wife home.

Coupe-tête sets the mug carefully on the floor, swallows, wipes his mouth on the edge of the towel.

COUPE-TÊTE Jean Mornet's wife.

JEAN Yes. Jean Mornet and his wife.

Coupe-tête rises quickly and quietly, pauses, takes up the wine bottle, examines the remaining wine, raises it toward his mouth.

COUPE-TÊTE Then perhaps we had better get some sleep.

DISSOLVE TO:

INT. CAR   NIGHT   CLOSE   EMILIE AND GEORGES

—traveling fast. Emilie and Georges in back seat. Georges wears Jean's clothes, has been drugged. He rouses. Emilie passes bottle of ether or whatever it is under his nose. He sleeps again.

WIPE TO:

EXT. MORNET HOUSE   NIGHT

The car stopped in front of Mornet house. Three shadowy men emerge, lift Georges out. Emilie speaks rapidly and efficiently to the German soldier driver in German. We distinguish the one word: PARIS.

DRIVER   Ja, Frau Mornet.

The car exits. The group turns toward the house, carrying Georges.

INT. MORNET KITCHEN

—shades drawn, etc. Mme Mornet, Marthe, Catherine, as Emilie and Coupe-tête, three others, enter, carrying Georges.

CATHERINE   Georges!

COUPE-TÊTE   *(panting)* Save it. *(to the men)* Over here.

CLOSE GROUP

Georges in chair.

EMILIE   *(to Catherine, harshly)* You're Catherine. He's just drugged. He's all right.

MME MORNET   Jean. Where is—

Her voice dies; she stares at Emilie.

EMILIE   *(to Mme Mornet, gentler)* You're his mother.

She approaches Mme Mornet, pauses, moves again, takes Mme Mornet's hand, kisses it.

EMILIE   He is where he would be. He has saved his soul, even if he won't admit it. *(she turns to Catherine again)* He's in that cell. Where would he be? How else would your husband be there in that chair? Didn't you realize that as soon as you saw him? His mother did.

CATHERINE   You lie. Georges didn't—

EMILIE   Don't worry. That's why he's drugged. He wouldn't have left that cell either, otherwise. But he can't stay here. Maybe they have already found out which one they have—

COUPE-TÊTE   And never a truer word. We are only waiting for His Reverence and the cart.

INT. COMMANDANT'S OFFICE, MAIRIE   CLOSE

Priest at desk, the young spectacled precise German lieutenant behind it. The lieutenant examines a paper.

LIEUTENANT   Permission to bury ———— Quinnoneaux, called "The Flea"— *(he looks up)* That's that idiot.

PRIEST   They can die, too. Perhaps they have souls, too.

LIEUTENANT   He will not know it, dead.

He signs the pass.

EXT. STREET   NIGHT

The Mornet cart moving along street. Priest and another man on seat, a cheap coffin in the cart.

EXT. MORNET FARMYARD   NIGHT

The cart halted inside the Mornet farmyard. Coupe-tête and the others open the coffin, help the idiot out. He is young, timorous, uncoordinated, clumsy. They lift Georges into the coffin, close the lid. The cart drives away, leaving priest, Coupe-tête, the idiot.

IDIOT   Did I do all right, Father? I wish to save Brittany, but I don't wish to die.

PRIEST   You did well. You will not die. Go with Coupe-tête and sleep.

The idiot kneels, the priest blesses him.

COUPE-TÊTE   *(to idiot)* Come, then, since you have saved Brittany.

Coupe-tête turns away. The idiot follows. Coupe-tête pauses, turns back to look at the priest.

COUPE-TÊTE   Bless yourself, Father, if you can.

He and the idiot go on.

DISSOLVE TO:

EXT. ROAD   NIGHT

The cart halted by two German sentries with flashlights. They look into the cart. The driver hands down the pass. The German holds his light on it, hands the pass back to the driver, steps aside.

    SOLDIER   Pass on. To Quimper. With the body of Quinnoneaux, called "The Flea." Pass on.

                        DISSOLVE TO:

EXT.   CLOSE   DAWN   EMPTY COFFIN

—hidden in bushes.

                        DISSOLVE TO:

INT. COMMANDANT'S OFFICE

The German captain and the small lieutenant at desk, the priest before the desk, the idiot being held between two German soldiers, trembling and frightened.

    IDIOT   Father! You promised me—

    PRIEST   Peace, son. You have done your duty. You will not suffer.

    LIEUTENANT   Yes, he has done his duty. That was all we wanted.

He speaks in German to the soldiers. They release the idiot. The idiot watches the priest.

    PRIEST   *(to idiot)* Go. You will not be harmed.

The idiot scuttles out. The lieutenant rises, barks an order in German to the soldiers. They fall in on either side of the priest. The lieutenant barks another order. The soldiers wheel stiffly to advance, the priest between them. The lieutenant barks another order. The soldiers and the priest begin to march. The priest's face is quite calm.

EXT. THE SQUARE

The whole village has gathered. The faces are grim, tense. A file of soldiers enters, the priest among them. A repressed

sound goes up from the people, stops. The priest is marched
into position against a wall. The soldiers leave him.

MED. CLOSE   PRIEST

Soldiers in b.g. The German captain in b.g.; the lieutenant in
f.g. with paper.

> LIEUTENANT   For assisting in the escape of the con-
> demned French traitor and prisoner, Mornet, Guillaume
> Riom, Priest, is hereby sentenced to execution. Signed:
> _____, Commissioner of Police, Paris.

He folds paper, turns stiffly, approaches the priest. The repressed sound comes again from the people.

CLOSE   PRIEST AND LIEUTENANT   CAPTAIN IN B.G.

The captain gives an order in German. The soldiers half-
present their rifles. The sound from the people ceases. The
captain speaks in German to the lieutenant. The lieutenant
answers, turns to the priest.

> LIEUTENANT   *(watches priest's face)* You have German, eh?

> PRIEST   Yes. The captain told you to beware. I tell you that
> also: Beware!

> LIEUTENANT   Of what? Of sheep? We could have used
> you. For your advantage and that of these cattle, too, with
> whom you threaten us. We already have a better hostage
> for this Mornet in Paris now. But we do not want a hostage.
> We want Mornet. And he will return and we will get him. I
> was given this authority.

He takes out the paper, tears it and drops it. The scraps float
toward the priest, who draws his gown aside as if to keep them
from touching him. The lieutenant watches.

> LIEUTENANT   So—*(he stares at the priest)* So.

He jerks his hand up suddenly. The captain speaks sharply in
German. The lieutenant pays no attention.

> LIEUTENANT   *(to the priest)* Heil Hitler!

> PRIEST   I will tell you what one of your own priests once
> told your fuehrer: "God, not you, is my leader."

The lieutenant jerks out his pistol. Another sound from the watching people. The captain moves, speaks again in German.

LIEUTENANT *(glares at priest)* Heil Hitler!

The priest spits in the German's face. The lieutenant shoots him. The priest falls. A sound from the people. The captain speaks sharp and loud; the soldiers aim rifles.

REVERSE ANGLE

The villagers, paused, the faces grim, threatening, unafraid.

DISSOLVE TO:

EXT. BRETON COAST

—favoring the sea. A small sailboat standing away from the coast, bound for England.

FADE OUT.

FADE IN

TITLE: July 14, 1942.

DISSOLVE TO:

ARC DE TRIOMPHE, PARIS

An aeroplane bearing the cross of Lorraine. [Nungesser flew a Spad through the arch in '20–'22, etc. I don't know whether the British F/Lt. took a Beaufighter through or not.]

DISSOLVE TO:

CLOSE SHOT JEANNENEY AND HERRIOT

A voice over scene reads the joint letter they wrote to the Vichy parliament.

VOICE . . . that liberty should ever perish from the land where it was born and spread to all the world. . .

DISSOLVE TO:

MAP OF FRENCH CHANNEL COAST

PAN TO:

A TOWN ON COAST

[Research for this by date.]

DISSOLVE THRU TO:

EXT.   CLOSE   COUPE-TÊTE   NIGHT

—gunfire, searchlights, etc. Coupe-tête crouching behind a corner as Commando men run past. Each time a group passes, Coupe-tête shouts.

 COUPE-TÊTE Mornet! Georges Mornet!

The men run on. Coupe-tête looks after them. Another burst of firing comes. He crouches, peering out. Three men run past. Coupe-tête steps out to intercept them.

 COUPE-TÊTE Georges Mornet! Est-ce que vous avez vu—

 SOLDIER *(in English)* Get out of here, old man!

The three British soldiers run. Coupe-tête follows.

CLOSE

A German soldier whirls, tries to raise rifle. Three men fling themselves on him. All go down. A grenade bursts. After the flash, the soldier lies dead, Coupe-tête beside him, the three British soldiers bending over them. Coupe-tête opens his eyes. Another grenade bursts. The three men snatch Coupe-tête up, exit.

BEACH   CLOSE   COUPE-TÊTE   DAWN

Fire in b.g., shots, etc. Coupe-tête lying on beach, landing barges in b.g. Commandos with blackened faces enter, firing backward toward land. Several men bending over Coupe-tête. A British officer pours brandy from a flask into his mouth. Coupe-tête opens his eyes, takes the flask in his own hand, is about to drink again, pauses.

REVERSE ANGLE

Coupe-tête looking up at Georges. Georges's face is blackened, smudged with sweat, etc.

 COUPE-TÊTE It's a boy.

GEORGES What?

COUPE-TÊTE Your son. What else do you think I am doing here? Bah! They will never beat us, so long as Frenchmen continue to replace themselves after one visit home.

GEORGES None of us had better be here long.

COUPE-TÊTE Go then.

Georges looks quickly about, points, rises. Four men pick Coupe-tête up.

CLOSE BEHIND A HUMMOCK

The men put Coupe-tête down.

COUPE-TÊTE Now a grenade—pistol—something.

GEORGES What will you do with a grenade or a pistol?

COUPE-TÊTE What did I do with them in 1914?

Georges gives him a grenade. The men exit. Coupe-tête crouches in his hole, listening. Sounds off scene. He turns over, grimacing, raises his head, peers out, pulls pin of grenade, throws it, ducks back. The explosion comes—a burst of machine gun fire. Coupe-tête raises his head cautiously, peers out.

A PARTY OF GERMAN SOLDIERS ON BEACH   COUPE-TÊTE'S ANGLE

—looking this way and that. They decide on a direction, exit.

CLOSE   COUPE-TÊTE

He sinks back in his hole. His hand fumbles at his pocket. He takes out the officer's flask, makes himself comfortable, drinks.

DISSOLVE TO:

MONTAGE

TITLES: SEPTEMBER   OCTOBER   NOVEMBER

—DISSOLVING one into another to:

1943

DISSOLVE TO:

INT. THE RUINED TOWER-CAVE   NIGHT

Coupe-tête and all the other faces which we know, and many more until the cave is crowded.

>   **LEADER**   They will tell us when. The word will come. Then we must light beacons for them—beacons to lead them.

>   **A MAN**   We have no beacons.

>   **LEADER**   Yes. We have. We have—

DISSOLVE TO:

FULL SHOT   AERODROME RUNWAY   ENGLAND   TWILIGHT

Bombers are taking off, one after another.

INT. OPERATIONS OFFICE   A SQUADRON OF FRENCH PILOTS

De Gaulle and Georges and squadron commander, adjutant, etc., about loudspeaker.

>   **RADIO**   Badger to Corridor. Over.

>   **RADIO**   Corridor to Badger. Good hunting. Over.

>   **COMMANDANT**   They are leaving the coast now. Soon they will be over France—

>   **GEORGES**   Over Germany, sir.

>   **COMMANDANT**   Yes. Over Germany. But not forever.

>   **GEORGES**   Not for long.

>   **COMMANDANT**   Yes. Not for long.

INT. MORNET KITCHEN

Coupe-tête peering out window. Marthe, Mme Mornet, and Emilie knotting bundles of what they can carry. Catherine holding the child. All are dressed to leave the house. A faint distant light appears beyond the window. Coupe-tête turns quickly. Emilie stops, glances up at him.

>   **COUPE-TÊTE**   Yes. It is time.

He hurries out. Emilie follows. The others gather up bundles and exit.

EXT. STABLE   CLOSE   COUPE-TÊTE AND EMILIE   NIGHT

—as they set fire to the stable, hay, etc.

CLOSE   MME MORNET, CATHERINE WITH CHILD, MARTHE

—with bundles, favoring stable as it begins to blaze. Emilie and Coupe-tête enter and Coupe-tête takes some of the bundles. They exit. Other faint fires begin to spring up, shouts, shots in distance.

CLOSE   GROUP

—all on a hill, favoring the countryside, fires blazing about it, faint shouts, shots.

COUPE-TÊTE   Who said there would not be beacons?

INT. COCKPIT OF A BOMBER IN FLIGHT OVER FRANCE

The dark countryside is spotted with fires. Others spring up as the pilot speaks into mike.

PILOT   (*into mike*) Fires. They are springing up every-where.

INT. SQUADRON OPERATION OFFICE

De Gaulle and others at loudspeaker.

RADIO   They are lighting the way for us.

CLOSE   LETTERS ON A WALL

—name of a factory making German munitions. Air raid sirens begin, A.A. fire, etc.

DISSOLVE THRU TO:

INT. FACTORY   CLOSE   JEAN

—favoring a long interior, half-finished guns, etc.; as the French workers pause, an alarm bell ringing, sirens from out-side, gunfire coming nearer as the raiders approach, the faces showing exultation. German soldier-guards excited, alarmed. Jean begins to sing the Marseillaise. Other voices take it up. The bombs begin, more voices singing.

Robert Buckner   November 19, 1942

William Faulkner   De Gaulle Story

Dear Bob:

Let's dispense with General De Gaulle as a living character in the story.

We will not only be free of the disadvantages and obstructions whose loss will be a gain, we will gain the freedom to make a picture which the American audience whose money will pay for it will understand and believe and not find dull.

If we use him as a living character, we must accept the supervision of his representatives, and at least satisfy them, even if we can't please them. Being Free Frenchmen and working for a tough cause, they are naturally more interested in the progress of the cause than in a mere American made and financed -- and distributed and looked-at and paid admissions by -- moving picture. They want to see a piece of Free French propaganda, not a moving picture in which those who see it will recognize their own human passions and griefs and desires. They want to make a document in which everyone who sees it will have to see what a Free Frenchman holds to be the true and important events of France's downfall, not a story which will create in the hearts of the foreigners who will buy the admission tickets a feeling of warmth and affection and pride toward the people like themselves who suffered from the fall of France and have struggled and resisted and are rising from it.

To make the picture under this supervision, we must either please them and nobody else, or probably please nobody at all. Because I don't believe that the audience for which it is being made, which must like it for it to make a return on its cost, will understand it. For this reason: These supervisors, being Free French, will insist upon an absolute adherence to time and fact, no matter how trivial the incident nor imaginary the characters acting it, and regardless of the sacrifice of dramatic values and construction or the poetic implications and overtones. And being Frenchmen, they will insist upon trivialities (to an American, just as minor American customs would be trivial to a Frenchman) of French life and differences in French customs which to an American are not only unimportant but dull, colorless, without warmth, until after a while an American might begin to think that perhaps the French people got what they deserved, after all.

Let us have a free hand with it. Let's accept with gratitude advice and information as to fact on all occasions,

16. Memo from Faulkner to Buckner

November 19, 1942

De Gaulle Story

(2)

but let us keep to ourselves the discretion to choose among these facts, choose those which we want to use and tell them in American terms, in the language (not just the diction but in the way of thinking and believing) of us who are making the picture and of those whom it is the purpose of the picture to move or please or instruct, or perhaps uplift even by reaffirming in them the value of human suffering and the belief in human hope.

Any historical hero, angel or villain, is no more than a figure-head of his time. He is only the sum of his acts, only the sum of the little people whom he slew or raised, enslaved or made free. He becomes colorful and of dramatic value only after he has been dead for years, because only then can a dramatist make him dramatic without challenge from the people who knew him in the flesh and who insist on fact.

Let's dispense with him as a living character in the picture. Let's tell what he has done by means on its poetic implications, in terms of some little human people, with their human relationships which an audience can understand, whose lives and destinies were affected, not by him but by the same beliefs that made him De Gaulle.

It seems to me that any Free Frenchman would be glad to help us in this, not by obscure ukase and prohibition, but by grateful advice when requested of him.

What's your reaction to this?

OPERATIONS OFFICE

De Gaulle, Georges, others listening to the radio.

> **RADIO**   More of them! More of them! You can almost hear them, like voices singing! All Europe is blazing, blazing. . .

FADE OUT.

THE END

VI

Related Documents

Faulkner's Abstract of "Free France"

Faulkner's abstract of the plot and theme of "Free France," c. August 1942, ribbon typescript, 1 page.

This is the story of Free France, told in the simple terms of a Breton village: the collapse of France and the hopes and struggle for rejuvenation as seen through the eyes of villagers, told by means of village characters who are themselves the common denominator of France. The village is the strophe, with its passions and bafflements and divisions of brother against brother and blood against blood, that it may continue to exist as a symbol of home, security, happiness and peace which is man's heritage; France is the antistrophe, with its passions and bafflements and division of Frenchman against Frenchman in the national terms of a people struggling to survive and to keep alive their traditions and glory as a nation. It is a thesis that lust and greed and force can never conquer the human spirit.

Deleted Scenes

Three scenes that Faulkner subsequently deleted or revised in completing the expanded story treatment of "Free France," c. August 1942, mixed ribbon and carbon typescript with holograph corrections, 28 pages.

[The Syrian Incident]

FADE IN

A concentration camp in October, 1940. Jean is among the prisoners. A group of them plot to escape. Jean has continued to preach collaboration on all occasions, even with the suffering of the various peoples in the camp under his eyes constantly. He sees no chance of being free himself or of any of the others being free until the war is over and peace returns. And the only chance he sees for peace is for the conquered peoples of Europe to stop striving against the conqueror, until at last the Germans will have to empty the concentration camps for their own benefit: to keep the land producing, commerce alive, etc. By resisting, by making attempts to escape, they will merely put off that day so much longer.

He learns by accident of the escape plan. He talks against the attempt. The men who plan to escape know Jean's ideas on the subject and they do not trust him. They believe he might even report them to the Germans through his conviction that by doing so he is ultimately protecting the conquered countries from further vengeance and suffering. When they discover that Jean knows of the plan, some of the escapers wish to kill Jean to protect themselves. Others of the escapers refuse to do this. Jean is a Frenchman; he will not betray other Frenchmen. But the violent part cannot be convinced of this. Finally the two groups compromise. One group will not kill him; the other group will not leave him behind. So he must go with them, whether he wants to or not.

They invite him to go. He refuses. He explains his reasons: if they escape, it will merely prolong things, even this one tiny drop in the bucket. It will bring down just that much more German anger on the conquered countries and perhaps even upon the individual families and kin of those escaping, and if not on their own kin, then upon people who are not even related to them and who are completely innocent, which will be that much worse. The violent party wishes now to kill Jean at once, no more argument. Again the mild group saves him. But they dare not leave him behind. Even if he will not tell on them, the police might torture information from him. Or perhaps the news of the plan will spread further yet from Jean and so when the time comes, there will be so many of them trying to escape that the whole plan will destroy itself by its own weight and all of them will be caught.

They overpower Jean by force and take him with them. When

he realizes that they will not leave him behind, he ceases to struggle and goes along rather than jeopardize the escape of the others by his actions. But he is still opposed to the idea. He is not thinking of himself. He is willing to lose his life or keep it, either one, to do what he thinks is best for the security of France and Frenchmen.

They escape from the camp. They cannot try to return across Austria and Germany both to France, so they go south and east. Now that they are out and the die is cast, Jean works harder than anyone to keep them together and protect them and get along, even though he still believes they are doing the wrong thing. It becomes necessary to kill a German soldier. Jean refuses to take any part in it, gains still more of the distrust and even contempt of his companions. One of them is wounded. Yet it is Jean who takes care of the wounded man, risks his life to get the man into a house where he will be hidden and cared for and protected until he recovers.

They reach Syria, still hunted, starving. Now they can join the British and the French who have refused to accept Vichy. The others take it for granted that this is what they will do; they have fled and hidden halfway across Europe to do this. But Jean refuses to go with them. The men of Vichy are the chosen leaders of France. He will join them. He reaches a garrisoned town on the Vichy French frontier. Now he feels that he will be safe. To his surprise, he is taken for a spy or at least a suspect and thrown into the guardhouse. Later the commandant examines him. He learns that the fort is waiting an attack from the Free French, from other Frenchmen. This cannot be. Frenchmen must not fight Frenchmen. He realizes that this is exactly what is going to happen if the Free French appear. He is given a gun and posted to a company. He is not even given any choice to be a conscientious objector: the garrison has neither the time, food nor inclination to support an idle noncombatant guest.

Now Jean begins to see the difference between the Free French whom his brother chose, and the Vichy men whom he had believed to be right. The men he escaped from the prison with, like his brother Charles, seemed to have no troubles of conscience. They seemed to know exactly what they wanted to do. They had no doubts whatever. They were all moved by one single clear burning desire and will. They had willingly accepted all hardship and risk of death, even the possible visiting of German vengeance upon their helpless and innocent kin and people and land, to continue to fight. The men whom he had now joined, whom he had believed to be in the right, seem sullen, undecided, distrustful even of one another. He realizes that the private soldiers do not even dare discuss and reveal their true feelings to one another, that they are held in the Vichy ranks not by any conviction that this is right to do, but merely by the old vested authority of the braided caps of the officers and the threat of the machine guns which the officers control and which the men know the officers will not hesitate to turn on them at the first sign of revolt.

His company relieves guard at an outpost several miles from the fort. The post is attacked by a company of Free French. Jean says Frenchman must not fire at Frenchman; they must not, they cannot do this. There is some reaction from the other privates, but they are still under the domination of the officer's authority. The attackers appear and begin to advance across the open toward the works. Jean springs out of the trench, faces the trench, his arms spread, shouts at the men that they must not shoot. The officer appears, draws his pistol and orders Jean back into the trench. A man cries, "Look! Look!," etc. The attacking party is advancing at a walk, their rifles slung on their backs where they cannot even reach them, their empty hands held out. In front walks their officer, carrying an upended rifle with a small French flag fastened to the butt. The Vichy officer speaks to a sergeant, who jumps out of the trench and flings Jean down into it and jumps in himself.

    VICHY OFFICER   Halt!

The line of attackers advances steadily, walking.

    VICHY OFFICER   Halt, Frenchmen!

The line advances steadily. The Vichy officer looks about at his men. At the last resort he will not ask them to fire. He leaps to a machine gun, shoves the crew away and swings the gun to bear on the approaching troops. Then he refuses to fire on them. He locks the safety on the gun and stands back from it as the Free French enter the works. Both officers are very rigorous with one another. The Vichy officer asks that his men be allowed to return to the fort. They exit.

The fort. The troops which surrendered the outpost are arrested and disarmed and marched away to the guardhouse.

Commandant's office. The officer has been stripped of his insignia and faces the commandant and other officers. He is not yet permitted to speak. An aide reads aloud the article of war covering the crime, and its punishment: cowardice and treason and death.

Parade ground. The mutinied troops, bareheaded and unarmed, are paraded. Five men are called out by name. Guards fall in and march them away.

The officer and the five men are lined up before a firing squad. The whole garrison is present. But the commandant has not arrived. The officers become anxious. The second-in-command sends an aide for the commandant.

Commandant's office. The commandant stands looking out the window as the aide enters, tells him they are waiting, asks for orders. The commandant orders the aide to cancel the execution, have the battalion paraded and order all men who will not support Vichy France to leave the fort before sundown. Aide exits. Commandant crosses to desk, rings for orderly. The orderly enters. The commandant orders his horse. Orderly exits. The commandant takes off his medals, lays them on the desk, takes a pistol from the drawer, exits.

CUT TO:

Desert. Night. The outpost commander and fifty or so men are crossing the desert, unarmed, with water bottles, and food. Jean is one of them. They have before them the long journey across Syria and then Egypt, to reach the Sudan where France is still free. They find a saddled horse grazing, recognize it, follow its tracks and find the commandant dead, the pistol in his hand. They know what he has done and realize why. They bury him, put up a marker: For France. They go on.

DISSOLVE TO:

England. De Gaulle's office. An aide is telling De Gaulle about the Syrian outpost, how at the last Frenchman refused to fire on Frenchman.

> **DE GAULLE**   They can never conquer us. They can only destroy our bodies. The body is nothing. It has taken the dying of many men to create France; through the dying of many men France will continue to live and be free.

CUT TO:

[The Brazzaville Scene]

FADE IN

Brazzaville, Africa, November, 1940. De Gaulle holds a ceremony in which the Tchad and the Cameroons pledge formal allegiance to Free France.

Charles is with him. Charles is sent on a mission to a frontier outpost on the edge of the desert. One night a small party of ragged men approach the outpost and are welcomed in. They are the officer and what remains of the men who left the Syrian fort. Jean is among them. They are ragged, unarmed, starving, only a handful of them left. But they are still indomitable. They have crossed Syria and the sea and then all the African desert, evading the enemy at night, to reach a land where France is still free.

Charles finds Jean. Charles is amazed to see him at all, and overjoyed to find him in the company of men who have voluntarily suffered this hardship to escape from Vichy. But he always knew that Jean would see the light at last, as all Frenchmen must when they have any chance to. But he finds that Jean is still not quite convinced. They talk alone a short distance from the camp, at night. Jean explains what has happened to him, trying to rationalize it not only to Charles but to himself. He believed that the only course to take was collaboration. He found that not only all his family but most of the people, too, were against him. But for their sakes he still stuck to his guns. Still trying to serve what he thought was the greatest good for the village and the rest of his family, he voluntarily surrendered to the Germans, risked death and received a concentration sentence, in order to protect his family and village. Even in the concentration camp, among all the suffering there, he still tried to collaborate, by suffering and acquiescing, not to anger the Germans any more and so prolong the war. Then he was forced to escape in order to preserve men who were opposed to what he believed. As soon as their safety was assured, he returned to his allegiance to Vichy. When he did so, he was sent out with a gun to shoot at other Frenchmen; when he refused to do this, he was sentenced to death. He saw that the people who seemed to believe as he believed were at cross purposes with one another. He saw one man (the commandant) take his own life in order to keep from killing other Frenchmen. The only men he knew who seemed to have a clear simple purpose were the men who believed what he, Jean, believed was wrong. So who knows what is right? Who can tell him, etc.?

CHARLES I know a man who can tell you.

JEAN Who is that?

CHARLES General De Gaulle.

JEAN General De Gaulle? Can I talk to him?

CHARLES *(proudly)* Any Frenchman can talk to him. If he ever saw you before in a French uniform, he will even remember you.

JEAN He never saw me before.

CHARLES Then let him see you now. It will be the same as if he had always known you. Come on.

Brazzaville. Armistice Day, 1940. Flags, etc., decorate the buildings.

Charles brings Jean to De Gaulle. De Gaulle understands Jean's trouble before Charles can finish explaining. De Gaulle sends Charles out and he and Jean talk as man to man, no rank or convictions either between them. De Gaulle is calm, reasonable, sincere. He talks simply and quietly, letting Jean talk as he will. He neither tries to browbeat Jean nor sell him a bill of goods. He lets Jean prove to himself how there is nothing else he can do now but put in with Free France, since he is now proscribed by the Germans and repudiated by Vichy.

> **JEAN**   But if I can change completely, reverse, up here— *(taps forehead)*—what can this—*(taps breast over heart)*—be worth to your movement?

> **DE GAULLE**   I have never doubted the heart of any French-man. That's what I have been speaking to ever since I myself had to leave France.

Exterior. De Gaulle reviews troops in an Armistice Day parade.

De Gaulle broadcasts his first Armistice Day address. He says he has a message to all Frenchmen, which he is going to allow one of his Free French soldiers to speak. Charles comes to mike.

> **CHARLES**   You, Chopine, old robber of radios—

DISSOLVE begins. Voice carries over to:

Statue of World War soldier in village square, a few meager field flowers at base of it. Voice carries over:

> **VOICE**   I know you can hear me because that big lug of yours never misses anything that hasn't to do with work—

DISSOLVE TO:

Int. wine bin. Mme Mornet, Catherine, Chopine, cook, a dozen villagers listening to the radio.

> **VOICE**   Tell our mother and wife and Marthe that our son and brother is with us, too.

FADE OUT.

[The Escape Plot]

Night. The wine bin. Men from about the district have gathered. They tell Charles of dozens of such dispersal points hidden about, camouflaged as villages, pastures, woods, etc.

Charles will return to England. A general raid will be made; each hidden field must be lighted at the last minute to guide the raiders, and the people must be warned. A sound naming the day and hour will come over the radio. Chopine has been on watch outside. He enters hurriedly. A German patrol is outside. The men scatter. Charles is caught and taken to jail.

Catherine is convinced that Jean spied on the house and is at least responsible for catching Charles, even if he did not report him. Mme Mornet does not reveal whether she believes this or not. She still reveals nothing, because Catherine is in an hysterical state. Mme Mornet is trying first to calm her. Catherine thinks of going to Jean and pleading with him to save Charles. But she does not want to ask any favor of him, of a traitor Frenchman. She will ask Charles's life of a true German, but not of a false Frenchman who to save his own skin has made a doormat of himself for the country's oppressors, etc. She goes to see the German commander. Mme Mornet has no faith in it, but she can think of nothing else either. Catherine meets the Gestapo agent, too, gets nowhere.

She hurries to Jean in the capital city of the province. She seems to get nowhere with him, as she expected. She ends in violent recriminations and accusations against Jean, which he accepts, letting her exhaust herself. He tells her gently to go back home. He orders his car, attempts to help her from room. She will not let him touch her. She goes out with a soldier, returns home.

Jean goes to the adjacent office of the district German military commander—a colonel. They have caught the spy who could have revealed to the English the position of all the new hidden dispersal fields. The colonel knows that the spy is Jean's brother. He is sorry of it, but the fortunes of war are the fortunes of war, and the payment which spies usually receive is a fortune of war, too. Jean agrees. He seems cold, contained as usual: his brother made his choice, and will abide by it. He states his request in the same frozen-faced way: to be permitted to see his brother. The colonel watches him piercingly.

COLONEL You can't save him. You will only jeopardize yourself by trying.

JEAN I know that. I have made my choice, too.

The colonel calls the commandant in the village by telephone, orders Charles's execution deferred pending the arrival of a messenger. Jean has prepared an order permitting him to see Charles. He lays it on the desk. The colonel signs it. Jean exits.

The village. Jean arrives in his official car. He goes to his mother's house. Catherine and Chopine are present. In her desperation Catherine is ready to clutch at any straw. She believes Jean has somehow saved Charles. Then she sees she is wrong, that he has not changed. She assails him bitterly again; leaves the room. Mme Mornet has remained calm. She cannot believe that Jean will let his brother die if he can help it. She examines his face.

MME MORNET You have saved him.

JEAN I won't need to. He won't die. He was still in uniform when they captured him. Technically he was still in open combat, not a spy.

MME MORNET These men are Germans. What do they care about technicalities, uniforms, decencies?

JEAN He will not die. I promise you.

He begins to talk, a little obscurely. Mme Mornet is too troubled to notice it at first, though Chopine does, begins to watch Jean. Presently Mme Mornet notices it. Jean talks of the hidden airfields, which must be protected against possible English raiders since they are of utmost importance if the English and Americans intend an invasion. They may even make the difference of victory and defeat, though very likely not, as the Germans are too well prepared and they want nothing better than for the allies to try to invade and lose a great battle, which will mean the end of England.

He tells about the young man in the Renault factory who gave his life and sacrificed that of many other innocent Frenchmen to England's ruthless savagery, for no purpose, too, unless it was for the pleasure of seeing a minor German installation destroyed. He talks so obscurely that Mme Mornet and Chopine begin to watch him, attentive and thoughtful. But they say nothing. He goes on to say that the English cannot raid by day because there are too many German fighters and A.A. guns, and they can do no harm at night because there will be no lights to show them where the fields are. Then he says that he must go. He tells his mother again that Charles will not die. He pauses, hesitates, says "Goodbye." Mme Mornet notices something in his tone. "Goodbye?" she says. "You mean you are going some distance? Away from Brittany?"

JEAN Yes. For some time.

He approaches her. Chopine watches him intently. Jean is suddenly diffident. Suddenly Mme Mornet realizes that he wants to kiss her. She kisses him; he is her son, too, whatever estrangement there might have been. And she is at peace again now. Jean turns to Chopine, hesitates, says goodbye again, exits. Mme Mornet looks at the door. Her face is peaceful.

MME MORNET He saved him.

CHOPINE Something did. Perhaps God. At least, I don't understand it.

Chopine exits, following Jean.

The wineshop. Evening. It is the wineshop heretofore patronized by peasants and laborers, now by German private soldiers. They have begun to gather for the evening, also a few villagers. Jean enters. Chopine follows him. Jean does not see Chopine. The proprietor and the other villagers know Jean. They, too, hold him responsible for Charles's capture; perhaps he has even come to supervise his brother's execution for his masters. Jean calls the proprietor to him, orders the back room cleared for his use. The proprietor leads Jean to the back room. A domino game is in progress. The proprietor breaks up the game, sends the players out. They look sullenly askance at Jean, who ignores them. The proprietor waits sullenly on Jean's order. Jean orders wine, and pen and ink. The proprietor exits. Jean takes the colonel's order from his pocket. We now see there are two papers: the written order, unsigned, and a blank sheet with the colonel's signature at the bottom. Someone enters, sets wine bottle and glass and pen and ink on the table, then still stands there until Jean looks up. It is Chopine.

Chopine does not ask what is going on. He merely is puzzled, watchful. He will believe Charles is saved when he sees proof. Jean thinks a moment, weighs the matter in his mind, decides to speak.

JEAN All right. Go to where the old viaduct opens in the woods. Wait there and you will see the proof.

CHOPINE That Charles is saved?

JEAN That he will not die.

Chopine stares at Jean.

CHOPINE Good. Go there and wait.

JEAN And do what you have to do.

CHOPINE And do what I have to do. Good.

He turns away. Jean stops him.

JEAN And say nothing beforehand and nothing after.

CHOPINE Nothing beforehand, and nothing after. To anyone.

JEAN To no one.

CHOPINE When have I talked?

JEAN Always.

CHOPINE What else shall a man do with his years? There is the hot blood of a youth. Then there is the comfortable stomach of middle age. After that, only the tongue for talking and old men's memories to prompt it. What else shall he do but talk?

JEAN But not this time. Not tonight.

CHOPINE Not this time, then.

Chopine looks at Jean, very thoughtfully.

JEAN Well?

CHOPINE This journey. It will take you far, eh?

JEAN Yes. Well?

CHOPINE   But goodbye is short. Farewell, then.

JEAN   To the good return, you mean.

CHOPINE   Have it so.

He starts to turn. Jean rises, extends his hand. Chopine looks at it, takes it.

JEAN   Take care of mother.

CHOPINE   While you are gone.

JEAN   While I am gone.

CHOPINE   Have I failed there, even if I do talk?

JEAN   No.

He tells Chopine to tell the proprietor to watch for the young German soldier whom Mme Mornet befriended, and to send him in as soon as he comes. Chopine says he will fetch the soldier; they are old acquaintances. Jean says no, to do as he ordered. Chopine exits. Jean takes pen and ink and begins to write on the paper. The young German enters. Jean informs him brusquely and shortly that he wants him to act as his orderly for a while, orders the German to return to barracks and arm himself and tell his corporal it is by order of the colonel, etc.

The soldier returns to barracks, is getting his rifle, etc. The corporal wants to know what for. The soldier says, detached orderly service with Meinheer Mornet, by order of the colonel. Jean is known, the procedure is all right. The corporal accepts it. The soldier returns to Jean. At last some of Mme Mornet's kin is accepting something of the debt he owes her.

Jean, the soldier at his heels, leaves the wineshop, the sullen faces looking after them as they go out.

CUT TO:

The street. Jean, the orderly at his heels. Jean stops. The orderly stops.

JEAN   You know why I chose you?

ORDERLY   Yes, meinheer. I have tried to repay. I—

JEAN   You can now.

ORDERLY   Yes, meinheer. I thank you.

JEAN   Maybe you won't thank me afterward. If you are struck, beaten perhaps. There will be nothing worse.

ORDERLY   I am a soldier. Beatings are nothing new to soldiers in war. I wish to pay.

They go on.

The mairie. Commandant's office. A sergeant on duty behind the desk, Jean and his orderly enter. Jean presents his forged order directing that the prisoner be surrendered to him. The sergeant hesitates.

SERGEANT   To take him out of this building? The Gestapo chief will have to okay it.

JEAN   You have the colonel's order.

SERGEANT   I can't help that. You can reason with a colonel. But try and do it with a Gestapo cop.

JEAN   All right. It doesn't matter. I just want to talk to him.

SERGEANT   Talk to him in his cell. Ask him if that's not private.

Jean becomes sharply an official, using his authority and the colonel's written order. He threatens the sergeant with the colonel. The sergeant is stopped by that. He says he will send an orderly to notify the commander that the prisoner has been removed from his cell.

JEAN   Send to him, then. We'll see what he thinks about the colonel's signature.

The sergeant speaks in German. A guard rises, takes up his rifle, exits. The corporal of the guard rises, beckons Jean's orderly to follow him. They exit.

Corridor outside Charles's cell. A sentry at the door. Jean's orderly and the corporal enter, approach cell door. The corporal unlocks the door, orders Charles to come out, turns him over to Jean's orderly. Charles marches ahead, the soldier behind him.

CUT TO:

Another corridor, a door at the end. Charles and the soldier march up corridor to the door; the soldier opens the door, gestures Charles in, shuts the door, takes his position before it.

CUT TO:

Interior of room. It is a plunder room, filled with junk: broken furniture, etc., piled about against the walls. Charles lies unconscious on the floor. Jean stands over him, holding a reversed pistol with which he has knocked Charles out. Charles did not have time to even see Jean. Jean removes his overcoat. Beneath it he wears a German private's tunic. He removes the tunic, stoops and swiftly begins to undress Charles, puts the German tunic on him, lays barracks cap beside him, puts on the battle dress, crosses to the wall and exposes a concealed door which opens into a narrow round stone stairwell, returns to Charles and takes a folded paper from his pocket and lays it beside the cap and takes a small phial of ammonia from his pocket and empties it on Charles's breast, beneath his nose. Charles begins to rise. Jean hides behind a pile of junk.

Charles rouses, shakes head, gradually recovers, sees the apparently empty room, begins to get up, sees the strange garments on him, then the cap and the folded paper beside it, picks up paper and as he does so he sees the half-open door, which he had never seen before. He looks at the note:

> You may have 30 minutes before
> they find you are gone. Don't
> stop at your home. Go on to
> England and do what you have
> to do.

Charles recovers, listens at the door he entered, hears nothing, crosses to the other door, exits. Jean emerges, goes to the first door and opens it.

CUT TO:

Corridor. The young German at the door. The door opens, Jean emerges. The soldier looks at him, pauses, recognizes him, shows astonishment, starts forward and looks through the open door. Jean's overcoat lies on the floor. Beyond it the hidden door stands open. The young German comprehends.

SOLDIER Du—du—Meinheer—

JEAN Hush. Forward.

The soldier recovers. His face becomes frozen again: a soldier. He falls in behind Jean. They march up corridor toward CAM-ERA.

                                          CUT TO:

Corridor outside cell. Jean and soldier enter. Jean enters the cell, the sentry locks the door. The soldier turns, marches out. His face is dazed, fixed.

                                          CUT TO:

The guardroom. The young soldier, still frozen of face. He has been stopped by the sergeant, who wants to know where Jean is. Something is wrong, but the sergeant has not yet had time to find out what. The commander and the Gestapo enter. The sergeant attempts to recount what has happened, holds out colonel's order. The Gestapo flings him back, rushes out. The commander takes the order, pauses only a moment, follows the Gestapo. The sergeant orders the young soldier ahead of him, follows, too.

                                          CUT TO:

Corridor before cell. Gestapo and others enter, Gestapo orders cell opened, a man in Charles's battle suit sitting in the cell with his back toward the door. Gestapo enters, followed by commander, grasps Jean's shoulder, jerks him around, recognizes him, jerks out his pistol to shoot, but the commander catches his arm, stops him. Gestapo glares wildly about, rushes out, shouts at the young soldier who still stands with his frozen martyr's face. Gestapo knocks the soldier down with his pistol. Commander shouts an order, three or four soldiers run out.

                                          CUT TO:

The room from which Charles escaped; the hidden door is still open. The soldiers rush through it.

CUT TO:

The woods. Night. The end of the viaduct, weed-grown. Charles emerges, looks about. Chopine steps forward. Chopine recognizes Charles first, before Charles recognizes him. Charles doesn't know how he got free, but Chopine has understood it. He tells Charles shortly that it was his brother who saved him.

CHARLES My brother? Jean?

CHOPINE Yes.

Charles begins to get it, too. He doesn't know how Jean hopes to work it, but someone will have to be the fall guy. He wants to go back; he will save Jean, at least not let Jean sacrifice his life for him. Chopine stops him sharply and harshly, too. There is no time. Charles has a job to do by getting free; there must have been some reason why he, Charles, stuck his head in the noose after getting it out twice. He tells Charles Jean will be all right; Jean hasn't wasted his time sucking up to Germans for nothing, and for Charles to get going. He stops, listens. They hear the Germans in the viaduct. Now Charles realizes he must go on.

CHOPINE That's right. Go to England and get your bombers and blow them up. But don't wait here to hold a boxing match with them.

CHARLES Then you clear out of here, too.

CHOPINE I will. Don't you worry about me. Beat it, now.

Buckner Memorandum, August 10, 1942

Warner Bros. Inter-Office Communication from Robert Buckner to Faulkner, August 10, 1942, ribbon typescript with typed signature, 2 pages.

Dear Bill:

This is just a suggestion for a possible scene.

I find that De Gaulle was actually fighting in a tank at the time of the story in which we have him doing this. It was right after the collapse of the Belgian armies when De Gaulle had asked Renaud and Pétain for three divisions of tanks and two divisions of infantry. With these he promised to halt the German advance on the left flank where the big breakthrough was being made. Instead of this, however, they sent him only a division and a half of tanks. With these De Gaulle fought the German mechanized army to a standstill and held them at bay for fifteen days, covering the retreat of the British armies to Dunkirk and saving both the British and the French armies from overwhelming disaster at that point.

But in the middle of this tank battle De Gaulle was suddenly and inexplicably called to Paris by Reynaud. This was at the height of the battle and De Gaulle was enraged at having to leave his men. But naturally he obeyed the orders of the President of the French Republic, returned to Paris and went into conference with the Ministers. Despite his desperate pleading to return to the front, this was denied him, and instead he entered a series of futile, fruitless conferences with the badly unnerved French politicians.

Conspicuous among this group was the Countess de Portes, who was Reynaud's mistress and is now thought to be as largely responsible for the disgraceful collapse of France as any other one person. The Countess de Portes, a Fascist, who was very probably in the pay of Germany, was urgently advising Reynaud to surrender France to Germany and quit the struggle. She was also urging that Pétain be retained as Provisional Leader of the French people during the Armistice which she proposed. Among the Ministers present at these talks were the traitorous Bonnet and Marquet, both of whom were also urging Reynaud to surrender. Also present was Mandel, the Mayor of Bordeaux,[1] who had come to Paris to urge Reynaud to continue the fight at any odds.

De Gaulle stepped into the midst of this lovely little mess; his pleas to continue the fight got him nowhere, particularly against the insidious influence of the Countess de Portes, who had Reynaud very much under her influence. Impotent and helpless, De Gaulle soon realized the futility of the situation and knew that France was lost. It was at this point that he quit the conferences, hurried to England and saw Churchill. He went to Churchill in a plane with an English general. I forget just who it was,[2] but it wasn't Gort. We can check this with Research.

Alone in London, De Gaulle went to a public telephone and called Churchill. He got straight through to Churchill and Churchill was willing to see him at once. Upon arriving at 10 Downing Street, Churchill offered De Gaulle any possible assistance and De Gaulle asked for only one thing, permission to use the radio microphone. Somewhat surprised, Churchill granted this request and for the first time De Gaulle spoke directly to the French people, telling them for the first time the true situation and that he was continuing the fight. Then he returned by plane with Churchill to Bordeaux. From there on you know the rest of it.

I thought this might possibly be useful to you.

ROBERT BUCKNER

[1] Adrien Marquet, not Georges Mandel, was Mayor of Bordeaux.
[2] General Spears escorted De Gaulle to England.

Buckner Memorandum, September 1, 1942

Warner Bros. Inter-Office Communication from Robert Buckner to Faulkner, September 1, 1942, ribbon typescript with typed signature, 1 page.

Dear Bill:

I suddenly got word that I must go back to New York this coming Thursday noon, to visit Ambassador Davies on the MISSION TO MOSCOW project,[1] and while I want to have a good talk with you before Thursday, if possible, this is just to cover us in case I don't.

If you complete your full treatment of the De Gaulle story by Friday or Saturday, I wish you would bring the material up to Betty so that she can assemble the first three full copies. She will know who to give them to as I have already instructed her. Then I have told Geller[2] that I wish you would begin im-

mediately next week on the actual screenplay, without waiting
for any word from De Gaulle, which in any case will take several
weeks. I will have Betty airmail me a complete copy of your
treatment so I can read it on the way back and if there are any
points to be changed we can quickly catch them. I will probably
be away about ten days or two weeks at the most.

I'll try to see you before I go.

Bob

---

[1] Joseph E. Davies, American ambassador to the Soviet Union from 1936 to 1938, was
the author of *Mission to Moscow*, published in 1941. The controversial propaganda film
based on that book was produced by Buckner and released by Warner Bros. on April
30, 1943.

[2] James J. Geller was head of the Warner Bros. Story Department.

Tixier Critique

Critique of Faulkner's story treatment supplied by Adrien Tixier,
undated [c. September 1942], unsigned carbon typescript, 5 pages.
[The bracketed numbers refer to page numbers of the present
volume.]

Observations on Inexact Details

Page 1. [13] The whole army was in alert in May 1940. It
should have been doubly impossible for Jean and Georges to be
on furlough in these days.

In a "village in Brittany" it is quite impossible to conceive
the presence of a "cook." The cooking is certainly made by Mrs.
Mornet. And even if it is a small town, then the maid is just a
maid doing all kinds of jobs.

Page 2. [15] The discussion on the cost of the Maginot Line
is irreal. Everybody in France knew, even a Breton peasant, that
the Line had cost billions.

The words "France is not Brittany" is an insult for the Bretons who are among the most ardent patriots in France. German propaganda alone used such phraseology and the so-
called autonomists were German-paid agents without any

following. Even if a maid could be stupid enough to say such a phrase, Madame Mornet could not tolerate it one second.

Pages 2 and 3. [15] The books of General De Gaulle had no circulation outside of technicians and certainly nobody in such a place had even heard of them.

Page 5. [16] In a cafe in France one does not play dominoes but cards or billiards.
The mayor of a village knows the cost of the Maginot Line.

Page 6. [17] Certainly Georges could not find in a cafe two persons having read General De Gaulle's books. If a discussion on offensive and defensive should have been held in the cafe, nine persons out of ten should have been for offensive and nobody should have taken the defense of defensive. Everybody thought that our generals were excellent, our armament complete and superb and that they were just playing with the enemy, waiting to strike at the right moment. Every armchair tactician is for offensive anyway.

It must be made clear that the De Gaulle conception of the tank system which resulted in the panzer division had nothing to do with such discussions. A complete study of the De Gaulle ideas is necessary before to proceed with such a discussion in a village.

If Madame Mornet is a peasant, she should not wear a "dressing gown."

Page 8. [19] It is impossible to say that "There is no hint everywhere [sic] of war" in a country where more than four million men were away in the army, where all men between twenty-one and forty-nine were mobilized. And if this "village" is on the sea (as it seems later when there is a raid), it is still worse, as all the sailors were at work on the blockade.

Page 10. [20] The battle for Holland and Belgium lasted a few days. The news of invasion came first. The bombardment of Rotterdam was not yet known. There was no hint of a retreat; on the contrary. The French and the British army were advancing through Belgium. The bad news were not made public for several days, and in the beginning the people thought on the contrary that good news was to be expected.

Pétain was not generalissimo. Gamelin was still the head of the allied armies. It is the 15th of May that De Gaulle (who was a colonel at the head of a tank regiment in the East) is called by Reynaud to expose his ideas to Gamelin at the Chateau of Montry; Reynaud had then obtained for De Gaulle the nomination as a general.

De Gaulle accepts to try with the Fourth Division to fight, although Weygand, named generalissimo then, refuses to give him the regular weapons he wanted to get.

Page 11. [21] Orders are given to tanks by radio or brought by motorcyclists. The episode of cigarette butts (taken from Barrès's book) belongs to this author and is probably very accidental. This battle (at Laon) is the 18th and 19th of May.

Page 12. [22] The battle of Abbeville 30 and 31st of May was not directed by De Gaulle from a tank. We shall ask from General De Gaulle himself the scheme of the battle and its real march.

Page 13. [23] The seventh of June, General De Gaulle is called to Paris and offered the portfolio of Under-Secretary of War by Reynaud. He accepts without discussion. There is then a Council of the Cabinet in Paris, the 8th of June. The battle of the Somme is lost and the French army under Weygand is in retreat; De Gaulle asks Weygand to tell his line of retreat, his scheme of resistance, and cannot get an answer nor any precision.

The story about Madame de Portes is very much exaggerated and cannot be taken seriously. She was not a Mata-Hari nor anything of the kind. The episode mentioned by Barrès happened anyway much later and not in Paris. After the council, De Gaulle goes to London to discuss with Churchill.

The Reynaud Cabinet anyway cannot be presented as entirely defeatist, Reynaud being the only one for resistance. In Bordeaux one week later, ten ministers will vote against the armistice, including men like Mandel and Campinchi who were much more resolute than Reynaud and upheld General De Gaulle's plea for resistance.

The Mayor of Bordeaux, Marquet, had not access to the meeting. He was a friend and partner of Laval, became his

Minister and is one of the worst figures in French Parliament. He was nicknamed "Loyola," so unreliable he was.

Page 13a. [23] The eighth of June in London after seeing Churchill, De Gaulle did not speak to the French people by radio.

In Paris the city was extremely calm and preparing for defense. The departure of the government was ignored by the population and, most of all, nobody thought that the city should not be defended; on the contrary.

The eleventh of June there is another meeting of the Cabinet in Tours. Weygand wants to continue retreating toward south without offering any plan for a fight. De Gaulle wants to create two centers of resistance, one in the East (in the Viges where an army, the fifth, is intact), the other in Brittany. Reynaud accepts De Gaulle's idea and decides to go to Brittany with the Government. Under the pressure of the high command, he yields and abandons De Gaulle's plan.

The 13th at Tours, Weygand announces that the war is lost and that an armistice must be sought. Reynaud asks Churchill to authorize France to ask for an armistice. Churchill refuses.

De Gaulle insists that the war is not lost, that the fight can and must go on.

Without taking any decision concerning the armistice, the Government decides to leave for Bordeaux and to continue the retreat.

The 15th of June in Bordeaux the Government is again in Cabinet meeting. Weygand insists for an armistice. De Gaulle insists for fighting, asks instructions to transport most of the army in North Africa. No decision is taken. De Gaulle is sent again to London to see Churchill.

16th of June in London. Churchill offers union between France and England. De Gaulle wires the big news to Reynaud in Bordeaux.

The cabinet rejects the proposition by 13 voices against ten, decides to ask for an armistice.

Reynaud resigns. Pétain is called to form a new cabinet. General De Gaulle comes back by plane from London in the night from 15th to 16th June.

16th and 17th of June in Bordeaux. De Gaulle pleads frantically for resistance in North Africa. Seeing that the attitude of the high command is hopeless, he leaves for London in General Spears's plane. Lord Lloyd was in Bordeaux, not Churchill.

Page 13d. [26] Before he left France, De Gaulle did not address any appeal to the French people. He was certainly in danger of being arrested and had to leave fast.

The departure of pilots for Africa and England could happen only after the 17th of June. Before the demand for an armistice and De Gaulle's appeal from London, the aviators were in service and fighting to the last minute. Leaving the territory then would have been desertion and for no reason. Troops were still resisting in many places.

Page 14. [27] There was not yet any headquarters for De Gaulle in London then. He spoke, I think, from a BBC studio. Anyway, his original speech has to be used, and not an imaginary one. His text is not only better but already historical.

Page 16. [28] The presence of Jean in his own town makes him a deserter, as the French army was not yet demobilized. He is represented as acting for the sake of discipline. How could he have crossed France through the German army? Georges is technically deserting to join De Gaulle. It is for that technical reason that the De Gaullists have been court-martialed in absentia.

Being still a soldier, Jean, if found in his village, should have been made a prisoner by the Germans and sent to a camp. It was anyway too early to speak of collaboration. There was not yet anything of the kind, except for traitors trained in advance, fifth columnists.

Page 28. [35] De Gaulle received very soon a great mansion from the British government. He had with him the soldiers from Narvik, who were very well equipped, and the men from Dunkirk. These men were given free choice and those who decided to go to Vichy were given passage on French boats. There you could utilize the discussions, often violent, between the French soldiers who did not agree on De Gaulle.

Page 29. [36] The intervention of the beggar is bizarre. The De Gaulle call for arms had been widely publicized by the British government and orders had been immediately issued to all coast stations to direct the French escaped from France to camps or to the Headquarters.

Page 31a. [38] Armistice Day is the 11th of November and the Bastille Day is the 14th of July. The first review has been extremely decent. No ragged men or mob of refugees. It has been filmed by the news.

Page 33. [40] There was not yet any underground movement in France and General De Gaulle had not yet established his contacts in France.

Page 36. [42] Jean was an aviator, not a fortress officer. It is a little bit exaggerated to place the two brothers suddenly facing each other in one encounter in Syria.

Page 38. [44] Jean is now quite a prefect.

GENERAL IMPOSSIBILITIES

If Georges is sent in mission from London, he is, as all secret agents, strictly forbidden to see his family.

Forced labor for the workers did not yet exist then.

De Gaulle has always avoided to pretend being the head of the people and the head of a government.

The two important achievements of De Gaulle have been the organization of fighting forces mostly in Erthyrea, in Lybia, in Africa, and the reorganization of the underground under his leadership. These are the two points which are paramount in his work. We can give all the necessary documentation on these two aspects of the Fighting France [*sic*]. The straightening of the French public opinion has been due to a gigantic effort which has been followed day after day, helped by a tremendous organization, radio propaganda, pamphlets, agents sent by plane, radio communications organized, etc.

The importance of Brazzaville, the Congo, the Tchad are also very interesting to consider and to emphasize.

Buckner Report

Summary report from Robert Buckner to Faulkner, undated [c. September 1942], unsigned ribbon typescript, 4 pages. [The bracketed numbers refer to page numbers of the present volume.]

Free French Story

(Incorporating criticisms by Tixier, Fighting French Representative in Washington.)

Page 1. [13] The brothers' furlough from the army should be only a brief 2 or 3 day leave and not 2 weeks. Tixier says that the army was on an alert order at this time and they were expecting a German attack. No 2-week leaves were given anywhere in France during this period. In connection with this, it might be remembered in all the earlier village scenes not to have too many young soldiers on leave but only two or three at the most.

Page 1. In a Breton peasant family there is no cook. The mother does all the household duties and there are no servants and no dressing gowns for Madame Mornet.

Page 1. Change Chopine's name to a typical Breton name.

Page 2. [15] Don't emphasize Breton nationalism, only their provincialism. I think this is a valid criticism. Not many people realize the racial and political difference between Breton and French, and this may be confusing to an American audience. I would suggest rewriting this section of dialogue since the confusion would come very early in the story otherwise.

Page 2. Check with Research on the actual or the approximate actual cost of the Maginot Line. I think it was greatly in excess of 3 million francs.

Page 5. [16] Tixier informs me that dominoes are not played in Breton cafes, but "pelote," a card game.

Page 9. [19] Tixier says it is important to correct the statement that there was no hint of war in the peaceful Breton village. Of course I realize you meant it as a phrase of poetic license, but he says there definitely was a hint of war during this May of 1940. There would be no young men left in the village except those young men on leave. All had been mobilized. The town would contain only old men, women and children. I think we may have overemphasized the peaceful background, for the French were actually very much disturbed in spite of the

Maginot Line. Already they had an instinctive distrust of certain leaders and politicians.

Page 11. [21] Tixier went into quite some detail at this point
to emphasize a certain historical fact. He says that at this time
France had over 3000 tanks but that the Army High Command
didn't believe in concentrating them, as De Gaulle advocated
for years previously, but instead had diffused them throughout
the army as support for Infantry, with only a few tanks for each
division. In 1929 there was quite a scene between De Gaulle
and the French National Defense Council when De Gaulle was
defeated on his idea of grouping Armored Forces for offense
and defense. His proposal was flatly rejected by Pétain and
Weygand, both of whom resented his interference with the organization of the Army as set up by the High Command. Only
Paul Reynaud backed him up at this time and Reynaud remained his strongest advocate in the political ranks. As you
know, De Gaulle had always advocated armored divisions as
intact and independent Panzer Forces. This was not general
knowledge in France, even at the time of May, 1940. Only a few
tank soldiers who were close to De Gaulle and who had heard
his ideas at first hand believed in him. The mass of French
people knew nothing whatever about the split between De
Gaulle and Pétain.

I don't know where you can fit this into the story as it is
presently constructed, or if it is needed to be so definitely
stated, but Tixier feels that in fairness to De Gaulle, his position
even as early as 1929 should be made clear somewhere in the
story. Perhaps Charles (or Georges as he is now called, I believe)
could present these facts a little more in detail in the scene in
the cafe, if you feel it does not hold up your movement.

Page 13. [23] Tixier says that the week of June 2nd to 8th
was the crucial one in French history and should be given more
clearer exposition in the story. He feels that De Gaulle's part in
this period of France's capitulation was more important than
we indicate and suggests that we check our research material
more carefully. As you can see, and this was a general criticism,
he feels that we have not enough of De Gaulle in our story, and
he is possibly right. We can discuss this together and decide how
much more of De Gaulle we think the story can hold without

slowing it up. He says that during the week of June 8th to 18th, De Gaulle went twice to London advocating further resistance by the French Army. He breaks down this period into three suggested scenes:

1. In Paris between De Gaulle and the Generals.
2. His advocating resistance in Brittany.
3. Bordeaux in the final fight.

Page 13E. [26] Tixier says that we are definitely off the track in our representation of De Gaulle's first days in London following the collapse of France. While he admits the dramatic value of our scene he feels that it is so inaccurate it is dangerous to let stand. There are too many people who know the facts, and particularly in England we would be open to serious criticism of the picture. The facts generally seem to be these:

De Gaulle's first loyal supporters in England were the troops who came back from Norway with the British after the fiasco evacuation of Narvik, etc. These French soldiers were in good shape, well equipped and with reasonably high morale in spite of the situation in France. Then shortly after, many others came to England with the British after the evacuation of Dunkirk. The Vichy Government (I don't know whether it was actually "Vichy" at the time or just the Pétain element) sent representatives to England with the permission of the British Government to ask these French soldiers to return to France and not to join with De Gaulle. These Vichy agents went to the various camps in England and pleaded with the troops, many of whom succumbed to the arguments and returned to France. At this time De Gaulle, trying to stop this movement, also appeared at the camps and argued for his cause.

This is possibly as dramatic a scene as we have, although on another plane. It suggests a possible scene between De Gaulle and the Vichy representatives in the camps making their separate pleas and the troops making their decisions. In any case, I think we should correct this important fact, namely that the troops who first joined De Gaulle were not a scattered handful but several thousand who were well uniformed and equipped. I don't think this will lessen the dramatics too greatly and since they are accurate facts I think we should concede them. It might be well here to check these facts more carefully for details.

Mr. Diamant-Berger, here in Hollywood as the official Fighting French representative, will be available to us for conferences and Tixier tells me that Berger is fully informed of all these details. If not, Tixier offers to supply the facts himself.

Tixier is sending out a complete point-by-point criticism of the entire treatment, which should be in our hands shortly. I will have it translated at once and we will go over it together.

This is as far as Tixier and I went in the criticisms, since he was sending out the fuller report and I thought that up to this point we could save time by incorporating as many of these facts in the present screenplay as you have written.

As I told you yesterday on the telephone, Tixier feels that we should play down the Syrian incident but had no immediate suggestion as to what would replace it. I gather this was a very sensitive affair with the Fighting French.

He also feels that we have made the German soldier too sympathetic and he is possibly right. I always felt that the character was a little sympathetic and served no really vital purpose except in plot, and I think we can circumvent that.

He also feels that we should make much more of the Underground Movement in France, particularly in the later part of the story, for that is the most important thing which De Gaulle and his men are doing. He tells me that this organization consists of three divisions, and that all French men and women sympathetic to the De Gaulle cause are organized into one of these three branches:

A. Sabotage
B. Intelligence
C. Military

He will elaborate on these separate details for us.

He also tells me that there is a regular plane service between France and England, with 5 or more planes each day. In fact he says that the plane service is much better now than it was prior to the war. All throughout France, both in the occupied and unoccupied territories, there are secret airfields where these planes land and take off. The planes come over at night with the British bombing squadrons so that the sound of their motors will not be detected individually. As they near their destination they drop out of the bombing squadron, cut off their motors, and glide down to the secret airfields. Here the plane barely comes to a stop as the passengers jump out and those waiting to return to England jump quickly into the plane which immediately takes off again. Tixier tells me that when he was in London two months ago he had lunch with a Frenchman who had had breakfast in Paris and who had dinner that night in Vichy.

Warner Bros. Research Department Memorandum, September 30, 1942

Warner Bros. Inter-Office Communication from the Research Department to Faulkner, September 30, 1942, ribbon typescript signed by Hetta George, 3 pages.

The chronology of Charles De Gaulle's activities during 1940 which follows has been gathered from various classifications in the index to the London *Times*. We have not attempted to photostat any of the items listed from the newspaper as it seemed best to have you scan the chronology first and indicate which of the items listed you would like to read. We have included the page and column numbers for future reference.

Up to June 7th, he was Undersecretary for Foreign Affairs in France.

In London

June 19	Broadcast a message to French people urging further resistance	6c	
20	Formed National committee—broadcast	5a	d*
24	Cashiered; court martial threat	6e	
	Broadcast	2e – 6d	
25	" Address	6c	
26	Visits British Foreign Office	6c	
27	Plans for formation of Legion & centre for armament & scientific research in Great Britain	6a	

	28	Formation of Legion	6c		
	29	Received British recognition	6f		
July	1	More on British recognition			
		Correspondence	5e		
	3	Ordered to return to France	3d		
	8	Recruiting office opened; inspects			
		French volunteers	2d	4*	
	15	Attends ceremony of July 14th			
		celebration	2a		
		Sentenced in absentia by France	6		
	20	Addresses meeting of sailors	4e	3g	4*
	25	Luncheon in honor	7a		
		Opened new London Headquarters	4f	6	
	29	Visits wounded soldiers	2c		
Aug.	3	Death sentence promulgated	4c		
	2	Broadcast appeal to French Canadians	2d		
	5	Broadcast	2c		
	6	Emblem of Red Cross of Lorraine			
		adopted	2d		
	7	More about emblem	3d	4*	
	8	Agreement with Great Britain signed	4e		
		Exchanged letters with W. Churchill	9b		
	9	Broadcast on War Guilt trials	3f		
	10	" " " " "	3f	4*	
	10	Luncheon in honor	7a		
	12	Inspects aircraft of French Air Force			
		in Great Britain	2b	4c	4*
	13	Broadcast	3c		
	17	"	3e		
	23	French aircraft surrendered to			
		Germany	3e		
		Broadcast	3e		
	24	More about surrender, another			
		broadcast	3d	4*	
	26	Gen. Larminat joined De Gaulle	4g		
	28	Chad Territory refuses to capitulate			
		Germany	4g		
	29	More about above	3a	4*	
	30	Spontaneous adherence to De Gaulle			

	of people of Chad Territory	4d		
30	Cameroons pledge allegiance	4d		
	Spontaneous adherence of Cameroons people	4d		
	Gen. Catroux joins him	4d		
31	Appealed through Red Cross for books for wounded Frenchmen			

Sept.
7	Broadcast message to Tahiti	3d		
16	Message to King George when Buckingham Palace bombed	4e		
18	Article on Catroux joining De Gaulle	3d		
20	Gen. Eon joins De Gaulle	4f		
23	Message to M. Sautot, newly appointed governor of New Caledonia	3c		

Oct.
9	Visits Africa—broadcast message	3c		
10	" " " "	3e		
11	In French Cameroons	4f	4c	4*
14	Exchanges messages with Churchill	3c		
	In Duala	3c		
15	" "	3e	4*	
23	In Chad Territory; meeting with Catroux	3d		
28	Assumed powers of Free French Govt.	4c		

Nov.
7	Formed Comite de Liason Franco-Britannique	2d		
4	Exchanges messages with Metaxas	3c		
5	" " " "	3c	4*	
24	Broadcast message re Hour of Silence	3e		
26	Received by Churchill	4f		
27	Broadcast	3c	4*	

Dec.
9	Inspects Free French Naval Bases in Great Britain	3c		
11	Deprived of French citizenship	3e		
20	Reception	7b		

Please let us know if you would like to have any of these items photostated or further investigated.

Herman Lissauer by
/s/ Hetta George, Asst

French Research Foundation Chronology

Chronology of events prepared by French Research Foundation, Inc., 405–413 North La Cienega Boulevard, West Hollywood, California, undated [c. October 1942], unsigned ribbon typescript, 6 pages.

1. Chronological events in French Cabinet from Daladier's resignation to Reynaud's resignation:

Daladier's Cabinet falls March 21, 1940

March 22, 1940   Reynaud accepts President Lebrun's call.

March 23   The Chamber greets the new Cabinet icily: it is known that the Radical party, in spite of Daladier's presence in the War Office, had a majority hostile to Reynaud.

March 26   Reynaud goes to London and signs with Chamberlain a pact of non-separate peace between France and England.

April 2   Georges Bonnet is trying to rend the Ministry from within. The Radical-Socialist party sends a delegation to Daladier to ask: "When are you going to trip Reynaud up? The sooner the better."

April 6   Under pressure from the Radical-Socialist party, a debate is scheduled to open on April 8th at the end of which Reynaud ought to be overthrown.

April 8   At 7 o'clock in the morning, Reynaud sends for Daladier and the Minister of the Navy. Promises the Minister of Norway the assistance of France.

April 13   Hitler momentarily saves the French Cabinet. Seeing the invasion of Norway, the Senate rallied behind the government after a declaration by Reynaud in which he may be said to have fashioned for himself a springboard from these events.

April 22   The secret debates at the Senate on the 18th and at the Chamber the following day have strengthened the Government's position.

April 25   Reynaud is trying to prevent Italy from entering the war.

May 2   On learning of the defeat of the Franco-British expedition in Norway, Mandel (Minister of the Interior) says: "From catastrophe to catastrophe we will go on to final victory."

May 7   The position of the Reynaud Cabinet, which was improved with the invasion of Denmark and Norway, is secretly known to be most precarious.

May 10   Reynaud makes peace with the right wing of the Chamber. He includes Louis Marin and Ybarnégaray as State Ministers. While in London, Chamberlain is resigning and Churchill is at last to come into power.

May 16   Reynaud wants to displace General Gamelin. Gamelin has stated before the Prime Minister, the President of the Chamber, and the President of the Senate (Herriot and Jeanneney) that he no longer answers for the security of the Government and advised its evacuation.

May 17   Indignation against the Commander-in-Chief and against Daladier increases hour by hour in the Chamber, and the deputies are now ready to sacrifice those whom they have maintained for years in the highest offices.

May 18   Reynaud has obliged Daladier to leave the Ministry of War but has asked him to take the portfolio of Foreign Affairs. Reynaud takes on the Ministry of War but has so little personal influence when so much is needed that he asks Marshal Pétain to become Vice-President of the Ministers' Council. Pétain accepts. Mandel is given the Ministry of the Interior. General Giraud is placed in command of a group of armies. The immediate departure of Gamelin is expected.

May 19   Reynaud asks Weygand to succeed Gamelin. Alexis Léger, Secretary General of the Foreign Affairs, is displaced.

May 21   Giraud (General) has been taken prisoner. The Army of the North and the British Army are now cut off from the bulk of the French Army; a disaster seems no longer avoidable. Reynaud, in a speech to the Senate, criticizes the "old school General Staff": "To our classical conception of war, a new conception is opposed, that which calls principally for planes and motorized units. It could not be stressed more clearly that the official thinkers of the 'Ecole de Guerre' have been taken by surprise and have lacked imagination."

May 22   Churchill has been to Paris and saw Reynaud and Weygand at the Ministry of War. Dramatic interview. The B.E.F., being surrounded, wishes to be evacuated as quickly as possible from the north of France and returned to England.

May 25   Weygand displaces 15 generals. Mandel is displacing prefects and arresting Fifth Column accomplices and decides that everyone shall work 52 hours a week in all ministries.

May 27   Reynaud has been to London to see Churchill and has mentioned the possibility of an armistice. There have been 2 Cabinet meetings, the second one provoked by the King of Belgium's decision to ask for an armistice.

June 1   Reynaud is pursuing two parallel policies: in his speeches he advocates resisting to the bitter end, but does not always act accordingly.

June 4   Reynaud attempts to persuade the Senate that he has done everything to forestall the menace which grows day by day from the Italian Fascist Government, but this conciliatory attitude only encourages the aggressor of the eleventh hour.

June 5   Reynaud telephones to President Roosevelt asking for thousands of planes.

June 6   Another Ministerial reshuffling. Prouvost (editor of *Paris Soir*) becomes Minister of Information; Baudoin, Under-Secretary of State for Foreign Affairs; and De Gaulle, Under-Secretary of State for War.

June 9   The Administration has received orders to pack up and go. Paris has been declared an open town and is to be put under the safeguard of Mr. Bullitt until the invader's arrival. Mr. Biddle will follow the French Government to Tours so that another representative of the United States will be in permanent contact with Reynaud.

June 10   Italy declared war on France. Reynaud telephones once more to the President of the United States. Churchill comes to Tours, Reynaud tries to make it plain that all is lost from a military point of view. Several members of the Cabinet think that France should solicit an armistice and ask England to release the obligation taken not to conclude a separate peace.

June 12   Meeting of the Council of Ministers. Weygand declares that there is nothing left to do but ask for an armistice.

June 13   New interview between Churchill (who also sees Mandel) and Reynaud. Reynaud explains why France is compelled to ask for armistice. Reynaud makes a last and pressing plea to America for "a cloud of planes."

June 15   The Government arrives at Bordeaux. At a Cabinet meeting Reynaud is of the opinion when the fate of the French Fleet is discussed that it should be given to the United States as a "gift to the cause of Liberty."

June 16   Resignation of the Reynaud Government. Albert Lebrun, President of the French Republic, appoints Marshal Pétain as Prime Minister.

2. *Why did Reynaud resign and what were the actual influences that brought him to that decision?*

The public had received scarcely any information. The fall of the Reynaud Cabinet and the constitution of the first Pétain Government were announced over the radio.

While Reynaud, Mandel and a few others were considering and preparing their departure for North Africa to continue the fight, Laval and his gang, underhand, were preparing their Coup d'Etat.

Reynaud's plans were opposed by Pétain, Prouvost, Pomaret, Bouthillier and Baudoin. Baudoin, as Under-Secretary of State of Foreign Affairs having had the first information about Reynaud's plans, divulged it, thus allowing Laval to create a kind of hypnosis of fear against the present government.

Among the defeatists, Camille Chautemps executed a maneuver which President Lebrun was unable to overcome.

At the last Cabinet meeting, Mandel protests vehemently against a policy of surrender, and strongly reprimands Chautemps for his attitude.

Pétain, handing his letter of resignation, at the same time hands the Civil Government the General Staff's ultimatum (abandon the fight).

Churchill's proposal of a "union between France and England" reopens the discussion. Reynaud maintains that France cannot, without failing to her honor, reject her ally's proposal.

It is Chautemps' cry, "We are not going to become a Dominion," which sways his colleagues to his opinion.

Reynaud, abandoned by the majority of his Council (an extremely small majority) who wants an armistice, gives his resignation to President Lebrun at 10 p.m.

3. *Where was Reynaud's Cabinet and what was the date of resignation?*

Bordeaux, June 16, 1940.

4. *Where was General De Gaulle at the time of Reynaud's resignation?*

June 15   Left by plane for London. Came back to Bordeaux on the 16th. That night, he learned, by way of a broadcast, the resignation of Reynaud's Cabinet and the coming into power of Pétain.

5. *Did De Gaulle have any actual words with Reynaud or plead at the time of Reynaud's resignation?*

No, he did not see Reynaud, who did not have anything more to say. De Gaulle understood it was the end. He went to the Town Hall where the ministries were installed. He was looking for a place where it might still be possible to act, to plead once more for the continuation of the fight. Reynaud and his crew were out of the game. It was not they who would answer the English Government's proposal for welding together the two largest empires in the world.

BBC Radio Addresses by De Gaulle

Texts of three of General De Gaulle's BBC broadcasts provided to Faulkner by either the Warner Bros. Research Department or the Free French representatives, c. September 1942, carbon typescript, 4 pages. [Faulkner made no use of a fourth De Gaulle speech made available to him.]

First Call by General De Gaulle in London

I, General De Gaulle, speaking from London, invite the French officers and soldiers, who may be in British territory, now or at a later date, with their arms or without their arms, I invite the engineers and the workers skilled in the manufacture of armaments who may be, now or in the future, on British soil—to get in touch with me.

Soldiers of France, wherever you may be, arise.

Second Call by General De Gaulle in London

At the present hour all Frenchmen understand that the ordinary forms of power have disappeared.

In the face of the confusion of French arms, in the face of the disintegration of a government fallen under subjugation to the enemy, in the face of the paralysis of all our institutions, I, General De Gaulle, French soldier and chief, assume the right to speak in the name of France.

In the name of France I make the following formal declaration: Every Frenchman who is bearing arms has a sacred duty to continue resistance.

To lay down arms, to evacuate a military position, to relinquish even the smallest slice of French land to the enemy would be a crime against the nation.

Soldiers of France, wherever you may be, arise.

Message Sent by Radio from De Gaulle to Pétain After the Armistice

Marshal Pétain, it is a French soldier who speaks to you over the air waves, over the ocean. Yesterday, I heard your voice, which I know so well. I was moved. I listened to what you said to the French people to justify what you have done.

You depicted first of all the military inferiority which caused our defeat. Then you said that, faced with a desperate situation, you took power in order to obtain an honorable armistice from the enemy. Next you declared that there were only two alternatives in the face of the conditions imposed by the enemy: accept them and remain in Bordeaux, or refuse them and take refuge in the empire to continue the war. You thought it your duty to stay in Bordeaux.

Finally, you recognized that the fate of the French people would be very harsh. But you called on the people to sustain themselves by hard work and discipline.

In truth our military inferiority has been terrible. But what was the source of our inferiority? It arose from a bad military system. France was struck down, not at all by the number of the German forces, not at all by their greater courage, but solely by the enemy's mechanized striking power. Every man who fought in the army is aware of that. If France did not have an equal mechanized force, if she had equipped herself with an army built along purely defensive lines, whose was the fault, Marshal?

You, who were the head of our military organization after the war of 1914–1918, you who were generalissimo up to 1932, you who were Minister of War in 1935, you who were the highest military personage of our country, did you ever support, urge or demand that the necessary changes be made in this bad system?

However, on the basis of the glorious services that you rendered during the last war, you have taken upon yourself the responsibility of asking for an armistice.

You were led to believe, Marshal, that an armistice, demanded of soldiers by the great soldier that you are, would be honorable for France. I think you must have a clearer view of it now. This armistice is dishonorable. Two thirds of our territory occupied by the enemy—and what an enemy! Our entire army demobilized. Our officers and soldiers captured by the enemy to remain prisoners. Our fleet, our planes, our tanks, our arms handed over intact so that the enemy may use them against our own allies. The country, the government, you yourself reduced to slavery. We didn't need you, Marshal, to obtain and accept such conditions of slavery. We needn't the conqueror of Verdun. Anybody would have done as well.

But you thought, you said, that you could, that you should subscribe to such terms. You considered all plans for continuing resistance in the empire absurd. You considered the efforts that our ally the British Empire is making and will continue to make negligible. You rejected beforehand the great amount of help offered by America. You played a losing hand, threw in your cards, emptied our pockets as though we didn't have a single trump left. There plain to be seen are the effects of the profound discouragement, the disintegration of the will to resist, of our home forces. And, in the same breath, Marshal, you call upon France—a France surrendered, pillaged and enslaved—to go back to work; to build anew and rise from his ruins. But in that atmosphere, by what means, in the name of what do you expect her to rise again under the German jack boot and the Italian heel?

Yes, France will rise again. She will rise in liberty. She will rise in victory. Throughout the Empire, throughout the world, even here, French forces are forming and organizing. The day will come when our arms, reforged far from home but well sharpened, will join those of our allies and perhaps still others and will bring us home in triumph to the soil of the nation. Then indeed we shall remake France.

Warner Bros. Research Department Memorandum, October 13, 1942

Warner Bros. Inter-Office Communication from the Research Department to Faulkner, October 13, 1942, ribbon typescript signed by Hetta George, 1 page.

Herewith a list of typical Breton names:

Surnames	*1st names—Men*	*1st names—Women*
Carnac	Jean	Marie
Kereon	Henri	Albertine
Guezennec	Louis	Anne
Thegonnec	Pierre	Mathilde
Plehec	Michel	
Laennec		
Basdavant		
Guerin		
Trouin		

We were not very successful in finding any first names that appeared to be typically Breton, they seem to use the well-known French variety; the surnames are more typical insofar as they seem to follow Breton town or place names.

The nicknames will take further reading and will probably follow the pattern of the usual French diminutives. We will try to send you some of these tomorrow.

Herman Lissauer by
/s/ Hetta George, Asst

Buckner Memorandum, November 9, 1942

Warner Bros. Inter-Office Communication from Robert Buckner to Faulkner, November 9, 1942, ribbon typescript with typed signature, 1 page.

Dear Bill:

Here is the information that I talked about to you over the 'phone.

Berger suggests that we have Georges come home, in the sequence in which he is married, as an agent of De Gaulle who has perhaps been on a mission south of Brittany to contact one of the underground cells. He missed the plane connection or the plane was captured and he escaped. He is now working his way back toward the Channel Coast and England. His Breton village is on the way and he stops over here for seclusion and to gather some information from the local underground sympathizers.

Berger suggests that the purpose of Georges's mission in contacting the underground cells is to gather their feelings about De Gaulle and take them back to him. The local underground members want to know whether De Gaulle is a democrat and exactly what he stands for.

Following this construction, in the later scene where Georges comes to Paris, the representatives of the underground have met there to hear De Gaulle's answer as brought by Georges. He reads De Gaulle's statement to them and they vote to act in a united effort with De Gaulle. Berger will supply the actual text of this statement.

Bob Buckner

Diamant-Berger Critique

Henri Diamant-Berger's critique of the first complete draft of "The De Gaulle Story," undated [probably early November 1942], ribbon typescript with typed signature, 19 pages. [The bracketed numbers refer to page numbers of the present volume.]

It seems that the two brothers do not convey any strength to the story; first their love for each other is only a matter of speculation, nothing being indicated to establish it seriously; second their social position, their characters have so many differences that it is clearly understood on the contrary from the first minute that they will be opposed on everything. Where is thus the conflict? Now that the character of Jean is better delineated, Georges seems rather uninteresting and Jean, who has become the hero of the film, is really shown as too stupid for words; he is the only one not to understand what is happening; never a man in his position should be treated by the Germans as he is treated without revolting, and the Germans have never treated collaborationists that way; on the contrary.

The only surprise in his case is that it takes him so long to realize that he will go to De Gaulle, as the spectator knows it from the first minute.

The indications about the opposition between Brittany and France are utterly inacceptable, inadmissible and even insulting. The insistence with which they have been maintained after our first objection is rather curious. These stories of Brittany have appeared until now only in the German propaganda. It is at least surprising to find them so importantly laid off in a scenario of this kind. Not one word of that kind can be put in the mouth of a Frenchman, Britton or other. This is absolute and definite.

The details around which the story evolves are so insignificant that they cannot be part of a story whose magnitude is the first condition. Particularly the story of the food packages is childish and does not provide any dramatic or human interest. The whole incident is involved and uselessly complicated—and for what result?

The works of Charles De Gaulle are extolling offensive and are not a study of the Schliessen plan of invasion through Belgium which had been already used in 1914, which were known by Gamelin and Weygand, expected by them. Two million men, including the whole British army, were on the Belgian frontier, and the attack through Belgium and Holland had been discussed in full length by every paper in France for months. There had been already two alerts during the winter, and the refusal of the Belgian King Leopold to cooperate with the general staff in the preparation against the offensive is the real cause of the success of the German army. Treason or stupidity, history will decide, but it was Weygand who had with him the last discussion in Brussels in 1937 regarding this.

De Gaulle's contention was that no fortifications could stop an army with a spearhead of crushing tanks, while the French high command was only interested in pursuit tanks; the actual defeat of Rommel is the illustration of the French general staff's idea of a tank battle (with the difference that Montgomery had air superiority). Anyway, De Gaulle was of the opinion that the Maginot Line could be broken by a frontal attack and wanted tanks to attack the Siegfried Line, or to counterattack any German move in the north plains. What Georges says about the general's idea is the proof that he has not read or not understood his ideas on tactics.

The same can be told about the plea of De Gaulle before the ministers; he advocated the formation of two groups of tanks to attack the German army on the rear from the west and from the east; the retreat of the government of Brittany was the best way to be under the protection of the British fleet; always faithful to his theories, De Gaulle was for offensive, for attacking the enemy with what was left of the French resources.

Other remarks made previously stand more forcibly than ever; this applies particularly to the scene of Madame de Portes who jumps into the middle of the scene without being introduced and without any reason; the character of Reynaud is still vaguely indicated; he is shown as a man of action and his undecision which leads to the catastrophe is not shown nor explained.

We have indicated that the double furlough in the beginning was impossible with the armies under alert as they were; the attitude of the mayor is inadmissible, first toward his servant; we are no more in the last century; no maid would accept to be treated that way today. The same remark applies to the prearranged marriage; no girl would accept to be promised to either of the brothers, and such a discussion in her presence and in the presence of the two brothers is radically impossible from every angle; the attitude of Georges refusing to take her home is unpolite and against all French traditions.

The scene in the cafe is nearing ridicule. What is a constable in France? We don't know. No mayor has the power to have a man arrested, and most of all a soldier. Georges then is furious against his brother who has not uttered a word.

Later, Georges comes back to his family against the most serious orders for secret agents to visit their families. No reason is given for this grave disobedience. On the contrary, a man who is committing such mistakes is therefore shown as the best agent General De Gaulle can find to send to Paris, and there, he starts again with his brother, giving himself practically to the enemy, jeopardizing his mission, just to have a useless talk with his dubious brother.

Another incomprehensible effect is the man who is sent to forced labor in Germany, when there was no forced labor, and whom we find later in the Renault factory in Paris, wherefrom he could very easily escape and go back home, if he wanted.

General De Gaulle disappears practically from the story after the first third, and the Fighting French movement with him. This was the strongest objection made by London on the first story and it should be even more stronger in the second which has practically nothing to do with De Gaulle nor with the movement.

De Gaulle does not insist on having his "part" increased, but he thinks that he can lend his name and personality [only] to a picture which shows the accomplishments done by his movement and being at least spiritually inspired by his activities.

Nor our military achievements are indicated as suggested in the London note.

It seems that this second scenario, although more complete in certain aspects, have [sic] gone more far away from the right track than the first one, and it seems that radical changes have to be considered to make it acceptable.

Suggestions for changes in the story

The story could open with the Council of Ministers in the

crucial day of the battle, and with the introduction of De Gaulle, of his first silent listening, and then bursting into a plea for action. Sent to London, he convinces Churchill that British troops have to be sent back to France, etc.

The efforts of De Gaulle for offensive, his fight to balance the influences applied on the weak Reynaud, to convince his former "boss" Pétain, his colleagues, etc.

Then, when his call comes from the radio, we see the principal personages of the story when they listen to him for the first time. We could then have all the men and women who shall be used in the following scenes and present them in these days.

I suggest that Jean should better be an industrialist who has stayed in Paris, a reactionary man who thought he was a patriot, but very much upset by the social progresses and the fear of an imaginary revolution. His son (I think the conflict would be much more important between a father and his son than between two brothers) his son Georges is in the army and made a prisoner, has escaped to Paris where he joins his father.

The father decides to collaborate and the son, although educated in the same principles than his father, escapes to join the F.F.F. But he is ashamed of his father's and adopts an assumed name. He becomes one of the aces of the new air forces, always somber and trying to redeem his father's activities which are now widely known by his exceptional bravery, always volunteers for danger.

Jean has in his own factory the birth of an underground organization. We can see through this factory and the principal workers, foremen, engineers, the sabotage at work, and also we might have hostages shot, all the scenes of occupied France. Jean is working in close cooperation with the Germans. He believes in their victory, he despises the British forces and ridicules the idea of an American intervention; besides, he hates the Russians.

Georges is shot down over France in a fight and parachutes to safety. Saved and protected, he comes to Paris to meet a man who is going to England, and there we can imagine that he is mixed with the last underground meeting, coupling this with the fact that he knows that his father's factory will be bombed, that the girl he loves (who might be the daughter of a foreman, working herself in the factory) is in danger.

It seems that we could have there grouped all the elements of a violent conflict with opposed sentiments and contradictory feelings, both between son and father, between love and duty. The last effect should be perhaps the father taking over the job for his son, who has been made a prisoner by the Germans or wounded or killed, then coming to De Gaulle who could explain definitely his position.

This is not an outline of a story but a suggestion of a series of situations which could permit more to show what is going on in a family, in a factory, in Paris, and also in the army.

Page 2 [93] First allusion to the cost of the Maginot Line. Really nobody cared about the cost of the line, which had been part of the military budgets every year for the preceding years, and I have *never* heard any discussion about it. It is a fact that in France nobody ever tried to economize on war budgets, that never any amount was refused to the army for their expenses; the line was built to allow the reduction of the duration of military service to one year, and nobody regretted such an expense which kept the boys home one year more.

There is a frequent mistake in American commentaries about the line, when they speak of the Maginot Line spirit. The line was supposed to give us full security in peace time and to let us live without the fear of a surprise attack, and it worked: it certainly gave us eight months which could have been employed to prepare an offensive. But the Maginot Line spirit was comparable to the American spirit that, protected by the oceans, it is safe to expect time to be working for you and not to make a feverish effort because you are protected against any danger in the meantime. The French (and British) idea in these days was not to disrupt the normal life of the country, not to stop civilian activities, and to integrate the war effort into a kind of semi-normal life. It meant: "Under the protection of the line, we can choose our own date for an offensive, spare life and suffering for our soldiers, build what we need and start *our* war in the moment we shall decide."

Again and again, I must stress that the common people of France were anxiously awaiting for an offensive and that the campaign actually made here for a second front is nothing compared to the excitement of the French people who even wanted to help Finland, to increase the Narvik effort, to attack Italy, etc.

The demoralization in the army (which has been greatly exaggerated) was mostly impatience and annoyment to be immobilized, building pill boxes and concrete trenches, doing maneuvers, when they all expected a victorious march through Germany. If you want to show discussions as they were in these days in French villages or small communities, they were between partisans of immediate offensive and partisans of delayed offensive, the latter stating that we better leave the conduct of the war to the technicians, that we had the best generals in the world, the best army, the best armaments and that the high command was very wise to prepare its attack, while the blockade was weakening Germany who was already so much rationed, etc.

There was also something like a tendency to "life as usual, business as usual." Why don't send they back home the men who are mobilized for nothing? For farm work, for factory work?

Page 5 [96] De Gaulle's theories had not much to do with the Belgian invasion. The invasion through Belgium had already been used by the Germans in 1914. Until 1937, the Belgians were our allies and their system of defense was part of ours. In 1936 the king Leopold—already betraying or stupid—did adopt a neutral policy. The Canal Albert Line, built on the Maginot principle, became a different system and there was no more cooperation between the general staffs of the three countries. In 1937 Weygand, after a visit to Leopold, advised the Government not to rely any more on the king of Belgium and the work was started on the "small Maginot Line" in the North. But the job was done by military workers instead of civilian enterprises used in the real Maginot Line and it was very inferior to the Eastern Line. During the first months of the war, part of the army was used to build concrete systems of defense, in the North and along the Belgian border, where everybody could imagine that the attack should come. It had been from the first minute the theory of Gamelin, who still today pretends that he should have staged another Marne if he should have kept command.

The whole British army and big French masses were constantly in the North where two alerts were given in the winter, but Leopold—always traitor or stupid—refused any cooperation, any consultation between the staffs. He even built fortifications on the French frontier and divided his armies in two parts, one facing France, the other Germany.

Anyway, the Canal Albert was supposed strong enough to hold the enemy for ten days. It lasted four hours. Then Leopold called the French and British armies for help (again was it deliberate treason?) and they rushed rather imprudently into a sort of a trap.

It is there that the theories of De Gaulle proved their striking reality. De Gaulle extolled offensive. He was against defensive war, pretending that no fortifications on earth could be made strong enough to resist to divisions made of crushing tanks. He had invented what has been called "panzer divisions" by Guderian who did proclaim very honestly that he was inspired by De Gaulle's book in organizing the instrument which the Germans used to destroy resistance, even installed in concrete fortifications.

De Gaulle in a report to the French high command in October 1939 (during the war) wrote: "Any defensive force that relies on static resistance of the older type would be doomed for destruction. Only mechanized force is able to break mechanized force. In the present conflict, as in those that have preceded, inertia spells defeat." He also was a strong advocate of youth in the command, criticizing the old generals and asking for young chiefs.

The French high command was not in the same opinion. General Giraud told *me* and even wrote me in his own handwriting, in November 1939, a letter which concluded, "One has a tendency to exaggerate the role of the tanks in modern warfare." They were still in the opinion that the tanks should be used as in the last war to pursue the retreating armies. So they had their tanks (mostly light tanks) scattered among the armies in very small groups to be helping the infantry in the fight and after the first clash. What De Gaulle had insisted upon was the creation of independent armored forces with their complete units, comprising tanks, anti-tank guns, anti-aircraft guns, working like spearheads to crush the enemy lines in a point and then pushing their advance as far as they could. The other theory did not work, and his worked—but in the hands of the Germans. In every discussion he had during the dramatic days of the battles, he asked for a regrouping of the existing tanks with anti-tank guns and anti-aircraft guns. He did improvise twice such groups, although he never had the guns he asked for, and scored two very serious victories. Then his ideas were demonstrated exact both by the German action and by his own. And the hate of the general staff for him became more acute and venomous, because he had been right when they were wrong.

Page 6 [96] Georges says that De Gaulle is in Syria. De Gaulle was in France. His sojourn in Syria had been years before the war.

What he says about generals and admirals calls for a distinction. Naval officers were never discussed and were not so old. Their tactics could not be criticized as they were actively working on the blockade with the British, and even today no reproach has been formulated about their action on the seas.

Page 11 [100] Coupe-tête (I suppose this is a nickname, as there has never been a name like that in France, and if it is a nickname, it should be explained. A nickname has generally some reason, some origin. Otherwise, it is confusing), Coupe-tête speaks bluntly of this prearranged marriage. When he says that the mayor should make up his mind which one he wants—before the youngsters, that should be enough to break all ideas of marrying for the three youngsters. Love or illusion of love is necessary, and a girl or a boy who marries to please papa or mama is outmoded and considered as stupid, lifeless. It is true that the families are taking great interest in arranging marriages of interest between families of even standing, but they keep it a secret from the young people always, leaving to them the illusion that they are conducting themselves their own lives, using the classical ruses to help them to meet, to stay alone, etc. Never a French girl and two French boys presented as normal beings and even sympathetic, intelligent, could accept the idea of "being married."

Page 12 [101] The French tradition of politeness should

make utterly impossible for Georges and Jean to even hesitate to take Catherine to her door. Their mother could not admit it, nor would they forget to offer their services and insist even. To act otherwise would be completely rude and even insulting.

Page 13 [102] In the country cafe, the indications that the laborers are respectfully in the background is far from being accurate. The cafe is, all over France, the real democratic place; and if the mayor can be shown some deference if he is old or even very rich, or even in certain places, if he is the noble of the place, it does not resemble to any withdrawing in the background. In a village, everybody who goes to the cafe is equally sharing tables or benches. If there are social differences, in a more important village, there is another cafe where the "elegants" or the "rich" go by themselves, or there is a club (in small towns), but if they go to the same cafe, here they are perfectly equal.

Page 14 [102] The mayor knows that if a man is in his village, it is on a regular furlough and there is no reason for him to question the right of a soldier to be there. Mostly Jean is a lieutenant and would not accept such an inquiry from a civilian.

Page 16 [104] Again about the Maginot Line. The mayor is right when he says that the Maginot Line has kept the enemy out of France, eight months, not one year. The discussion, to be sensible, could be about the impregnability of the line (which after all was not taken by direct assault and resisted very efficiently even after the armistice was signed).

Page 17 [105] I suppose that the "constable" is the "garde-champêtre." He has no authority to arrest a man for whistling. He has not even authority for such cases and in a cafe where everybody is free to talk and whistle. The mayor is no sacrosaint; he is elected and should be more polite with his own electors. First he cannot order any arrest on any such ground. The "garde-champêtre" would not even consider obeying, and the assistants should throw him out of the place if he were crazy enough to start such a scene. The only thing he could do is when the gendarme comes in, to accuse Georges of having "held defeatist talks in a public place," or of having made scandal being drunk. But there are witnesses who should testify of the contrary, except if the dialogue is arranged so that Georges insults all the men present and keeps saying things which should from a certain angle be objectionable, attack for example the high command in definite words, saying that the generals are too old and stupid, that we have no armaments, no aviation, no tanks. Everybody believed we had a superior armament and thousands of tanks, that our relative inferiority in aviation was compensated by British superiority, etc. On this ground the discussion could become general and rather violent, Georges being accused of undermining the morale of the people. Then the gendarme could advise him to go home and to keep silent.

Note that the people were not afraid of any attack. They were expecting it and rather eager to see it come, at least, and to hear about some fighting where they generally thought that we should beat the Germans. Anyone saying that we could be beaten should have been violently accused of being a "communist" or a "defeatist," and in these days that was in certain cases enough to justify an arrest. But in such a small village, the son Mornet is too well known, his family too popular, his mother and brother too much respected to go that far. Jean's intervention would be enough to protect him, and that could be justly the reason for his resentment against Jean, who probably should agree with the other's opinion but would certainly interfere to save his brother from trouble.

Page 20 [107] The patronne knows certainly very well the sons Mornet and has no fear for their good credit. Furthermore, in page 15, Georges has paid already [for] his drink.

Page 21 [108] Georges is furious against Jean who has not uttered a single word during the whole discussion except to protect him against the mayor's insulting words and accusations. He did not criticize one of his words, nor accused him of anything. Even his silence is not indicated as a disapproval.

Page 24 [111] Here Coupe-tête starts his phrases opposing France to Brittany. Such phrases seem directly quoted from German propaganda and are insulting both for Brittons and Frenchmen alike. There is perhaps no place in France where patriotism is so developed and unselfish than in Brittany,

Clemenceau's and Briand's country. Even as jokes they have to be carefully avoided.

Page 25 [111] No maid today would accept to be treated as the mayor treats his maid. And before guests it is extremely rude. Madame Mornet should resent it and Catherine could not let it go, nor anyone of the others.

Page 26 [112] The remarks about the planned marriage are still more valid for the mayor's speech and Madame Mornet's answer. The mayor speaks like in Molière's time, but three centuries have elapsed and no man, no father could talk that way, today, in front of his daughter and of the proposed husbands.

Page 27 [112] His references to the Maginot Line are still in the same line that the scenes before, although a little bit more in the line of discussions about the phony war. If the preceding discussions are arranged, this one will of course follow the arrangement.

Page 29 [114] De Gaulle was not the only one to be right, if he ever discussed the point.

The constable or "garde-champêtre" could mention the call for help which came that morning from the king of Belgium, but there was no fear in France, only big hopes in this day. There was this day a wave of enthusiasm and of confidence in the strength of our army. Our people never liked the trenches and the termite war. They all thought that the French soldier was more at ease in the open air and that in open air battles he would charge and win. They did not know a thing about the intervention of planes in the battlefield or about our inferiority in technique and armaments; for them, it was to be hand-to-hand fighting and in this kind of fighting we have always been much superior to the Germans. It was true this time too. Unfortunately the Germans had a technique which did not resort to hand-to-hand fighting except in very few occasions and the soldiers were soon disgusted to be dive bombed and crushed by tanks without mechanical nor aerial opposition.

General remarks on the first 34 pages

In this part of the script, the first objections made are still to

be sustained. The double furlough is impossible in the first days
of May. The army was in alert. The only technical explanation
could be that one of the brothers, Georges for example, had
been wounded and is convalescing. His brother, being in the
navy, could have been in the high seas for a while and, coming
back to Brest, could have found a way to jump for one or two
days to see his mother and his brother. On account of the tense
situation, Georges gives up the few days he had still to con-
valesce and joins immediately his regiment; and Jean, of
course, hurries to his boat.

The convalescence could be used to develop the love affair
between Catherine and Georges and to put some charm of the
country life into the picture of "life as usual in the phony war."
Your idea seems to show France unaware of the war and indifferent in the course of everyday life to its developments, and
that is partially true. The reason for it was the extreme
confidence of everybody in the final victory, among the people
at least. All our work in the propaganda was directed on this
line, and we succeeded only too well in building this feeling of
superiority, of confidence. Life was going on. People were worried because in every family soldiers and sailors were mobilized
(five million men out of a population of forty-one million),
which would represent for example in U.S.A. an army of sixteen million men. But the losses were very feeble at this time
(three thousand dead). No bombardments as expected. Practically not much rationing, and money was pouring with war
orders. The morale of the people was crushed when they
realized that all was different from what they believed and
expected. Then they began to be anxious and even to exaggerate the bad news, having lost their confidence in our informa-
tions. This shift from confidence to despair and credulity to the
worst was total and justified by our stupid overconfidence in
our chiefs who proved to be incapable. But in these days you
could without any exaggeration show a peaceful and happy
village, where love is a joyous affair and business and life normal.

Page 35 [120] It seems that it would be useful to date exactly
the events, as things did happen very fast and with a lot of
confusion in the minds of the actors and the spectators them-

selves. The first scenes seem to be around the fifteenth of May. The radio did not announce anything very seriously about the German advance. The news came vaguely and without any geographical precision; there was [sic] no throngs in the streets, no public meetings.

There were no loud speakers in public places, and Reynaud when he spoke in the radio spoke mostly at night; he never presented Weygand as another Foch and most of all the Somme was never mentioned. The exact words of Reynaud in his first speech can be found. I heard them and I remember him saying, "The enemy has opened a breach in our lines. We *have* stopped them. We shall stop others [the exact word he used was "colmated"]. General Weygand who is in charge of the war promises victory if we can hold one month. . . ."

I have no recollection of the session in the Chamber of the Deputies, but if there was one, it was not panicky nor even extremely violent. The name of De Gaulle was certainly not mentioned and if Reynaud should have mentioned anything, it would certainly have been his own proposition of law to create panzer divisions in 1934 and he was not the man to give his own pride and glory to another man.

There has certainly never been a public discussion on these theories, as everybody knew at this time that De Gaulle was right and even Gamelin had admitted it the fifteenth of May in Montry when he handed to De Gaulle the command of the first improvised tank group which stopped the Germans at Laon and saved Paris from an immediate thrust.

Page 40 [124] The king of Belgium was not made a prisoner of war. He chose to go back to his palace in Brussels and to stay there as a voluntary prisoner of war, "to share the fate of my people," as he stated.

The French were not evacuated in Dunkirk except some small units mixed with the British. Their army under the command of General Prioux was fighting in the North to protect the evacuation of the British army. Prioux was made a prisoner with the remnants of this sacrifice army. This sacrifice has been mostly heralded in anti-British propaganda later. The surrender of the Belgian king was the 28th of May. The battle of Abbeville, which practically saved the British from encirclement, was fought the 29th and the 30th. The Dunkirk evacuation was in the first days of June and finished, I think, the fourth or the fifth of June.

Page 41 [125] The staff officer speaks as if he had read the letter addressed to his chief, which is not a normal procedure. The letter from Reynaud is exaggerated (De Gaulle never pretended to have saved the army). It was not his role of designating De Gaulle's successor, which had to be chosen by the generalissimo.

Page 42 [126] Weygand was not a member of the Council and could not assist to the deliberations. He was summoned before the Council to speak of the military position.

Page 43 [126] The Council of Ministers was held at the Foreign Affairs, at the Ministry of War or at the Hotel Matignon, never in the Parliament's building. No voices from outside could be heard and certainly not the noise of the Parliament, one mile away.

Page 45 [129] Churchill speaks French fluently and understands it perfectly.

The Government decision to move to Tours was taken the 9th of June, and there was no decision made public about Paris declared an open city before the 11th or the 12th. The 10th Paris was still preparing its defense; and the 11th, when I left, nobody knew anything about the decision. I had seen the troops leaving during the night and I did not even know that they were leaving for good.

De Gaulle had certainly no reason to go to the Parliament, but to Reynaud's cabinet at the Ministry of War.

Page 46 [130] Reynaud refused to let Churchill speak to the Council of Ministers although Churchill insisted to do so. He saw Reynaud but not the others in group.

In the Tours meeting the highlight was the quarrel between Weygand pretending that Paris was already in rebellion and that the communists had occupied the Elysée. Mandel told him it was a lie, called the prefect of police on the phone who confirmed that Paris was calm and peaceful, deserted and without any troubles. Then Weygand told Mandel: "Of course, you, as a Jew . . ." but he could not finish his phrase as Mandel insisted immediately for public excuses which were made at once by Weygand.

Page 48 [131] De Gaulle wanted to establish a double base in the East and in the West, let the corridor [be] opened for the Germans, group one thousand tanks in two separate corps and attack them in the rear.

Pétain's remark is unconstitutional and inadequate. De Gaulle was Under-Secretary and General and had every right and reason to speak as he wanted.

Page 50 [133] I don't know where it can be found that the first republic did never conquer Brittany. Brittany was part of France since five centuries during the revolution and was French territory since the first days of France. There was never any tentative of withdrawal from the French unity but a refusal to accept religious laws and the fall of the king. Half of the Brittons (the blues) were for the Republic and the others (the Chouans) were for the king and the priests. They fought each other. Hoche at the head of the troops restored order and Carrier in Nantes ended the revolt by ferocious execution. It had lasted only one year and it was serious only because in the same time the Prussians were attacking with the royalists from the East.

We have already objected very strongly to the sudden appearance of Madame de Portes who irrupts suddenly into the story without being even presented and explained.

Page 54 [136] General De Gaulle was not at all mentioned in the communiques announcing the formation of the Pétain ministry. He left, as many others, when he saw that the situation was desperate and that Pétain was ready to accept the German terms, but he disappeared without being even suspected of trying to do what he did. Otherwise he should have been probably arrested. His call from London came as a surprise to the government.

After his call from London, there was just a vague communique stating that De Gaulle had spoken in his personal name and not on behalf of the government. Many persons were thinking at that time that De Gaulle was still minister of the war—and in fact he was still legally and is still legally today—and that he was in agreement with Pétain. Then the government issued a second communique in more energetic terms, blaming him and asking the French people not to take his call into consideration.

The rage against him and the trial in absentia came later.

Page 70 [148] Syria was the last to be conquered. Before, the colonies who joined De Gaulle were
1—The New Hebrides
2—French possessions of India
3—French Pacific possessions (Tahiti-New Caledonia)
4—The Tchad
5—The Gabons
6—Congo and the Cameroons (Equatorial Africa)
7—Syria
8—Saint-Pierre and Miquelon

Page 71 [149] Catroux joined De Gaulle in July 1940, one year before the Syrian campaign. He was Governor of Indo-China, refused to accept the armistice but could not get British nor American help to defend Indo-China against Governor Decoux, named by Vichy to replace him. Then he escaped and came to U.S.A. and therefore to London, but he had advised De Gaulle from U.S.A. and perhaps even before of his intention.

Page 79 [154] The Oran episode happened a few days after the armistice had been signed, around the fifth of July 1940.

Page 81 [156] Napoleon had never to conquer Brittany. He refused, on the contrary, to be in charge of the campaign against the royalist rebels, and Hoche was designated. Napoleon preferred (he was then Bonaparte) to stay idle than to mix in a dirty and bloody civilian war with fanatics and priests.

Page 82 [156] The attitude of Madame Mornet is absolutely unbelievable. Why does she keep silent before her son's utterances is in opposition with everything we have seen and will see from her. She has no reason, if she disapproves it, and she certainly does, not to speak her mind.

Page 83 [157] Jean cannot be on duty from the navy without being from Vichy. No official works directly for the Germans. All nominations are still made by Vichy—with German approval mostly for the occupied zone, but Vichy is still the administration and this is particularly true for the navy officers who have been given civilian jobs.

Page 87 [160] There is absolutely no reason for Jean not to send food to his mother. The question might be how he gets it, but there has never been any law or rule to stop sending food when you can get it.

Page 92 [164] The name of Doriot is the name of a very well known traitor.

Why does Emilie explain that Jean is from Brittany? It is not customary in France to speak constantly about anyone's province or birthplace.

Page 95 [166] The custom of washing the dishes while the guest is still there is typically American. She should never do it before he has left.

Page 100 [170] The game about the Germans to be killed is utterly obscure for us and has extremely surprised London. I don't understand either its meaning. These men could perhaps gamble in some dangerous mission to accomplish immediately, but this speculation on the future is—for us—involved to the extreme. The situation of the peasants under oppression is no joke, and there is something extremely shocking—for us—in this joke. Especially the heavy way they continue the joke and insist on it for pages.

Page 105 [174] A music teacher in a small village would starve.

Page 108 [176] There was no forced labor in this time. Forced labor appeared a long time after.

They do more serious sabotages than to destroy a box of truffles. The whole thing is not taking seriously enough the atrocity of their lives. It is no joke. It is slavery, but also murder of isolated soldiers and destruction of crops, derailment of trains. They would not lose their time in such petty jokes when there is a job to be done. Especially in Brittany, they are rather serious-minded and the sense of humor is not their dominant quality. They are strong, stubborn and somewhat moody. This kind of scene could be laid in a Pagnol atmosphere in Marseille, not at all in Brittany, a harsh and silent country. Coupe-tête alone speaks more than one thousand Bretons in one year.

Page 110 [178] The disobedience of Georges is so serious that it cannot be admitted. Such a visit is so strictly forbidden that his coming is quite a crime.

Page 111 [179] The reelection of President Roosevelt was known in France the very day he was elected and hailed everywhere with parties and celebrations. But at that time— November 1940—The underground had practically not yet started and De Gaulle was only trying to promote it. The reason given by Georges for his insubordination against his orders is extremely weak and even does not mean a thing.

Page 114 [181] A priest has no right to marry people in France. The religious benediction has absolutely no legal value, and he is even forbidden very strictly to give it to people who have not been married. The marriage is only a civilian affair and can be performed only by the mayor after ten days of bans. But the mayor can relinquish the bans in case of emergency. Religious ceremony has absolutely no legal significance in France. They are not married and the child will be illegitimate.

Page 117 [183] The stealing of the food is an exploit for children, not for grownup men. It must be known that it is not in the country that they lack mostly food. It is in the towns. The peasants have all the food they produce and do not hesitate to keep for themselves what they grow and what they need. They don't care so much for luxuries and delicacies. The food problem in the cities comes from the fact that the Germans take everything and that the transportation is a problem which they have been unable to solve. There has even been food which has perished in Brittany and Normandy because there was no transportation. The black market finds everything they need, because they have the transportation. And anyway they should never take this thing so seriously and so many risks for a few parcels of food. Always the same petty things in grave days.

Page 120 [185] The Renault factory does not use forced labor and the presence of Kereon is at least bizarre. If he wanted to go back to his village from Billancourt, nothing could stop him.

There is no apparent slavery around the factory, and the Germans don't show much of military machine around. The workers might be controlled, but when they leave the factory, they go home to their family house, go to the cinema or to the cafes. They cannot leave because they need money to live and if they leave, their ration cards are taken away from them, but Kereon lives in the country. He should not starve because he should not have ration cards.

Anyway the factory has never been turned into a prison. Fifty thousand men are working there without barbed wires and Gestapo control.

Page 123 [188] They are not conscripted laborers. They are the laborers of Renault, who have always been working there and live in the city with their families.

They did not give any air raid alarm in the Renault bombing.

Page 124 [189] No French officer, even working for Vichy, would accept to be treated by a German that way. If after that scene Jean is still for Vichy, his character becomes unbearable and unbelievable. The Germans are extremely polite with the men who collaborate, especially if they are of some importance.

Page 125 [190] Georges is a young peasant, quite an ordinance. His choice as representative of De Gaulle for a political meeting with men who represent millions of important persons is really impossible. He can perhaps escort some important person or, if he has become so important and so extraordinary, it has to be explained and shown. The only thing he has done so far is to disobey orders and to take unnecessary risks for his personal pleasure.

Page 127 [191] Really the underground in Paris has other things to do than to have everybody concerned with one package of food somewhere in a village. They are printing and distributing tracts, organizing airfields, arming patrols, sabotaging, organizing escapes, building and equipping radio transmitters. They are facing death every minute, fighting for their liberation—not playing little jokes for a package of food.

Page 130 [193] I already mentioned that the U.S.-German war was before the Renault bombing. In fact the first real organization of the underground is dated back to December 1941, approximately about the same time.

Page 131 [195] Really the great De Gaulle agent acts like a foolish child with all the members of his family and forgets with a great regularity all the strictest orders and instructions. Why should he take such a chance and betray his party, his country, his duty just to see his brother? When Jean threatens him, Georges could so easily have Jean shot or imprisoned, and it is his duty not to let an enemy of France go and report him to the Germans. He is unforgivable for being such an idiot.

Page 138 [200] Coupe-tête has been in the other war and has crossed France already then.

Page 140 [201] Again, such a marriage is practically impossible in France. Ten days including two Sundays is the legal delay.

Page 148 [207] It is not Nungesser who flew a Spad through the Arch but a young aviator who crashed a few weeks later and died. The British fliers did not go through. The exploit could be done only with a very small plane.

Page 152 [211] The voluntary firing of barns and crops to guide the friendly planes is fully used in "Secret Mission," the Twentieth Century-Fox picture.

Page 153 [212] I don't see how Jean has escaped from the cell where we left him to be now working in a factory.

Faulkner Memorandum, November 19, 1942

Warner Bros. Inter-Office Communication from Faulkner to Robert Buckner, November 19, 1942, unsigned carbon typescript, 2 pages.

Dear Bob:

Let's dispense with General De Gaulle as a living character in the story.

We will not only be free of the disadvantages and obstructions whose loss will be a gain, we will gain the freedom to make a picture which the American audience whose money will pay for it will understand and believe and not find dull.

If we use him as a living character, we must accept the supervision of his representatives, and at least satisfy them, even if we
can't please them. Being Free Frenchmen and working for a
tough cause, they are naturally more interested in the progress
of the cause than in a mere American made and financed—and
distributed and looked-at and paid admissions by—moving picture. They want to see a piece of Free French propaganda, not a
moving picture in which those who see it will recognize their
own human passions and griefs and desires. They want to make
a document in which everyone who sees it will have to see what
a Free Frenchman holds to be the true and important events of
France's downfall, not a story which will create in the hearts of
the foreigners who will buy the admission tickets a feeling of
warmth and affection and pride toward the people like themselves who suffered from the fall of France and have struggled
and resisted and are rising from it.

To make the picture under this supervision, we must either
please them and nobody else, or probably please nobody at all.
Because I don't believe that the audience for which it is being
made, which must like it for it to make a return on its cost, will
understand it. For this reason: These supervisors, being Free
French, will insist upon an absolute adherence to time and fact,
no matter how trivial the incident nor imaginary the characters
acting it, and regardless of the sacrifice of dramatic values and
construction or the poetic implications and overtones. And
being Frenchmen, they will insist upon trivialities (to an
American, just as minor American customs would be trivial to a
Frenchman) of French life and differences in French customs
which to an American are not only unimportant but dull, colorless, without warmth, until after a while an American might
begin to think that perhaps the French people got what they
deserved, after all.

Let us have a free hand with it. Let's accept with gratitude
advice and information as to fact on all occasions, but let us
keep to ourselves the discretion to choose among these facts,
choose those which we want to use and tell them in American
terms, in the language (not just the diction but in the way of
thinking and believing) of us who are making the picture and
of those whom it is the purpose of the picture to move or please

KNOW ALL MEN BY THESE PRESENTS:

I,   __William Faulkner__   , hereby

certify that I wrote, created and composed and/or collaborated

in the writing, creation and composition of the story outline

and screen play

entitled "DE GAULLE STORY" and/or "FREE FRENCH"

(copy, identified by my signature on the first and last pages

thereof, being handed to Warner Bros. Pictures, Inc. herewith)

based on the life of Charles DeGaulle and the Free French
Movement,

and the original dialogue used therein, as an employee of

Warner Bros. Pictures, Inc., pursuant to an agreement of

employment dated   __July 27, 1942,__

in performance of my duties thereunder and in the regular

course of my employment; and that said Warner Bros. Pictures,

Inc. is the author and entitled to the copyright and all

other rights (including the moral rights of authors) therein

and thereto, and with the right to make such changes therein

and such uses thereof as it may determine as such author.

     IN WITNESS WHEREOF, I have hereunto set my hand

this 29th day of   __June__   , 1945.

                         William Faulkner

Subscribed and sworn to
before me this 29th day of
    __June__   , 1945.

Augusta J. Weisberg
    Notary Public
    My Commission Expires July 29, 1947.

17. Contract between Faulkner and Warner Bros.

or instruct, or perhaps uplift even by reaffirming in them the value of human suffering and the belief in human hope.

Any historical hero, angel or villain, is no more than a figure-head of his time. He is only the sum of his acts, only the sum of the little people whom he slew or raised, enslaved or made free. He becomes colorful and of dramatic value only after he has been dead for years, because only then can a dramatist make him dramatic without challenge from the people who knew him in the flesh and who insist on fact.

Let's dispense with him as a living character in the picture. Let's tell what he has done by means [of] its poetic implications, in terms of some little human people, with their human relationships which an audience can understand, whose lives and destinies were affected, not by him but by the same beliefs that made him De Gaulle.

It seems to me that any Free Frenchman would be glad to help us in this, not by obscure ukase and prohibition, but by grateful advice when requested of him.

What's your reaction to this?

TEXTUAL COLLATION

Page.Line	Volume	Manuscript
5.10	sees	see
8.17	represent	represents
12.8	mean	means
13.1 and through-out Chapter II	Georges	George
19.2	for	from
20.16	kits	kit
23.1	defeatist	defeative
25.12	tell	tells
29.7	saving	savings
40.29	has	have
41.4	reaches	reached
42.18	holds	hold
47.14	destroy	destroys
48.5, 23	off	off of
49.24	recklessness	reckless
50.14	is	are
54.9	their	the
54.33	Catherine and Georges's	Catherine's and George's
56.18	villagers	villages
58.28	safely	safe
60.34	have	has
71.10	De Gaulle	De Gaulle's
75.25, 26	know	knew
81.5	opportunists	opportunities
82.17	do	does
83.14	carries	carry
84.32	whom	who
84.33	has revealed	revealed
85.13	incognito	incog.
86.37	than	rather than
119.30 and throughout	———	Blank
157.16; 283.28	toward	to
177.11, 13, 18, 21	Guezonnec	Guezennec
188.26; 308.23	youngish	younging

399

Page.Line	Volume	Manuscript
216.12	widow's takeover	widow take over
232.19	He	She
279.18	dies	die
296.36	mettle	metal
307.9, 10	before one	before two
307.18	past one	past two
310.11	MOELLENS' . . . MOELLENS	DORIOT'S . . . DORIOT
311.8	had	and
320.12	Moellens	Doriot
323.11	three others	Guezonnec, two others
330.3	crowded.	crowded. Guezonnec is the leader.
330.4, 8	LEADER	GUEZONNEC
337.37	men	man

Friday. Saturday.
return to the car again.
can wax the floors again.

MARTHA:

I can?

SARAH.

Yes. You. I'll be
them. Or something
them rubbing wax on

MAR

At neither of whi
hurt yourself. G
over seen, and G
back home where
help you. Perh
together can d
industrious

Mah. What
ing after
need no he
Catherine

Mmh!
Catheri

And L
Geor
I wi
Ther
At